RELIGIONS FOR TODAY

RELIGIONS FOR TODAY

THIRD EDITION
OF
RELIGIONS OF MAN

Roger Whiting

MA DLitt FRHistS Dip Ed
Formerly Head of History Department, King's School, Gloucester

STANLEY THORNES (PUBLISHERS) LTD

First published 1983 (as *Religions of Man*)
Second edition 1986 (ISBN 0-85950-655-X)
  Reprinted 1987
  Reprinted 1990
Third edition 1991 (as *Religions for Today*)

British Library Cataloguing in Publication Data
Whiting, J.R.S. (John Roger Scott) *1933–1990*
  Religions for today.–3rd. ed.
  1. Religions
  I. Title   II. Whiting, J.R.S. (John Roger Scott) *1933*–1990.
  Religions of man
  291

  ISBN 0-7487-0586-4

Typeset by Alan Sutton Publishing, Gloucester
Printed and bound in Great Britain at The Bath Press, Avon

CONTENTS

PREFACE

A Third Edition has become necessary as a result of the continuing popularity of this book in schools, among adult study groups and with the public in general. Some sections have been expanded, while further changes have followed from my growing maturity in handling this difficult subject. I found my thoughts crystalized in Leslie Newbigin's *Foolishness to the Greeks* and in the 1989 Hibbert Lecture by Bede Griffiths, both of which relate the religions of the East and West to one another.

Fulfilment in modern Western culture is found in secular pursuits, personal achievement, possessions and the individual's right to have personal values, or beliefs. In the 'public world' of society, science is felt to supply all the answers society needs. Alongside this factual 'public world' attitude, there is the 'private world' of personal values in which individuals are free to believe what they will. These values originated in the American Declaration of Independence ('The Right to Life, Liberty and the Pursuit of Happiness' – originally, 'of Property'), later embraced in the French Revolution's well-known slogan and the trades unionists' 'My Rights!', and more recently in Mrs Thatcher's 1987 statement that 'there is no such thing as society, only individuals and their families'. Thus secular Western materialistic democratic culture freely allows individuals their own personal values, which include the right to atheism, agnosticism, or any religious belief, provided that the holding of such values does not impinge on other citizens' differing values. Therefore, although there is an 'established Church', in the UK, the State must be neutral to allow others to pursue their freedoms under the slogan of 'Freedom and Democracy'. The vast bulk of National Curriculum subjects prepare the student for the 'public world' of facts, leaving, *it seems*, only Religious Education to supply the personal values so necessary if we are to rise above mere materialism in our Pursuit of Happiness. Hence the importance of religious studies in today's curriculum.

Any militant missionary religion is bound to be dissatisfied with a culture which is materialistic, secular and pluralistic. With its 'Greed is the Creed', such a culture brushes to one side the spiritual dimension of life. In a 1989 survey the EC's youth, asked to list the three things most desired, put 'health' first, 'happy marriage' or 'family relationship' second, but, while the rest of European youth put 'secure job' or 'rewarding career' third, British youth put 'money'. A sad reflection on the success of Western materialism's propaganda. Perhaps fear of such materialistic culture encouraged the rise of Iran's theocracy, an over-miltant attempt to ensure that the spiritual side of life is placed above the material.

So where is God in the modern world? The Western Semitic religions (Judaism,

Christianity, Islam) claim God is personal, the creator and transcendent ruler of the universe, so creating a gulf between heaven and humanity. In the East, the Buddha would not even *speak* of God. Taoism vaguely refers to the Way, while Hinduism finds 'infinite eternal reality' near to hand in Brahman. In the West, God is transcendent, almost unreachable but, in the East, God is close-by, the very ground of being. Hinduism does not proclaim pantheism, but pan*en*theism, god is *in* all. Aquinas agreed with this when he said that God is *in* all things, His essence being in every particle of life, and so close-by in all creation.

It is argued that Western religions have de-sacrilized nature by making God so transcendent – by separating the Creator God from his creation. The sense of sacredness is removed from all life, hence Western ecological abuse today (though Semitic religions stress that humans are God's tenant-controllers of the earth). In the East there is no such division, *everything* has its sacred aspect. While in the West, God is masculine, in the East the feminine aspect (Shakti) is prominent, so balancing the understanding of the whole creative process in life.

In the West the soul is separated from God by the gulf of sin, while in the East, God and the soul are in each other. St Paul acknowledged this when he said, 'In Him we live and move and have our being'. The Western concept of a person's structure is body, soul (psyche, psychological organism) and spirit. In today's Western materialistic culture the concept of the spirit (that link between God and humanity) has been virtually lost, leaving only a belief in a body–soul structure. In contrast Hindus see the atta as the spirit in all creation. We need to recognize the idea of a common humanity, and so look beyond a world filled with individuals in competition with each other.

Another major East–West division is over the subject of the Godhead becoming incarnate, entering the world of time and space. For Christians, there is only one incarnation, Christ, but for Hindus there are many appearances (avatars) of God on earth, perhaps one every age. These different viewpoints result from different concepts of *time*. Hindus see time as cyclical (including transmigration) with avatars regularly coming to renew the process. But in the West, time is linear; the universe has one beginning and one end. The Second Coming heralds the end of history. Add in each Western religion's claim to exclusive revelation about the 'Truth', and inter-religious quarrels arise. In the East, the Buddha saw the danger of disputes about 'God' and refused to use the term, while Hindus concluded that God was too great to be named. Each religion is a revelation of God in its culture and historical situation. All religions need to recognize this restriction in their presentation of 'Truth'.

Finally, what is the ultimate destiny of humanity? For Hindus it is moksha, liberation from space and time, suffering and death, via the purification of transmigration's many lifetimes on earth. Christianity solves the problem of a person dying 'too soon' for purification by seeing humanity as a community of people redeemed by Christ. We are not individuals, but part of the human community of God. Fallen and redeemed humanity absorbs individuals into itself, 'As in Adam all die, so in Christ shall all be made alive.'

Does the individual survive into eternity? Clearly the body does not. It is unlikely that the soul (psyche) can survive without the body. But the spirit can, as it links humanity with divinity – people with the infinite and eternal Godhead. It is claimed that the whole universe is a web of interpersonal relationships and that all humans are made in the image of God. So all are integrated into God in eternity – as Hinduism proclaims. The Godhead created the world out of love and redeemed it by love. Nibbana is the mystery of that love, hidden in the depths of our hearts – not remote, but everywhere in life's suffering. Love is the reality hidden within us, which gives meaning to life – as Christ on the cross revealed.

In his Foreword for the First Edition, Professor John Bowker stressed there were three reasons why Religion was as important a subject to study as Maths or Physics. First, religions are extremely dangerous, as countless evils have been done in the name of Religion, ranging from tortures and holy wars, to the subjection of outcasts, slaves and women. Religion is also at the root of divisions in Northern Ireland and the Middle East, for example. Religion may not be the *sole* cause of such divisions, but it can contribute. So a peaceful world needs citizens who understand what the passions of Religion are about.

Secondly, religious belief has been an inspiration for the greatest achievements in art, poetry, music, architecture, etc. Religion is an enormous creative power. In every age it changes its forms of appearance and expression, as it has always done. Thirdly, religions are concerned with the ultimate, endless things of life. As Professor Bowker put it, 'If it *is* the case that your life can find its rest in God and can abide in Him/Her for ever, it is obvious that the issues which religions set before us are a great deal more important than a choice between cornflakes and porridge for breakfast'.

Of course, religions may be making false claims – perhaps there is no reality correctly described as God. That does not mean an investigation on our part is not worthwhile. Exploration, the keynote of this book, is what matters. The real question being asked is not, 'Which religion is true?' but 'What is true about you as a human being?' We know that we have a range of physical and mental abilities; that we can have spiritual experiences such as love. 'Religions,' wrote Professor Bowker, 'describe what those states are and the ways in which you can enter into them; and . . . that we are also capable of entering into a union with God'. Religions offer us that possibility, that exploratory challenge.

'So this book is not asking of you, or even expecting, that you should be committed to one religion or another; but rather that you should be alive to the whole possibility of what it may mean to be human. The important thing to remember, as you follow or join in this exploration, is that these issues and possibilities *matter*.' Possibly all the roads described in this book lead to the same truth, but we cannot be sure. All roads do not necessarily lead to London simply because they are roads. Thus religions are not automatically, or necessarily, true simply because they claim to be religions. 'If it *is* possible to be religiously right, it must also be possible to be religiously wrong.' So there are issues of truth and choice along the road.

Roger Whiting

A word of warning. Handling the history of religious wars, massacres, etc., in a multi-racial society poses problems. Often human weakness, economic problems and other factors contributed to such atrocities. The danger lies in equating a religion with the bad patches in its history.

HOW TO USE THIS BOOK

The topical structure of the book is designed to produce a closer comparison of the religions concerned than would be possible if they were dealt with separately. However, the chapters have been subdivided religion by religion so that you can follow the study of one religion from beginning to end without difficulty, if so desired. The index is also a glossary for quick reference to technical terms, and states which religions are referred to in each case.

You can use this book in three ways:

(1) by *topics*, as arranged chapter by chapter
(2) by *religions*, taking religions in turn, chapter by chapter
(3) by a *combination of religions and topics*, starting with Chapter 1, and then by religions for Chapters 2, 3 and 4, ending with the remaining chapters by topics. This might be found to be a better way of ensuring that the basics of each religion are clear at the outset.

ACKNOWLEDGEMENTS

In 1984 a Goldsmiths' Company Travelling Scholarship for Teachers enabled me to travel to India, Sri Lanka, Hong Kong and Japan to study religions by living in ashrams, temples and monasteries. My thanks are due to the following who helped me in a variety of ways:

Salvation Army Information Services; Hindu Centre, London; London Buddhist Centre; R. El-Droubie, Minaret House, Croydon; Sikh Missionary Society; Sikh Cultural Society of Great Britain; J. H. Pennington; Bish Chaudhuri; Rev. J. B. P. J. Hadfield; Canon J. R. Harwood; P. Leung Kwong Ha; Tim Ball; Prof. John Bowker; Clive Lawton of the Board of Deputies of British Jews; Salvation Army Gloucester Corps; Society of Friends, Gloucester; Rev. R. J. Stephens; Stanley Rosenthal, British School of Ordinary Taoist Zen; Dr Stewart McFarlane, Department of Religious Studies, Lancaster University; T. Singh Bedi; Rev. C. Birch, National Shrine of Our Lady, Walsingham; Choinin Pure Land Temple, Kyoto; Divine Life Society Sivananda Ashram, Rishikesh; Dr H. El-Elssawy, Islamic Society for the Promotion of Religious Toleration; Michael Glickman; Rev. M. Griffiths, Shrine of Our Lady, Walsingham; Dr M. Hall, MUFRU, Birmingham; Karma Ling Tibetan Buddhists, Edgbaston; Myoshinji Rinzai Zen Temple, Kyoto; Nanzan Institute of Religion and Culture, Japan; Prinknash Abbey, Gloucestershire; Ramakrishna Vedanta Centre, Bourne End, Buckinghamshire; Rissho Kosekai, Tokyo; Dennis Rose, Rockhill Hermitage, Sri Lanka; G. S. Sidhu; Tenrikyo, Tenri City, Japan; Vispassana Bhawana Meditation Centre, Delgoda, Sri Lanka; Rev. Tim Yau, Taoist Master, Ching Chung Koon Temple, Hong Kong.   Roger Whiting

In addition, the author and publishers are grateful to the following for permission to reproduce material:

The Baptist Times (p. 214, left) • Barnaby's Picture Library (pp. 142, 153, 159, 185, 193) • Hulton Picture Company (pp. 16, 125, 161, 163, 211) • The British Library (pp. 82, 88 right) • Church Information Office and the United Society for the Propagation of the Gospel (p. 241) • Church Missionary Society and Canon J. R. Harwood (pp. 131, 170) • *Gloucester Citizen* (p. 198) • Director, Cheltenham Cemetery (p. 242) • Gloucester Photographic Agency and King's School, Gloucester (p. 196) • *The Guardian* (p. 88, left) • Hong Kong Tourist Association (p. 189) • ITC Entertainment Ltd (p. 25) • *Jewish Chronicle* (p. 195) • G. K. Johnson (p. 234) • Lutterworth Press (pp. 179, 222), reproduced from *Understanding your Sikh Neighbour* by Piara Singh Sambhi • Methodist Church Press Service (p. 215) • Ann and Bury Peerless Slide Resources and Picture Library (p. 9) • Percy Thomas Partnership (p. 165) • Popperfoto (pp. 102, 144, 164, 178, 183, 186, 228) • Religious Society of Friends (p. 128) • Canon C. Rhodes (p. 214, right) • The Salvation Army (pp. 59, 61, 172, 173)

1
WHAT IS RELIGION?

You, like everyone else, have needs which crave to be fulfilled. Hunger and thirst are your two most basic needs. But you also long for the love and care your parents and friends can give you. If your needs are great, you, and your friends and relatives, may be hard-pressed to find the answers or supply the help you are looking for. Life can produce great sorrows – incurable diseases or deformities; loneliness; poverty. Overwhelming forces, such as war, famine or homelessness, may affect you. The death of a loved one can bring grief to you.

Why is life so unfair? When will suffering end? How can I feel loved? How can I cope with fear or loneliness? What can I do if I have done something wrong? Do I really matter in such a big universe? What will make me really happy? Do science and materialism really provide satisfaction in life and solve all problems?

Too often life seems to be pointless. Of course it is not always so – it can be exciting, varied and fulfilling. Then arises the question of whom ought you to thank for health, love, happiness and success?

1. *Select three of the questions listed in the second paragraph which you think are the most important and say why you have chosen them. Why is it difficult to answer them? Can you think of any more questions?*

Your human needs and reactions are also religious ones. If the doctor cannot cure your illness, you can seek the help of some great power we call God. Lonely, you can turn to God for comfort. Afflicted by some disaster you can look to Him for protection, help and guidance.

When we are perplexed about what we should do – about a career step or how far to go in a relationship with a close friend – we seek assurance by looking for the *truth*. Rules of behaviour for the good of all are laid down by all religions. Religions create in us a *seriousness* about evil and point to its existence in life. But they also offer the power to resist it. Upset at death, we turn in our grief to the hope that God has arranged another life beyond this one. If a further life exists, it will help us to understand that our present life will be resolved and rewarded later on.

No matter where or when Man has lived, his religious needs have always been the same:
● Strength, to bear life's sorrows
● Protection, to survive
● Assurance, in time of doubt
● Faith, to soothe his conscience

● Conviction, to face life's dangers
● Sustaining courage to cope with fear and loneliness.

But he also needs to know the very purpose of his existence on earth. Whichever way you look at it, the existence of anything is a mystery. Why on earth does anything exist? Indeed, why in the universe does anything exist? Why does the universe itself exist? Is there some purpose behind it?

All of these are hard questions. Science can help us to understand the causes of things such as diseases or how to reach the moon, but when we ask *why* anything exists at all we may well feel baffled.

Some people believe that only the material (atoms, etc.) in the universe exists. According to them, if we explain how this works we have explained all there is to explain. Even emotions of love and hate could be explained in terms of physics if we could work out all the equations. 'Life' is a complicated system but animals are just rather special machines. Man is an animal, which is just an extra-special machine.

2. *In what ways are you like a machine?*

3. *Are people really robots?*

People who hold these views are often called materialists. Some of them would call themselves atheists. The word 'atheist' means 'one who does not believe God exists'. An agnostic is someone who says we cannot tell whether God is real or not. Some people who reject the idea of God call themselves humanists. They say that humans have no need to worship and that Man is self-sufficient. In contrast to atheists and humanists, many people have a *religious* view of the world.

The great religions of the world have grown up (or been revealed to Mankind by God) over many centuries. Not only do they seek to supply answers and aids for us, but they also show us how to give thanks and praise for all that we have and enjoy. At different times in our lives we all need help, or want to express our joy and thanks, or want to try and solve the mystery of existence. It is worthwhile learning from the experience of millions of others by studying these religions.

When you were small and were learning to walk you often needed urgent assistance. Quickly you reached out for your parents' hands. This was because you had faith, or belief, in their ability to help you. Without this belief you would not have made the effort to grab their hand, for it would have been a pointless gesture.

We all have beliefs, or faith, in something, or somebody. It is natural to do so. We could not cope with life if we did not.

Belief in the ability of someone to help you may make all the difference. If you are seriously ill and you have faith in your doctor your morale will improve and this will aid his skill. If you are to look to a greater power, God, then you will have to be prepared to make an effort to believe in Him to start with, just as you did in your doctor.

People's beliefs change as their knowledge increases. Twentieth-century Man believed that travel to the moon was possible and he got there, whereas nineteenth-century Man did not have that belief. Twentieth-century Man believes in germs, whereas early nineteenth-century Man did not. Before Charles Darwin explained his theory of evolution, people believed that the story of Adam and Eve was literally true. People's beliefs in superhuman power have changed too.

Primitive Man was being sensible when he believed there were unseen 'spirit' powers at work causing earthquakes or floods. Seeing an unusual object or some display of the powers of nature, he tended to be fascinated and overwhelmed. This made him worship the object or powerful force so long as it impressed him. In this way he 'created' gods in his mind for a while – 'momentary gods'. He used his imagination to make up poetic stories about these spirits and why they behaved as they did. These myths served to make them even more real to him. He concluded that it would be wise to please them, for clearly a volcano's explosion or drought showed they could get angry. Surrounded and often threatened by forces which he seldom understood, Man tried to penetrate the mystery of life.

Some came to believe that there were gods controlling specific parts of nature – for example, the rain, crops, thunder and so on. These can be thought of as 'nature gods'. Because primitive Man was so dependent on nature, which could often be hostile, he devised ways to keep these gods happy.

Medicine men (shamans) developed charms, rituals and sacrifices to satisfy them in the hope that the tribe would be protected and get the rain its crops needed. Today we have come to know so much more about the earth that these beliefs seem very primitive. But if you stand on top of a mountain and survey the view or look at the raging of the sea or the setting sun on a peaceful scene, you can still grasp that sense of awe at the wonders of nature which primitive Man felt. We can stand in awe too when the scientists explain to us the gigantic scope of the universe or the microscopic atoms that compose the simple things around us. A sense of awe is still part of our life. Who made all this? Who could have designed it all on such a gigantic and such a minute scale and built in an evolutionary pattern of such complexity? Why was it all made? Will it go on for ever? What is the meaning of life? What is Man's place in the universe?

We get the idea of 'the holy' or holiness – that extra-special something, a kind of covering or atmosphere, which is above and beyond mere worldly things and ways: 'Holy, holy, Lord God Almighty . . .' 'God' is a word people use to describe the Being or creative energy who created the universe. It is said that such a Being must know everything and have unlimited power. In comparison we seem minute and unimportant. It would be surprising if we could know all about God. But we can have some ideas about Him. We might find our ideas agree with those of someone living on the other side of the world or we might not. If we pool our ideas and experiences we are bound to learn something. That is the purpose of this book.

Questions to bear in mind as you read on are: Who am I? What am I? Is there a God? What is God like? What is real? What is reality? Is there a purpose in living? Is there an afterlife? What is evil? What causes things to happen the way they do? What is the good life? What is true happiness? Is there such a thing as bad luck?

Where did the world come from and where is it going?

4. *Select three questions from those listed above which you think are important and say why you have chosen them.*

5. *What characteristics have these questions in common?*

Obviously the knowledge we acquire over the centuries makes us re-think our beliefs. Modern medical knowledge makes the medicine man's magic unnecessary and the contraceptive pill has challenged traditional codes of sexual behaviour. Earthquakes can now be scientifically explained, whereas John Wesley in the eighteenth century saw them as God punishing the wicked. The Russian Communist astronaut Yuri Gagarin reported that he could not see God anywhere in outer space in 1961. Perhaps he thought Christians believed in an aged man on a throne surrounded by angels and the souls of the dead. If that is your idea of God, then you will soon find you must think again.

In spite of modern knowledge, we humans are still superstitious. You may take a lucky charm into the exam room, just as country folk in Hong Kong cross the road at the last minute so that evil spirits following them can be killed by the traffic, or Maltese busdrivers leave the driver's seat to St Christopher (the patron saint of travellers) and lean over to drive from the next seat.

Religions have to cater for all kinds of human needs and skills. They must answer the queries and challenges of the brainy and yet guide the simple-minded at the same time. They must supply encouragement and comfort. They usually provide a means by which believers can understand something of the Supreme Being and help them to make contact with the Being through prayer, ritual and service. They may devise a form of worhip so that the worshippers feel they are doing the right thing and succeeding in conveying their thanks and praise to the Being. Many religions are a sophisticated communication system between earthly man and the Supreme Being. But religions also need to give behaviour rules for their followers if they are to live in Fellowship. Religions have to be *organised* to ensure that the discovery routes they offer are handed on to future generations.

6. *What challenges might an intelligent person make to belief in God?*

7. *What comforts would someone look for in a religion?*

8. *Do you know of any religious rituals which could be described as sophisticated attempts to communicate with God?*

9. *What behaviour rules are essential for any religion?*

Religions inspire people with a creative urge. Music, pictures, sculpture, buildings and dances have been produced as a result of religious inspiration. Religions have dominated history – kings, politicians and soldiers have claimed that God supported their policies and actions. The sociologist and the psychologist can point to the important influence of religion in the lives of communities and individuals. Sometimes religions exploit people, or become big businesses with vested interests, and one must be alert to such dangers.

10. *List under these headings anything with religious inspiration behind it: (a) music, (b) pictures, (c) sculpture, (d) buildings, (e) dances.*

11. *Briefly describe incidents in history where (a) kings, (b) politicians, (c) soliders have claimed God supported them in their policies or actions.*

12. *(a) In what way can a religion support the structure of community relations and promote community values by expressing them through a set of symbols and practices? (b) Does your local church or temple do so? In what ways?*

So what are the basic ingredients of a religion? Consider this list.

(1) They look for the 'something else' or 'somebody' beyond the world of senses and scientific measurement. This 'something' or 'somebody' controls all.

(2) They have great figures, men of vision who seem to perceive the 'something else' more than other people.

(3) They all express themselves in the written word trying to encapsulate what they believe in.

(4) Each religion gives to its own people advice on how to behave and what to do to draw close to the 'something else' or 'somebody'.

(5) Religions are often practised by people coming together in common worship at special places.

(6) Religions often bring people together at special times for particular celebrations.

(7) All religions hold special funeral ceremonies and grapple with the problem of whether there is life after death.

In this book we shall be looking at each of these themes. Our journey will take us all round the world and we shall see how fascinating Man's response to the 'something else' actually is. We shall see too how important that response is to Man. For a religious person it is all-demanding. A person who believes in God feels called to serve and honour Him, often to the point of death.

SYMBOLS

Symbols hint at something; they express thoughts or feelings; they remind us of important truths and aid us on our way through life. There are four different types of symbol:

(1) *Nature's elements*. Light points to goodness, truth, knowledge, understanding and so to divine power. Christ is the 'Light of the World'. 'Allah is the light of the heavens and the earth'. Hindus pray to Brahman, 'from darkness lead me to light'. Water stands for purification. Christian baptism is a fresh start in life. Shinto misogi purifies one. Islamic wudu cleanses one before prayer.

(2) *Symbolic badges, or signs*. Each religion has its own, reflecting an aspect of its faith.

(3) *Gestures*. Prostration during Islamic rakat shows a humble wish to obey Allah. Making the sign of the cross reminds the Christian of his Founder's sacrifice.

(4) *Ceremonies*. The matzoth at the Passover reminds Jews of God giving them food when they needed it. The Sikh langar stresses sharing and Christian communion includes the words, 'This is my Body'.

All these symbols are explained in the text; see the index to find them quickly.

2
GODS AND MEN

Religions must begin in some way, at some time, but how and when? You will find that the answers will vary from religion to religion. The origins of Hinduism and Shintoism are now lost in the dim past. Taoism was started by a legendary, mysterious figure called Lao-Tse. Judaism emerged from the experiences of Noah, Abraham (or Ibrāhīm) and Moses, while a rich Prince started Buddhism by running away from home. Christianity and Islam were revealed through two men of humble origins, Jesus and Muhammad. The former is seen by his followers as the Son of God, while the latter claimed to be the bearer of God's word in the Qur'ān or Koran. Sikhism (more correctly called Gurmat, 'instruction to the gurus') was founded by the son of an army officer, Guru Nanak, who turned his back on his planned career. The time over which these eight religions began is approximately three thousand years: 1500 BCE–1500 CE.

Although the racial, economic and social backgrounds of these holy men are different, they must have all possessed an inquring mind and an ability to see to the heart of the great mysteries of life. They could see the truth and make sense of the meaning of life and could also do something else. They were able to explain and communicate what they had found to others. Those others would be able to see the truth for themselves, through prayers or ritual.

From then on it was up to their followers to organize their members into groups with rules, customs and buildings, together with systems for governing and money raising. This development often led to arguments so that splinter groups were formed. Thus today a religion may have different sections in it.

What had the holy men discovered which they felt compelled to tell others about? Some were convinced that a multitude of gods and goddesses must exist. Obviously they would live something like human lives, even to the extent of showing human passions and squabbling amongst each other. To believe in many gods is called polytheism. Each god or goddess is in charge of running some part or aspect of the universe. Gods of rain, sun, battle and fortune are but a few of them.

Others argue there is only one God who controls everything. This belief is called monotheism. In this case the God must be all-powerful, all-knowing and absolutely perfect if He is to create and control the whole universe. He is likely to be just and possibly fierce, or He may be loving and caring. Not only will He rule the universe but He will lay down rules of behaviour for those who would serve him. Although invisible, He will have some kind of personality which humans can understand and make contact with.

Buddhism and Taoism are exceptions because they argue that there is *no* God in the sense that other religions have one. Nevertheless, a way of life exists which one ought to follow if one wishes to find that truth.

It is now time to start on our world-wide journey to try to solve the mysteries of life and see if we can find the truth.

HINDUISM

Background. Hinduism dates back to 1500 BCE in India and it has no single founder. The word 'Hindu' comes from the river Indus, which in Sanskrit is Sindhu. The ancient Persians pronounced this as Hindu, and so all the people in that area were called 'Hindus'. This means that the word is really a geographical term and not a religious one. It would be better to call the religion 'Vedantism', meaning the 'knowledge of God'. It has also been called Sanātana Dharma ('eternal truth'). Today's 406 million (400 000 in Britain) Hindus recognize 330 million gods and goddesses behind whom is Brahman (pronounced BRAH-muhn). Only Brahman is seen as ultimate reality.

The Universe. The vital point to grasp is that for Hindus creation goes in cycles – a universe is created, flourishes and ends, to be replaced by another one, and so on. The cycle takes an immense time span (4 320 000 years) to work through (see p. 254). Thus the universe is not a 'one-off' creation. Secondly, God does not create it out of nothing, but out of Himself, then sustains it with His power, rules it and judges its inhabitants' behaviour, and at the end of the cycle draws it all back into Himself before recreating it. The assumption is that a fresh start is needed periodically.

When the 'energy' involved is in a static condition – before the universe was even in 'seed-form' – it is called Brahman. When it starts evolving into creation, that is, becomes active, it is called Shakti. The 'energy' is one and the same. If Brahman is seen as fire, then Shakti is its burning power. In turn Shakti is personified as the female, or wifely and so inseparable, side of a God. Female energy is seen as more powerful than male energy and it is the source and sustenance of all creation, whether at the level of matter, life or the mind. It explains the relationships of mind and matter for ultimately it is one and the same energy (see Tantra, p. 78). Each god has his main Shakti and often many more consorts too.

Brahman. Hindus see God in the impersonal, neuter, form which they call Brahman, as well as in the personalities of all their gods and goddesses. We are all part of the impersonal form and eventually we will return to Brahman (see pp. 229 and 231). Brahman is described as the 'ultimate, holy power', the one great spirit God, the supreme soul of the universe. Brahman is present everywhere and is like a powerhouse 'lighting up' all the other gods and goddesses. Thus the gods reflect or illuminate the greatness of Brahman for us. Brahman is not a person and should be referred to as It. A man's atta, or atman (soul), is Brahman and it will eventually recognise this fact. Here is an attempt to describe Brahman.

OM or AUM symbolizes what is beyond speaking of, Brahman, the ultimate reality.
✙ the swastika (Sanskrit for 'well being') is an ancient good luck symbol of prehistoric Indus civilization linked with Ganesha, patron of fresh endeavours.

'infinite in the east ... in the south ... in the west ... in the north, above and below, and everywhere infinite ... unlimited, unborn ... not to be conceived'.   (Upanishads)

Because Brahman is so mysterious and impersonal It has made Itself manifest (clear to people on earth) in the forms of different gods and goddesses in a much more personal way. Because Hindus believe that God is always creating, they conclude that whatever is created eventually fades away or is destroyed and new creations are necessary. So there are three gods (Triad, group of three) responsible for this cycle of events.

They are Brahmā (pronounced brah-MUH), the creator, Vishnu, the preserver and Shiva, the destroyer. Sometimes they are represented as a three-headed god, the Trimūrti, 'triple form'.

Brahma, the creator god. His eyes are closed in meditation and he holds a rosary and spoon for rituals, a book for the knowledge he gives and a water pot for creation. Why has Brahma got four heads?

Brahma represents the ball of fire from which the universe developed. He is shown with four heads representing the four Vedas (pp. 74–5), the four yugas (p. 254) and the four Varnas (p. 96). It is also claimed he needed them to search for his daughter who had hidden from him when he wanted to seduce her. His Shakti is Saraswati, patroness of literature, music and learning.

Vishnu, the preserver god, has appeared in nine forms (avatars) already and is expected to appear in a tenth one. He comes periodically to encourage people to worship more readily (Bhagavad Gītā; 4:7–8). The world passes through cycles connected with his life. A 'year of Brahman' is 360 days; a life of Vishnu is 100 'Brahma years'. We are now in Kali yuga, which began in 3102 BCE and will last 432 000 'Brahma years'. Whereas Jews and Christians believe that the Messiah comes but once, Hindus believe in many 'messiah'-like appearances, as Vishnu's nine forms show:

(1) *Maysya, the Fish God.* He came to save Manu (primeval Man), who, like Noah, was caught by a world-wide flood. His fish horn pulled the cable of Manu's boat to save it.
(2) *Kurma, the Tortoise God.* He recovered the valuables lost in the flood.
(3) *Varāha, the Boar God.* He is the symbol of strength who delivered the world from the power of a demon who had carried it down to the depths of the ocean.
(4) *Nara-Sinha, the Man-Lion God.* He saved the world from the demons.
(5) *Vāmana, the Dwarf God.* He too saved the world from demons. His wife was Padmā (Lotus).
(6) *Rāma, Son of Brahman.* He used an axe to stop the tyranny of the warrior class over the priestly class of Brahmins.
(7) *Rāma-chandra, the perfect man.* He rescued his wife, Sita, from the tyrant King of Sri Lanka (see p. 76).
(8) *Krishna, the Hero God.* As a boy at Vrindaban he played naughty tricks before growing up to be a cowherd, when he chased all the gopis (milkmaids) and stole their clothes when they were bathing. Later he appeared as the Buddha (see (9) below). He married Rukminī whom he rescued on the day she was to wed a king she disliked.
(9) *the Buddha, the founder of Buddhism.*

Vishnu, the preserver god. He often holds a conch shell for the five elements, a discus ring (cosmic mind), a mace (intellect) and a lotus flower (evolving world).

At the end of the Kali-yuga, Vishnu will come again as Kalkī, as the world will be depraved and need reforming. It is said he will come on a white horse, with drawn sword to destroy the wicked and save the good. Rāma and Krishna are by far the most popular of these avatars of Vishnu and his followers put a white 'U' (Vishnu's right foot, the Ganges' source) with a red 'I' (for his wife, Lakshmī) in between, or three vertical sandal paste lines on their foreheads. To support Vishnu is known as Vaishnavism, which involves Bhakti Yoga (see p. 99). Lakshmī is shown in a dark colour as his wife but yellow when representing fortune and wealth, or pink for compassion, or white for purity. Whenever her husband Vishnu came to earth she would come too as his wife; for example, as Sitat when he was Rāma-chandra. Vishnu represents all that is male in life and Lakshmī all that is female.

Vishnu as the boar god.

Krishna and the gopis. What trick did he play on them? His love for the gopis sym-bolized God's love for the soul of mankind. His flute is God's voice calling the gopis, his mystical brides, from worldly things.

Shiva, the destroyer god, lurks on battlefields and cremation grounds and wears a garland of skulls. His hair, representing the Himalayan foothills, supports the river Ganges as it falls from heaven.

It is claimed that the Ganges flowed through the sky, white as the Milky Way, and when Shiva caught it he saved earth from destruction. It is known as the Triple-Path River as it flows in the three worlds of heaven, earth and the nether world (at the point where it enters the sea). It should not be forgotten that the Ganges basin supports 300 million people. He has three eyes to see the past, present and future. He has four hands. Two hold the balance between construction (holding the drum of creation) and destruction; the two offer people salvation and protection. The one pointing to his toe (the soul's refuge) indicates there is no need to fear. Round his body is a serpent for the endless cycle of recurring years. He dances on the back of a demon (Ignorance) which must be destroyed if souls are to be saved. Shiva's dance keeps the universe alive with its energy. He is sometimes shown in the middle of a flaming circle standing

Lakshmi as goddess of prosperity here stresses fertility and female beauty.

Shiva, the destroyer god. Why has he three eyes and four arms?

for the universe. He destroys time and things which are old and worn out, so allowing new things to be born. Thus he is also the god of fertility. The crescent moon is his forehead and his neck is dark blue from swallowing poison at the churning of the ocean to save the earth. To support Shiva is known as Shaivism. Both involve devotion by bhakti yoga (see p. 99).

Shiva supporters put three white ash or cow dung horizontal stripes on their foreheads and wear a rudraksha (necklace of large beads) and carry a trident (pinaka, symbolizing lightning) and water pot. They let their hair grow long and ragged. Shiva's wife, the beautiful Pārvatī (power), is also known as Khakti. To support her is called Shaktism and her supporters use red turmeric powder to mark their foreheads. This represents Shiva's third eye and when it is applied one says, 'May the eyes of my intuition open soon.' She is known as Mahadevi (Great Goddess) or 'the Mother'. As Durga or Kāli she personifies death and darkness.

God can appear to people in any form they like to worship and respond through that form. He can incorporate Himself anywhere at any time to guide people. Below the Triad are other gods who are limited manifestations of Brahman. Here are two such gods.

Ganesha, the god of fortune and wisdom. He lost a tusk in a fight and so often holds it as a stylus. His ears are large enough to hear all prayers. His whole tusk is Truth, the broken one is the imperfect world, but both belong to the same body. His trunk is Brahman and his belly full of created worlds.

Ganesha. His name can mean Lord of the Ganas (a tribe of demi-gods attending Shiva) or Lord of the Categories (gana; hence, everything in creation) or gaja, meaning both elephant and the origin and end of all (hence God). He is the god of fortune and wisdom. He is also the god of obstacles, either removing them or putting them in front of people. He is shown as a pink or yellow elephant and may be chubby and good humoured with sweetmeats in his hand or the stern doorkeeper of the universe equipped with hatchet and noose. His statue is found at city gates, temple doorways and house doors.

One story of how he came to have an elephant's head is that he was originally moulded from clay by the goddess Pārvatī to guard her bathroom door. Her husband, Shiva, was so furious when Ganesha stopped him entering that he cut off his head. Afterwards to calm his upset wife, he cut off the head of an elephant belonging to Indra, the rain god, and put it on him.

Another version is that Pārvatī made an image of a child with an elephant's head for fun, threw it in the Ganges and this brought it to life. Ganesha's body can represent human microcosm aiming for macrocosm (elephant's head); then the fact that they are known as one unit is significant. The body represents the individual, while the head is the cosmic Truth, God; thus a person though apparently limited to this earth is in essence part of God. The noose of attachment and the goad of anger which he often holds points to the fact that our misery will increase if we misbehave, but if we surrender our worldly attachments and anger to Him we will find refuge. His vehicle is a mouse (mūsaka). As a mouse creeps stealthily so self-centredness can overcome us.

Hanuman the monkey god is the son of Pavana, the Wind, and so is able to fly. He came to help Rāma-chandra defeat the king of Sri Lanka because he could jump from India to the island. His monkey army formed a bridge for Rāma and Sita to return to India (p. 76).

Lokapālas, protectors of the world, form the third group of gods. Among them are Agni (Fire); Varuna (Space); Pochama (Smallpox); Rudra (Storm); Indri (War). They are exceptional humans who have risen to be officers of power in the cosmic creation scheme. New officers are appointed in each creation cycle.

Finally there are village gods, who are either very limited manifestations of Brahman, or the deified forces of nature or outstanding humans.

A Hindu believes personal devotion (bahkti) to a god will enable him to reach out to Brahman. Businesses and shops are named after gods, e.g., Shri Tama Motor Cycle Shop or Arjuna Cafe. Naturally pictures of such gods will be on display there.

1. *Draw pictures of some gods.*

2. *Put the word Brahman in the middle of a page and then draw spokes outwards and on the end of each spoke put the names of different gods. This should help you to see Brahman's relationship to the gods.*

3. *List four words which could be used to try to describe Brahman.*

Hanuman rescues Rama and Sita. Who is he trampling on?

SHINTOISM

Kami. Shintoism is a Japanese religion meaning 'The Way (*to*) of the Gods (*Shin*)'. It began about 650 BCE but had no particular founder. Although it is said that Shintoists worship some 8 million kami, i.e. gods, spirits or sacred objects, '8' simple means an unlimited number as the Japanese for '8' is λ, the lines at the bottom of the character spreading outwards to suggest myriads. It is claimed that gods, people and the whole of nature are related in that they all have a kami-nature, the same divine 'blood'. This does not imply nature worship, but nature awakening in people a sense of the divine at the heart of everything. Shintoism is a sense of the mysterious at the heart of life, a desire to commune with it and a willingness to place dependence upon it. Hence the belief in the power, beauty and goodness of life itself. 'Kami' has a whole range of meanings, such as 'someone who possesses superior power', 'is pure like a clear mirror', 'mysterious', 'marvellous', 'reference', 'an invisible power', 'soul' and so on. All people can become kami spirits in the end. So Shintoists do not have to worship God as Christians do, because they believe there is no definite line dividing them from kami spirits. However, they must show respect to kami as they are close at hand.

Torii represents a bird perch, as birds helped gods in mythology; a temple gateway.

To some extent it is possible to list different kinds of kami, according to what they do:
(1) Invisible powers — spirits of creativity, fertility, productivity.
(2) Natural phenomena — wind, thunder, rain.
(3) Natural objects — sun, mountains, rivers.
(4) Certain animals — fox, dog.
(5) Ancestral spirits — spirits of the dead.

In fact a kami can be anything which makes a person feel awe or reverence. The kami can work in one of two ways:

11

(1) Local area control – 80 000 (implying an unlimited number) Ujigami (family) kami each protect particular areas of Japan. Originally they were the ancestors of leading families in these areas. Everyone is a parishioner (ujiko) of a particular ujigami.

(2) Special protection provided by kami responsible for particular things such as help in exams, protection of insects.

Kami like to lodge in unusual rocks, trees or grottoes, but especially in the home. There are toilet kami, fire kami, and oven kami.

Story of creation. Shintoism is not just a primitive nature worship religion, for it sees all creation as one. This can be understood by following its story of creation which implies that the universe came in to being by condensing out of chaos. Originally the world was divided into two parts; the pure top part (heaven) and the impure lower part (earth). Izanagi (a male spirit) and Izanami (a female spirit) stirred the impure part with a spear and made an island and landed there to get married. They peopled the island with kami of trees, herbs, winds and so on. When Izanami died and began to rot in the land of death, Izanagi followed her, but she was so upset that he had seen her in a decayed state that she divorced him. In disgust, Izanagi washed himself in the sea and from his right eye came the moon goddess, and from his left eye, the sun goddess, Amaterasu, and from his nose the storm god, Susanoo, so continuing his creative work. The point is that life is stronger than death.

Amaterasu, known as the 'Great-Sky-Shiner', was insulted by Susanoo, who had destroyed her ricefields, so that she went into the Cave of Heaven and the world became dark. Other kami enticed her out with a mirror hung on a sakaki tree. Thus day and night came into existence. She sent her grandson, Ninigi-no-Mikoto, to rule Japan and his grandson became the first emperor. The emperors were regarded as divine until 1945 CE. The Isé temple (see p. 153) houses the mirror given to Ninigi by Amaterasu.

Thus there is a firm link between this world and the Age of the Kami as we shall see later. It is a religion without a creed – you do not have to hold certain beliefs. You can be a Shintoist without having to understand its teachings. You simply live them in your daily life, for it is a faith which expresses an attitude of joy in accepting life and nature as it is. There is no struggle between good and evil to face. In the West Man's struggle with a hostile environment led him to see the world as a symbol of his own sinful nature. Shintoism's aim is to help people live in this life. It is a love of life itself, with ritual purity as the only concern (see pp. 104-5). You are free to think almost entirely as you wish, and there is an unlimited variety of rituals to perform. Shintoism is hale and hearty because it is so adaptable and tolerant. As the kamis' heavenly world is just a better version of this world, Man does not have to try to obtain salvation by entering it. Salvation comes by bringing the kami into the human world of daily life.

4. *Draw a series of pictures to tell the story of creation and the lives of the kami gods down to the first emperor.*

5. *Draw six things the Shintoists thought kami controlled.*

TAOISM

Origins. Legend has it that Taoism (pronounced 'Dowism') originated with Huang Ti, the Yellow Emperor of China in approximately 2697 BCE, but the true founder was probably Lao-Tse as he formulated its teaching. Lao-Tse, or Tao-Tzu, was born about 604 BCE and is said to have lived for 160 years. His name means 'Old Master' because it is claimed that he was born aged 60 years with white hair after being conceived by a shooting star and carried in his mother's womb for 28 years. He lived in central China and looked after the emperor's documents. Although his teachings are the foundation of China's age-long survival, he believed civilization was the beginning of mankind's downfall.

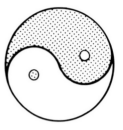

Yang and Yin, the balancing powers of heaven and earth; all life is a harmony of these two forces.

Some people say he was a recluse, a hide-away, while others claim he was sociable. In the end he decided to leave China. At the Hankao Pass the gatekeeper persuaded him to write down his beliefs before he left. In three days it is claimed he produced his 5000 characters (words) known as the Tao Te Ching (The Way and its Power, see pp. 79–80). Then off he rode and was not seen again. He never preached to anyone or organized a religious group, so that Taoism rose from his book alone.

Taoism's aim is to preserve life and avoid injury. In its first phase it followed Yang Chu's (440–360 BCE) idea that the way to achieve this aim was to live the life of a recluse, so avoiding enslavement to the world's evils. But such an escape method cannot avoid all evils, for example, illness; so in its second phase Lao-Tse said one must find the laws that make life change and then follow them and make use of them. He thought civilization was the beginning of Man's downfall. He did not believe there was a personal Creator behind everything, but an impersonal Tao instead. Tao Te Ching is about the path, Method or Way (Tao) and the Power (Te) that enables one to follow it. The Way has three meanings:

(1) It is the mystery of mysteries behind everything in the universe. It is so overwhelming that we cannot grasp what it is by using our normal senses. We can only grasp it through mystical insight, and even then it is impossible to put into words what we have seen. Nevertheless the impersonal Tao is the reality behind all existence. But put another way, Tao is the only world, as there is no supernatural World. So there is nothing supernatural about the impersonal Tao. It has no pre-knowledge nor memory of people or events and it must not be seen as similar to God in the way the Jews, Christians or Muslims talk of Him. Tao does not care for its creation and so people cannot pray to or displease Tao. Like Brahman, Tao is the ultimate source of everything, but Brahman is eternal and timeless, whereas Tao is not, for it is forever changing. Tao is not merely the source, but also the flow and terminus of all things.

(2) Tao is also the way the universe works: the driving force which makes nature work; the way which brings order and sense to all life, so preventing chaos. Nature is always changing, but it also remains the same, like the cycle of the sun. How it operates is explained in the Book of Chuang Tzu (see p. 80), which was partially written by Chuang Tzu (369–286 BCE). The system is called Yin-Yang. (It will be explained Chapter 5.)

Jade Emperor.

Matzu.

Lao-Tse.

Three figures in Taoism. What does Lao-Tse mean? Who does the Jade Emperor rule over and why is he called Jade? What is Matzu's nickname?

(3) It is the Way we should order our lives so as to gear them to the way the universe works. Then life will go smoothly for us, for we shall not be struggling against its flow. To do this we must use the Power (Te) at our disposal.

Lao-Tse wrote, 'Tao gives birth to life. Te determines the individuality, growth, development, completion, maturity, protection and security of all things.' Te gives you intelligent power and vitality to live your life so that you can be self-sufficient.

But Lao-Tse's way gives no absolute guarantee of success, for unseen things may cause injury. The third and last phase of Taoism was taught by Chuang Tzu (369–286 BCE) who said you must not escape from society to the mountains as a recluse, but from this world to another world. He thought civilization was an artificial way of life which caused people endless work and sorrow. He refused to be prime minister when offered the post as he felt all forms of government were wrong. Individual freedom would bring contentment, while meditation would free one from emotional upsets. He said that ordinary knowledge is simply about the rights and wrongs of things, but there is a higher knowledge about the universe and one's place in it.

6. *What three phases did Taoism pass through? Who started each and why?*

The two types of Taoism are:
(1) *Tao Chia*, Taoist School of Philosophy (wise thinking) involving the use of the Power (Te) which enters our lives when we gear ourselves to the Yin-Yang Way (Tao) the universe works. Tao Chia works with, not against, nature (see pp. 106–7). This is the form which people in the West are interested in today.
(2) *Tao Chiao* (Teaching of the Way), Taoist Religion. This is really a separate movement with gods, temples and priests and the use of magic and alchemy. It arose because Taoism sought to enjoy life, so it aimed to lengthen people's lives to a great age and then gain immortality for them. This could be done, it was said, by seeking out one's lighter spirit or soul by means of breathing exercises (for example, breathing in morning mist) and lighter diet (vegetables, etc.) as meat and grain-foods nourished the three 'worms' of disease, senility and death. Immortality pills made of cinnabar (mercuric sulphide) were taken in the hope that they would turn into gold – in fact they killed some Taoists. Such ideas required belief in gods, temples and expert priests on hand.

7. *Under the headings: (a) Tao Chia, (b) Tao Chiao, list the differences between these two kinds of Taoism.*

Three Pure Ones, Taoist Trinity. During the Western Han Dynasty (206 BCE – 24 CE) Tao Chiao developed its three-tier heaven system.
(1) At the top was the Jade Emperor (Yu-Huang). Jade is a symbol of purity. He ruled a heavenly court with government ministries run by gods – Ministries of Thunder, Fire and Healing, as well as the Kitchen under Tzau Wang who rules everyone's domestic life. He reports to the Jade Emperor each year on everyone's behaviour (see p. 188). Kuan Tin, Goddess of Mercy, is very popular in Taiwan. She is pictured caring for a child as the protectress of women and children. Also popular is Matzu, or Ma-Chu, nicknamed 'Granny'. She originally

was a girl who set fire to her seaside home as a beacon for fishermen who were caught in a storm.

(2) Tao Chun (Ruler of Tao), the Lord of the Earth, who is in charge of Yin-Yang.

(3) Lao-Tse, Lord of Man, who founded Taoism.

A Taoist hell to avoid was also created. Thus Taoism came to consist of Tao Chia and Tao Chiao.

8. Draw a diagram to explain the three-heaven system.

9. Why should Westerners today be interested in Tao Chia and not Tao Chiao?

BUDDHISM

Siddhartha Gotama (or Gautama), the Buddha (563–483 BCE), was the son of an Indian prince of the Sakyamuni, or Shakya, tribe. The princedom was in the Himalayan foothills, 160 km north of Benares. Queen Maya realized she was going to give birth to a special child when she had a vision of an elephant entering her side. Legends of signs in the sky, earthquakes, flowers appearing out of season and miraculous healings surround his birth. It is said that as soon as he was born Siddhartha took seven steps and said in a lion's voice, 'I am the chief in the world. This is my last birth.' This refers to the fact that the Hindus saw him as the ninth incarnation of Vishnu (see p. 8).

His father had been warned not to let him see anything of pain, sickness and death, so he made sure that his son was kept within the palace grounds. Siddhartha grew up to be a great athlete. When he was 29 years old he managed to elude his father's guards on a number of occasions and so he saw the four signs (The Four Passing Sights) his father feared; namely, an old man, a sick man, a corpse and a monk. Now he knew that the world contained suffering, old age, death and the peace which could come from living as a monk.

He decided to leave his wife, son and 40 000 dancing girls and set out to find the causes of suffering and how to cure them. His departure is known as the Great Going Forth. For six years he wandered around seeing religious teachers and trying yoga exercises (see pp. 97–101), but got nowhere. He fasted until he collapsed, and this led him to conclude that this was not the way. Clearly one's body could not escape disease, old age and death.

Now aged 35, he reached the town of Gaya on a tributary of the Ganges and sat down under a Bodhi or Bō-tree, which means tree of enlightenment. He vowed to stay there at this 'Immovable Spot' until he understood all. The evil spirit Māra, King of Passions, tempted him with three voluptuous daughters, Gaiety, Caprice and Wantonness, who said, 'For you are in the prime of youth and vigour. Turn now your thoughts to love and take your pleasure. Look upon us, behold our cheeks and see how perfect are our forms . . .'. Then Māra sent an animal army with weapons but they had no effect either. When these failed, he showed him death amidst hurricanes, rain and boiling mud. After this experience the 'Great Awakening' occurred, when Gotama realized that suffering could end and there was a path away from it. Now he took the name of the Buddha, the Enlightened

The Buddha's hand positions indicate turning the wheel of the dhamma. He is seated on a lotus flower which symbolizes purity. Notice the hump of enlightenment on the top of his head, and the extended ear lobes, symbol of renunciation. Hand positions are called mudras.

One, the 'Ideal Man'. Earthquakes are said to have taken place for a week at this point. He sat there for 49 days in rapture for now he knew the cause of suffering or dissatisfaction and how to cure it.

He believed that a person can move from one category of manhood to another:

(1) Ordinary or unenlightened category.
(2) Enlightened category, a new species or category of Man.

Everyone has an embryo of enlightenment in him. If properly nurtured, this embryo will develop and enable one to become an enlightened, ideal person. Such a person has supreme knowledge, love, compassion and energy. So you must have faith in your ability to enlighten yourself. His Four Noble Truths and Noble Eightfold Path for life will be explained later (see pp. 113–15).

The Buddha preached his first sermon in the deer park at Sarnath near Benares to the five holy men who had earlier deserted him. Then for more than 40 years after this he travelled as a missionary for nine months of each year and stayed in a monastery for the three rainy months. He spoke in a popular way, easy for people to understand, unlike the Hindu brahmin priests. He used stories and parables to illustrate his points.

The dying Buddha with Burmese monks discussing their faith. What did the Buddha die of?

He was over 80 when he died at Kusinara (Kushinara) in North India. His death was the result of eating some poisonous mushrooms. He died lying on his side, and for this reason many statues, like the one below, show him in that position.

10. (a) *Compare Māra's temptations of the Buddha with the devil's of Jesus (Matt. 4:1–11; Luke 4:1–13).*
    (b) *At what stage in their lives do these temptations take place?*
    (c) *What effect do they have on them?*
    (d) *Are there any other aspects of the Buddha's life, or methods, which seem similar to those of Jesus?*

The Buddha has been described as one of the greatest personalities of all time. He had a warm patient heart for people but faced problems in a cool, careful way. He made things seem very simple, speaking to the level of his audience. His teaching was about how to solve the problems of this life until you could eventually reach the truth after a series of lives on earth.

He said the Hindus were wrong in thinking there were *immortal* gods, and so there was no need for sacrifices, rituals and prayers to them. So there was also no need for priests. Man had no immortal soul; instead his personality consisted of ever-changing components that would die with him (see pp. 237–8). Thus he challenged much of what the Hindus taught.

The Wheel of the Law, stressing the Eightfold Path to Nibbana.

11. *Briefly recount what the following events mean in Gotama's life:*
    (a) *Four Passing Sights*
    (b) *Great Going Forth*
    (c) *Immovable Spot*
    (d) *Great Awakening.*

JUDAISM

God's Creation. The Jewish story of creation is told in Genesis 1. God is said to have created the universe, starting with a shapeless mass, within a week: 1st day—created light, dark; 2nd day—created sky and water; 3rd day—arranged the earth and seas and created plant life; 4th day—created the sun, moon and stars; 5th day—the fish, birds; 6th day—animals and the first man (woman came shortly afterwards); 7th day—God rested. His concern for His creation was shown early on, when He ensured Noah and his farm stock's safety in the ark during the Flood (Genesis 6–9).

Abraham. Judaism is the religion of the Jews. The word comes from the name of their original Middle Eastern kingdom of Judah or Judea. The Hebrew name for God is considered too holy to use except in prayer, and the term Hashem (the Name) is used at all other times. They believe that God made a Covenant (contract) with a farmer called Abraham in about 1800 BCE (Gen. 17:1–8). As a result he uprooted his family, workmen and flocks and left Ur near the Persian Gulf for Haran, 500 miles (805 km) to the north-west. He then felt that God directed him to Canaan (Holy or Promised Land) later called Palestine; and here God made it plain to him that he would protect his people. Being a man of absolute obedience to his God, Abraham was prepared to sacrifice his son Isaac when told to do so. This was just a test, however, and Isaac succeeded his father. His passive leadership provided a period of consolidation so necessary after

Abraham's religious revolution. In turn Isaac's son, Jacob, took over as the third of these Patriarchs (avot). From him came the twelve tribes destined to conquer the Holy Land. By an angel's command his name was changed to Israel and so his descendants were called Israelites.

This was how a small obscure people began their great history. They ignored the worship of many gods going on around them and came to grasp the point that there was only one God, who judged people fairly yet firmly. He was far more than a nature god (see pp. 20–1). Nature god worshippers simply took care to please their gods to ensure that they themselves stayed alive contentedly. But God was prepared to direct the course of events, the course of history, in order to care for them, provided they would serve Him. Life for the Jews is not an illustration, as Hindus believe earthly life to be, but the arena in which God works out His plans.

Star of David, Magen David, a seventeenth-century CE symbol. The Menorah was the earlier symbol.

Moses. The Jews were not always fortunate. They became slaves of the Pharaoh of Egypt until Moses rescued them, around 1300 BCE. When Pharaoh had ordered the death of all Jewish baby boys, Moses' mother had hidden him in such a way that Pharaoh's daughter found him and adopted him. But when Moses was a young man he killed an Egyptian slave-master and had to flee across the Red Sea. Here God spoke to him and told him to return and rescue the Jews. God sent plague after plague on Egypt but Pharaoh refused to give in, even when He threatened to kill all the first-born children in the land. Moses alerted the Jews to kill lambs which the Egyptians held sacred, and smear the blood on their front doorposts. Also when the slaughter occurred it might then be assumed that the houses had been visited. After the slaughter Pharaoh told the slaves to go. Then he changed his mind and sent his army after them but they got across the Red Sea which was parted by God. The Egyptian army perished as the waters returned. The journey is known as the Exodus. *En route* for the Promised Land the Jews camped near Mount Sinai of Horeb. Moses climbed up to talk to God and returned with the Ten Commandments, the Tablets of the Law, on stone tablets (Exod. 19:20, see p. 122). These and other rules, which became known as the Oral Laws, he pressed on them to make them worship their God, and none other, and behave themselves. The making of the Israelites into the 'people of the covenant' was a new and original step amounting to a contract between God and a whole people. Thus Moses became Moshe Rabbenu, Moses our Teacher. Tradition has it that he also received the whole Torah and later wrote it down (see p. 83). This meant that the Torah not only had divine origin, but existed from the beginning of creation. It marked the Jews as God's people who were to settle in the Promised Land and gave them all they needed to know about God and their relationship to Him (Gen. 12; Exod. 19). The point to grasp is that there is no evolution in Jewish religious ideas, as the Torah gave all from the dawn of creation. Anything coming after it is a commentary on it, not new revelation.

> *Remember the Torah of Moses my servant that I commanded him as Horeb for all Israel, laws of faith and laws of justice.* (Malachi 4:4)

To mark these events a Tabernacle, a portable tent, was set up as the first house of worship (Exod. 26–7), known as the Ohel Mo'ed, Tent of Meeting, or

Mishkan, God's abode. God spoke to Moses in it. Inside, separated by a veil, was the Holy of Holies containing the Ark of the Covenant holding the Tablets of the Law, the menorah (see p. 192) and shewbread (offered bread). From then on a priesthood (kehunnah) was established to replace the system of heads of families performing sacrifices.

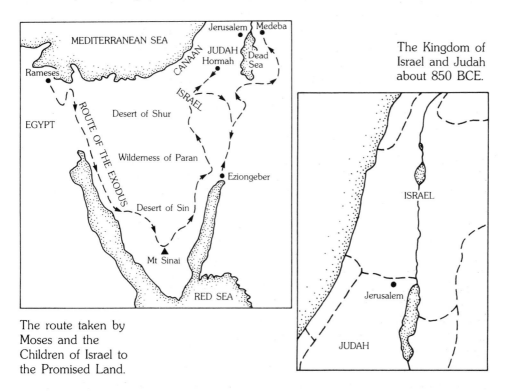

The Kingdom of Israel and Judah about 850 BCE.

The route taken by Moses and the Children of Israel to the Promised Land.

Kings and Prophets. After 40 years of nomadic life the Jews crossed the Jordan into the Promised Land. To help them settle down after a strong tribal period, kings were appointed, starting with Saul (1020–1005 BCE). Under King Solomon (965–925 BCE), their kingdom started its golden age with the building of the first Temple to house the Ark at Jerusalem. They saw God in those days as one who was slow to anger, but kind and forgiving while still prepared to punish. On Solomon's death, the twelve tribes split into two kingdoms, Israel in the north and Judah in the south. The Jews were ruled by good and bad kings. Some of the bad ones allowed idol worship, but men aware of God (prophets) called the people back to the true God. One of these was Elijah who lived in the ninth century BCE. He showed God's power by calling down fire from heaven against idol worshippers.

Diaspora (Dispersion) is the term used on a number of occasions in Jewish history, when military defeat and enforced exile pushed the Jews into other lands. Travel and trade have also led to dispersions. In 722 BCE, Assyria overran and deported the inhabitants of Israel and in 586 BCE the Babylonians deported those in Judea. During this long period they were inspired by prophets or wise men, who unfolded the riches explicit in the Torah so that they would know how He regarded them.

Prophets interpreted God's will so as to fit events of their time. They predicted the consequence of the social situation; as political and social commentators, they denounced social inequality and evil and criticized extravagance and idolatry. Their role was to forth-tell (tell forth God's will) rather than foretell the future like fortune-tellers.

Amos (active 760–746 BCE) was a herdsman. He preached that God would punish His Chosen People because their behaviour was a sin against Him. God expected people to behave in a good moral way or He would judge them; sacrifices would be of no use without good behaviour. Another prophet, Hosea (active 750–735 BCE) stressed the people's lack of faith in God, while pointing out that He did forgive repentant sinners as He was a God of Love.

Isaiah (active 735–701 BCE) claimed that God used the Assyrians to punish and purify the Jews and that the purified 'remnant' would survive. He forecast the coming of a human Messiah-King who would rule stongly, yet gently, and so deliver them. His arrival would change people's characters.

Jeremiah (active 627–580 BCE) stressed that God dealt closely with individuals as they were precious to him. A person's sin would separate him from God. He prophesied defeat when Judah and Egypt planned to revolt against Babylon and so was imprisoned as a traitor. In 586 BCE Nebuchadnezzar II destroyed the Temple and during Israel's Exile (586–538 BCE) synagogues which previously had played relatively minor roles became the main religious and community centres.

Ezekiel (active 593–571 BCE) saw these setbacks as God's fair judgements on a sinful people, for He was a worldwide God who controlled kings. Ezekiel encouraged the Jews to appreciate that each individual was responsible for his own fate and was not affected by any bad behaviour of his ancestors. The Exile was a result of the present nation's sins, not those of an 'earlier generation', so there was hope for the future. He had a vision of a redeemed people and a rebuilt Temple. In 539 BCE Cyprus of Persia did allow the Jews to return and rebuild their Temple.

The book of Isaiah covers two distinct periods and this has led some people to believe that Isaiah predicted the later events; others have concluded that there was a Second Isaiah (Deutero-Isaiah) about 550 BCE. This latter Isaiah said that God's judgement was over with the end of the Exile. God was not only magnificently great but gentle too. He argued that through the purification suffering of the servant-people (Israel seen as the Suffering Servant of God) all nations would turn to the new Jerusalem, as they would see God's righteousness shining through Israel's experience. Thus he saw Israel as the light for all nations to follow as Abraham and Moses had done (Gen. 12, Exod. 19). The idea also existed of a period of rule by the Messiah, meaning 'Anointed One'. After this would come the 'End' when all would be judged. They thought the Messiah would be an outstanding human being, but not a divine one.

The era of the prophets had been one in which Israel was accused of sinfulness.

Sin for Amos was the social injustice and exploitation he saw around him, while for Hosea it was a lack of faith in God and sexual licence. Isaiah saw sin as rebellion and pride; Jeremiah saw it as backsliding and corruption; Ezekiel, as stubbornness and profaneness and the Second Isaiah as Israel's blindness to God's will. All cried, 'Repent!' and offered a new start if Israel responded.

After the Exile the Temple was rebuilt and by the middle of the fourth century BCE the Torah's requirements on behaviour were again strictly upheld. Certain Jews called Zealots expected the Messiah to lead a military movement against the occupying Roman army. In the opinion of Jews today the Messiah has still not come. This marks them off decisively from the Christians, who see Jesus as the Messiah, although a different type of Messiah from the one the Jews expect. The Jews realized God was not a nature god in any way as He created everything. The sun, moon, mountains and rivers have no gods in them as they are all part of God's creation; His existence does not need to be proved to Jews; they take it for granted. People are created in His image, however, and so must demonstrate His justice and mercy by treating others similarly. The world is God's gift to people and they must treat it as such. People are free to choose whether they will respond or not. Jews do not reject the world and live as monks for they believe God meant them to enjoy His world. This world is not essentially evil and is not to be rejected.

12. State briefly why the Jews believe they are a people selected by God for particular care in return for their religious duties to Him. Does their history justify their claim?

13. List all the points made describing God and His ways, attitudes, etc, and say which prophets made which points. What points do you consider the most important and why?

14. (a) Does God intervene in history or has He no control over what men do or what natural events and disasters occur? (b) Give examples, ancient and modern, great or small to support your opinion.

15. When the Jews suffered, their leaders said it was God's judgement on them and so it was their fault for not keeping to the contract or covenant with Him. Why do you think the leaders said this rather than saying it was God's fault and He had let them down?

16. (a) Why did God need prophets to explain what He and His methods were like?
(b) What might have happened to Judaism if there had been no prophets to give God's attitude to matters when problems arose?

CHRISTIANITY

Jesus. But what makes the beliefs of Christians distinctive from those of Jews and Muslims is their acceptance of Jesus as the Son of God, and not just as another prophet (John 14:9; 20:28; Mark 1: 10–11). Jesus is unique in being

The Cross is a symbol of Christ's sacrificial death for mankind.

both God and Man. Christians argue that the Jewish prophets had merely paved the way for the coming of God's Son to make the truth clear and provide a way of salvation (the saving of the soul from sin and its entrance into heaven) for mankind. Jesus' perfect example showed people what God wanted them to be like (Mark 1:14–15).

They look back at the Second Isaiah's reference to a Shepherd caring for his flock and argue that Isaiah produced a new solution to the mystery of suffering when he said that someone could suffer for another's sins, 'He was wounded for our transgressions (sins)'. Jesus' first disciples (followers) who were Jews accepted the Jewish idea of a Messiah as an Anointed One, an earthly king of a new religious age, not as a saviour of all mankind. That idea was begun by Paul (see p. 54). Jesus himself never claimed to fulfil such Old Testament prophecies, though he probably thought of himself as the final prophet. Nor, it seems, did he think of himself as existing before his earthly birth; the idea that he was eternal and part of the Trinity Godhead (see p. 24) grew up after his crucifixion.

Jesus was born in Bethlehem, probably sometime between 2 and 6 BCE. (Our 'AD' calendar is not completely accurate. BC means 'Before Christ' and AD 'The Year of the Lord'. Today the classifications BCE 'Before the Common Era' and CE 'Common Era' are becoming accepted.) According to the stories of his birth he had a human mother, Mary, but no human father. His Virgin Birth (implying conception by the Holy Spirit and not a man) is called the Incarnation, and it involves the eternal Word (Logos), of God coming to earth in human form. So it is claimed that he was both God and Man when he was on earth. Mary was told that God's Holy Spirit (Paraclete, Comforter) would overshadow her and she would conceive a son. Some Christians argue that Jesus had to be conceived without a human father because he was uniquely the Son of God.

17. *Interview the innkeeper about the events connected with the couple who arrived seeking shelter and whom he put in the stable (Luke 2:1–20; Matt. 2).*

Jesus seems to have lived a quiet life as a carpenter until he was about 30 years old. Then he led his missionary life for some three years until the closing events of his earthly life. His missions began when he was baptized by John the Baptist and received God's Spirit (Mark 1:1–11). He was immediately put to the test by the devil – Satan – before starting his teaching career (Matt. 4:1–11).

Who is baptizing whom?

Moving among social drop-outs, Jesus concentrated his teaching on the rapidly approaching coming of the longed-for reign of God on earth, the Kingdom of God. He told special stories (parables) which stressed that the 'zero hour' was near and people must make a decision to trust God completely. Coming into Galilee he said 'The time is fulfilled and the Kingdom of God is at hand; repent and believe in the gospel (good news)' (Mark 1:14–15). It is claimed that Jesus cured the lame and the blind miraculously, as signs that the age of salvation was dawning (Matt. 8:1–14; 9:1–8, 18–31). His exorcisms (expelling of evil spirits from people) marked the opening assault on the forces of evil (Matt. 8:16, 28–34; 9:32–34).

18. *Give brief summaries of (a) cures, (b) exorcisms done by Jesus. Comment on what interests or surprises you about them.*

19. *Jesus compared the Kingdom of God to a number of things including a mustard seed, treasure and a fishing net (Matt. 13:31–49). Explain the Kingdom in terms of (a) a mustard seed, (b) a fishing net.*

Jesus urged Jews to respond to the coming of God in the person of himself (Matt. 10:37–42; 11:28–30), stressing the matter was urgent. This led him to press everyone who believed in him to adjust their behaviour quickly (Mark 1:4–15). His followers should love others without exception he argued. Their relations with each other must match God's with them (Luke 6:32–36; Matt. 5:43–48). The more they loved the bad characters of this world, the more they would appreciate God's love for all people (Matt. 25:24–46; Luke 10:29–37). He stressed that a person's attitudes and motives counted most of all (Matt. 15:11–20; Mark 7:1–23) and he set high standards for his followers to copy (Matt. 5:5–9, 21–24, 27–32, 38–48; 6:1–4, 24–33; Luke 18:9–14). But he offered salvation as the prize (Matt. 7.21; 18:1–5; John 5:21–24; 6:48–51, 54; 11:25–26; 14:6).

20. *(a) Look up the Bible references given above and summarize Jesus' teaching on (i) good behaviour, (ii) salvation.*
(b) How can a Christian obtain salvation?

Like some other Jews, Jesus simplified the Jewish Law by reducing it to two commands, 'Love God and love others as much as yourself' (Mark 12:28–31; Luke 6:27–28). He taught his disciples (followers) that they were God's sons rather than His slaves. They could approach God in intimate, personal ways as Father (Matt. 6:7–18; Luke 10:21; 23:34, 46; John 14; Rom. 1:7). He gave them the Lord's Prayer, which begins with the common Jewish formula, 'Our Father in heaven'. One modern version of the Bible gives the Lord's Prayer as follows:

> *Our Father in heaven, we honour your holy name. We ask that your kingdom will come now. May your will be done here on earth, just as it is in heaven. Give us our food again today, as usual, and forgive us our sins, just as we have forgiven those who have sinned aginst us. Don't bring us into temptation, but deliver us from evil. Amen* (Matt. 6:9–13)

(Amen is a common ending to prayers which means 'so let it be'.)

Palestine in the time of Jesus.

When he appointed twelve disciples as followers and aides it seemed to some a sign that he was about to start a Messianic community (God-like community run by a saviour) to replace the Twelve Tribes of Israel (Matt. 4:18–22; 10:1–42; Mark 1:16–20; 3:14–19). Once, he was transfigured (that is, he appeared in glory, like a vision) to three of the twelve. Under these circumstances it was not surprising that his controversial views and huge outdoor meetings attracted the attention of powerful Jewish religious leaders. They feared their people might be misled with false hopes. The political situation did not help as the Romans were occupying the land and Jesus' efforts might be seen as aimed at starting a popular nationalist uprising. The result was that the Jewish leaders pressed the Roman governor, Pilate, to find him guilty of pretending to be the expected Messiah (political and religious king) when he entered Jerusalem in triumph (Mark 15:2, 9, 26). Anticipating arrest, he had invented a unique commemorative-style meal for his followers when he broke bread and blessed it and wine at the Last Supper (Mark 14:22–25; see also Exod. 24; Isa. 42:6). However, his view of the Messiah

The Last Supper.

differed from that of the Jews (see p. 21) for he saw his role in terms of the Suffering Servant of Isaiah (Isa. 42:1-2; 49:1-6; 50:5-9; 52:13-53:12): 'He was despised and rejected of men . . .' Jesus saw his mission as one which involved suffering and death for the sake of others. He came 'to minister, and to give his life as a ransom for many' (Mark 10:45) and so re-establish the good relations between God and people which had been broken by sin.

The difficulties of securing a conviction and sentence at his political trial can be seen from all the problems which arose from the time of his arrest onwards (Matt. 26:45–27:27; Mark 14:41–15:15; Luke 22:47–23:25; John 18:1–19:16).

21. *Summarize the trial sequence, from the time of Jesus' arrest until Pilate's condemning him to death, using any two of the Gospel accounts. What differences can you find in the two accounts you have selected?*

Jesus was flogged before being made to carry the beam of the cross from which he was crucified, so paying the supreme sacrifice of surrendering his life for others. His disciples put his body in a tomb (Matt. 27:26–61; Mark 15:15–47; Luke 23:25–56; John 19:16–42). These events are commemorated by Good Friday. His suffering and death are referred to as his Passion. Christians believe this sacrifice provides them with a way of achieving redemption (reconciliation with God) for their sins.

22. *Summarize the story of Christ's last hours, from when Pilate handed him over to the troops to his burial, using any two of the Gospel accounts.*

Two days after Good Friday Jesus' body had disappeared, the stone in front of the tomb having been rolled away. All that remained inside were the bandages that the body had been wrapped in. The disciples were in some confusion, the more so when Jesus appeared to them alive again. He was not a ghost as the wounds he had suffered were there to touch. Traditionally it is believed that he ascended bodily into heaven for, as the unique Son of God, he could not end his life like others (Matt. 28; Mark 16; Luke 24; John 20–21). His rising is commemorated by Easter Sunday and his ascension on Ascension Day. Christians believe that one day he will come again to rule in glory – the Second Coming, the Parousia.

23. *Give brief descriptions of all his appearances after he rose again. Comment on what interests you or surprises you.*

The Trinity. Before he left his disciples Jesus gave them instructions to carry on his mission. He promised to send them God's Holy Spirit to aid them, and this promise was fulfilled (Luke 24:29; John 20:21–22; Acts 2:1–33, 38). This led to the teaching that God is Three-in-One (Tri-unity, Trinity): God the Father, God the Son and God the Holy Spirit (2 Cor. 13:14). The Godhead can appear to us in three forms just as water can be ice, liquid or steam, namely God *over us* (the Father), God *with us* (the Son, Christ), and God *in us* (Holy Spirit or Ghost). The first viewpoint stresses God's immeasurable greatness before which all should bow humbly. The second shows His love for mankind in sending His Son. The third provides His followers with comfort and guidance. God is one being or 'substance' but can be 'seen' as three 'persons' or 'channels' of communication. Some Christians tend to emphasize one viewpoint more than the others, so they disagree in some ways about how God should be approached and what the Christian life should be.

24. *The Jews claim that God controls history and they are His Chosen People, while Christians claim that God entered history personally in the form of Christ. What is the difference between these views and the effect they have?*

25. *Jesus was a poor man who travelled only some 90 miles (145 km) from his birthplace, wrote no great books, lived and worked with the poor and outcasts, and died a criminal's death; yet he altered the course of history as the founder of Christianity. Why? How?*

26. *It is claimed that Jesus freed people from three intolerable burdens: (a) fear, even of death, (b) guilt over sin, (c) selfishness, and that he gave them a new birth into life. (See 1 Pet. 1:2–25; Rom. 3:9–31; 5:3–6:11; Gal. 5:19–24.) How could this be so?*

Jesus on the cross as depicted in a modern film.

25

Muhammad and Allah. Islam means 'submission to God'. God is called Allah (Allah; Al = the; Lah = God), and submission to Him will bring peace. The prophet Muhammad ('highly praised') was born in the trading centre of Makkah (or Mecca) on Monday 20 August 570 CE. His father had just died and his mother died when he was six. As an orphan he was sensitive to human sufferings. He started work as a shepherd boy for his uncle, Abu Talib. In 594 CE he worked for a merchant and the next year he married his widowed employer, Khadijah. He was 25 and she was 40. They had a number of children, all but one of whom died young. But it was a happy marriage.

Muhammad was a gentle, sensitive and helpful man who traded honestly. He was known as the 'upright, trustworthy one' (Al-Amin). He was disturbed by the lawlessness and immoral behaviour of those around him and their futile idol worship. Possibly he heard of the Jewish and Christian beliefs in one God and the importance these two religions attached to their holy books. Certainly he must have turned over in his mind the problems of his countrymen. Then in 610

The main areas of Islam today (shaded). Muslims face towards Makkah when praying. Which compass direction do they face from

(a) London
(b) Rabat
(c) Tehran
(d) Dacca?

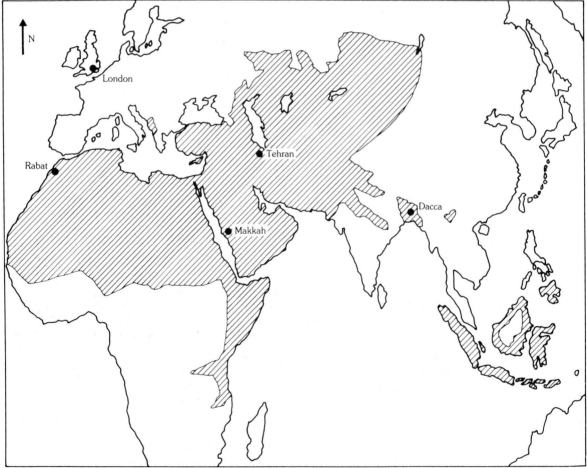

CE, during one of the all-night vigils he used to keep in caves or the wilderness, he had a revelation from the angel Gabriel:

> He came to me while I was asleep, with a piece of brocade whereupon was writing, and said, 'Recite, in the name of thy Lord who created man from clots of blood. Recite! Thy Lord is wondrous kind, who by the pen has taught mankind things they knew not'. So I recited it, and he departed from me. And I awoke from my sleep, and it was as though these words were written on my heart . . . When I was midway on the mountain, I heard a voice from heaven, saying, 'O Muhammad . . .'. I raised by head . . . to see, and lo, Gabriel in the form of a man, with feet astride the horizon, saying, 'Muhammad! thou art the Apostle of God and I am Gabriel.'

Terrified, Muhammad ran home. His wife thought he must have been chosen as a prophet. His first revelation was on Lailat ul Qadr, the Night of Power, and it is commemorated during Ramadan (see p. 142).

In a number of revelations Muhammad received the Qur'ān, or Koran, from Gabriel. 'We have made this Qur'ān easy for you in your own tongue' (Qur'ān, Surah 44:58) so 'that you may understand' (Qur'ān, Surah 43:3). So for the next few years Muhammad preached about Allah, the One and Only God, the Compassionate and Merciful, to the tribesmen who came to Makkah on business or as pilgrims to the Ka'ba (see pp. 143-4). The people of Makkah worshipped natural objects made of stone and wood. He warned them that this was idol worship and they would suffer on the Day of Judgement (see pp. 243-4). His views were a threat to the trade centred on the idol worship there. Also he called for higher moral standards, which was unpopular. His claim that all were equal in Allah's eyes was dynamite to the class-ridden people of Makkah. So opposition to him built up and he and his few followers were pelted and stoned.

Note Muslims often add 'peace be on him' after referring to Muhammad or other prophets; sometimes abbreviated in books to 'pboh'.

27. *What evidence is there that Muhammad received the Qur'ān from Allah rather than writing it himself?*

28. *Why were Muhammad's views rejected at Makkah?*

By 619 CE, 200 had accepted Muhammad's message. They were mainly slaves or poor workers. In 622 a group from Yathrib (later called Medinā-al-nabī, City of the Prophet) asked him to help the faithful there. His journey to Medina is called the Hijrah or Hegira ('breaking with old ties'; 'migration') and Muslims date their calendar from this turning point in their history. AH 1 means Anno (Year of) Hegira 1. On the way Muhammad and a friend hid in a crevice as people from Makkah tried to find them. His frightened friend said, 'We are but two.' 'No,' said Muhammad, 'We are three for Allah is with us.' After three days in hiding they escaped.

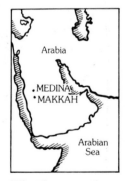

What happened at Medina and Makkah?

At Medina Muhammad preached about Allah in opposition to the idol worship, which he regarded as a special sin, called 'shirk'. He ceased to be a despised

The Star and the Moon which guide desert peoples. Islam guides (star) and lights (moon) the way through life.

preacher and became in turn a statesman, judge, and general teacher. He was a religious and a political leader which meant that his judgements could be seen as Allah's commands pronounced by His prophet (nabī). Muhammad's prophethood (Risalah, Rasul) to the Arabs is thus most important, as there had been earlier prophets to the Jews and Christians. He called for an end to idol worship, immorality and alcoholism. He developed Medina as a rival trade centre to Makkah. In addition, he hoped that Jews there would accept the message and see him as their leader as he too preached about one God. But they rejected him and said no Arab could be their leader. At Medina he issued the first charter of freedom of conscience in human history when he said that Jews (and Christians) 'shall ... practise their religion as freely as the Muslims.'

Muhammad's wife died in 620 CE and the custom of the land led him to accept that he could have several wives. Nine or 14 have been mentioned. When he married Zainab, who was divorced from his close friend Zaid, he emphasized the acceptance of divorce. He married other women when he was between 55 and 60 years old, sometimes to cement relations with various tribes and sometimes to shelter widows during periods of war. He raised the status of women and insisted that sex should only take place within marriage (see pp. 219-20). Muhammad was a man of burning sincerity and magnetic personality.

If he was to establish Allah's rule on earth Muhammad believed he would have to set up an independent state based on Allah's laws. This meant fighting for Medina's independence from Makkah. Thus until his death in 632, battles took place from time to time. The fighting he regarded as jihad (holy struggle) for the faith, which would lead to life in Paradise for those who fought in it. In 624 at the battle of Badr his 300 defeated the Meccans' 900 (Surah 8:11-12, 42-44), but they suffered at Uhud in 625 (Surah 3:120-126, 143-154) when 9000 attacked their 700. Muhammad was wounded. But in 630 his 10 000 captured Makkah easily. He destroyed all 360 idols, as they were connected with human sacrifices, and then circled the Ka'ba there before rededicating it to Allah.

29. *Jihads are of two kinds. The Greater Jihad is the struggle to purify oneself. The Lesser Jihad is a war fought in the last resort after all peaceful attempts have failed. It is not an aggressive war.*
    (a) What wars have been fought by people in the name of their religion?
    (b) Do you think they were justified today?
    (c) Do people who fight in holy wars usually win?

Muhammad died in 632 CE. Whereas Jesus had emphasized that God is a Father of His people, Muhammad stressed His compassion as the majestic powerful God who shows mercy. Muslims' prayer is an act of submission to Allah. Islam means 'submission' and Muslim 'a surrendered man' (active participle of 'Islam'). They think Christians go too far in thinking they know His nature when they call Him Father. They deny that Jesus is God's Son as that would reduce God to human level, they claim. They deny that the Holy Spirit is part of the Godhead, saying spirit is part of God's creation. They stress the 'oneness of Allah' (Tauhīd, Tauheed, Tawhid).

The Muslim devotion to Allah is expressed in Surah 1:

> *In the name of Allah, the Merciful, the Compassionate.*
> *Praise be to Allah, the Lord of the worlds,*
> *The Merciful One, the Compassionate,*
> *Master of the day of doom.*
> *Thee alone we serve, to Thee alone we cry for help!*
> *Guide us in the straight path,*
> *The path of them that Thou hast blessed,*
> *Not of those with whom Thou art angry,*
> *Nor of those who go astray.*   (Surah 1)

30. *Compare this prayer with the Christian Lord's Prayer on p. 23.*
     (a) Have they any points in common?
     (b) What different pictures of God do they conjure up in your mind?

The Qur'ān describes Allah, with 99 'Beautiful Names'. The key names are Compassionate, Merciful, First and Last, Almighty, Creator, Giver of Life, Provider, Guider, Forgiver, and Judge. Father is not one of the 99.

Islam's three basic beliefs are Tauhīd (Oneness of Allah before whom one should bow); Risalah (prophethood – Allah sent prophets to guide people); and Ākhira (life after death, which implies that people are accountable for their lives on earth).

SIKHISM

Guru Nanak (1469–1539 CE), the founder of Sikhism (meaning 'discipleship'), was born in Talwandi village, now called Nanakana Sahib, in Pakistan. His father, Kalu, was a well-known official and a Hindu. At Guru Nanak's birth the midwife saw a dazzling halo around the boy's head, and this lead a local brahmin (Hindu priest) to say that Guru Nanak would be a great man, a king or a guru (wise teacher). Stories about his birth are called janam sakhi. His father took him away from school early on when he spent too much time thinking about God and not doing his work. He was given a brahmin tutor instead. Guru Nanak asked him 'Can you tell me, sir, why should I be a Hindu at all? Is it not good to be just a man?' Kalu and the brahmins were very annoyed at this and Guru Nanak was packed off to be a cowherd.

One day he fell asleep under a tree and the cattle got into a cornfield and ate the crop. The angry farmer took the cattle away and told the police chief who in turn set off with Kalu to find Guru Nanak. When they got to the field they found the corn was as good as ever! It seemed like magic and Guru Nanak came to be accepted by many as 'a man of God'. When he was a teenager he had Muslim as well as Hindu friends. When Kalu told him off for having Muslim friends, he replied, 'There's no Hindu or Muslim. We are all brothers.' Kalu was angry because Guru Nanak kept giving away his clothes, books, food and money to poor boys, and so he decided he must put his son to the test. He gave him 20 rupees to go to a city and set himself up as a merchant. But Guru Nanak used the opportunity to preach his friendship-faith as he went through the villages and when he got to the jungle he used the money to buy food for 20 hermits who lived there praying to God. Returning home empty-handed he was slapped by Kalu.

Mother Tripta Devi with baby Nanak.

At 18 Guru Nanak got married and became a storekeeper. One day he went to the river to bathe and did not return. Three days later he was found at prayer. He said God wanted him to work for Him. He was asked if he meant for the Hindus or the Muslims, and he replied both as they were brothers in God's eyes. He then began a 30-year missionary journey in which he covered thousands of miles on foot. To emphasize his concern to bring Hinduism and Islam together he wore the yellow robe of a guru and the turban and beads of a Muslim. He was inspired by Hindu bhaktism and Muslim sufism. For his God was personal, unlike the impersonal Brahman.

In one village he stayed with a carpenter, Lalo, and shared his simple food. A rich man, Bhago, invited him to a feast and he went reluctantly, taking some of Lalo's simple food with him. When everyone had gathered, Guru Nanak stood up with Lalo's food in one hand and Bhago's in the other. He squeezed the two handfuls and from Lalo's came drops of milk and from Bhago's blood. He said that this was not magic but the truth. A poor man's food was clean as it was worked for. A rich man's was not clean as it was obtained not by honest work but by making others work until they dropped. Bhago quietly bowed low before Guru Nanak and promised to treat his workers better in future.

When he went to the Muslim holy city of Makkah, Guru Nanak lay down to rest in such a way that his feet pointed towards the Ka'ba. This made an official, Rukandin, furious as Guru Nanak's position insulted Allah. Guru Nanak apologized and asked, 'Could you turn my legs in the direction in which there is no God?' but each time Rukandin moved him round and looked up he found the Ka'ba was still in front of Guru Nanak's legs. Rukandin was dumbstruck. Guru Nanak told him, 'God does not live in one place. He lives everywhere.'

Guru Nanak eventually reached Hardwar on the river Ganges. A crowd were splashing water in the direction of the sun where they believed their ancestors now lived. Guru Nanak started splashing water in the opposite direction and got told off for being so stupid. He replied that his farm 300 miles (483 km) away had not had any rain for a year and he was sending it water. They asked him how could the water possibly reach his farm and he pointed out that theirs had a much longer way to go to reach the sun! So the people stopped and listened to him and he told them to serve the living and not the dead.

On one occasion, Guru Nanak was travelling through Bengal, and one village refused him and his companion the food they had begged for, whereupon he said, 'May these people stay in this village for ever.' At the next village the two were given food and he prayed, 'May the people of this village scatter.' His companion was puzzled and asked him why he blessed the bad and cursed the good. Guru Nanak pointed out that he wanted the example of the good villagers to be spread around, while the bad ones should be confined where they were so that they did not spread their bad customs.

Eventually, Guru Nanak gave up his journeyings and started a farming commune. He knew he had to choose a successor and after a hard day's work he thought of a test which would help him choose wisely. A heap of wet, muddy grass was lying in the fields and he asked his two sons to carry it home. 'What for? We don't need it at home', said the elder. 'It is wet and muddy and will spoil our

Guru Nanak.

clothes,' said the younger, and added 'Ask one of your Sikhs.' Nanak replied that his sons should work as hard as his Sikhs. Immediately a Sikh, Lehna, ran forward and picked it up. Guru Nanak was now convinced his sons were too proud and lazy to become his successors, but he decided on a further test. Another day he dropped a rupee into a deep pool of cold, dirty water. No one, including his sons, wanted to get wet to recover it. But Lehna jumped in and got it without complaining. After a while Guru Nanak asked him if he felt cold and Lehna replied, 'No, I don't, my Lord. I enjoy working for you. It keeps me warm.' That evening Guru Nanak appointed him his successor, naming him Angad (literally 'my limb', myself). During the night Nanak died.

31. What are the main events in Nanak's life which particularly interest you? Why?

32. Compare the ways in which Jesus and Nanak preached or demonstrated their beliefs.

Khanda, the two-edged sword in the centre, symbolizes God's concern for truth and justice. The two Kirpans represent his temporal and spiritual powers. The circle (Chakra) is God's Unity, the continuity of life and the equality of all.

Creation. Guru Nanak explained that 'There was darkness for countless years. There was neither earth nor sky; it was His Will (Hukam). There was neither day nor night, neither sun nor moon. God was in deep meditation. There was nothing except Himself.' Then he willed the creation of the universe. He did so to please Himself and enjoy its spectacle. It is not an illusion (maya) as Hindus see it, although it will not last for ever. God dwells in it and transcends it.

Akal Parkh, or Akal Purakh. Sikhs (literally 'learners') believe in God whom they call Akal Parkh ('Immortal'), Waheguru ('Wondrous Teacher'), Sat Guru ('The True Guru') or Ek Onkar ('Bodiless' One, God). Guru Nanak wrote, 'There is one God ... the All-pervading Creator, without fear, without hatred, immortal, unborn, self existent! God sustains all and is a personal God who is close to men's hearts. He controls history.' Nanak wrote:

> By His writ some have pleasure, others pain,
> By His grace some are saved,
> Others doomed to die, relive and die again.   (Japji)

Guru Gobind Singh, tenth guru, made his view of Akal clear when he wrote, 'God has no marks, no colour, no caste and no ancestors, no form, no complexion, no outline, no costume and so He is indescribable. He is fearless, luminous and measureless in might.' Of Man's relations with God he wrote:

> As sparks flying out of a flame
> Fall back on the fire from which they rise,
> As dust rising from the earth
> Falls back upon the same earth;
> As waves beating upon the shingle
> Recede and in the ocean mingle
> So from God come all things under the sun
> And to God return when their race is run.   (Swayye)

Notice that Akal does not become incarnate, that is He does not come to earth in any human form, but He is called Father. Guru Ajan (1563–1606) said, 'He dwells in everything; He dwells in every heart.' Sikhs treat the Guru Granth

Sahib (Sikh holy book, see pp. 91–2) with devotion, as the Christians treat their Bible and the Muslims their Qur'ān. Guru Nanak believed the truth could be found along different paths and different religions were like different languages

33. *Compare the Muslim idea of God with that of the Sikhs. Is the Sikh idea nearer that of the Muslims or the Christians?*

34. *Make a table listing the words or phrases used to describe (a) Brahman, (b) the Jewish God, (c) the Christian God, (d) Allah, (e) Akal Parkh. Then add a further column (f) with words or phrases which appear in all the other columns. Finally add a column (g) containing words or phrases you would use to describe God.*

35. *Who or what are (a) Brahman, (b) Brahma, (c) Vishnu, (d) Shakti?*

36. *Which god is shown with an elephant's head? Give one explanation as to how he came by it? Why are his large ears so important?*

37. *What does the word Buddha mean? What was Gautama's father's religion? Beneath what did Gautama sit when he was seated at the Immovable Spot?*

38. *Who moved from Ur to Canaan when his God told him to do so? Who led his people from slavery and what was the escape event called?*

39. *Jesus is referred to as 'The Only Son of God'. What did early Christians mean by this? Why do Muslims reject this description?*

40. *What do Akal Parkh, Waheguru, and Ek Onkar mean? Which religion do they refer to?*

41. *Why is Shiva shown dancing in the centre of a flaming circle? What does the circle represent?*

42. *Which is the main symbol used by Christians? Why is it central to their faith? What year was Muhammad born and in which country? What does his title Al-Amin mean? Name the religious leader born in Talwandi, Pakistan.*

3
HISTORY

We cannot understand any religion today without knowing something of its history because history develops and affects a religion. The problem is that followers may not be really true to their chosen faith, but still claim that they are acting 'in good faith'. Religious wars have been only too frequent over the centuries, but do they really represent the gentle, loving faiths they claim to champion? What may start as a defensive act may become an offensive one. An offensive campaign might even be pursued on the grounds that it is religiously good for the faith to overcome other faiths. Often such arguments conceal a lust for power or a fear of invasion and do not really represent the true faith at all.

Ideally the followers of different faiths today should acknowledge that their predecessors did make mistakes, claim too much, and act too ruthlessly. Unfortunately there is a human desire to explain away the blackspots rather than face them head on. So you must take care when you read this chapter not to jump to unfair conclusions and too easily condemn a faith for what *some* of its followers did in its name. The important thing is to value the faith itself and have sympathy for the followers who, like everyone else, find it is very difficult actually to put a faith into practice in a wicked world.

HINDUISM

Harappan or Indus (Hindus) Valley Civilization (2500–1500 BCE). This covered much of NW India. Brick-built cities with straight streets and elaborate water supplies existed. People worshipped mother goddesses.

Aryan Age. From 1500 BCE onwards the Aryans ('Noble People') entered India from the north west in search of new cattle pastures. They had no difficulty in defeating the Harappan valley civilization as they used a new weapon, the horse-drawn chariot. They brought with them the Sanskrit language, but as they could not write, they had to learn their scripture, the Vedas ('Knowledge'), by heart. They preferred male gods (Vedic Polytheism) to the natives' female ones, preaching about reincarnation, karma and Nibbana. They built no temples, being satisfied with temporarily sanctified ground for their ritual sacrifices in a nomadic way. They intermarried with the natives and between 800 and 500 BCE their priests came to dominate the people while their rulers were campaigning so that three classes of Aryans or Twice-born developed: (1) priests (2) warrior nobles (3) the people (see p. 96). A fourth class accounted for the non-Aryans. About 500 BCE some came to see that there was really one god, Brahman, and all other gods were below him (*see Upanishads*, pp. 74–5). They preached that deliverance from rebirth could come by using the Jnana (Knowledge) yoga method (pp. 97–9) rather than by performing rituals.

1. *What effect did the Aryans' conquest of the Indus valley area have on the development of Hinduism and class structure?*

About 300 BCE the Rāmāyana (p. 76) marked a revival of the polytheism of the Vedic gods, Vishnu and Shiva, using the Bhakti (Love) Yoga method (p. 99) in reaction to the Brahman one-god idea. Vaishnavism developed *c*.600 CE with its idea that God visits earth in different forms or incarnations (p. 8). Shaivism, stressing hermit-like service to Shīva and belief in this one god who stands for life's energy, followed 200 years later in South India (pp. 8–10). Tridandrins, who are ascetics, carry Shīva's weapon, an iron trident, around. The three prongs symbolize bodily, worldly and heavenly suffering. Some Shaivites came to follow Shankara (788–820 CE), whose Advaita Vedānta teaching claimed that Brahman is the only god. Advaita means 'not-different', so denouncing the false teaching that God and the human soul (atta) are not one – in other words, teaching that the soul is part of the godhead (Brahman-atta) and Man should spend his life seeking to find his atta, preferably by using Jnana Yoga.

The idea of the Great Mother (Shakti), Shīva's wife, sometimes seen as Durgā or Kālī, is favoured by other Hindus. She is seen fighting demons and gods yet she is worshipped by women wanting children.

2. *What is the difference between Vaishnavism and Shaivism?*

3. *Trace the conflict between various groups over the question of whether there is ultimately one god or more.*

Muslim Domination. Muslims entered India and in 1206 set up a sultantate at Delhi, covering a large area. The Muslim Mughal emperors reigned from 1555 to 1858. Many Hindus turned Muslim, while others were satisfied with the emperors' patronage of brahmins and their temples. The Emperor Akbar (reigned 1560–1605) was particularly kind to them, while Aurangzeb (reigned 1658–1707) was ruthless against them. Thus Hinduism became a rather secretive religion kept going by brahmins.

British Rule. The East India Company gradually took over the running of Bengal and other parts of India in the eighteenth century. But the British were not absorbed into Indian life the way the Aryans and Muslims had been. Many Indians feared the influence of Christian missionaries who saw the construction of the railways as a means of spreading that faith. When cartridges were greased with pig fat (unclean for Muslims) and cow fat (holy to Hindus) feelings burst out in the Indian Mutiny, 1857.

Brahma Samāj. Some Hindus realized that their faith needed modernizing to make sense for the new urban middle class. The founding of Brahmā-Samāj (The Society of One God) by Ram Mohan Roy (1772–1833) followed in 1828. This Bengali Brahmin, who had worked for the East India Company and studied Islam

and Christianity, saw the need to respond to Western ideas. His aim was to purify Hinduism by concentrating on its devotional rather than mystical side. So he denounced idol worship, the caste system and suttee, the custom of burning widows on their husbands' funeral pyres. He translated some Hindu scriptures into English and used hymns in worship. Eventually he died in Bristol. Although the Samāj did not attract large numbers it did modernize Indian thinking and start social reforms, so Ram can be called the father of modern India.

Ramākrishna (1836–1886) was a Brahmin priest of Kālī's Temple, Calcutta, who despised formal education and who fell into trances in which he felt he was in touch with the Divine Mother (Kālī). Using the Vedantic Yoga paths of Jnana and Bhakti (see pp. 97–9) he asserted that all religions lead to the same goal. Krishna, the Buddha, Jesus and Allah were all names for the same energy or reality. By using simple sayings and stories he taught that Hinduism was universal and not just for Indians.

Sri Ramākrishna.

His chief disciple Swami Vivekānanda (1862–1902) founded the Rāmakrishna Mission with its headquarters at Belur in Calcutta in 1897. He was a Bengali university graduate and sannyāsin. He was an excellent organizer as well as outstanding preacher. He travelled to the UK and in 1893 made a big impact on the Parliament of Religions, or World Congress of Faiths, meeting at Chicago. He gave Indians a pride in their own culture and disillusioned Westerners the idea of looking to India for the Truth. He taught that everyone was potentially divine and should work to unleash the unlimited power that was within him. The Mission does educational, charitable and hospital work as well as its religious mission. It has a centre at Bourne End, Buckinghamshire staffed by two swamis, one Indian and the other English. This centre is a place of worship, meeting, education, and friendship for those wanting to follow Vedantism whether they be Indians or not.

4. Compare the effects of the Mughal Empire and British Rule on Hinduism.

5. Write an article for a newspaper on the life and work of Ram Mohan Roy or Vivekānanda.

6. How did Rāmakrishna turn Hinduism from simply being an Indian faith into a worldwide one?

Swami
Vivekānanda.

Sri Aurobindo Ghose (1872–1950) took his degree at Cambridge before he became involved in violent nationalism which led to his arrest by the British. While detained he had a deep religious experience so that when released he started an ashram (religious community). Influenced by Rāmakrishna and Vivekānanda he argued that Hinduism was a universal faith. He introduced 'integral yoga' to bring together religious and 'worldly' pursuits. Instead of following the ascetic way of Hindu yoga, he saw the need to bring daily life and religion together. He wrote *The Life Divine* which attracted Westerners to his ideas.

Mahatma (Great Soul) Gandhi (1869–1948), a Vishnu supporter and lawyer, preached ahimsā (non-violence) leading to understanding Sat (Truth) by means of Satyāgraha (holding on to Truth). This would not only resolve conflicts but in

his opinion be an act of devotion to the Truth. He went in for hand-spinning as a religious act as well as a remedy for India's economic dependence on Britain. Inflict suffering on yourself, for example by fasting, rather than on your opponent, was his theme. For him the opponent was the British Government and his fasting pressurized the Government into granting independence in 1947.

He aimed to re-interpret the class system in the light of ahimsā and so championed the outcasts, whom he called Harijan (children of God), both as a social reform and as a means of purifying Hinduism (see p. 96). This division of India into Hindu and Muslim states (India and Pakistan) led to his fasting and finally to his assassination by an extreme Hindu in 1948.

Other new presentations of Hinduism have interested Westerners. The Maharishi Mahesh Yogi introduced his Transcendental Meditation in the 1960s. Claiming that no religious beliefs were necessary, he told people they could reduce stress in their lives by 20 minutes' meditation a day. Bhakti Vedāntā Swāmī (1896–1977) brought his modern version of the fifteenth century CE Bhakti Chaitanya sect – called the International Society for Krishna Consciousness – to Europe and the USA. His shaven-headed, yellow-robed followers chant the mantra 'Hare Krishna' as a way of achieving ecstatic union with God. Music and dance are important to them.

7. *Why should Westerners find these presentations of Hinduism interesting and helpful?*

Mahatma Gandhi.

Migration. In the nineteenth and early twentieth centuries British firms with overseas interests recruited Indian workers to build railways in East Africa, grow rubber in Malaya and sugar in the West Indies. There were no large communities in Britain before 1947 – until then students and doctors were the main immigrants. Hindus came in large numbers following independence in 1947 and their expulsion from Kenya, Uganda, Tanzania and Zambia in the 1960s. Immigration Acts have since restricted the flow into the UK. Today half the sub-post offices of London are run by Hindus, while Birmingham, Manchester, Leeds, Bradford, Leicester, Coventry and Nottingham have big communities. There are some 400 000 in the UK today. They have opened 100 temples which provide them with cultural, food and education centres as well as places of worship. Sometimes a temple has to cater for different sects. Most are dedicated to Krishna or Rāma, and some to Shiva. Religious observances have had to be adapted to the English working week and lack of temple priests has given an important role to organizations like the Rāmakrishna Movement or the Ārya Samāj (Vedic Mission). The latter was founded in 1875 by Dāyananda Sarasvatī (1824–1883), a brahmin who laid down rules of behaviour, included modern scientific ideas and said the Vedas revealed there was one God. He called for a non-hereditary class system based on individual merit. He felt the West had much to learn from Hinduism and India nothing from Western faiths. Punjabi Hindus usually follow this sect.

Followers of Bhakti Vedāntā.

His point of Westerners learning from Hinduism is borne out by the steady stream who visit the Divine Life Society ashram beside the Ganges and Rishikesh founded by Swami Sivananda (1887–1963). He wrote that Hinduism 'is more a

League of Religions than a single religion with a definite creed . . . It prescribes spiritual food for everybody, according to his qualification and growth.' As a doctor he included a free hospital as well as a publishing firm in his ashram. The society has branches in Britain and other lands.

8. *Write a brief biography and summary of the work of Ram Mohan Roy, Rāmakrishna, Vivekānanda, Sri Aurobindo Ghose, Dayānanda Sarashvati. What have they or their groups in common?*

9. *Draw a map of the UK and mark in the main centres of Indian communities. Underneath say what role their temples have in such communities*

10. *Modern Hindu groups aim to show Westerners that their civilization was not necessarily the best. With examples, show how Hinduism has attracted Westerners today.*

SHINTOISM

Early Days. At its outset Shintoism did not even have a name, it was simply a way of life. It acquired its name when the need arose to distinguish it from Buddhism and Confucianism which influenced primitive Japan in the sixth century CE. Until then Japanese religion was unorganized and consisted of a mixture of agricultural cults, nature and ancestor worship, and magic. Villagers worshipped their founding ancestor and the village chief was both religious and political leader. The Yamato rulers (fourth to seventh centuries CE) unified the country and this led to the setting up of a nationwide system of rites and myths centred on Amaterasu.

Early Kami worship had been performed in temporary enclosures (himorogi) marked by a sakaki tree branch in the middle and bounded by straw rope (shimenawa) with an entrance gate (torii, see pp. 152–4). Then permanent shrines were established containing houses (honden) for the kami. When Buddhism arrived, the Buddha and bodhisattas, or bodhisattvas, were seen as foreign kami. From the eighth century CE the two religions fused to some extent; Shintoism was seen as the religion of life and Buddhism that of death – hence the customs today of having a Shinto kamidana (p. 105) and a Buddhist butsudan (p. 236) in homes. Dual Shinto (Ryōbu, or Shimbutsu) identified kami with bodhisattas. Shrine-temples (jingūji) were built within Shinto shrines for Buddhist priests to perform their rituals. This amalgamation (Shugendō) ended in 1868.

11. *Describe what Shintoism was like before the sixth century CE and how it changed when faced with Buddhism.*

Popular or Folk Shinto lies at the root of Shintoism. It has no doctrine but concentrates on rituals which are a part of community and individual life in Japan. In early days this meant honouring good kami while taking care to calm bad kami. Worship in the home, at the kami pillar marking the village entrance and at the shrine were all important. Taboos such as unlucky days for marriages are still taken seriously. In almanacs every day is classified under one of six kinds. Omens, divinations, petitions, magic words and amulets play a part. During an annual festival everyone is involved, as it is believed that a single family alone cannot satisfy the kami. Groups (kumi) are important too. The youth group takes part in weddings, the old people's in reciting 'Amida Buddha' (*see* pp. 45–6). Associations of worshippers (kōsha) are formed to proclaim a particular aspect of faith. These have led to the so-called 'new religions' (*see* pp. 39–40).

12. *Explain with examples the words omen, divination, amulet. Do British people have similar customs? Give examples.*

State Shinto. The Meiji rulers (1868–1912) realized that modernization of the country was essential when the feudal Edo era collapsed in 1868. Also there was a need to develop a positive national identity to cope with foreign trade demands and internal discontent. The obvious solution was a national religion centred on emperor devotion as he was a descendant of Amaterasu. So Buddhism was separated from Shintoism and downgraded, while Shintoism was integrated into the power structure of the new state. Its priests became government officials with privileged status. A Department of Shinto Affairs was set up and its work included propaganda and education. Other religious groups had to have government authorizations to operate. Thus State (Kokka) Shinto was the political creation of the Meiji. It was a combination of Imperial House (kōshitsu) Shinto and Shrine (jinja) Shinto. The former was centred on the rites performed by the emperor for his ancestors' spirits, while the latter was concerned with the rituals performed by the communities at their local kami shrines.

13. *What did Shintoism gain by becoming State Shinto? What difference would it have made to the lives of its priests and the upkeep of its shrines?*

14. *Should a state use a religion to assist it? What advantages would a government get from having a state religion to hand? Name any other religion which has been taken over by a state today or in the past. What advantages and disadvantages has this relationship given to (a) the religion, (b) the state?*

Sect Shinto (kyōha) was a new classification announced in 1868 for the 13 sects which the Meiji did not want to incorporate into State Shinto. These sects had been started in the nineteenth century by the charismatic personalities who were trying to relate religion to the needs of their time. As they have flourished since World War II, they will be considered below.

15. *What is meant by a charismatic personality? Give examples from any country or religion.*

Twentieth Century. During World War II State Shintoism had led to fanatical devotion to the emperor and the war. Kamikaze pilots' suicidal attacks on their targets are well-known; notice the term begins with 'kami'. On 15 December 1945 the USA Commander-in-Chief, on occupying Japan, stopped all state support and control of Shintoism. Religious freedom was official policy. Kamidana (god shelves, see p. 105) were to be removed from schools and offices and priests reduced to private citizens. The Directive said nothing about how Shintoism was to be organized in future, which left 100 000 shrines in confusion.

The Japanese were deeply shocked and a partial collapse in behaviour standards followed. Then came a reaction in favour of Shintoism with sympathy for its priests. On 3 February 1946 the Association of Shinto Shrines was formed and most shrines joined it. Shrines are now run by their priests and worshippers' committees. By 1961, 180 shrine kindergartens were open, so marking Shintoism's move into education.

16. *How did State Shintoism help the Japanese war effort? Why should the end of State Shintoism shock and confuse the Japanese so much? Why do you think the USA made its Directive?*

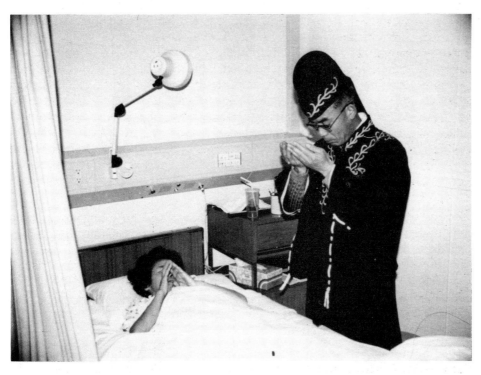

Faith-healing by Tenri-kyo priest who states patient's name and illness before passing his hands over the diseased part.

New Religions. The rapid growth in towns and industry since 1960 has turned Japan from a rural to an urban land. This has been a blow to village-centred Shintoism. The big cities are too crowded for traditional festivals. Uprooted people feel frustrated by the lack of human fellowship. Traditional religions seem to be of little help. Christianity is too foreign, while Buddhism traditionally centres on death. Consequently the 'new religions' provide the answer today by offering concrete solutions to immediate needs. Their members are conspicuous because they are so confident and happy. They offer help to those in distress, with faith healing alongside medical care.

The newcomer is looked on as the 'child' of the recruiting member. Newcomers are encouraged to bring a friend next time, so putting them in the place of a 'parent'. Many sects argue that deliverance from misery comes with winning more new members. Their founders were often women who felt themselves possessed by a kami. Revelations were made such as the claim by Nakayama Miki (1798–1887, foundress of Tenrikyō (Religion of Heavenly Truth)) that

Tenri-kyō lecture by priest to new members.

Risshō Kōsekai – Hoza circles meeting in the training hall of a Risshō Kōsekai branch.

humans were created at Tenri City. The city was built to mark the spot she indicated. This sect's magnificent buildings are spread throughout the city and include a hospital for faith and medical healing and a museum of discarded medical aids. Risshō Kōsekai (Society to Establish Righteousness and Foster Friendship) is a lay Buddhist sect founded by Nagunuma Myōkō (1889–1957) and Niwano Nikkyō (1906–). It offers similar care for its members' problems. The politically alert Sōka Gakkai (Creative Education Society) has made a big impression with its propaganda.

Today the Religions League of Japan includes Buddhist, Christian, Shinto and 'New Religions' associations and there is a Japan Council for Interfaith Co-operation. Of 35 million Shintoists, some 17 million belong to the Kyōha sects.

17. *Medical care in civilized countries gets better all the time. (a) Why do you think that faith healing attracts so many to the 'new religions'? (b) What does a religion need to offer a busy city worker today?*

18. *Shintoism flourishes in Japan today. Why do you think this is so?*

19. *Unlike Hinduism, Shintoism has stayed the religion of one people. Why?*

TAOISM

The early history of Taoism has been dealt with in Chapter 2.

Chang Tao Ling (34–156 CE), a Tao Chiao priest, claimed he had had a vision of Lao-Tse and had made a treaty with all the spirits. He had got control of their powers by identifying their names and functions in his *Auspicious Alliance Canon Register*, and so achieved immortality. A masterly organizer, he called himself the first Heavenly Master. He began the Five Pecks of Rice Sect (followers had to give him five pecks). He set up a Taoist 'papacy' centred at the Dragon and Tiger Mountain, Kiansi, South China by passing on his secrets to his son and grandson. Its folk-medicine, magic and alchemy fulfilled the needs of the peasants providing them with hope in their primitive world. It offered the Tao (Way) to the three targets of happiness, wealth and long life. Those who confessed their sins did penance by repairing roads for 100 paces, etc. The sect's rituals can be found in *Tao Tsang*, the Taoist Canon, 1436 CE (p. 80).

20. *Why did peasants take to Chang Tao Ling's teachings?*

Confucianism (Confucius 551–479 BCE) was challenged by Taoism in the second century CE. Confucianism said well-ordered government benefited people, whereas Taoism said it took away their liberty. Confucianism expected people to be respectable and conventional, while Taoism offered freedom for the individual. Confucianism was for the city-dweller who today would buy bottled milk while Taoism was for the country folk who would prefer milk from the cow. There was no heaven, hell or immortality in the former, while the latter offered a world of wonder, mystery and immortality. Thus Taoism offered an alternative to the monotony of Confucianism's respectability. It allowed the businessman and peasant a form of escapism.

21. *How did Taoism offer escape for the hard pressed worker? Should a religion offer escape from daily life or help to cope with it?*

Neo-Taoism. In the third and fourth centuries CE this led the Neo-Taoists of Tao Chia led by Hsiang Kuo (d.213) to stress the importance of one's emotions. They introduced the romantic spirit (Fun Liu) into Taoism in contrast to Lao-Tse who had taught people to control their emotions. They argued that institutions and moral standards are always going out of date and so spontaneity and naturalness should guide people.

22. *(a) Give examples of moral teachings going 'out of date' in this century. (b) Why have they 'gone out of date'? (c) Can any moral teachings be always 'in date'? Give examples and say why you have chosen them.*

23. *What are the advantages and disadvantages of living life spontaneously and naturally?*

Buddhism's challenge in the Ching Dynasty, 265–420 CE. In contrast to Tao Chia's Neo-Taoism, Tao Chiao's priests developed a rival temple and ritual system to outdo the Buddhists. While Buddhism saw life as an ordeal to be escaped from, Taoism searched for the elixir of life to prolong it with its enjoyments, privileges and powers. In its efforts to 'sell' its faith Tao Chiao descended to using more and more magicial techniques and offering a greater range of gods, charms, cures and exorcisms than its rival. In practice the ordinary Chinese cared little for the distinctions of these two faiths, simply making use of the service of either when the need arose. Meanwhile Tao Chia got closer to

Buddhism and the outcome was Buddhism's Ch'an (Zen in Japanese) meditation system, (see pp. 119-21).

24. *(a) How did Tao Chiao try to attract followers from Buddhism?*
    (b) What effect did this have on it as a religion?

Taoism's heyday. While peasants tended to turn more to Buddhism, the educated and ruling classes preferred Taoism. From 440 CE it was the state religion while Buddhism was temporarily suppressed, and it had state patronage, especially in 574–591 CE and 618–907 CE.

Taoism today. In Communist China many temples were adapted for secular use or demolished. But in 1957 a Communist-controlled China Taoist Association was founded and some temples were repaired. In 1978 the Chinese People's Congress guaranteed religious freedom and the Political Consultative Conference now contains 16 representatives of various religions who serve as a department of religious freedom. In Taiwan Taoism was revived in 1945 after its suppression by the Japanese during World War II. In 1965 the National Taoist Association of the Republic of China was set up to supervise 480 organisations involving 2745 temples, 1300 priests and 3 300 000 worshippers. Most priests are 'Red headed' ones of the Spirit Cloud sect, using mediums, although some are the 'Black-headed' ones who do not use them. In Hong Kong Taosim is alive and one of its flourishing temples is Ching Chung Koon ('evergreen', so 'long life') of the Sect of All Truth Dragon Gate, founded in 1949. It runs free schools, clinics and homes for the aged, (see p. 156).

It is difficult to say how many Taoists there are today, but there may be 30 million. In the west there is a growing interest in Tao Chia and many English bookshops stock books on it.

25. *Communism denies the existence of God. Why do you think it has allowed some opportunity for Taoism to survive in China?*

26. *(a) In what ways has Hong Kong's Ching Chung Koon temple shown how Taoism can adapt to modern urban life? (b) Many Chinese who worship there have come from Communist China. What can the temple offer them in particular?*

BUDDHISM

The first 500 years, 500–0 BCE. Emperor Ashoka (273–232 BCE) gave his patronage to Buddhists, so transforming them from a small sect of monks to an all-Indian religion. His son, Mahinda, took the faith to Sri Lanka c.240 BCE, where it became the state religion. Only Buddhists could become kings there and the island was held to belong to the Buddha himself. During this period the first Buddhist writings began to be collected (see Chapter 4).

27. *How was the spread of Buddhism helped by rulers?*

Second period, 0–500 CE. Theravāda (The way of the Elders, Thervādins) also called Southern Buddhism, centred on Sri Lanka and spread to Burma, Laos,

Kampuchea, Indonesia and Thailand. It taught that the Buddha was simply a human who had pioneered the way to Nibbana, or Nirvana (pp. 113–15) so showing others how it could be done. As he got there entirely on his own achievement, others must do likewise. Individuals must work their way along the river of life on a 'small vehicle' (Hīnayāna) and achieve Nibbana for themselves, aided only by the Buddha's teachings. They will then become Arahats, ones who have achieved Nibbana. The word Hīnayāna was first applied to the Theravādins as a term of abuse by the breakaway section called Mahāyāna or Northern Buddhists.

Mahāyāna ('the Great Vehicle') was a new trend in Buddhism at the beginning of this period. It took its name from a story in which people used vehicles to get away from a burning house, symbolizing the world. Whereas the Theravādins claimed one could only escape from this world by individual effort, developing the wisdom of an Arahat, the Mahāyāna Buddhists claimed escape was possible for all people who put their trust in the eternal Buddha. But this implies that the Buddha can be worshipped almost as a god. Theravādins argued that prayer to the Buddha was pointless as he had been swallowed up in Nibbana (p. 115).

The new movement arose in N.W. and S. India because of foreign influence and because lay people wanted equal rights with the monks. Roman and Greek influence made Mahāyāna Buddhism fit for export and so it spread along the silk routes into Central Asia and then to China, Japan, Tibet and Korea. Mahāyānists were more effective missionaries than the Theravādins, as they were prepared to adapt their teachings and monastic rules while the latter were not. They also realized the importance of introducing medical care into their missionary work as

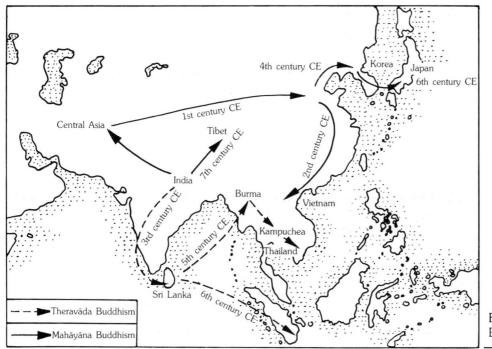

Early Spread of Buddhism.

43

Christian missionaries did in Africa in the nineteenth and twentieth centuries. This meant relaxing the monastic rule about monks not being doctors. Mahāyāna Buddhists realized the need to produce new books to cope with new ages, populations and social problems and so they set out to do this, as will be seen in Chapter 4. But they insisted that these writings were the very words of the Buddha, although he was long dead. They argued that he lives for ever and reveals his teaching periodically, but claimed that their books had in fact been the Buddha's earthly lifetime preachings stored away for 500 years in subterranean palaces.

27. *Summarize the difference in Theravādin and Mahāyāna beliefs. Which countries did each spread to?*

Bodhisattas, or Bodhissattvas. Instead of salvation being only for the few who can become Arahats through wisdom, a new way is worked out in which compassion ranks equal with wisdom. Instead of trying to become an Arahat one should strive to become a Bodhisatta. This term usually refers to one who has perfected wisdom yet voluntarily defers entering Nibbana, remaining instead on earth. It is used also of one who has vowed to cultivate the six pāramitā (perfection) methods – generosity, moral behaviour, patience, persistence, meditation and wisdom – for the benefit of all beings.

28. *What is the difference between an Arahat and a Bodhisatta? What does one have to do to become them?*

29. *Write down dictionary definitions of compassion, wisdom. Discuss their differences and decide whether one or both are ways to the Truth.*

True Bodhisattas are prepared to share all the merit of goodness they have collected from their countless lives of self-sacrifice with other people so as to help them. Consequently they are regarded as saint-gods to whom one can pray. A popular Bodhisatta is the God of Mercy (Kuan-Yin in Chinese, Kannon in Japanese). Although essentially male, he can also assume female form to help the needy. The importance of faith in a Buddhist's life is increased by encouragement to pray to Bodhisattas.

Manushi Buddhas (man buddhas) once lived on earth but have now reached enlightenment through meditation. They are in Nibbana beyond the reach of anyone's prayers. Gautama is the most famous Manushi.

Dhyani Buddhas (meditation buddhas) are beings who have never been on earth. They live in Nibbana but will share their happiness and help anyone who prays to them. They are pictured as monks with calm, kindly faces. Amida, Lord of the Western Paradise, is a dyhani buddha. He is worshipped by the Chinese and Japanese as it is believed he will take them to paradise, by-passing the effects of people's earthly failings if they call on his name (pp. 45–6).

Buddhism reached China via the silk routes in the 60s CE, to be welcomed by the Han emperor Ming. It became the faith of traders, merchants and shopkeepers. By 400 CE, 1300 Buddhist scriptures had been translated into Chinese. With imperial patronage Buddhism was soon firmly established, in spite of its monastic call challenging the all-important family obligations of the Chinese, or the way it seemed to encourage baseless superstitions. The opportunity of becoming a monk during the confusions following the fall the Han dynasty in 220 CE aided it. The chance for lowly lay folk finding Nibbana was equally attractive. Also the Mahāyānists did not forbid the recognition of Chinese gods.

30. *Why should Buddhism attract traders, merchants and shopkeepers first?*

31. *How did Buddhism's concentration on the life of monks threaten Chinese family life?*

Pure Land Buddhism was begun in 402 CE by the Chinese ex-Taoist monk Hui Yuan (334–416) but it did not become a definite sect until later (see below). Meanwhile in Sri Lanka the Theravāda Sangha (monks) decided learning was more important than religious practices so that intelligent monks concentrated on book work, leaving the weaker ones to do full-time meditation.

Third period, 500–1000 CE. Tantric ('systematic') Buddhism began in the first century CE in North-West and South India. It took account of the popular belief in spirits, demons and ghosts and magical practices linked with them. The Buddhists did not use magic to acquire power, but to free themselves from powers which affected them. Instead of Arahats or Bodhisattas, the Tantra concentrated on Siddhas, magicians. While Mahāyāna literature was available to all, the Tantric literature of secret documents was only for the chosen few to read. This new method was called the Vajrayāna, Diamond Vehicle. Tantric Buddhists are drawn to their faith through mysticism, an esoteric approach. They rely on union with a Bodhisatta via the 3 M's – Mudra, symbolic gesture with hands and fingers; Mantra, a formula or words; Mandala, cosmograms (diagrams of the universe), visual aids such as sacred diagrams or magic circles. In the circles cosmic and spiritual forces are represented by symbols or pictures of deities. Properly understood these images can free followers of their deeply hidden fears or passions. The Nyingmapa ('Old Ones') sect seek to cultivate sensual pleasures so as to pass beyond them and eliminate the 'self' in them. So they break normal taboos in a ritually controlled way in order that experiences may enable them to detach themselves from selfish cravings. The pleasures concerned are known as the 5 M's: Madya, wine; Māmsa, meat; Matsya, fish; Mudra, hand gestures; Maithuna, sexual union. It must be stressed that this does not mean that they led immoral lives, in fact quite the reverse. Enlightenment is represented by the union of female (wisdom goddess) and male (material world) in the ecstasy of love.

Mandala in five colours. Spaces represent gods. The centre is the sacred magic place which the user concentrates on. It is the point where the self and the divine fuse; the outer points are fragments of personality.

32. *Why did Tantric Buddhists use magical methods? How do their ideas differ from the Buddha's?*

Pure Land Buddhism. 500–800 CE was the most prosperous period for Buddhism in China. Tao-ch'o (562–645) founded one major sect, Ching-t'u (Pure Land of the Western Paradise) which promised salvation to those who call on the name of Amitābha (Japanese – Amida; Eternal Life) Buddha, Lord of the

Amida (Amitābha in China).

Western Paradise. Enlightenment is by faith in the Bodhisatta's merits, and not through your own merits (p. 44). Legend has it that a man called Dhammākara-biksu vowed that when he attained Buddhahood he would create a Pure Land and save all who wanted to enter it. In due course he became Amitābha Buddha.

Different sūtras describe the Pure Land in different ways. One says, 'There is a pond made of seven jewels, which is filled with the pure, crystalline water of the eight virtues. The bottom . . . is covered with golden sand. On the edge . . . there is a beautiful building of gold, silver, emeralds and crystal.' Today some think this is like a fairy tale, a fantasy world, but they forget that such a land is not of this world. It is another world beyond early people's concepts. The sūtras try to explain the unexplainable, the ideal spiritual world, in material terms. It is a world of wisdom, compassion, peace and harmony. Faith in Amitābha Buddha will enable you to by-pass kamma's, or karma's, effect of rebirth (p. 239) and go straight to this land.

Amidism's success lies in the simple way to obtain salvation in a magically restful land which it offers ordinary people faced with the bustle of life. The only virtue required is faith.

33. *What does Pure Land Buddhism offer? How can one obtain what is on offer? Does having faith in Jesus as a Saviour seem similar to Pure Land Buddhism?*

Ch'an (Japanese, Zen) meditation movement was founded possibly by the legendary Bodhisharma or Bodhidhamma in 520 CE but more likely by Huineng (638–713) who felt that the aids to salvation in the form of sūtras (rules, sayings), images, and rites lost sight of the goal of the faith. He wanted a much more simple approach to enlightenment. He insisted that salvation could not be found by simply studying books. Instead meditation was the key. Because the Ch'an movement was against book work, its leaders distrusted the distorting effect of words and tried to induce enlightenment in their pupils by nonsensical remarks (kōans) and beat them with sticks (pp. 119–20). Although these techniques were designed to bring a spontaneous reaction, as they became routine methods they lost a lot of their value. Buddhahood was to be obtained through instantaneous enlightenment. Hīnayāna no longer seemed to produce any fully enlightened people (Arahats) and Mahāyāna Bodhisattas still has to pass through almost endless preparation to become Buddhas.

In the seventh and eighth centuries people were impatient with those who taught that enlightenment came in the dim future. Quicker results were wanted. The Ch'an claimed their followers were attaining enlightenment all the time in this very life. But they used a new word *wu* (Japanese, *satori*) for being aware of enlightenment. It was achieved by a new type of 'saint', a rōshi. So after Theravādin Arahats, Mahāyāna Bodhisattas, Tantric Siddhas, there were now Ch'an or Zen Rōshis.

This form of Buddhism became divided into those who believed in sudden enlightenment called Lin-chi (Rinzai in Japan) and those who believed in slower enlightenment, Ts'ao-tung (Sōto in Japan) (p. 119).

34. *Why had people become impatient with trying to become Arahats or Bodhisattas? How could one become a rōshi?*

Buddhism reached Korea in 372 CE and became the state religion in the sixth century. From Korean Buddhism went to Japan in *c.*552 CE and was accepted after a struggle with Shintoism. In the Heian period (794–1186) two important sects came from China: (a) Tendai was founded in 805 by Saicho, called Dengyō Daishi (767–835), and it argued that both meditation and faith were needed to become a Bodhisatta, as either on its own was inadequate; (b) Shingon ('true word') founded in 807 by Kōbō Daishi (774–835) had elaborate rituals as it believed outward acts changed one inwardly. But in the tenth century travelling preachers were bringing the message of Amida's saving grace in a language ordinary people could grasp, as we shall see (p. 239).

Tibet. Here Buddhism began *c.*650 CE but did not take root until a century later. It became divided into two Tantric sects, the Nyingmapa ('Old Ones') known as Red Hats, and the reformed Gelugpa ('Virtuous Ones') or Yellow Hats. The latter are ruled by a reincarnation of the Bodhisatta Avaolokita, known as Dalai Lama ('superior person'). As they feel it is essential to be ruled by a Bodhisatta they search for a boy who is such an incarnation on the death of their leader. Mahāyāna and Ch'an Buddhism also appeared in Tibet.

35. *What do you think Shingon meant by claiming outward acts changed one inwardly? What examples can you give?*

Fourth period, 1000 CE to present day. Buddhism died out in India about 1200 largely owing to Islamic invasions. Once it lost royal favour, the people ceased to support the Theravādin monks, who then left for other lands. Also Buddhism, being a tolerant and flexible religion, had to some extent simply been absorbed by Hinduism.

Theravāda Buddhism came to dominate Burma (state religion in 1961), Indo China, Thailand and Kampuchea. One Thai monastery runs a successful course for heroin addicts. This shows Buddhism is adopting the idea of getting involved in social welfare. In Korea Buddhism flourished especially under the Koro dynasty, 1140–1390. The abbots (bonzes) became powerful and used magic to intrigue ordinary people. One son in four had to become a monk but in 1392 Confucianism took over and monks lost their privileges.

36. *How did Buddhism come to lose its importance in (a) India, (b) Korea?*

In Japan new sects changed Buddhism between 1160 and 1260. Jōdo-shū (Pure Land Way) was developed by Hōnen (1133–1212) who said sincere chanting of 'Nembutsu' ('Hail to Buddha Amida') could save one, as it amounted to vocal meditation, whereas traditional Buddhist disciplines were too hard for people of his time.

Hōnen.

>   *Have no further doubts; Rejoice greatly in your hearts, knowing that*
>   *you will become Buddhas.*   (Lotus Sutra)

At Chion-in Temple, Kyoto, Japan, which is the head Jōdo temple, Nembutsu and sūtras are chanted from 5 a.m. onwards. Occasionally elaborate ceremonies are held by gorgeously robed priests. The temple publishes a quarterly bulletin in English. Hōnen's disciple, Shinran (1173–1262), founded the True Sect of the

Kannon.

Pure Land (Jōdo-shinshū), when he stressed that Amida's compassion was such that all people were already saved even if they did not realize it. It was Amida's decision to save people and not their faith in him which counted. He also stressed that there was no real difference between monks and layfolk and so he started the movement for married priests.

A typical Japanese development of Buddhism is the sale of omamori (amulets, talismen) to protect one. They come in little bags which can be hung from belts or kept in handbags. One temple even advertised expensive ones in a 'girlie' magazine, an action one would not expect of the Catholic Church advertising a St Christopher medallion! Kannon (from which Canon cameras get their name) is a Bodhisatta found everywhere as a road safety talisman.

37. *How does the Lotus Sūtra quoted above express the spirit of Japanese Buddhism?*

38. *Compare Nembutsu with Christianity's Salvation by Faith teaching (see pp. 127–8).*

Nichiren (1222–1282) founded a fiery nationalistic sect in 1253 in Japan which demanded the end of all other sects. Today 30 million belong to its newer subdivisions, particularly as a reaction to American occupation after World War II. Risshō Kōsekai, a lay Buddhist society and Sōka Gakkai have already been mentioned on p. 40. The Rinzai and Sōtō Zen sects developed in the twelfth and thirteenth centuries (see p. 119). The Samurai took up Rinzai and gave rise to Bushido, the Way of the Warrior. After 1500 Buddhism lost out to Shintoism and nearly died out in the nineteenth century. But in this century, it has revived and involves two-thirds of the population. Zen has aroused interest in Europe and the USA today. Throssel Hole Priory, Hexham, Northumberland, is a flourishing Sōtō centre in England.

Tibetan Buddhism was the victim of Communism which took over Tibet in 1950. The Dalai Lama fled with 70 000 supporters to India in 1959. As a result, Tibetan Buddhism has spread to Europe and North America and a group thrives in Birmingham today. Buddhism also suffered from Communism in China. In the 1960s the Cultural Revolution led to the sacking of some monasteries, but Buddhism survived and many monasteries and relics were protected on State Council orders. In 1978 the People's Congress allowed freedom of religious belief, and in 1980 the Chinese Buddhist Theological Institute was reopened (it had been closed in 1966). Forty monks, aged 18–31, began a two year course there before returning to their own temples. In 1984 Peking announced that 200 temples and monasteries would be restored by 1988. So Buddhism survives in China though it is not yet free from restrictions.

The Buddhist Society was founded in England in 1906 and the London Buddhist Society in 1924. There are 200 Buddhist groups in the UK today. There are now 250 million Northern Buddhists (Taiwan has seven and a half million, served by 7750 priests in 2520 temples) and 50 million Southern Buddhists in the world. Buddhism has sustained itself for five centuries longer than Christianity with little recourse to violence or underhand methods, a considerable achievement.

39. *What has Buddhism to offer Westerners which makes it so attractive these days?*

The Temple era ends. Antiochus Epiphanes (The Illustrious) IV of Syria sacked Jerusalem and defiled the Temple when the Jews refused to accept his nominee as High Priest. This led to a revolt led by the Hasmonean family in 167 BCE, resulting in the cleansing of the Temple by Judas Maccabeus (The Hammerer) in 165 BCE (see Hanukkah festival, p. 194).

From 63 BCE to 200 CE the Jews were under Roman domination. However, they did call Herod 'King of the Jews' and allowed him to start rebuilding the Temple in 20 BCE. It was finished in 62 CE. In this period the minority Sadducee party controlled the Jews. They collaborated with the Romans, rejecting the oral law (laws passed on by word of mouth). Opposed to them were the Pharisees (Separatists) who felt the Torah (see p. 83) needed constant interpreting to reflect changing conditions in society. They believed God wanted people to use their reasoning powers to go on interpreting his design for the universe. This meant they must keep updating their religious laws by majority verdict in assemblies of their leaders (hakhamin, sages, later renamed rabbis). They carefully recorded any minority's opinion in the Mishnah (see p. 85) in case it might lead to a future new decision. Thus they accepted that differences of opinion were inevitable and did not condemn each other for 'heresy' (holding non-acceptable beliefs) as Christians did. They believed no more prophets would appear until the Messianic age. The Pharisees regarded the hereditary Temple priests as just ceremonial officials. Anyone could become a hakhamin (a synagogue's leading figure) provided he studied religion, history and science. His religious duties involved making legal judgements and preaching without payment, while earning his living in some job. Their authority was not divine but simply based on their knowledge. They were not 'hypocrites' as depicted in Matthew's Gospel, but are often referred to as 'lawyers' in the New Testament.

There was a hope at this time that a Messiah would come to restore independence and in 66 CE a general revolt started. But the Romans took Jerusalem in 70 CE, destroyed the Temple and sacked the High Priest and the Sanhedrin (Council). Jerusalem ceased to be the heart of Judaism and the Sadducee partly collapsed. The revolt continued for three years around the rocky fortress of Masada. The Romans cut it off from relief and when they finally captured it they found the 960 Jews there had committed suicide.

40. *How many times was the Temple built and by whom? In what way was its existence crucial to Judaism?*

41. *What effect did the Romans have on Jewish history?*

The post-Temple era. With the Jews dispersed, it became more important to rely on the Torah. Hillel (The Elder), the Pharisee President of the Sanhedrin, took the lead between 30 BCE and 10 CE. This kind, lenient peace-lover started to sort out the oral law (halakhot) to go alongside the Torah. His pupil Johanan (Jochanan) ben Zakkai was smuggled out of Jerusalem in a coffin and started an adult school at Jamnia or Jabneh. It was here that the term rabbi (master) came to be used to refer to those teaching the faith, and the school ensured that Judaism could survive the loss of Jerusalem. Arguments over what interpretation the oral law was to have led to the Council or Synod of Jamnia, c.100 CE. It settled that Hillel's interpretation, rather that that of Shammai, his old colleague, was correct. It drew up the official list of books to be included in the scriptures and rejected others.

42.   Why should the Torah become more important when Jerusalem was lost?

Akiva (Akiba) Ben Joseph (40/50–135 CE) was one outstanding rabbi who arranged legal teaching by subject matter, so sorting out opinions on what the Torah meant. This enabled the brilliant Judah (Yehuda) ha Nasi (The Prince, Patriarch, 135–217 CE) to compile the Mishnah (see p. 85) as a basic textbook of the Oral Law.

43.   Give as many reasons as possible for the concern shown over the law.

A rebellion against Rome was led by Simon Bar Kokhba (Kakhba), 'Son of the Star' (Num. 24:27) from 132 to 135 CE. He was the last rebel and an outstanding military leader. He liberated Jerusalem, but not for long as the Romans recaptured it and then killed him. Akiva, who had called him the Messiah, had his flesh torn off by the Romans. Half a million Jews died, their religion was banned and the name of Jerusalem obliterated. So ended any form of Jewish independence.

44.   Diaspora means 'dispersion' and it can apply either to a forced or to a voluntary movement. Identify the dispersions referred to in this section and say what caused each.

Jews living in exile turned to the Gaonim (excellencies), the heads of the Babylonian academies, when they wanted guidance over how to live their lives correctly. So many queries were answered that the collection became known as the *Responsa*. Such collections continue to be made today. *Karaites* (Readers of the Scriptures) were a Jewish sect active from 750 CE. They were founded by Anan ben David, who was dissatisfied with the way rabbis claimed to be the sole interpreters of the Law. Like the Sadducees, he accepted only the authority of the Torah. The trouble was that he began to interpret the Torah himself and so produce his own Oral Law. His plea that Jews should search the Torah thoroughly – and not rely on his opinion – led to his followers arguing as to what the Torah meant. It was to avoid such arguments that the Talmud (see pp. 84-5) had been compiled in the first place! The term Karaites came in after this time. The sect spread throughout Israel, Egypt and Europe in the eleventh and twelfth centuries CE, but then waned as the Rabbanites (Rabbis' side) produced good leaders like Maimonides and because the Karaites had such a strict interpretation of the Law. This sect still exists today.

45.   Why do you think the Karaite movement was successful but then waned?

Moses ben Maimon, Maimonides, nicknamed Rambam (1135–1204), was born in Spain and began his career as a distinguished doctor in Egypt. He wrote books which popularized the Mishnah, and arranged the Laws in an orderly fashion. His *Guide of the Perplexed*, 1190 CE, helped to solve problems worrying the thoughtful Jews of his day. He also listed Thirteen Principles of Belief which is the nearest statement to a creed which Jews possess. They believe in (1) God as Creator, Provider (2) His oneness (3) His spirituality (4) His eternity (5) Worship due solely to Him (6) The Prophets' teachings (7) Moses as chief prophet (8) The Torah is His revelation (9) The Torah is unchangeable, eternal (10) God is all-knowing (11) Reward and punishment for all (12) The Messiah will come (13) The dead will be raised.

46. *Compare the Thirteen Principles of Belief with the Creed in the Christian prayer book. What have they in common and what do they differ on?*

Jewish Mysticism. In thirteenth and fourteenth century Spain Jews emphasized the belief that one can have some kind of direct 'vision' of divine things. They started from the Kabbalah ('that which is received', tradition), books not contained in the five books of Moses, searching them for hidden meanings. Their main book was the *Zohar* (Splendour) which said one could grasp ten ways of experiencing God, but that He Himself is beyond comprehension. It gave mystical meanings to the Torah and used astrology too.

The Hasidism, or Hasidic revivalist movement (hasid means pious) made mysticism popular in the eighteenth century. Using the *Zohar* Baal Shem Tov ('Master of the Name', 1700–1760), a dynamic Polish miracle-worker, stressed the presence of God in everyday life. He called for passionate devotion to God, to be found in the ecstatic joy of dancing, singing and praying. Their circular dance represents the dance of the Righteous Ones round God in heaven. For the deprived, frightened Jews of Eastern Europe he offered an emotional, devotional alternative to the rabbis' worship through study method. The illiterate could experience God as much as the educated. The movement's leaders were called zaddikim (saints) or rebbes. Today the Hasidim are uncompromising defenders of Orthodox Judaism, identifiable from the black coats they wear. Although some once played a prominent role in the movement, they no longer do so.

47. (a) *Why should some feel that mysticism is the only way to reach God?*
    (b) *What advantages and disadvantages does this approach have?*
    (c) *Compare the Muslim sufi approach (p. 64) to that of the Hasidim.*

Liberal Judaism. In the late eighteenth and early nineteenth centuries, German Jews found their way of life suddenly beginning to change. For a long while they had lived in walled ghettoes, isolated from other townsfolk. As they acquired more freedom they found they had to cope with the opportunities of university education and new scientific ideas which seemed to conflict with the Torah. Faced with opportunities and pressures, a third of Berlin Jews turned Christian to improve their chances. If Judaism did not quickly respond to the changed situation it would lose out.

The Liberal movement was a response to this situation. David Friedlander (1756–1834) argued that the Torah contained God's 'teaching' rather than His 'law'. Its rules on good behaviour must be obeyed, but those on rituals such as Sabbath observance were not divine. They should alter as times changed. The Torah contains some primitive ideas and errors which need updating, he said.

Abraham Geiger (1810–1874) stressed that Judaism is progressive, not static, the result of slow evolution and not a miraculous movement of revelation. So its scriptures must be studied critically, using modern scientific knowledge. For example the parting of the Red Sea should be seen as a legend, not a miracle. For him, truth was not unchanging, but progressive. Also Judaism was a universal movement, 'A Light unto the Nations', and not simply for the Jews alone. He thought a Messianic age would come.

The result of these ideas was an explosion of sweeping changes in ceremonies and customs, such as the dietary laws. Hebrew prayers were translated and organs and family pews introduced in synagogues (see p. 161). In fact much of what was swept away returned in the 1930s. The Hebrew Union College, USA, founded by Isaac Wise in 1875, started to ordain women in the 1970s.

48. *Religions which rely on a basic teaching, revealed by God and written down in a holy book, must either stick rigidly to that book or be prepared to criticize it and argue that what it reveals needs altering as times change. (a) Is this true? Explain what this statement means using examples in Jewish history. (b) Compare the Jewish attitude to the Torah with the Christian and Islamic attitudes to their holy books.*

Reaction to Liberal Judaism came in two movements (a) Reform Judaism; (b) Orthodox Judaism.

Reform Judaism originated in Germany, under Zachariah Frankel (1801–1875), when it was felt that Liberal Jews had gone too far. Reform Jews disagree as to whether the Torah is the only revelation of God to Man, and they do not believe it is all God's work and so divine. They think God may want all the ritual rules kept and so try to apply them in modern ways, as we shall see. They do not look for a Messiah in Jerusalem. They want to stress Judaism's historical basis. The sect caught on in the USA where it now has one and a half million followers. In the UK the term Progressive Jews covers the Liberal 'left' and the Reform 'right' of non-Orthodox Judaism, while in the USA Conservative Jews are midway between the UK Orthodox and Reform Jews; their Reform Jews are midway between Reform and Liberal Jews in the UK.

Orthodox Jews are those who believe that God revealed to His Chosen People all they needed to know in the Torah, once and for all. Its 613 instructions (mitzvot) must be interpreted and obeyed. The best-known interpretation of them is the Talmud (see pp. 84–5). These instructions cover behaviour and diet, as we shall see. Orthodox Jews believe God is all-powerful and all-knowing. Samson Raphael Hirsch (1810–1888), a German Rabbi, encouraged them to acquire a secular education and absorb Western Culture as many were emigrating to America. The majority of British Jews are Orthodox, under the leadership of the Chief Rabbi of the United Congregation of the Commonwealth.

Zionism. The nineteenth century saw a growth of nationalism and minority rights, and this encouraged Theodore Herzl (1860–1904) to call for a Jewish state when speaking in Basle in 1897. This Eretz Israel (Land of Israel), the Promised Land, should be Palestine which is in the strategic and politically

Theodore Herzl.

important strip linking Africa and Asia. A few Orthodox Jews believed the Messiah's arrival should precede the start of the State of Israel, and most Liberal Jews originally rejected Zionism as cutting across their belief that Judaism was a universal movement. Today Liberals support Israel. The dream was not to be fulfilled easily, but early in the twentieth century Tel Aviv began as the first entirely Jewish City. In 1917 the British foreign secretary, Balfour, issued a Declaration saying that Britain supported the idea. Palestine came under British control after World War I. Then the Jews began to move in more and more, the number rising from 55 000 in 1918 to 450 000 in 1939, so forming 30 per cent of Palestine's population. In the 1930s and 1940s British governments tried to stop further immigration because of Arab reaction. Terrorism followed and the UNO was called upon to divide the land between the Jews and Arabs in 1948. A Jewish government then became established in Israel and Orthodox standards (kosher food in the army, no public transport on the Sabbath, etc.) were maintained. The Jewish State was born.

Palestine and Jordan in 1948.

49. *How important is Eretz Israel to the Jews? Remember the role of the Jerusalem Temple centuries earlier?*

Anti-Semitism refers to the descendants of Noah's son, Shem, and effectively means an anti-Jewish policy. In Russia the periodic bouts of anti-Semitism were called by the Russian word, pogrom. In the late nineteenth century and early twentieth century the aim was to force one-third to emigrate, one-third to become Christian and one-third to perish. Jews were blamed for the attempted revolution of 1905 and for siding with the enemy in the Russo-Japanese War. At the Tsar's orders a forgery called 'Protocols of the Elders of Zion' was produced saying that the Jews planned world conquest. Although Lenin was against anti-Semitism, Communism has made life very difficult for many Jews.

The Holocaust. In the 1940s Hitler exterminated six million Jews in concentration camps in order to 'purify' the German race. This destroyed the largest population of Jews in the world; one-third of all Jews died, including one-tenth of 'coloured' Jews in North Africa. Of the 11–12 million Jews left in 1945, about five million lived in the USA, while 250 000 were in Displaced Persons' Camps in Europe. In all one and a half million needed a new haven. 150 000 went to the USA, many stayed in Europe, and by 1958, 850 000 survivors had joined the new state of Israel.

Children who survived the Auschwitz death camp.

There are some 12 million Jews today of whom 330–350 000 live in Britain (and there are 300 synagogues). Jews believe that all religions have their routes to God and that Judaism is a good route for themselves. There are Jews of all races and nationalities.

Sephardim and Ashkenazim. Two long-standing sides of Judaism still make themselves felt today. Sephardim is the Hebrew for Spanish Judaism (the Jews were expelled from Spain in 1492). Ashkenazim is derived from Ashkenaz, the great-grandson of Noah (Gen.10:3), who was said to have settled in what is now Germany; hence the word means Jews from Germany or Central and Eastern Europe. There are three factors which explain why the division took place.
(1) *Anthropological.* When the second Temple was destroyed, 70 CE, the Jews in

the north headed north, while those in the south headed west. Both were said to have intermingled with the peoples of the lands they entered, though Jewish racial purists deny this.

(2) *Religious traditions.* From the Babylonian exile onwards some remained linked to Babylonian rituals, customs and pronunciation as they went from North Africa to Spain, while others became more Palestinian in outlook as they headed for central Europe.

(3) *Environmental.* The Sephardim were affected by Islamic Spain and the Ashkenazim by Christian Germany.

Today the Sephardim make up 17 per cent of the world's Jews, but half of Israel's population. Furthermore, they are the poor citizens there and have sometimes been called 'blacks' by the Ashkenazim.

50. State briefly why the Jews believe they are a people selected by God for particular care in return for their religious duties to Him. Does their history justify their claim?

51. When the Jews suffered, their leaders said it was God's judgement on them and so it was their fault for not keeping to the contract or covenant with Him. Why do you think the leaders said this rather than saying it was God's fault and He had let them down?

52. (a) Summarize the main differences so far mentioned between Orthodox, Reform and Liberal Jews. (b) Why do Orthodox Jews insist that the Torah's rules must all be kept while other Jews say they can be changed?

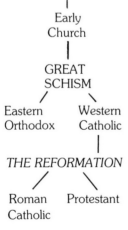

CHRISTIANITY

Early Days. St Paul. An ambitious man called Saul of Tarsus persecuted Christians before he was converted and changed his name to Paul. This small, bow-legged, large-nosed man was imprisoned and shipwrecked during his extensive missionary journeys. His New Testament letters explained the new faith for those who abandoned the Old Age of evil for the New Age of the Messiah. Paul was to use his international background of being a Jew by birth, a Greek by culture and a Roman by citizenship to open up the new faith to all people and not just Jews (Acts 9:1–22). This split the movement for a while over whether Gentiles (non-Jews) becoming Christians had to observe the whole Jewish Law, since Christianity was the fulfilment of Jewish history and not really a new religion. Jesus' brother, James, who headed the 'Jerusalem church', wanted observance, but Paul said Christ's coming made this no longer necessary. Sinful people cannot live up to the Law and 'saved' people do not need it, maintained Paul. In fact Gentiles, sympathetic to Judaism and not wanting to be circumcised and obey the whole Law, could become 'God-fearers' (Jewish sympathisers), accepting the less demanding covenant (deal) that God made with Noah and his sons (Gen. 9).

It was Paul who raised Jesus' status from that of an earthly Messianic king to Christ (Greek for 'Anointed One'), the timeless cosmic king of the universe. He argued that people were affected by original sin which had become inborn in them (Rom. 12:21). To overcome this you must believe Jesus is the Christ and be baptized, as his self-sacrifice on the cross atoned for (pardoned) this sinfulness (Rom. 6:3–11). The resurrection was his triumph over sin in this world (Rom. 5:18–19). Paul's point was that belief in Jesus, rather than acceptance of the Jewish way of life, was the key factor. Contemporary 'mystery cults' claimed their gods died and were resurrected to bring life and salvation for their followers. While Gnostics (knowledge-holders) were beginning to claim that special knowledge and angelic help, not faith, were needed if you were to be saved. They claimed the world was an evil creation to be escaped from, and not God's good creation. Paul believed the world had been 'captured' by evil and needed rescuing by an outside power, Christ. While 'saved' was not even in the Jewish vocabulary, for Paul it was essential because humans had become so wicked. He saw the Old Testament as a coded message pointing to Christ's coming to unlock the code for all to understand. Paul claimed the Law (Torah) was but a temporary rule of life – to convince people it was impossible to be good by their own effort – until a saviour came to provide the solution. Though Paul saw Jesus as the one with special knowledge who died and was resurrected for the sake of all mankind, he was probably not affected by the ideas of the mystery religions of Gnosticism. People could justify their claim to be saved by faith as God had made a promise to Abraham based on faith long before the Law had been written. Now it was made really clear by Christ's life, death and resurrection, claimed Paul.

The spread of Christianity under St Paul.

Whereas in the Gospels Jesus is a man *with* a message, in Acts and the Epistles, he himself *is* the message. When the Messianic age was expected daily, he was its *agent*, but when it did not happen, he became the centre of worship. An earthly human historical Jesus became an eternal Christ above and beyond worldly history. Christians, whom Paul had taught should live in a kind of ready-for-the-End state (1 Thess. 4–5; 1 Cor. 7 – no time to get married unless you felt an overwhelming urge to do so), had to gradually adopt a love-your-neighbour lifestyle which would last for centuries.

53. *Read the New Testament about Paul's life and sayings and then write a reconstruction interview with him about the new Christian faith he proclaimed.*

Apostles' Creed. When early Christians were baptized they needed to make a statement as to what they believed in. Eventually these baptismal creeds were formalized into the Apostles' Creed. It is a simple statement of belief in God as the Father, Son and Holy Spirit, together with the main facts about Jesus. Later on, the Nicene creed was drawn up to lay down certain points of belief such as Christ being of one substance with the Father. Among early Christians the ex-pagan St Justin Martyr (c.103–165 CE) defended his new faith by explaining their way of life to Romans who believed all the rumours they had heard that Christians were man-worshippers and immoral. His reward was martyrdom at Rome.

Origen (185–254 CE) pioneered the critical study of the Bible, pointing out that it had three levels of text: (a) literal, (b) moral, (c) allegorical or spiritual.

The Apostles' Creed

I believe in God the Father Almighty,
Maker of heaven and earth:
And in Jesus Christ his only Son our Lord, Who
was conceived by the Holy Ghost, Born of the
Virgin Mary, Suffered under Pontius Pilate, Was
crucified, dead and buried, He descended into hell;
The third day he rose again from the dead, He
ascended into heaven, And sitteth on the right hand
of God the Father Almighty; From thence he shall
come to judge the quick and the dead.
I believe in the Holy Ghost; the holy Catholic
Church; the Communion of Saints; The Forgiveness
of Sins; the Resurrection of the body, And the life
everlasting. Amen.

The Nicene Creed

I believe in one God,
The Father Almighty, Maker of heaven and earth,
and of all things visible and invisible:
And in one Lord Jesus Christ, the only-begotten
Son of God,
Begotten of his Father before all worlds,
God of God, Light of Light, Very God and Very
God.

Begotten, not made, being of one substance with
the Father, by whom all things were made:
Who for us men and for our salvation came down
from heaven, And was Incarnate by the Holy Ghost
of the Virgin Mary, and was made man,
And was crucified also for us under Pontius Pilate.
He suffered, and was buried,
And the third day he rose again according to the
Scriptures,
And ascended into heaven, and sitteth on the right
hand of the Father.
And he shall come again with glory to judge both
the quick and the dead: whose kingdom shall have
no end.
And I believe in the Holy Ghost, the Lord and giver
of life,
Who proceedeth from the Father and the Son,
Who with the Father and the Son together is
worshipped and glorified, who spake by the
Prophets.
And I believe in one holy Catholic and Apostolic
Church.
I acknowledge one Baptism for the remission of
sins:
And I look for the Resurrection of the dead,
And the life of the world to come. Amen.

(Book of Common Prayer)

---

54. *'Every religion needs a creed.' Is this so? What are the effects of having, or not having, a creed?*

55. *Who were the Apostles? Why were the facts mentioned about Jesus' life on earth so important to Christians? What is the word, other than God, used to describe the Father, Son and Holy Spirit all together?*

Catholic and Orthodox Churches. Over the centuries Christians have become split into many different denominations and sects – some major, some minor. The first split, the Great Schism, 1054, resulted from the Roman Empire breaking up into eastern and western parts. The Christians of the Eastern or Byzantine Empire looked to Constantinople as the centre of what became known as the Orthodox Church (Greek: ortho 'true'; doxa 'belief'). This Church became divided into fourteen self-governing Churches under Patriarchs (senior bishops), for example those of Constantinople, Jerusalem, Russia and Greece. They allow their parish priests to marry but not their bishops. There are now 100 000 Orthodox Christians in Britain, as opposed to 4 million Catholics in 3000 parishes.

The Western European Christians came to see Rome as their centre. Their head is the Pope. He is supported by a college of cardinals (senior bishops) from all over the world. When a Pope dies the cardinals are locked up in the Vatican (Pope's palace) until they have elected a new one. No Roman Catholic clergy are allowed to marry.

Medieval Church. St Benedict of Nursia (480–543/7) developed the idea of the life devoted entirely to God. His Rule required his followers (monks) to take vows of poverty, chastity (not marry) and obedience and to concentrate on prayer and work. Their base, a monastery or abbey, also served as the hospital, school, library and charity centre for its area. Women who wished to follow a similar life became nuns in a convent.

What is the haircut style called?

Gloucester Abbey cloister washbasin.

Protestant Churches. In the sixteenth century some Christians broke away from the Roman Catholic Church. These groups are called Protestants because they protested for one reason or another against the Pope's power and his Church's teachings. Protestant churches also allow their clergy to marry. A German called Martin Luther (1483–1546) was one of the first to challenge the Roman Catholic Church in a period known as the Reformation. In 1517 he pinned his 95 theses (arguments against the failings of the Catholic Church) to the church door at Wittenberg. He criticized the sale of indulgences which let the buyers off purgatory's punishments and excused the Church's worldliness. He said Christians did not need the Virgin Mary or the departed saints to mediate for them, as they could make use of the Holy Spirit's grace if they had faith in Jesus. Thus he removed the medieval custom of praying to God via Mary and the saints, and rejected the Catholic claim that, to be saved, one must accept the traditions set by Councils and Popes, as well as faith in Christ. This teaching is called Justification by Faith – you are saved by your faith in Christ. He was condemned at the Diet of Worms, 1521, and went on to start the Lutheran Church.

John Calvin's action in Switzerland in 1536 led to the start of the Calvinist Church. In 1534, in the reign of Henry VIII, the Church of England broke away from Rome to become England's national or 'established' Church, with the sovereign at its head. Twenty-six of its leading bishops now sit in the House of Lords.

Society of Jesus – Jesuits, 1540. While Luther and Calvin reinvigorated the Church in one way, St Ignatius of Loyola (1491/5–1556) did so in another way for the Catholic Church. Recovering from a wound, this Spanish soldier saw the need for a new style crusader, dedicated to spreading the faith to new areas. While Luther found his peace by rejecting the Church's medieval traditions for primitive Bible Christianity, Ignatius found his by revitalizing those traditions. His Jesuits were to take the three vows of monks and a fourth vow to obey the Pope unquestioningly. They were to be a healthy, handsome, intelligent and eloquent team, ready to act as the storm-troops of the Counter Reformation – a reform of the Catholic Church in counter-attack on Luther and Calvin. By 1556, 1500 of them were in action in Europe and the New World. In England they failed, in spite of running an underground campaign for years in Elizabeth I's reign. Jesuits are active today wherever there is suffering in the world, such as Latin America where the poor face great problems. In the 1960s London Jesuits called for the ordination of women to increase the numbers of priests in the world.

56. *Monks and nuns are still active in the Catholic Church today. Are their lives similar to those of medieval times? What do they do today?*

57. *Compare the reform movements of Luther and Ignatius. You could do this either in the form of an essay or by reconstructing an imaginary meeting between the two of them, in which they explain and argue their cases.*

58. *Why did Catholic houses contain 'priests' holes' in Elizabethan England?*

The Rev Carol Anderson, rector of All Angels Episcopal Church, West Side, New York – the Episcopal Church is an offshoot of the Church of England.

The Church of England is divided into dioceses (large geographical units) presided over by bishops, who are based at cathedrals. Church government by bishops is called episcopacy. There are some 13 250 smaller units called parishes which are under the control of parish priests (rectors or vicars). Deans are in charge of cathedrals and are aided by priests called canons, archdeacons supervise the clergy and church property over set areas; deacons are trainee priests; curates assist parish priests. The governing body of the Church consists of bishops, clergy and laity (ordinary members). It is called the General Synod. Today the Church has a shortage of priests and is trying to face up to the question of whether or not to have women priests. Just as with the sixteenth-century Reformation, so now a kind of 'Second Reformation' is taking place in how the Gospel is 'ministered' to members and how worship (liturgy) is held. Unpaid priests (NSMs – Non-Stipendary Ministers, 'stipend' means salary), who volunteer their services after they have done their everyday job, and 'readers' (men and women volunteers), now take many of the services. Soon there will be as many readers as priests. 'Framework for Faith' courses help church members learn more of their faith so they can proclaim it. The new prayer book has changed the meaning and content of the services, so stressing the joy of the Christian life and the community feeling among members. There are 1 559 000 active Church members today.

There are various 'nonconformist' denominations, known as Free Churches, which have broken away from the Church of England.

59. *In 1900 25 235 parish priests cared for 3½ million members. Today 10 480 care for 3 million, aided by 1000 NSMs and 7000 readers. How would you replan the use of available 'manpower' to cope? Your plan may have to be very radical! What problems will have to be overcome?*

The Baptists (founded in England in 1612) insist on adult believers' baptism (see pp. 213–14). They are supervised by the superintendents. Their chapels are run by ministers (clergy) and their congregations.

The United Reformed Church was formed in 1972 with the coming together of the Congregational and Presbyterian Churches, some 2000 churches in all with 129 000 members. It is run by a General Assembly, 12 synods and numerous distinct councils. It is normal to have women priests in this church.

John Wesley (1701–91).

The Society of Friends (Quakers) was founded by George Fox in the 1660s. There are about 18 000 Friends in Britain, worshipping in 450 meeting houses. They have no clergy, but elect members to be elders and overseers to take charge of meetings. They have local, district and national meetings. They have no set form of service, no sacraments and no creed, but trust in God's Spirit to guide them.

The Methodist Church came into being as a result of the work of John and Charles Wesley. They separated little by little from the Church of England in the late 1700s. There are some 40 million Methodists worldwide, 1 321 000 in Britain. The Methodist Church is divided in 33 districts and some 900 circuits each under the direction of a superintendent minister. It depends greatly on some 20 000 lay/local preachers to maintain Sunday worship. Ordained ministers serve in a circuit for an initial period of five years, subject to renewal. Women have been allowed to become ministers since 1974.

The Salvation Army was founded by William Booth in 1865, and it now has 3 million members using 111 languages in 83 countries. Its leaders hold 'military' style ranks with a general in overall command. Lieutenants, captains, majors, etc. are its ministers. They are posted every three to four years from one citadel ('fort' or base) to another. There are 1250 citadels in Britain. Men and women can become officers, but officers must marry officers if they wish to marry. They specialize in the care of the rejects and failures of society, and march into battle with their bands against evils such as drink, drugs and poverty. Their Missing Persons Bureau traces some 10 000 missing people a year. They accommodate 200 000 homeless each night and provide 2000 million meals a year in Britain.

From top: Salvation Army captain. Collar patches of lieutenant and captain (*top*), major and lieut-colonel. Epaulets of major (*left*) and captain (*two stars*). A lieutenant has one star.

The Pentecostal Churches consist of the Elim Church, founded in 1915 with 2500 in 310 congregations, the Assemblies of God in 1924 with 60 000 in 541 congregations, and the West Indian New Testament Church of God with 20 000 in 74 congregations. They concentrate on the gift of the Holy Spirit at Pentecost (Acts 2:1–4). In addition to adult baptism they expect members to be baptized by the Spirit, and speaking 'in tongues' occurs at their services (see p. 199). This emphasis on 'Baptism in the Holy Spirit' has spread to other churches in what is known as the Charismatic Movement. Pentecostalists also believe that people can be 'devil possessed'. This means that they are controlled by the devil or evil spirits, causing sins such as drunkenness and violence, or severe illness. Some people can remove demons and this is called exorcism.

Ecumenical Movement, the movement for the recovery of unity among the churches. In 1910, 1200 non-Catholic Christians representing missionary societies and different churches met at the Edinburgh World Missionary Conference to work out ways to unite the churches and set about the evangelization of the world. It led to the founding of the International Missionary Council, 1921, and the 'Faith and Order' Movement. Eventually, after several further conferences, the World Council of Churches was formed in 1948 at Amsterdam. Here 147 churches from 44 countries were represented, but few Orthodox churches were there and no Roman Catholics. However at subsequent meetings the Orthodox joined in 1961 and the Catholics sent observers in 1968. The WCC's aim is to bring the churches closer together and to help member-churches face up to their differences and find out what they have in common.

Vatican I, 1869–1870, saw the announcement that the Pope was infallible – could not be challenged or faulted – when he spoke *ex cathedra* (officially). In 1950 Pius XII pronounced that the Virgin Mary went bodily up into heaven and did not die on earth although this was not recorded in the Bible.

Vatican II, 1962–1965, marked a new ecumenical spirit in the Catholic Church. Its main aim was to improve pastoral work. Today the old Latin mass has given way to a modernized mass said in the local language of the people, with the priests facing the people and with members of the congregation aiding in the distribution of the elements. Liberation Theology has flourished in Central America where the Church has become identified with the downtrodden. This has drawn the Church into politics. There are signs of a swing back to traditional ways and in 1985 the Pope and his bishops were assessing what should be done next. One controversial issue is that of contraception, which the Pope has pronounced a serious sin.

Pope John Paul II.

Christianity began as a missionary religion to proclaim the 'good news' and has swept across the world over the centuries. It has numerous missionary societies today attached to its different churches. The Church Missionary Society of the Church of England is one example. It has hundreds of workers preaching, educating and healing in different parts of the world. There are 983 million Christians in the world today divided among 20 800 Christian denominations.

60. *Make a table of the different Christian churches and denominations under the headings: (a) name, (b) when started, (c) main features.*

61. *What important developments have occurred in the Roman Catholic Church in the last 150 years and why?*

62. *What are meant by the following terms? (a) ecumenical, (b) ex cathedra, (c) infallible, (d) vicar, (e) bishop, (f) citadel, (g) charismatic.*

63. *Describe Christian missionary work in any one part of the world. How is it organized and promoted? Does it try to meet up with, or reject, traditional culture and beliefs? Why is it successful? Or, why is it not successful?*

More than a cuppa

. . . on an international scale The Salvation Army provides **352** children's homes and nurseries, **481** hostels for the homeless and transient, **117** homes and centres for the treatment of alcoholics, **130** hospitals, clinics and dispensaries, **36** maternity homes, **10** institutes and centres for the blind, **10** leagues for the deaf and dumb, **21** homes and institutes for the handicapped, **110** remand, probation and approved homes, also schools, **874** primary, secondary and vocational training schools, **150** industrial homes and workshops, **3** leprosaria, **150** holiday homes and summer camps, **18** convalescent homes, **10,000** missing persons traced and found each year, **96** community centres, **15,175** evangelistic centres.

The cost is enormous. In order to help others

THE SALVATION ARMY

continues to need your help.

Salvation Army fund-raising poster. To what extent do the details given show that a 'military' style campaign is needed?

Spread of Islam. Unlike many religions, Islam spread like a hurricane, so that between 635 and 651 CE Egypt, Palestine, Syria, Iraq and the Persian Empire were overrun. A nomadic tribal existence was a feature of the Arabs' lifestyle, and aided the rapid extension of Islam. Inevitably Islam became divided into sects, largely for political reasons. When Muhammad died, his friend Abu Bakr was elected his successor (kalif or caliph) instead of his cousin Ali. Abu Bakr (kalif 632–634) united the Muslim tribes and gathered the seven different dialect pieces of the Qur'ān together. Omar or Umar (kalif 634–644) captured Damascus, Jerusalem and Egypt. The Mosque of Omar, the Dome of the Rock, was built on the site where the Jewish Temple in Jerusalem had once been. This was a traditional spot for prophecies to be made. He set up Qur'ān study schools. Othman, or Uthman (kalif 644–656), Muhammad's son-in-law and of the Umayyad family (see below), proved to be gentle and tolerant. Egyptian Muslims murdered him, although he had ordered a single-dialect (Quraysh) text of the Qur'ān to be compiled. Ali (kalif 656–661), also Muhammad's son-in-law, was assassinated by a Khārijite (see p. 63). He had established a tradition of scholarship.

The speedy expansion of Muslim power was a result of the determination which belief in Allah gave them, and novel military tactics, riding camels to make swift attacks from desert camps. But wealth and power beyond Arab dreams proved a challenge to them, as did the hordes of new converts.

64. *Make a list of the four 'right-guided' kalifs and what was achieved in their times.*

Division among Muslims. The role of the kalifs and successive leaders was to cause the major split into Sunnis (orthodox) and Shi'i, Shi'a or Shi'ite (followers of Ali). Sunnis, who make up 80–90 per cent of Muslims today, claim that none can succeed Muhammad in his nature or quality (wilaya) as a prophet as the Qur'ān said he was 'the Seal of the Prophets'. So his successors can only be guardians, kalifs of the faith. By a process of consensus (ijma) the community elects its kalifs from Muhammad's Quraish, or Quraysh tribe. This was the procedure used for the four right-guided kalifs mentioned above. Muhammad's examples and teachings constitute the Sunnah (customs) way of life to be followed.

Muhammad
|
Ali
/   \
Sunni   Shi'a

The Shi'a who live mainly in Iraq, Iran, Lebanon and India, supported Kalif Ali but refused to accept the earlier kalifs as they were not blood relatives. Both the Shi'ite and Sunni consider the Qur'ān infallible (i.e. it cannot be faulted), but the Shi'ites also believe in the infallibility of the imāms, successors to Muhammad in their interpretation of the Qur'ān claiming that they were as sinless as he. They say there were 12 or 7 imāms.

65. *Explain clearly the difference between Sunnis and Shi'a Muslims.*

Umayyad Sunni Dynasty, 661–750 CE, witnessed the reign of eleven kalifs of the Umayya family in their new capital of Damascus. Their first kalif was Muawiya, nephew of Uthman. Ali's younger son, Husain (626–680 CE), led the Shi'ites against him but he was cornered in Karbalā (Kerbalā) in Western Iraq in

680 CE. His head was carried to Damascus in triumph. As a result, Karbalā became a place of Shi'a pilgrimage and in the month of Muharram a festival centres round his golden-domed shrine and the blue-domed one of his half-brother Abbas who died with him. Black tents are erected and unshaven pilgrims wear mourning clothes. Preachers recount the tale of Husain, while some followers pull out their hair and cut themselves. A Passion Play re-enacts the end of Husain, with prophets and angels foretelling the events of his life. Visiting the shrine is said to give protection from fire and flood and rosaries of clay tablets to be worn on foreheads during rakat (see pp. 138–41) are purchased. The city is full of tombs of Shi'as who place a high value on being buried there.

66. Why is Karbalā so important to the Shi'ites?

Under the Umayyads Muslim power spread to North Africa and Spain but was halted by the French at the battle of Poitiers, 732. The Umayyads also occupied Persia (Iran) and Afghanistan and crossed the river Indus in modern Pakistan. Their raids were more for booty than to make converts. Those they conquered were allowed to follow their own faiths, although they often became Muslims to gain first-class citizenship benefits. The Khārijites ('seceders') withdrew support from Ali and opposed the Umayyads, believing the kalifs should be democratically chosen. They were very criticial of the lax morals that developed as the Umayyad power grew. They argued that faith in Allah alone does not make one

Map showing Islamic expansion to 750 CE.

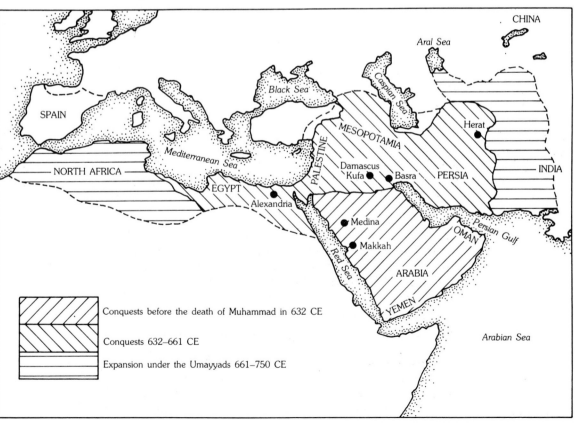

Conquests before the death of Muhammad in 632 CE

Conquests 632–661 CE

Expansion under the Umayyads 661–750 CE

a Muslim; one must do righteous deeds too. Hence a jihad (holy war) should be fought against backsliding Muslims themselves. The Khārijites are the oldest sect to reject orthodox Sunni ways and they still exist in North Africa today.

Abbasid Sunni Dynasty, 750–1055, defeated the Umayyads, and ruled from Baghdad. Under them there was a Golden Age of prosperity and trade increase. Libraries and centres of learning were established throughout the Islamic world, before the dynasty fell to the Seljuk Turks in 1055.

Fātimid Dynasty, 909–1171, claimed descent from Fātima, Muhammad's daughter, the wife of Kalif Ali, and ruled in Egypt from Cairo. They came to rule North Africa, Sicily and Syria until overthrown by the Turks.

67. *Summarize the development of Islam during the Umayyad, Abbasid and Fātimid dynasties. How did each dynasty end?*

Twelvers and Seveners. Meanwhile divisions appeared among the Shi'as. The majority, the Imāmis, who live in Iran, became known as the Twelvers as they said there were 12 imāms. The last, the Mahdi ('the guided one'), the Master of the Age, vanished at the age of eight in 880 CE. He is seen as the 'hidden imām' who did not die but will reappear as the messiah Muhammad al-Mahdi. However, his guidance can be sought through his agents, mujtahidun or ulama ('doctors of the law') of whom the most senior in Iran are the ayatollahs ('Sign of God'). Ayatollah Khomeini became famous in Iran in the 1980s for his championship of the faith. They have the right to interpret the Shari'a and make religious rulings. Imāmis also abound in Iraq, Yemen and parts of Syria and Pakistan. A rival sect is the Seveners, Sab'iya, or Isma'ilis, who claim it was the Seventh Imām, Isma'il, who disappeared and who will return. Hence they are called Isma'ilis. They hold mystical beliefs centred round the number seven – seven prophets, seven imāms, etc. They have become divided into the Mustālians in the Yemen and India and the Nizāris in Syria, Iran, Afghanistan, India and East Africa. They total over 10 million.

The Druze are an Isma'ili sect started by Darazī (d.1019), who are to be found in Lebanon, Syria and Israel. Their Hidden Imām is the Fātimid kalif called Hakim. The Assassins whose correct name is Hashishis ('self-sacrificers') are a sect (founded by Hasan ibn Sabbāh) living in Pakistan, India and East Africa. At the time of the Crusades they would drug themselves with hashish and then murder their enemies.

68. *The Shi'a Muslims look for a Messiah's coming; so do the Jews and Christians. Explain what each religion expects of its messiah.*

Sufis ('wearers of undyed wool', hence austere people) are a mystical sect. Their burning love for Allah draws them closer to Him through the use of self-control and denial of worldly pleasures. They concentrate on prayers, using the subha (see p. 175) to aid their feelings of gentleness and peace, as well as spiritual exercises such as dances which involve whirling round and round ('whirling dervishes'). They began in the seventh century among the Sunni and there are numerous different groups now, including some in Britain.

Ahmadiyya was founded in 1889 by Mirza Ghulam Ahmad (1839–1908) at Qadian, near Lahore, who proclaimed himself the Messiah-Mahdi of the Christians and Muslims and the Hindu Avatar. Convinced of his prophetic abilities, he challenged Christians and Muslims to prove him wrong, but they declined his contests. Although he represented Islam at debates on comparative religion, he was turned on by other Muslims who rejected his personal claims. The present Kalif is based at their London Mosque at Southfields. Their 10 million followers have mission houses, schools and medical centres in many parts of the world.

Salafiya, the movement for pan-Islam, was founded by Muhammad Rashīd Ridā (1865–1935), an editor. It was a puritan movement which rejected the guidance of the ulama. Rashīd denounced the secular way Kemal Ataturk modernized Turkey, for example.

Recent history. Islam, once the fastest-spreading religion in history, is now growing fast again. Modern states such as Pakistan, and Iran (under Ayatollah Khomeini), are concerned to apply Islamic law. In the Middle East, Arabs have realized the power of oil and use this to gain influence in non-Muslim countries, regardless of colour or race. In a sense this is a kind of modern jihad, a light to the Islamic truth. In the unorthodox Black Muslim movement in the USA, Islam attracts many who feel downtrodden. There are now 387 mosques in Britain, where 1½ million of the world's 854 million Muslims live. Birmingham has 100 000, Bradford 80 000 and East London 50 000. Five to ten per cent of British Muslims belong to the Shi'a sect, almost all the rest are Sunnis. The largest single Islamic country is Indonesia with 100 million. Forty million (15½ per cent) of Russians and 17 million (2 per cent) of the Chinese are Muslims.

In the twentieth century immigrants to Western Europe were largely temporary workers wanting to raise money to send home before going back themselves. However, the 1962 Commonwealth Immigration Act in the UK and the 1972–74 West European legal changes closed the door to further immigration, with the result that temporary immigrants sent for their families and became permanent settlers. This influx of women and children led to a big increase in mosque building and a rush of problems involving health, education and social services. In Britain charity status was obtainable to Muslim associations and political participation was allowed. This had led to much pressure to ensure that single-sex Muslim-only schooling, among other things, are accepted as religious requirements. The Islamic Society for the Promotion of Religious Toleration in the UK was started to correct many misunderstandings about Islam that appear in the media.

69. *Locate the mosque in your area and find out whether it was purpose-built or adapted. Are there any special provisions for education of Muslim children in your area? If so, what are they?*

Muslims do not see the history of a state, its culture or its religion, as something which is continually developing and improving. History is seen either as cyclical or as in a decline since the 'ideal' days of Muhammad and the four kalifs. Thus human society is essentially the same as in Muhammad's time. It is right to use the writings of that period, because Islam already possesses in the Qur'ān and Sunnah *all* the religious and moral knowledge required for the whole human race for all time. As Islam is seen as the final and entirely self-sufficient religion, the ulama (*mullahs* in Iran) claim to interpret that knowledge. They call for a return to the Qur'ān as the answer to what they see as the threat of Western irreligion and depravity. Thus history is at the mercy of religion and moral truth as Islam presents it. For them, the world is seen as divided between the Muslim sphere and the 'sphere of war', that of non-Muslim lands with whom only temporary ten-year treaties may be made.

Bahā'īs. In 1844 a Persian Shi'a, Ali Muhammad (1819–1850) known as Bāb ('The Gate' – leading to the truth) said he was the Messenger of God sent to proclaim the coming Messiah. He was executed for the threat he posed in Persia. Then in 1863 Bahā'u'llāh ('Glory of God'; 1817–1892) claimed to be the Messiah heralding a new era. He publicized his teachings widely. This led to the 40 years' exile and imprisonment. He taught that Moses, Zoroaster, Jesus, the Buddha, Krishna and Muhammad had all received divine revelations before his own. He rejected polygamy, slavery and the jihad. His followers, the Bahā'īs, spread beyond the Islamic world and are to be found in the UK today.

Believing in the oneness of religion they call for a world-wide community under a world government with a single world language to promote human unity, so ending racial, religious and class prejudice. They also point to the harmony of religion and science, and to the equality of the sexes. The Bahā'ī religion, though derived from Islam, claims to be independently revealed. Bahā'īs do not regard themselves as Muslims, though they revere Muhammad and the Qur'ān. Orthodox Muslims look upon the Bahā'īs as heretics, and attack them because they challenge Muhammad's role as the final prophet to whom Allah revealed the Qur'ān.

70. *Show how the idea of Jihad is linked to important Islamic beliefs and principles.*

SIKHISM

The Ten Gurus
Guru Nanak: see pp. 29–32.
Guru Angad (1504–1552). In 1539 Angad became the second of the Ten Gurus (teachers), men who had achieved moksha (spiritual liberation, freedom from rebirth). They are seen as perfect men who have been sent to earth to preach God's message. Guru Angad set up religious centres to teach Sikhism and popularize Punjabi for the purpose, as it provides a better language to use than the outdated Sanskrit. The script used is called Gurmukhi (Guru language, literally 'script used by the blessed'). Sixty-two of his hymns are in the Adi Granth.
Guru Amar Das (1479–1574) took over in 1552 in spite of his age. He emphasized the importance of the langar (see p. 179) to encourage Sikhs of all castes to mix together. This strengthened their brotherhood. He set up 22 manjis (preaching centres, like dioceses) to systematize the growing Sikh

faith. There were 146 Masands (missionaries) in charge of the manjis, which sent offerings to Goindwal, on the river Beas, and Sikhs gathered there at the festivals of Baisakhī, Maghī and Diwali. The town's centrepiece was the baoli, a pilgrimage well reached by 84 steps which Guru Amar Das built. He composed Anand Sihib, a hymn used on all religious occasions.

Guru Ram Das ('Slave of God', 1534–1581) followed his father-in-law in 1574. He founded the Sacred Sarovar, the Lake of Immortality, at the new trading city of Amritsar ('Pool of Nectar'; see p. 179). A humble, pious man, he put missionary work on a sound basis.

Guru Arjan (1563–1606) was a teenager when he became fifth Guru. He founded the Golden Temple (Harmandir) at Amritsar, in 1589, with its four doors open to all classes and creeds, unlike Hindu temples with their single doors (see p. 150). He got a Muslim holy man to lay the foundation stone of what was the Sikh's holiest building, but he was to end his life as the first Sikh martyr at the hands of the Muslim Emperor Jahāngīr. The Emperor had asked him to include praise of Muhammad in the Guru Granth Sahib and when he refused, he had boiling water and burning sand poured on him. When he tried to bathe the blisters in the cold river Ravi, he was swept away to his death. Thus Arjan's time marked a turning point in Sikh history, namely the start of the Sikh struggle against the Muslim state.

Guru Har Gobind (1595–1644), his son, took to wearing two swords, the Meeri (Temporal), and the Peeri (Spiritual) swords, indicating political and spiritual power (see p. 31). He built the Akal Takht in Amritsar. He organized a Sikh defence system and won three battles. Thus Sikhism became more militant.

Guru Har Rai (1630–1661), the grandson of the sixth Guru, was only fourteen when he succeeded. His period was a peaceful one partly because he avoided the intrigues of the Muslim Mughal court, and partly because he kept an army ready as a deterrent.

Guru Har Krishan (1656–1664) was known as the Child Guru, being only five years old in 1661. Hence he is loved by Sikh children and students. He soon died of smallpox.

Guru Tegh Bahadur (1621–1675) was a devotional man rather than a soldier although his name means expert swordsman. He travelled a lot before the Emperor Aurangzeb had him beheaded at Delhi for refusing to become a Muslim. Aurangzeb, a fanatical Muslim, had altered his great grandfather's policy of religious toleration to one of ruthlessness.

Guru Gobind Singh (1666–1708), was Tegh Bahadur's son. He realized that a strong organization was essential if Sikhism was to survive. So in 1699 he called the Sikhs together at Anandpur. He stood in military uniform, with drawn sword in front of a tent, and cried five times, 'Is there any one of you who will give his head to prove his faith in me? I want a head!' One Sikh got up and said, 'Lord, you can have my humble head. There can be no greater gain than to die under your sword'. Guru Gobind took him into the tent; a thud was heard and blood flowed out. Guru Gobind emerged with dripping sword and cried, 'Is there any other true Sikh who will offer his head?' Twice more he called and another came forward. Five times this frightening ritual was enacted before he and the five emerged alive and well. The Five Loved Ones (Panj Piares, see p. 221), as they are now called, were all dressed in saffron uniforms and carried swords. To an

Guru Gobind Singh.

astonished audience he announced that the five, who came from different classes, were now his brothers in this cause, as they had passed the toughest test.

He declared his intention to start the Khalsa ('pure ones') army of soldier-saints, a brotherhood in which all were equal. They took the surname Singh ('lion') and demonstrated their equality and unity by consuming amrit (sugared water) and revised the five Ks (Kakars, Symbols) in a ceremony (see p. 222). He used the world 'amrit' as it referred to the 'water of immortality' in the lake around the Golden Temple, Amritsar, as he could not reach the old city but wanted his followers to possess its essence.

Twenty thousand Sikhs were then 'initiated' into the Khalsa that day. He told them they must never shrink from the enemy, but help the poor and protect the weak. They must not smoke or use drugs and should not cut their hair. Turban wearing would make them so distinctive that they would not be able to deny their faith in the face of danger. His chief aim in creating the Khalsa was to ensure democracy in Sikhism; none should be a sole guru in future. As the Masands had become greedy and corrupt, he told the Khalsa they could dismiss the bad ones. Thus the Masand Missionary System came to an end.

71.   Write a one-act play on Guru Gobind Singh's founding of the Khalsa. Read about the five Ks on p. 222 before doing so.

The fighting continued and Guru Gobind Singh's four sons sacrificed themselves for the cause. The two youngest, aged nine and seven, were bricked up alive in a wall at Sirhind in 1704. Guru Gobind Singh died in 1708, stabbed by a Muslim retainer. Although involved in much fighting, he was a patron of the arts and poetry and a learned man. He was known to his followers by numerous descriptions, some of which have been translated as follows:

> Pious, Profound, Perfect and Princely Prophet,
> Painstaking, Prominent, Powerful, and Pitiful Patriot,
> Platonic, Practical, Prudent and Pacific Philosopher,
> Progressive, Popular, Proficient and Prolific Poet,
> Promising, Predominant, Patient and Potent Politician
> Paternal, Polite, Pleasant and Peaceful Personage.
>
> Subtle, Serious, Sober and Stately Seer,
> Sympathetic, Strong, Soothing and Successful Saviour,
> Sweet, Supreme, Sacred and Simple Saint,
> Scientific, Sound, Shining and Significant Scholar,
> Skilful, Sensible, Sagacious and Sane Statesmen,
> Selfless, Stout, Splendid and Steady Soldier,
> Sincere, Silent, Superfine and Social Sage,
> Smiling, Shielding, Striking and Spiritual Sovereign.

72.   Take two or three other letters of the alphabet and see how many words you can write down which could be applied to Guru Gobind Singh.

73. *What happened when an Islamic army and a Khalsa met in India? See if you can find out both for Gobind's period and the late 1940s.*

The Guru Granth Sahib, the holy book, now became the tenth perpetual guru.

Sikh history after the Ten Gurus

Banda Singh (1670–1716) was appointed as army commander by Guru Gobind Singh and with his supporters (Bandais), avenged the death of Guru Gobind Singh and his two sons by destroying Sirhind, killing all oppressors. But support for him declined when it seemed he wanted to be recognized as a guru. After he had suffered defeats, the Mughal Emperor had him beheaded. A period of acute suffering followed and the Sikhs fled to the Himalayan foothills. But organized in two Dals (platoons), they hit back. Merciless killing took place on both sides. But 30 000 were massacred in the Wadda Ghallughara (big holocaust) at Malerkotla in 1762 by Ahmad Shah's Afghanistan raiders, and the Amritsar temple destroyed. Eventually the Sikhs under the leadership of Lehna Singh drove Ahmad away. To fight the Mughals and the invading Afghans, they had regrouped in 1765 into twelve misals (militias), ranging from 100–20 000 strong. They met twice a year at Amritsar to plan their operations in a democratic way. After they had won the Punjab, they became rulers.

In 1799 Ranjit Singh (1780–1839) wisely absorbed the misals into the Khalsa, as they had come to rival each other. A small, ugly, one-eyed man, Ranjit Singh proved to be a good ruler. Known as the Lion of the Punjab, he rallied a disunited people, employing Muslims, Hindus and Europeans. Fanaticism and bigotry were replaced by fairness and justice. He had the Golden Temple rebuilt with copper gilded plates, hence 'Golden'. He signed a treaty of friendship with Britain, 1809, but in 1845–46 the British captured Lahore and annexed the Punjab in 1849.

Sikhism in the twentieth century

In 1906 and 1907 some 4000 Sikhs emigrated to Canada, only to find to their disgust that loyal British subjects from India were not welcome. Getting no sympathy from London, they announced the start of agitation to liberate India. In 1913, 200 Indians, mainly Sikhs, founded the Ghadar (Revolutionary) Party in Washington to expel British rule by any means. Three hundred then chartered the *Komagata Maru* and sailed to Vancouver, but although their papers were in order they were surrounded by warships and forced back.

In 1919 General Dyer massacred 321 men, women and children at Jallianwala Bagh. In 1920 the Shiromani Gurdwara Prabandhak Committee (Central Gurdwara Management Committee, SGPC) was formed and started to get control of the temples from the corrupt custodian priests (mahants). The Akālī Dal (Immortal Army) was a paramilitary organization supporting this demand. This led to the banning of the Kirpan (see p. 222) and so to widespread arrests. After the Akālī Dal was declared illegal, the Sikh Gurdwaras Act, 1925, gave the temples to the SGPC. These disturbed years had lost Britain the loyal support of the Sikhs.

In 1942 many joined the Japanese-sponsored Indian National Army and the Indian National Congress, calling for Britain to quit India. But the Sikhs were caught between the Congress Party's call for a united India and the Muslim League's demand for a Muslim Pakistan. The latter would mean the division of their Punjab. On 16 August 1946 the Muslim League held a Direct Action Day, slaughtering 6000 Hindus and Sikhs in Calcutta. Rioting followed elsewhere. In North West Punjab 160 Sikh villages were destroyed and in 1947 Sikhs rebelled. In the Punjab where 15 million Hindus, 16 million Muslims and 6 million Sikhs shared a common way of life, rioting was savage. The offical division of Punjab into two led to a mass exodus from the Western portion, now Pakistan, where they had owned 40 per cent of the land. Two and a half million Sikhs arrived as refugees in East Punjab, vacated by the fleeing Muslims. Most called for a Punjabi Suba (Punjabi-speaking state), but other Sikhs and Hindus rejected this. In 1966 Prime Minister Indira Gandhi set up a smaller Punjab than demanded, which led to further agitation for boundary changes. In 1984 she sent troops in to the Golden Temple complex which was held by the Akālī Dal, who had been organizing violent acts in despair. Sikhs were grieved and she was assassinated by her Sikh bodyguards in Dehli. Many Sikhs were killed in a Hindu backlash. The result has been a growing call for an independent Sikh state to the known as Khalistan. The name has no particular meaning, but it resonates with Hindustan and Pakistan. As yet Akālī Dal has not come out for such a state.

74. *What is behind the movement for Khalistan? How would its establishment help and hinder Sikhism?*

Emigration of Sikh men to Britain, North America and South and East Africa increased after World War II, many abandoning their turbans, beards and long hair to obtain acceptance. In the late 1960s wives and families arrived, gurdwaras were opened and turbans and long hair restored. In 1969 the Sikh Missionary Society was founded in Britain and numerous pamphlets offered to anyone interested. At weekends gurdwaras organized Punjabi lessons for their children. Sikhs in Britain today include a judge, JPs and local councillors. Those from the Far East and East Africa have an urban background and speak English well compared with those from India. Many live in Southall, Middlesex, as it is near Heathrow Airport, but other centres are Smethwick, Coventry, Hounslow, Birmingham and Wolverhampton. There are over 150 gurdwaras in the UK today. Of the 14 million Sikhs about 300 000 live in Britain.

Sikhism has incorporated Islamic monotheism, Buddhist ethics, Jewish concern for the family and the Christian concept of love and service, and done so within the Hindu framework of reincarnation. To this has been added equality for women. God's will (hukam) is sovereign and in the end will enable man to merge into God and end the cycle of reincarnation.

75. *Make a brief summary of the contribution of each Guru to Sikhism.*

76. *(a) Explain how and why Sikhism changed from a peaceful to a warlike faith. (b) Had it any choice in the matter?*

Sikh Khalsa leaders
with ceremonial
swords leading a
march to India
House, London.

77. *(a) Consider what it must have meant for Sikhs to abandon their turbans
     and long hair in order to obtain work. (b) What impact did the arrival of
     dependants in Britain have on the Sikh community? (c) What problems are
     likely to face Sikhs in Britain in the future?*

78. *Mahāyāna Buddhists and Christians showed their emphasis on compassion
     in their missionary work by bringing medical care with them. (a) What methods,
     besides preaching do religions use to attract new members today?
     (b) Should missionaries make their appeal primarily with the Truth they
     claim for their teachings, or by means of the by-products that come with
     their faith's organization?*

79. *Once a religion has become established it produces experts who guard the
     faith and pronounce on its interpretation in their age. Identify those who
     emerge as such experts in each religion; for example, Roman Catholic
     Popes.*

80. *Periodically a religion produces a reforming sect claiming the experts have
     developed their religion in a wrong way. (a) Identify sects that appear in this
     way. (b) Do they seem to have anything in common in (i) their criticism of
     their religions, or (ii) in what they propose as the solution?*

81. *Religions which are revealed to mankind by a founding figure or in a holy
     book are faced with the dilemma of either claiming what was once revealed
     is eternal, the only Truth and so cannot be changed, or admitting that the
     revelation needs to be adapted to changing circumstances. (a) Identify
     religions which have had to face this dilemma and say what they did in the*

circumstances. (b) Is a religion hampered or aided by having a fixed revelation of the Truth? Give examples of hampering and aiding before you draw a conclusion. (c) Is there evidence to support the argument that an unchanging faith requires followers to opt out of society (unless that faith is the state religion), while an adaptive one will allow its followers to live within the community? (d) Is the role of a religion to serve the Truth or the community?

82. If Truth is eternal and unchanging, is it essential that the Truth is presented in a fixed form, for example in a holy book? If change is allowed for, does that mean that there can be no eternal Truth for mankind to find?

83. Explain the origins of the Hindu caste system.

84. What is meant by (a) Arahat, (b) Bodhisatta? What is the difference between them?

85. What was the Hasidic movement? What had the rebbe to do with it?

86. Who was John Wesley and why was he an outstanding religious leader?

87. What is the function of the World Council of Churches and how did it come into existence?

88. What is the importance of Vatican II, 1962–65?

89. What makes Shi'ites different from Sunnis?

90. How many human-being gurus were there in Sikhism? Name two of them and say what they did for their faith.

91. What is meant by Alākī and Khalistan? Are they connected in any way?

92. Who was Swami Vivekananda and what did he do?

93. Why do some Buddhists call on Amida Buddha?

4
BOOKS TO READ

All the main religions of today possess holy books of some kind, often dating back a very long way. Holy books are usually ones which contain teaching revealed by God or gods and so they are of very special value to their religions. Their contents may have been built up over a thousand years, as with the Jewish holy books, or quite a short time, as with Islam's Qur'ān which was finished within 40 years. A religion's authoritative books are called its canon (lit. 'measuring rod').

We shall see that some religions revere their holy books so much as the very word of God that they will not allow them to be criticized in any way. Such books are regarded as infallible; that is, they tell the truth and cannot be faulted. People who believed the literal truth of such books are often called fundamentalists.

Holy books are usually given a place of honour in the worship building and may be ceremoniously carried in during services. Readings from them are considered most important and a sermon (instructive talk) may be based on a passage from them. This litugical (service) use of holy books will be dealt with more in Chapter 6. Most Hindus, Orthodox Jews, Muslims and Sikhs insist that when their scriptures are used in services they are read in their original languages as God revealed them in those languages. The contents of holy books are varied. They are likely to contain some historical facts as well as biographies of leading characters, rules to be followed, songs or poems to be recited, and myths. Myths are stories of God or gods, people and events. They are designed to explain matters which would otherwise not be easy to put into words. For example, the story of Adam and Eve explains the need for people to find God, ask His forgiveness and obey Him in future.

HINDUISM

Hindu sacred writings are of two types:
(1) Sruti, Shruti ('hearings'), which the rishis (holy men) heard from the gods. Thus they are eternal and were in existence when the rishis discovered them. They include the Vedas and the Upanishads.
(2) Smriti or Smrti ('memory'), which were remembered from generation to generation then written down by wise men. This means that they are considered as lower than the Sruti. If there is anything in Smriti which conflicts with Sruti, the Sruti point is taken as correct. They include the Mahābhārata, Rāmayana and the Laws of Manu.

BOOKS TO READ

Sruti. The Vedas ('Knowledge of God') consist of four collections (samhitās) recorded in Sanskrit between 1500 and 800 BCE. The first three samhitās are known collectively as the Trayī-Vidyā, Sāma-Veda, Yajur-Veda; the fourth is the Atharva-Veda.

The Rig-Veda (Veda of Praise or Royal Veda) is the most sacred and oldest. It consists of ten volumes (mandalas) compiled by the Aryans who conquered Northern India, c.1750 BCE. It contains 1017 hymns to nature gods, each made up of a number of verses (mantras). These hymns reflect the nomadic life of the people who cry out to their favourite gods as they charge into battle, rejoice in the sun's rising or feel lonely on a silent evening. Agni, the fire god, essential to all sacrifices, and Indra, the warrior god, are particularly worshipped as well as Varuna who directed rivers and fixed the position of the planets.

The Sāma-Veda (Veda of Chants) comprises hymns from the Rig-Veda to various gods arranged for the chanting priests to use in the Soma (hallucinatory plant) rituals of the Aryans in praise of Agni. The Yajur-Veda (Sacrificial Veda) contains prose prayers for domestic and public rituals, while the later Atharva-Veda (compiled by the priest Atharvan) corrects the pronunciation and errors of the Trayī-Vidyā with its incantations and magical texts for healing. It portrays the popular Indian religion and stresses the magical power of knowledge. The Vajur-Veda suggests the dawning truth of a single god behind the legion of gods and goddesses in this passage:

> *For an awakened soul Indra, Varuna, Agni, Yana, Aditya, Chandra – all these names represent only one basic power and spiritual reality.*

All the Vedas had subsequent additions made to them so that each can now be broken up into four parts. These can be used by Hindus following the four stages of Jnana yoga (see pp. 97–9). The original Vedas' Mantra-Samhitās, metrical poems of praise to gods for supplying prosperity on earth and happiness hereafter, are useful for brahma charyas (see p. 97). The Brahmana ('belonging to the brahmins') is a very detailed guide for performing sacrifices with explanations for them. The sacrifices serve three purposes: (a) gifts to persuade gods to give people long life, health and wealth, (b) sin offerings to remove guilt, (c) communal meals with the gods so that those who join in acquire the gods' virtues. Mythological material on the origin and development of the universe is included. This prose work was compiled between 800 and 500 BCE. It is suitable for the householder (grihastha) stage of life (see p. 98). Together the Mantra-Samhitās and the Brahmana form the Karma-Kanda ('work portion') of the Vedas.

The Aranyaka ('being in the forest') is for those who cannot perform ritual sacrifices as they live in the forest. It explains what lies behind rituals, and so deals with the inmost nature of people and the universe. The work is suitable for the hermit (vāna prastha) in the third stage of life as it deals with worship and meditation (the Upasana-Kanda) (see p. 98).

Lastly the 108 Upanishads ('sitting down near your teacher', i.e. for a session with him), were compiled between 800 and 300 BCE. Their subject is Jnana-Kanda (knowledge portion), the basic foundation framework of Hinduism; hence they form the most important part of the Vedas. They are also known as the Vedanta ('end of the Vedas') as they used to be the third section of the Vedas. Set in quiet forest glades, they consist of discussions and teachings that gurus (teachers) had with their disciples about Brahman, atta, karma, and transmigration. They answer the question 'Who are you?' by saying that you are not the clothes you wear, nor the things you eat, nor the face you have, your real self is your atta (soul), which you will find when you join Brahman. They stress that the millions of gods of the Vedas are really one, Brahman, which is the energy source behind them all.

> *In the beginning . . . this world was just Being, only one, without a second . . . It bethought itself: 'Would that I were many! Let me procreate myself!' It emitted heat. The heat bethought itself: 'Would that I were many! Let me procreate myself.' It emitted water. Therefore whenever a person grieves or perspires from the heat, then water is produced.*
>
> *That water bethought itself: 'Would that I were many! Let me procreate myself.' It emitted food. Therefore whenever its rains, then there is abundant food. So food for eating is produced just from water.*
> (Chandogya Upanishad)

The four Samhitās of the Vedas, 1500–800 BCE

Rig-Veda	Sāma-Veda	Yajur-Veda	Atharva-Veda
Veda of Praise	Veda of Chants	Veda of Sacrifices	Veda of priest Atharva
21 sections	1000 sections	109 sections	50 sections

Trayī-Vidya – threefold knowledge for

chief priest	chanting priests	sacrificial fire priests

The Sruti – the revealed books, their subjects and their uses for followers of Jnāna Yoga

BOOKS	SUBJECTS	FOR USE BY
Vedas' Mantra-Samhitās (mantra collection) 1500–800 BCE	Karma-Kanda (work portion)	brahma charyas (students)
Brahmana (Brahmins' treatise) 800–500 BCE		grihasthas (householders)
Aranyaka (Forest treatise) c.700 BCE	Upasana-Kanda (worship, meditation portion)	vāna prasthas (hermits)
Upanishads (Sitting with teacher) 800–300 BCE	Jnāna-Kanda (knowledge portion)	sadhus or sannyāsīns (holy men)

Life is a quest to overcome problems. They offer the yogas (ways) to salvation to enable you to find your atta and so cease to return continually to earth. For example:

From the unreal lead me to the real!
From the darkness lead me to light!
From death lead me to immortality!
He who inhabits water . . . fire . . . the sky . . . heaven . . . the sun
. . . the moon and stars . . . darkness . . . light . . . He is your Self
[atta], the Inner Controller, the Immortal.
(Brihadaranyaka Upanishad)

The Upanishads are suitable for the sadhus (holy men) to use in the last stage of life (see pp. 98–9).

Smriti. The Mahābhārata (Story of the War of the Bharatas) and the Rāmāyana (Adventures of Rāma) are long collections of stories (epics). They attempt to get to grips with the mysteries of chaos and misery in human life and show how order and purpose in life would eventually prevail. The book is recommended for Hindus who want to know what life is about. 'What is not in it is nowhere'. They stress Bhakti, the personal devotion to a particular god (see p. 99). They claim that history goes in cycles. The world starts in good order or righteousness (dharma) and then goes through four ages (yugas) in which goodness weakens until it is necessary for the gods to destroy the world and start again.

The Rāmāyana is set at the end of the second yuga, when goodness is still basically intact but under serious threat. The adventures were put together in Sanskrit by Valmiki, a wise man in about 300 BCE. Prince Rāma, heir to the kingdom of Ayodhya, is exiled when his step-mother tries to get her son made heir. Rāma, his wife Sita, and his brother are sent to the forest home of the demons. The demon king, Rāvana, abducts Sita and takes her to his island kingdom, Sri Lanka. Eventually monkeys, led by the monkey-god Hanuman, link tails to provide a bridge for Rāma to rescue Sita. Rāma (an avator of Vishnu, see p. 8) is the ideal good ruler whose faith withstands the demons' wiles. Sita proves her loyalty, when Rāma doubts it, by walking through fire. So good conquers evil by a display of manly courage, and a woman's virtue is maintained.

The Mahābhārata is the world's longest poem, consisting of three million words, and it is set at the end of the third yuga. It tells of a tragic war between two sets of cousins, the Pāndavas and the Kurus, or Kauravas, of the Bharata royal family, which ushers in the Kali yuga, the final age of disorder and wickedness in which we now live. It was compiled perhaps about 200 BCE by a vyasa (editor) who was told by Brahma to get Ganesha, the elephant god, to take it down at his dictation.

The Pāndavas and Kurus both wanted control of Elephant City, a kingdom whose ruins are near Delhi. The Kurus became jealous of the heroism and goodness of the five Pāndava brothers, sons of King Pandu and Queen Pritha, and tried to burn them in their palace. The Pāndavas, however, secretly hid in the forest disguised as brahmins. The story centres on how the five face the crisis. The eldest hates war and wants to turn from the world like a Buddhist monk. The second thinks only of fighting on, while the fourth and fifth are too young to help.

The third, Arjuna, dislikes war but is nevertheless a great warrior. Eventually he emerges from the forest to win an archery contest and hence a princess in marriage. He alone was strong enough to draw the bow and hit the eye of a revolving target five times. So the Kurus had to recognize the five were still alive and share the kingdom with them. But they succeeded in tricking them by a game of dice and after some years the war was renewed.

The climax is a section of the Mahābhārata called the Bhagavad Gītā (Song of the Lord) consisting of 700 verses written between 400 BCE and 100 CE. In it Arjuna hesitates before the final battle at Kurukshetra as he is shocked at fighting his relatives. He orders his chariot driver to withdraw, but the man argues with him. Gradually Arjuna realizes the man is in fact Krishna, the god, who has appeared to teach him the truth. Krishna argues that because the world is threatened with chaos it is Arjuna's duty to restore order and not simply fight for his own gain. He must face up to life and serve God as revealed in Krishna. What Krishna asks for is love. 'Just fix your mind upon Me, the Supreme Personality of the Godhead, and engage all your intelligence in Me. Thus you will live in Me always.' In Krishna, the impersonal Brahman became a personal loving god (Bhagavad Gītā 18:65–6). Krishna assures Arjuna that those who die in battle live eternally, for none really die. Thus Krishna points out that the discipline of knowledge (Jnana Yoga, see pp. 97–9) will teach him that his real self cannot be injured in battle and so he should fight as it is the duty of a Kshatriya, and that the discipline of action (Karma Yoga, see pp. 99–100) will teach him that right actions should be performed without regard for the outcome. He clinches his argument by pointing out that

Krishna as charioteer to Arjuna.

while the discipline of devotion (Bhakti Yoga, see p. 99) is the highest form of discipline it is also the means by which God becomes available for all, for bhakti comes from the word 'bhaj', meaning 'to share'.

So Arjuna, aided by Krishna, fights and wins over the Kurus with all their material forces. In a sense Arjuna represents Man's soul and the chariot his body while the chariot's motion is time and the battlefield the world. The story is one of Man's attempts to make sense of the world in which he lives. The poem commands personal devotion to a personal God and this form of life and worship is called Bhakti Yoga (see p. 99). In overcrowded, poverty-ridden India it is the most popular Hindu scripture today.

The Yoga-Sūtras (Yoga Exercises) were written in 100–200 CE (see p. 101). The Puranas ('old writings') were written about 1000 years ago to popularize the religion of the Vedas. They were written for ordinary people in a language of the time, illustrating the main religious points by means of stories about the world's creation, destruction and re-creation and the lives of the rishis, kings and gods.

The Laws of Manu ('man', a kind of Adam) has 12 books with 2685 verses, and was written in 200–100 BCE. It is also said that a rishi called Manu wrote the book. Here is its description of the creation of the universe:

> This (universe) existed in the shape of Darkness, unperceived, destitute of distinctive marks, unattainable by reasoning, unknowable, wholly immersed, as it were, in deep sleep.

> Then the divine Self-existent himself indiscernible, but making all this, the great elements and the rest discernible appeared with irresistible creative power, dispelling the darkness . . .

> He, desiring to produce beings of many kinds from his own body, first with a thought created the waters, and placed his seed in them.

> That seed became a golden egg, in brilliancy equal to the sun; in that egg he himself was born at Brahmā, the progenitor of the whole world . . . The divine one resided in that egg during a whole year, then he himself by his thought alone divided it into two halves; and out of these two halves he formed heaven and earth, between them the middle sphere, the eight points of the horizon, and the eternal abode of the waters . . . But joining minute particles . . . which possess measureless power . . . he created all beings.

The Laws of Manu also give instructions on what men may or may not do, marriage laws, diet rules, daily rites and laws, and so on:

> Coveting the property of others, thinking in one's heart of what is undesirable and adherence to false doctrines are three kinds of sinful mental actions. Abusing others, speaking untruth, detracting from the merits of all men, and talking idly shall be four kinds of evil verbal action.

The Tantra ('Rule System') are magical and religious books made up of talk between Shiva and Shakti about creation, destruction, worship, etc., in which the power of the female is dominant (see p. 7).

1. List the titles and main subjects of these Hindu books.

2. Draw a picture or series of pictures from some of the stories in these books.

3. *Explain how Hindus learn about the characters of their gods and goddesses from myths.*

SHINTOISM

Although the word 'Shinten' means 'a collection of sacred books', Shintoism has no holy book comparable to those of other religions, but is has got the Kojiki (Records of Ancient Matters) which was finished in 712 CE and covers events to 628 CE. It contains myths and historical stories about creation, gods, men, the nation, customs and ceremonies. The story of Izanagi and Izanami is in it (see p. 12).

The Nihongi or Nihon Shoki (Chronicles of Japan) gives different versions of the same creation myths and legendary figures as the Kojiki and covers to 700 CE; it was compiled in 720 CE. For example:

> Of old, Heaven and Earth were not yet separated . . . They formed a chaotic mass like an egg which was of obscurely defined limits and contained germs . . . Heaven was therefore formed first, and Earth was established subsequently. Thereafter Divine Beings were produced between them.

The purpose of these books is to make clear the origins of the Imperial Throne with its clan lineage.

4. *What does a religion lack if it has not got a 'holy book'? Why cannot the two Shinto books be considered as 'holy books'?*

5. *Are books of myths and legends any real religious help today?*

TAOISM

There are two main books from about 300 BCE and a collection of books compiled in the fifteenth century CE.

Tao Te Ching (Pronounced 'Dow Deh Jing') means The Way and its Power, or The Book of the Right Way. It is the basic guide book said to be written by Lao-Tse. It is like a popular bedside book today. If it was written by him, it would date from the sixth century BCE, but it was more likely written by an unnamed person between 350 and 300 BCE. It has 81 short chapters and teaches that there is a way (Tao) which if taken will show how a perfect balance in one's life can be reached. But it is a cryptic book, which has been understood in different ways. It teaches the way of the world and how to survive in it by means of humility, gentleness and not overstriving (see pp. 106–8). It proclaims the social ideal of a return to nature, arguing that the more one governs the less one achieves the desired result. Man can possess three great treasures, it claims:

> I have Three Treasures. Guard them and keep them safe. The First is Compassion. The Second is Moderation. The Third is Humility. Because of compassion, one will have courage. Because of moderation, one will have power to spare. Because of humility, one can develop talent and let it grow. (Chap. 3)
>
> By acting naturally, one reaps Nature's rewards. (Chap. 23)
>
> The intelligent man adheres to the genuine and discards the superficial. (Chap. 38)

If Nature's way is a joint process of initiating and completing, sowing and reaping, producing and consuming, can you rightly demand that you deserve always to play the role of consumer? (Chap. 10)

The inner self is our true self, so in order to realize our true self, we must be willing to live without being dependent upon the opinion of others. (Chap. 13)

Whenever someone sets out to remould the world, experience teaches that he is bound to fail. (Chap. 29)

Men should live according to nature and so it is opposed to too much government activity and too many laws. It is against war too.

He who by Tao proposes to help a ruler of men will oppose all conquest by force of arms; For such things are wont to rebound. Where armies are, thorns and brambles grow . . . And what is against Tao will soon perish. (Chap. 31)

Book of Chuang Tzu. It is thought that Chuang Tzu (369–286 BCE) actually wrote little of it. It was probably compiled by Kuo Hsiang in the third century CE. Its 33 chapters are made up of essays and stories, and it is important as it explains the Yin-Yang idea that nature is controlled by continuous transformations as the two forces rock to and fro. It is a witty and imaginative book which does not seek to reform society but pleads a spiritual freedom for the individual from his own mind rather than from rules imposed on him. It calls on readers to free themselves from their prejudices and self-centredness. Everyone should be free to develop his or her natural abilities.

Tao Tsang is a collection of books compiled in 1436 CE. It consists of 1120 volumes which contain material from much earlier centuries. It is divided into the San Tung (Three Vaults) and the Ssu Fu (Four Supplements). The first two San Tung contain texts for meditation and rituals, while the third has the 24 registers of the names and functions of the spirits discovered by Chang Tao Ling, the first Heavenly Master and founder of Tao Chiao, Religious Taoism. The Ssu Fu contains the Tao Te Ching and an alchemy section. The volumes have spiritual charts, illustrations, magical rites, charms, cures, blessings and hymns.

BUDDHISM

Tipitaka, or Tripitaka (Three Baskets) are the scriptures of all Buddhists written in Pali, which was the dialect they were in when they were brought to Sri Lanka in 247 BCE. Soon after the Buddha's death 500 monks met for the First Council in India to hear Ananda, one of his confidants, recall the Buddha's sayings and Upali, another confidant, to go through the rules of the Sangha (spiritual brotherhood, in this case the monks). All these were then checked and agreed upon so becoming the first two 'baskets'. The original texts have long since been lost and the earliest surviving fragments date from 250 BCE. The title refers to the way baskets of earth are passed from hand to hand in building, implying that baskets of wisdom or traditions are passed from person to person. Alternatively it refers to the baskets in which the palm-leaf manuscripts were kept.

The Sutta Pitaka (Teaching Basket) as it is called in Pali (or *Sūtra Pitaka* in Sanskrit) contains the teachings of the Buddha and his followers. Sūtra ('threads') refers to the threads linking the teachings into a common theme. It is divided into five sections. It also contains stories of the Buddha, a description of the 32 superman marks which he had on his body, and an account of his descent to the world to give us his teachings. In the Jataka there are 547 Birth Stories about his previous lives as a bird, stag, hare and man. As a stag he sacrificed himself to save the herd; as a hare he hurled himself into a fire to feed a starving brahmin. Finally, it contains the Dhammapada, the Way of Virtue, or Path of Teaching. Its 423 verses are often learnt by heart.

> *Do not speak harshly to anybody; those who are spoken to will answer thee in the same way. Angry speech breeds trouble, you will receive blows . . . To wait on mother and father, to cherish child and wife and follow a quiet calling, this is true blessedness . . . To give alms, to live religiously, to protect relatives, to perform blameless deeds, this is true blessedness . . . To cease from sin, to refrain from intoxicating drinks, to persevere in right conduct, this is true blessedness . . . Patience and pleasant speech, contact with holy men, religious conversation in due season, this is true blessedness. Penance and chastity, discernment of the noble truths and the realization of Peace, this is true blessedness.*

6. *Compare these statements with the Beatitudes (Blessednesses) given by Jesus in Matt. 5:1–12.*

The Vinaya Pitaka (Discipline Basket) gives the rules for monks and nuns.

> *Let him who desires to receive ordination first have his hair and beard cut off, let him put on yellow robes, adjust his upper robe to cover one shoulder, . . . and sit down in a squatting position; then he should raise his joined hands and say . . . The Three Refuges.*

It lists a monk's basic possessions and what he can eat.

The Abdhidamma Pitaka (Higher Teaching Basket) has long explanations and comments on the Buddha's teachings about philosophy and psychology. It defines things in detail. For example, 'right speech' (Step 3, Eightfold Path, see pp. 113–14) is listed as not speaking falsely, slanderously, harshly or frivolously. It tells the reader how to train his mind.

Milinda-Panha (Questions of King Milinda) was written in the first century CE and deals with the questions this Greek king put to the monk Nagasena about Buddhism:

> *The King asked, 'Is it true that nothing transmigrates, and yet there is rebirth?'*
> *'Yes your majesty.'*
> *'How can this be? Give me an illustration.'*
> *'Suppose, your Majesty, a man lights one lamp from another – does the one lamp transmigrate to the other?'*
> *'No your reverence,'*
> *'So there is a rebirth without anything transmigrating.'*
> *'Does the Buddha still exist?'*
> *'Yes, your Majesty, he does.'*
> *'Then is it possible to point out the Buddha as being here or there?'*

'The Lord has passed completely away in Nibbana, so that nothing is left which could lead to the formation of another being. And so he cannot be pointed out as being here or there.'

'Give me an illustration.'

'What would your Majesty say if a great fire were blazing, would it be possible to point to a flame which had gone out and say that it was here or there?'

'No your reverence,'

'In just the same way . . . the Lord has passed away in Nibbana . . . He can only be pointed out in the body of his doctrine, for it was he who taught it.'

Other Buddhist Books. The Mahāyāna, or Northern Buddhists, accept the Tripitaka but have other books as well. They are the Sūtras ('threads'), a collection of the Buddha's discourses. There are so many of them that no one has read them all. The *Diamond Sūtra* or *Scripture* compiled in the fourth century CE deals with the Buddha's knowledge and teaching. It says a Bodhisatta's job is to save all beings.

The *Lotus Sūtra* or *Lotus of the Wonderful Law* was written in the second century CE. It has been called the 'Gospel of half Asia'. It pictures the Buddha sitting on a Himalayan peak, announcing to thousands a new way for all to be saved. He points out that a Theravāda monk's life is too narrow, as it results in only a few being saved. From now on a large vehicle (mahāyāna) will enable all to cross the river of life to be saved. There are different methods, as there are many different kinds of people seeking Nibbana.

7. *List the names and summarize the contents of (a) Southern Buddhist and (b) Northern Buddhist books.*

8. *What is the difference between Sruti and Smriti?*

The Diamond Sutra.

JUDAISM

The TeNaKh (or Jewish Hebrew Bible) is the Old Testament of the Christian Bible, but in a different book order. The Greek translation is called the Septuagint (meaning '70') as it was translated by 72 people in 270 BCE. It consists of 24 books divided into three sections: (1) the Torah (Law), (2) Nevi'im (the Prophets), and (3) Ketuvim, Ketuvim (the Writings). The three capitals of TeNaKh stand for these three sections.

(1) *The Torah* meaning 'guidance' or 'teaching' is made up of five books: Genesis, Exodus, Leviticus, Numbers and Deuteronomy, known as the Five Books of Moses, as tradition says he received them while on Mount Sinai and subsequently wrote them down.

Genesis deals with the beginning of the universe and early life on earth. Exodus describes how the Israelites escaped from slavery in Egypt. Leviticus lays down rules on the jobs of priests and (among other things) how to deal with sacrifices and leprosy. Numbers deals with Jewish history from the time the Jews left Mount Sinai until they approached Canaan, the promised land, and shows how their leader Moses built them up into a nation. Numbers refers to the census taken at the time. Deuteronomy (the 'second book of the Law') reviews the events of the earlier books and concludes with some strong statements by Moses on how the Jews are to live. It includes the Ten Commandments (Deut. 5:1–22).

9. *Read Gen. 1–2 and summarize these chapters.*

10. *Read Lev. 5 and name the different types of sacrifice mentioned. Describe one of the types in detail.*

11. *Read Lev. 13–14 and state the main rules for leprosy cases.*

(2) *The Prophets* are books dealing with Jewish history from the time of Joshua. Holy people called prophets explained various aspects of God to the Jews and guided them in their understanding and worship (see pp. 20–1). The books include Joshua, Samuel, Amos, Isaiah, Jeremiah and Ezekiel. Jews regard the Torah books as more important than the Prophets, whereas Christians do the reverse.

(3) *The Writings* deal with human problems, such as family relations, social and business matters, manners and moral behaviour. Among the numerous books that make up this section is the Psalms, which deals with the whole range of human life at its best and worst. The book Ecclesiastes argues that everything in this world is impermanent and worthless. Pleasure is short-lived and wisdom gives a wise man no advantage over a fool when they both die (Eccles. 2:13–16). Wealth has nothing to do with merit or ability but just chance; moreover it cannot be taken with one at death (Eccles. 9:11). Good and bad people are treated alike so good behaviour seems pointless (Eccles. 9:2). Although earthly life is transitory and fleeting, it is not pointless; it is a riddle which we do not yet know the answer to. The Five Megillot (singular, Megillah) is the title given for five books, namely Esther, The Song of Songs, Ruth, Lamentations and Ecclesiastes.

12. *Produce some evidence for and against Ecclesiastes' arguments about life.*

Books of the Old Testament with the corresponding books of the Tenakh in italics

Genesis
B'reshit

Exodus
Ve Elleh Shemoth

Leviticus
Vayikra

Numbers
Be Midhbar

Deuteronomy
D'varim

Judges
Shophetum

Nehemiah
N'hemyah

Esther
Ester

Job
Iyyobh

Psalms
Tehilim

Proverbs
Mishlei

Ecclesiastes
Kohelet

Isaiah
Yeshaya

Zechariah
Zechariah

Apocrypha contains further short books

The Book of Job is the story of a good man who suffers horribly, so raising the question of why people suffer. It stresses that suffering is not the result of one's sins as the sinful often prosper and good suffer. It concludes that suffering is a mystery.

13. *Read (a) Pss. 5 and 12 and (b) Prov. 23:29–35 (on alcoholism). Summarize what they say in modern English.*

The Torah can also refer to the Prophets and Writings when it is used in the synagogue (see pp. 160–1). It is highly honoured by Jews as they regard it as a sacred object in the ritual. It sums up the learning, wisdom and love of God which is involved in their faith. The Torah scrolls, called sefer scrolls, containing the Pentateuch only, used in the synagogues, are handwritten on parchment. In the period 400–1000 CE Jewish scholars called Masoretes invented signs (teamim) to indicate the correct reading and chanting of the Torah. An interpretative Aramaic translation of the text is called the Targum.

Studying the Torah. It takes two years to handwrite a scroll and it costs £10 000.

Talmud. Second in importance to the TeNaKh is the Talmud (meaning 'teachings'). This is a huge collection of traditions to explain the Torah, as well as the Oral Law received by Moses and handed down by word of mouth from previous generations. It was completed in the fifth century CE. It is the main Jewish textbook for social and religious laws (Halachah, Halakah or Halahah) as it was compiled from the writings of over 1000 contributors. Its 63 sections contain legal rulings, stories, history, discussions between scholars, thousands of parables, biographies and humorous anecdotes in 6000 pages and three million words. All the non-legal sections are called Haggadah (narratives). The legal rulings, called Mishnah ('to repeat'), are collections, made by certain rabbis, dealing with the laws on agriculture, the Temple and sacrifices, cleanliness and impurity rules, criminal and civil law. The Gemara are the rabbis' explanations of the Mishnah, printed below each Mishnah. Rashi, or Rabbi Solomon (1040–1105), a French Jew, wrote a clear commentary on the Talmud, which young

Jews find easy to follow today. Here are some examples from the Talmud:

- *Give every man the benefit of the doubt.*
- *One good deed invariably leads to another; an evil deed always brings another in its wake.*
- *Do not threaten a child; either punish him or forgive him.*
- *A classroom should never have more than 25 pupils.*
- *When you encounter a child whose head is as solid as iron, you may be sure that his teacher did not have a pleasant way of explaining things.*
- *Always begin the lesson with a humorous illustration.*
- *There are four categories of pupil: the sponge – he absorbs and retains everything; the funnel – everything that goes in comes out; the sifter – he remembers the trivial and forgets the significant; the sieve – he retains the important and sifts out the incidental.*
- *Judge a man not according to the words of his mother, but according to the comments of his neighbours.*

The study, discussion and codification of the Oral Law continues today. Pirkei Avot (The Sayings, or Ethics, of the Fathers) is a collection of wise moral sayings on how you should behave, found in the 4th Mishnah, called the Nezikin. It is also included in the Jewish prayer book. Disused scrolls are stored in a genizah.

14. *Give your opinion on what the Talmud says about schools and schoolchildren.*

The Midrash (meaning 'to search out, expound') deals with legal, moral and devotional teachings, and includes the well-known saying, 'all is well that ends well.' It includes the oldest legends and fables of the Jews.

For Orthodox Jews the Torah and its interpretation, the Talmud, are the word of God and must be kept as divine. Reform Jews do not believe that God actually delivered the whole Torah and argue that human errors have crept in. They believe God is definitely concerned about its good behaviour rules, and maybe its ritual ones too. The Liberal Jews see the Torah as 'teaching' rather than 'law' and so argue that it can be changed. This means rituals are not divinely binding.

CHRISTIANITY

The Holy Bible (Greek 'biblia' means 'books') consists of the Jewish Old Testament (Old Covenant) in Hebrew and the New Testament (New Covenant) in Greek. The latter's contents were not finally decided until 367 CE. Although it was clear that certain books should be included there were a number on the borderline. Even today the Roman Catholic Bible contains a section of Jewish writings called the Apocrypha which are not accepted by Protestants. The New Testament consists of 27 books, including: (1) the four Gospels ('good news') named after early Christians Matthew, Mark, Luke and John, which recount Jesus' life on earth, (2) Acts of the Apostles by Luke, (3) 21 Epistles ('letters') mainly by Paul, (4) The Book of Revelation. The Gospels and Acts were all probably written at different times between about 60 CE and 100 CE. The

Bible on a lectern in a church.

Books of the New Testament

Gospels:
Matthew
Mark
Luke
John

Acts of the Apostles

Epistles:
Romans
1-2 Corinthians
Galatians
Ephesians
Philippians
Colossians
1-2 Thessalonians
1-2 Timothy
Titus
Philemon
Hebrews
James
1-2 Peter
1-3 John
Jude

Revelation

Epistles' dates vary from about 48 CE to about 140 CE, and Revelation was written in about 90 CE. By including the Old Testament in the Bible, Christianity is the only religion to include all the scriptures of another religion with its own.

The Gospels came to be written down for several reasons. The original eye-witnesses of Christ's earthly life were dying out, while the spread of Christianity made it impossible to keep in personal contact with all members and the persecution of Christians ordered by Emperor Nero in 64 CE gave a feeling of urgency to the matter. Errors would creep in if there was no book to lay down the truth. The gap between the Old Testament and the Epistles needed filling with the story of Christ's earthly life and the early life of the Church.

The four Gospels record Jesus's life and teaching. Their writers are called evangelists, which is a term also used today for someone who preaches the gospel. Matthew's, Mark's, and Luke's are similar because Mark's Gospel was probably used as a basis for the other two. Hence they are called the Synoptic ('one view') Gospels. Presumably each author wanted to give the story the emphasis which he thought would suit his particular readers. The result is that the Gospels are not straightforward biographies but books designed to proclaim Jesus as the expected Messiah, the Saviour whom God sent to mankind. We have already studied their content in Chapter 2 (see pp. 21-4). They contain numerous parables (stories with a meaning), healing stories and comments by Jesus. John's Gospel begins each chapter with a story about Jesus and then goes on to comment on it afterwards.

15. *Look in the Gospels for the birth stories of Jesus. Summarize them, pointing out how they differ.*

16. *Read Matt. 20:1–16 and then rewrite it in a modern setting in Britain.*

The 'Good News' was that the reign of God was near. All should repent of their sins, and Jesus had explained what was involved in starting a new life. Some may have thought he was about to start a national uprising against the Romans and the Gospels record the desperate attempts made to have him found guilty and condemned to crucifixion (death on a cross). They describe the event and then the astonishment of the disciples (Jesus' followers) when they find he has vanished from the tomb. Eye-witness accounts of the risen Christ are given.

Acts starts with Peter and his companions preaching the new faith and how a persecutor of theirs, Saul of Tarsus, becomes converted and is renamed Paul. Paul then goes on to bring the gospel to Gentiles (non-Jews) when he sees it has world-wide implications and is not a religion solely for the Jews.

17. *Read Acts 2:44–47. How did the early Christians live?*

18. *Read Acts 5:7–7:3; 7:51–60. Describe how the first Christian to die for his faith was handled by the authorities and what he said at his trial.*

19. *Read Acts 9:1–30. Put in your own words what happened to Paul. What explanations can you give of these events?*

The Epistles (epistolē is Greek for 'letter') are letters by Paul and others to groups of Christians they have started at Rome, Corinth, etc., and to friends such as

Timothy and Philemon. They explain Christian beliefs, and argue that Jesus is the Messiah whom the Jews expected. They claim he is God's Anointed One, the Son of God in fact. They present a new way of thinking about God, stressing that He is Love.

20. *Read 1 Cor. 7:26–40. What does this indicate about what early Christians thought was about to happen?*

21. *Read Eph. 3:1–11. State in your own words what Paul's message is. Why might it disturb the Jews?*

The Book of Revelation was written to encourage Christians who were facing persecution by Nero and other Roman emperors. Its strange visions of heaven and warfare cannot be taken literally.

Most Christians are prepared to analyse and criticize the Bible in an effort to find the truth from the fiction about their faith, although they hold it in respect and use it regularly in services. Sermons often explain its meaning. Christians regard Jesus as more important than the Bible, in contrast to the Sikhs, for example, who respect their holy book more than their founder.

English Translations. The Catholic Church had brought the Latin Vulgate version of the Bible to England. John Wycliffe (1320–1384), an Oxford professor, translated it rather inaccurately from this version. He claimed that the Bible was the only guide needed for a Christian. His Bible was banned after he became entangled in the Peasants' Revolt. William Tyndale (1490/95–1536) tried to make a better translation from the original Hebrew and Greek, but he was forced to leave England. His New Testament was published in Germany in 1525 but he was caught and burned before he could finish the Old Testament. A long while after the Reformation the *Authorised Version* was published in 1611 on James I's orders and this was followed more recently by the Revised Standard Version, both based on Tyndale's work. In the twentieth century several careful translations have been made.

The British and Foreign Bible Society, 1804, is one of many societies started to supply Bibles throughout the world. In 1946 Bible societies formed a co-operative called the United Bible Societies. In 1974 the Bible (or parts of it) was available in 1549 languages and 254 138 606 copies were distributed.

22. *What do Christians mean when they say the Bible is 'inspired'?*

ISLAM

The Qur'ān or Koran (meaning 'recitation') is the sacred book which Muhammad received as revelations from Allah via the angel Gabriel over a period of 20 years beginning in 610 CE, coinciding with the period of turbulence and development in Muhammad's life (see pp. 26–8). It became a book in about 650 CE when an official version was compiled. It is different from the other books we are considering because it is the only one collected by one person and has remained unchanged since its revelation. Hence it is important to read it in the original language. Muslims claim that the original copy is in heaven, so they call that divine copy, Ummul Kitāb, meaning 'Mother of the Book'.

ISLAM

It is a little shorter than the New Testament and contains 114 surahs (chapters) which, except for the first surah (fātihah), are arranged in order of decreasing length from Surah 2's 286 verses (ayats) to Surah 114's six verses. Events are described in reverse order, the shorter chapters dealing with earlier events and the longer ones later matters. Because of this some translations reverse the order of surahs.

It is claimed that the original Qur'ān is on a tablet beside Allah's throne in heaven and that every word is Allah's: 'There is no doubt in this book'; ' "I have perfected revelation for mankind", said Allah.' The Qur'ān is to Muslims what Christ is to the Christians, the Word of God, but in the form of a book instead of a man. Whereas the Bible is an 'omnibus' book of many parts, the Qur'ān is a single unit. It was revealed in *words*, not *ideas* left to man to put into words.

(a)

(b)

(a) Extract from a sixth-century Bible discovered in England in 1982.
The extract is from Ecclesiasticus and is in Latin.
(b) Extract from the Qur'ān. What is the language?

Muhammad could not read or write and so he could not have written the Qur'ān himself, argue the Muslims. He memorized it and dictated it to scribes. It is said that after Muhammad's death, Abu Bakr ordered Zaid to write it down and he did 'from pieces of paper, stones, palm leaves, shoulder-blades, ribs, units of leather and from the hearts of men'. In Arabic it is in rhyming prose and Arabic copies are used in mosques although translations are used in private. Because it is Allah's word no criticism of the text is allowed.

Every chapter except one begins, 'In the name of God, the Compassionate, the Merciful'. Chapters headed Makkah and Medina show where they were revealed, while others are after such names as Ibrāhīm, the Islamic name for Abraham, Joseph and Mary, or after animals, such as the Cow, the Ant and the Bee.

23. (a) Summarize how the Qur'ān came to be written and explain the layout of the book. (b) What is the proof of its divine origin?

Adam, Ibrāhīm, Joseph, David, Solomon and Jesus are referred to as prophets (nebīm) and honoured as true messengers of God. One nabī (sing. of nebīm) was sent to each community. Ibrāhīm revealed there was only one God; Moses gave the Ten Commandments, and Jesus ('Isa') gave the Golden Rule of 'Love your neighbours as yourself'. Thus Islam follows on from Judaism and

Christianity, paying respect to those religions, but also claiming that until Muhammad (rasūl, the apostle) received the Qur'ān the revelation of God was not complete. The prophethood (Risalah) era had reached its climax. Muslims claim that Judaism and Christianity are superseded by Islam:

> He has revealed to you [Muhammad] the Book with the truth, confirming the scriptures which preceded it; for He has already revealed the Torah and the Gospel for the guidance of men, and the distinction between right and wrong. Those that deny Allah's revelations shall be sternly punished; Allah is mighty and capable of revenge. Nothing on earth or in heaven is hidden from Him . . . It is He who has revealed to you the Qur'ān. Some of its verses are precise in meaning – they are the foundation of the Book – and others are ambiguous (or allegorical). Those whose hearts are infected with disbelief follow the ambiguous part, so as to create dissension by seeking to explain it. But no one knows its meaning except Allah. (Surah 3:3–7)

24. *How does the Qur'ān deal with the fact that some of its verses are difficult to understand?*

> This Qur'ān could not have been composed by any but Allah . . . It is beyond doubt from the Lord of Creation. If they say: 'It is your own invention', you say: 'Compose one chapter like it. Call on your false gods to help you, if what you say be true!' (Surah 10:37–40)

25. *Why will Muslims not criticize the Qur'ān?*

So far as Christianity is concerned the chief point is that Islam denies that Jesus was uniquely the Son of God. He is seen simply as a great prophet. Muslims refer to Jesus as Īsa, and Mary, his mother, as Maryam.

> Speak nothing but truth about Allah. The Messiah, Jesus, son of Mary, was no more than Allah's apostle . . . So believe in Allah and His apostles and do not say, 'Three' (i.e. Trinity) . . . Allah is but one God. Allah forbid that He should have a son. (Surah 4:171)

Jesus's birth is mentioned twice in the Qur'ān:

> When the angel said: 'Mary! God has chosen thee and purified thee and chosen thee above the women of the world . . . be obedient to thy Lord and humble thyself . . . God gives thee good news with a word from Himself whose name is The Messiah, Jesus, son of Mary, worthy of regard in this world and the hereafter, and one of those who are near to God . . .' she said, 'My Lord, how shall there be a son born to me as no man has touched me and I am not unchaste?' He said, 'So shall it be, God creates what He pleases: when He has decreed a matter, He only says to it, "Be", and it is.' (Surah 40–46)

> And she conceived him and then withdrew herself with him to a remote place. And the throes of childbirth compelled her to betake herself to the trunk of a palm tree. She said: 'Oh, would that I have died before this' . . . Then a voice called out to her . . . 'Grieve not'. (Surah 19:22–24)

It goes on to say that Jesus will heal the blind and lepers and bring life to the dead (Surah 3:18). But his crucifixion is denied.

*And [the Jews] saying 'We have killed the Messiah, Jesus, son of Mary,
the apostle of God'; and they did not kill him nor did they crucify him,
but he was made to resemble (one crucified) . . . and they killed him not
for sure'.* (Surah 4:157)

In fact, Muslims find it hard to accept that a prophet as great as Jesus could have
suffered such a humiliating death. Because of this, some Muslims argue that
someone who died on a cross was mistaken for Jesus. Others say he was put on
the cross but revived when placed in the tomb. Nothing on the resurrection or
ascension into heaven is mentioned.

26. Compare the Qur'ān's reference to Jesus' birth with those of Luke 1:26–55;
     2:1–20.
     (a) How does the Qur'ān suggest the birth was unique?
     (b) Why are the two versions of Jesus' birth vital to the two religions
     concerned?

27. How does Islam link up with Judaism and Christianity?

28. (a) Why would the reference to Jesus as the Messiah upset the Jews?
     (b) Is the meaning of Messiah different for these three religions?

29. Why must the Qur'ān deny the crucifixion and the resurrection of Jesus if
     it is to be taken as God's Word?

The Qur'ān's main message is that Allah is immaterial, invisible, almighty, the
creator, the merciful, the judge, the kindly one, the wise, the life giver, the
avenger, the forgiver. In all, 99 Beautiful Names are ascribed to Him. Man is
Allah's supreme creation for the great, good world he created. Man's soul lives
for ever. There will be a Day of Judgement. This will be considered in Chapter 9
(see pp. 243–4). Clear directions are given on worship, marriage, divorce,
women's position, fasting, almsgiving, pilgrimage and many other matters.
Although the Qur'ān may not be on display in a mosque, passages are used in
prayer. Friday sermons are based on it. Before reading the Qur'ān a Muslim will
always wash carefully. Many learn it by heart and are awarded the title of Hafiz.

Hadith. Besides the Qur'ān there is the Hadith ('saying'), the traditional sayings
of Muhammad which record the Sunna, the rules of life. There are three kinds:
(1) A saying of Muhammad.
(2) An action or practice of his.
(3) His silent approval of someone else's action.
They can also be classified as Sahih (sound), Hasan (good) and Da'if (weak) or
Saqim (infirm) according to how genuine they seem to be after extensive checking
by thousands of scholars. In the Sunna the details of when to pray and give alms
are spelt out as the Qur'ān says little beyond 'pray and give alms' (see pp. 137–8).
Several Hadith collections have been made and Bukhari's (810–870 CE) fills 97
books. He writes:

*Abdallah reported that 'Al-Fadl told us: 'Isma'il told us on the authority
of Yaha that he heard Abu say, "I heard Ibn Abbas say, 'When the
Prophet . . . sent Mu'adh to the Yemen, he [Muhammad] said to him,
'You will come upon some of the People of the Book [Jews, Christians],*

so the first thing you will call on them to do it to profess the Oneness of God . . . When they have learned that, inform them God has prescribed . . . five ritual prayers a day . . . inform them that God has imposed zakat [see pp. 137–8] on their possessions."

30. (a) *How many people passed along Muhammad's words orally before they were written down by Bukhari in the extract?*
     (b) *Why do you think some Muslims criticize the Hadith?*
     (c) *How are Muslims to treat Jesus and Christians?*

Sunni Muslims accept six collections of the Hadith while Shi'a Muslims accept their own five collections. The Hadith is open to criticism by Muslims. A teacher of the Qur'ānic and civil law is called a mullah.

SIKHISM

The Adi Granth ('original' or 'first' book) was compiled in 1604 CE by Guru Arjan and written down by Bhai Gurdas. It is regarded with great respect (see pp. 176–8). Guru Arjan collected the preachings of five gurus and several non-Sikhs and wrote them down in the Gurmukhi script. However, the vocabulary of the Granth Sahib contains words from several languages (Hindi, Gujurati, Marathi, Sanskrit, Persian, Arabic). The teachings include 5894 hymns by Sikhs, Hindus and Muslims in the 1430 pages. The hymns are called shabad, as they are divine words. The Muslim mystic Kabir (d.1518 CE) and the Muslim mystic Sheikh Farid (1173–1265) were contributors. This shows the Sikh's willingness to draw on the religious experience of other faiths. Guru Nanak had written over 900 hymns and Guru Arjan includes over 2200 verses of his own. They are arranged in 31 ragas (musical measures) so that they can be recited with music. Guru Gobind Singh completed the book by adding works by his father, Guru Tegh Bahadur. In 1708 he declared that the Guru Granth Sahib would be his successor as Guru of the Sikhs. It was then called Guru Granth Sahib (meaning, 'Holy Book, Guru'). Thus after ten Gurus there were to be no more gurus but the Granth Sahib would be the living voice to men. It is treated with great reverence and its pages are not touched by unwashed hands. When it is carried into a room, everyone stands and bows towards it. In its presence Sikhs are named, and married. There are no story sections in the Guru Granth Sahib. The subjects covered are:

(1) Religious – devotion to one God; the importance of the Guru; the need to purify oneself; the importance of karma (deeds) and the rejection of idol worship and the priesthood.

(2) Social and political – breaking down of the caste system; the importance of service to others, family life, etc, the need to stand up against a ruler's injustice; aid for the downtrodden; the gurdwara (temple) should be available for all religions and classes; free food (langar) for the needy; the need to contribute to the common cause.

At the beginning is the Mool Mantra (sacred chant stating Sikh beliefs):

> There is one God
> Eternal Truth is His name:
> The Creator and all pervading spirit devoid of fear and hatred
> Immortal and formless, unborn, self-existent,
> By the grace of the Guru, he is known.

On the beginnings of things, the Guru Granth Sahib proclaims:

> In the beginning there was darkness; there was no earth or heaven,
> naught but God's unequalled being. There was no day or night or moon
> or sun, no life, no voices, no wind, no water . . . no continent, no hills,
> no seas, no rivers . . . nor the Hell nor Heaven of the Hindus, nor birth,
> nor death, nor did anyone feel pain or pleasure. There was no Brahma,
> no Vishnu, nor Shiva of the Hindus. There existed but the one God.

It offers the following advice:

> Let compassion be thy mosque, let faith be thy prayer-mat, let honest
> living be thy Qur'ān, let modesty be the rules of observance, let piety be
> the fast thou keepest . . . the foolish who drink wine are the maddest of
> all. The true drunkards are those imbued with the name of God . . .
> Human birth is a rare fortune; it does not take place again and again . . .
> Pilgrimage, austerity, mercy, almsgiving and charity bring merit, be it as
> little as the mustard seed . . . Live amid the hurly-burly of life, but
> remain alert. Do not covet your neighbour's possessions. Without being
> devoted to God's name we cannot attain inner peace or still our inner
> hunger.

Few Sikhs own personal copies as this would involve setting aside a room in their home as a gurdwara (temple) to house it as they honour it so highly. It would also involve the owner in the daily task of having a pre-dawn bath before he reads it and then in the evening a further reading followed by meditation. For a long while the Sikhs resisted the printing of the Guru Granth Sahib as they felt this would lower its status, but now it has been translated into a number of languages.

The Dasam Granth is another collection of religious, moral and political poems by the tenth guru ('das' means ten) Guru Gobind Singh. A patron of poetry, he had 52 poets at his court. He wrote enough to fill 1428 pages. The collection making up the Dasam Granth was compiled in 1734 after his death.

An example of the vigour of his poetry is:

> Eternal god, You are our shield,
> The dagger, knife, the sword we wield,
> To us protector there is given
> The timeless, deathless, Lord of Heaven,
> To us all-steel's unvanquished might,
> To us all-time's resistless flight,
> But chiefly you, protector brave,
> All-steel, will Your own servant save.

For private devotions Sikhs use a collection of compositions by the Gurus called the Nit nem.

31. What criticisms of Islam does the Guru Granth Sahib make and what would Muslims think of these criticisms?

32. What Hindu beliefs are rejected in the Guru Granth Sahib? What would Hindus think of these rejections?

33. Make a table with columns headed: (a) religion, (b) holy book, (c) date of writing, (d) author, if known.

34. (a) Which religions take their basic book to be so holy as to be above criticism?
     (b) Why do they do this?
     (c) What effect might such a view have on their religion?

35. Describe the use made of their holy books by: (a) Christians, (b) Sikhs, during their services (see pp. 164-6, 177-8 for further information).

36. The scriptures of the world's religions are made up of very different types of literature. Illustrate this point by reference to the scriptures of two religions.

37. These scriptures say nothing about modern scientific achievements or twentieth-century social problems. To what extent are ancient religious scriptures relevant to believers today?

5
ON THE ROAD

Once you have become a member of a group or organization you are expected to obey the rules. If you do not do so, you will not get the full advantages of membership. Comparing the rules of one school with those of another can be an intriguing task as the difference may tell you a lot about the two schools, although by and large you will find the rules are similar. As you read this chapter compare each religion's rules. Ask yourself: what are the rules for? Are they designed to make you worship God properly or to ensure you live peacefully with your neighbour? The latter rules may be similar to those any country has to prevent crime. Do the rules suggest that good behaviour – a moral life – is an essential part of a life acceptable to God? Whereas a government makes laws on murder and adultery for the peace of the community, a religion may also do so because it claims God expects good behaviour.

Religions often insist that certain behaviour is required because it is 'God's will'. That 'will' is available to believers in the form of the religion's sacred books and teachings, which are often explained and enlarged upon by the subsequent writings of senior priests. Good behaviour and justice are essential ingredients for any religion. The problem is that duties often clash and sometimes sacred texts contradict themselves. The Bible contains views in favour of war *and* pacificism, celibacy *and* polygamy, socialism *and* capitalism. What did Jesus actually teach about divorce? Compare Matt. 5:31-2, Matt. 19:3-9, with Mark 10:2-12 and Luke 16:18. Experts think Mark 10:2-12 is the correct version. But because the Torah allowed divorce, the Matthew version was adopted by the church. This shows the need for people with authority to interpret what is to be done. Followers believe that such people of authority speak in the name of their God.

Realizing the problems involved in getting at the *true* behaviour required, Eastern religions approach the subject differently to Western religions. Hindu Advaita Vedanta's (see p. 34) idea of justice (dharma) claims that there are no absolute rules. The correct behaviour varies with the role in life you have to play, as well as what stage in life you are at. A priest should not kill, but a soldier should. A student should be chaste, but a married person not so. Each person has a traditional role, dharma, to perform. Thus society is held together. Advaita Vedanta argues that you do not act for fear of divine punishment, nor for heavenly reward. You simply get what you deserve (the law of karma, see p. 97).

Advaita Vedanta, Taoism and Buddhism explain that you can reach a state of liberation and enlightenment. By practising bodily, mental and emotional self-control, you will find inner peace. You will leave behind the conflicts in life, so that love *and* hatred, pleasure *and* misery, good *and* evil no longer bother you. By mastering these 'lower' aspects of life, you reach beyond them to the real happiness of being at one with God, the Truth. Such a liberated, enlightened person is not bound by rules and duties, but acts spontaneously from the joy of his or her faith, thinking automatically of the welfare of others. It is a state of being which is beyond earthly good and evil. While Western religions tend to treat people as if they are still children in need of disciplining, Eastern religions regard them as awakening adults.

But joining an organization has a purpose beyond that of obeying rules. A religious group is there to help and guide its members to find God or the truth about life here and hereafter. Each religion explains how to set out on life's journey. There is a right road to follow, they claim. If you step out along it you will 'get there in the end'. Not surprisingly, many religions means many roads are pointed out. But they may run parallel to each other. As the Vedanta Hindus say, 'God has made different religions to suit different aspirations, times and countries . . . One can ascend to the top of the house by means of a ladder or a bamboo or a staircase or a rope. So diverse are the ways and means to approach God, and every religion . . . shows one of these ways . . . The devotee who has seen God in one aspect only, knows Him in that aspect alone.' So let us examine the recommended routes and see what they have in common and what alternatives they offer.

HINDUISM

Rules. The Hindus have a set of clear-cut rules divided into two parts. The first part, Yama (abstentions, things not to be done) are:
(1) Do not destroy or injure anything
(2) Do not lie
(3) Do not steal
(4) Do not be envious
(5) Do not overeat or overdrink or over-indulge in sex.

The second part, Niyama (observances, things to be done) are:
(6) Keep yourself clean inside and out
(7) Be contented
(8) Practise self-discipline, tolerance, patience and mental calmness
(9) Educate yourself
(10) Try to surrender your mind to the Higher Power.

1. *Only Rule 10 refers to God; all the others refer to human weaknesses and characteristics. Only Rule 10 says 'try': the rest are orders.*
    (a) Why do you think this is so?
    (b) Should a set of commands include more about our relationship with God?

Class and caste. The Vedas teach that Brahman assigned separate duties and jobs to those who sprang from Purusha (the first Man)'s head, arms, thighs and feet. This means that every Hindu is born into a local or regional jati (birth caste group) and a national varna (literally 'colour') occupations class and must follow the dharma (duty) of that position. The four varna classes are:

(1) Brahmins, priestly class, but now containing teachers, chemists, doctors, etc, with varna colour of white. They represent the brains of society from Purusha's head. Sixteen per cent of Hindus today are Brahmins.

(2) Kshatriyas, warrior and ruler class, which includes civil servants and local authority workers, with varna colour of red. They represent the brawn of society from Purusha's arms.

(3) Vaishyas, or vaisyas, farmer, merchant and minor official class, with varna colour of yellow. They represent the stomach of society from Purusha's thighs.

(4) Sūdras, unskilled workers, with varna colour of black. Society's labourers from Purusha's feet.

Besides them, there are the pariahs or chandala, the 'outcasts' or 'untouchables' who do menial work.

The first three are called Aryans or dvija (twice-born) as they can take part in the Vedic rituals and have received the sacred thread (see pp. 202–4). The stages of life of a 'twice-born' man are called varnashrama-dharma.

A jati consists of about 1000 families with similar occupations, customs and marriage arrangements. Each village may have many jatis, one for each job, the landowner's jati being the superior one. Over three thousand jatis exist to cover all the occupational groups in India, and they are particularly important among the lower classes. Some jatis such as leather-workers, liquor distillers and butchers, for example, are regarded as 'impure' and thus 'untouchable'. Other trades are considered better, for instance, that of a tailor. The great holy leader Gandhi (1869–1948) did much to undermine this caste system by encouraging his followers to clean toilets, a job normally reserved for outcasts. He called 'the untouchables' Harijans, meaning 'God's people', but this is no longer liked as it can have other meanings. He also applied the Hindu idea of non-violence (ahimsā) to political activities as well as to its original purpose of non-violence against creatures (hence vegetarianism).

Hindu rules make various requirements depending on one's class. Brahmins may eat only rice cooked by brahmins, but vegetables cooked by anyone. The lower classes may drink liquor but brahmins may never do so. Once it was a brahmin's 'dharma' (rule of life, duty) to study, while a kshatrya should fight or rule, and so on. Hindus should follow their caste dharma unless they become sannyāsīns (see p. 98).

2. *Design posters to explain (a) the varna class system, (b) jati caste system.*

3. *Why do you think leather-workers, liquor distillers and butchers are in the untouchable jatis?*

4. *(a) Make a list of jobs done by British people today, together with rules that these jobs impose on them.*

(b) How does your list compare with that which would affect Hindus under their system?

5. *Comment on these Hindu sayings:*
   (a) He who is calumnious (given to slander) has the character of a cat.
   (b) A sacrifice is obliterated by a lie and the merit of alms by an act of fraud.
   (c) Never do to others what would pain yourself.
   (d) Children should be considered lords of the atmosphere.
   (e) Love is all-important and is its own reward.

The Hindu Paths. Hindus do not think about sinfulness as Jews and Christians do. Their gods and goddesses got married, had children, quarrelled, made friends, and so on. They were not concerned about sin in the way that God is for the Christian. So the Hindu does not see the need to start on the road of life feeling himself to be a sinner. Instead, he knows that he has a dharma to perform. If he does his dharma, he will be able to cope with dukkha (unsatisfactoriness of life). The law of karma (you get what you deserve) is ever in his mind.

The problem a Hindu faces is maya, which is the name for all visible things which we mistakenly assume to be 'real'. We think things are real when they are not. They are really all illusions as they will pass away one day. Chairs, houses, people, animals and so on are just illusions as they will not exist for ever. The word 'real' means something that will last for ever. Only Brahman is real. So the Hindu needs to follow the road to help him solve the confusion in his mind as he keeps thinking that things around him are real whereas they are only maya.

He claims there are four paths (yogas) or margas ('ways' or 'paths') which you can follow to obtain moksha (release from the worldly life; salvation). The discipline, or teaching, required to follow one of the paths is called sadhana. There are different paths for different kinds of people. 'Yoga' also means 'yoke', and, as a yoke disciplines and unites two animals for ploughing, so yoga disciplines a person and brings him into unity with Brahman.

Jnana Veda Yoga (Path of Knowledge or Realizing) is the shortest, steepest, hardest path up the hill of life. It involves stopping caring about things and people. It means using all the powers of your brain to distinguish what is really yourself inside you from what you appear to be. If you try really hard you will find your true self, your real self, called your 'atta', which amounts to finding Brahman. The white cow is sacred as it is the symbol of atta.

> *He is myself within the heart, smaller than a grain of rice, smaller than a mustard seed; He is myself within the heart, greater than the earth, greater than the heaven; He is myself within the heart. He is that Brahmin . . . He who inhabits the nose – the organ of speech – the eye – the ear – the mind – the skin – He is your self, the Inner Controller, the Immortal.* (Upanishads)

To follow this path you must divide your life into four sections (āshramas). In practice few reach the last stage, however.

Stage One, The brahma charya, or brahmachārīn (student or immature stage), is for 8–20 year olds, for study and character building. You must learn the rules of personal purification which involves bathing twice a day, good conduct, and so on. (See the sacred thread ceremony, pp. 202–4.)

> Let him not injure others in thought or deed; let him not utter speeches which make others afraid of him, since that will prevent him from gaining heaven ... Let him abstain from honey, meat, perfumes ... substances flavouring food, women ... and from doing injury to living creatures ... from the use of shoes and an umbrella, from desire, anger, covetousness, dancing, singing ... from fumbling, idle disputes ... and lying, from looking at or touching women. (Laws of Manu, 200 BCE)

6. What kind of person will you become if you follow these rules?

7. List (a) the rules you agree with, (b) the ones you do not agree with.

Stage Two. Grihastha (householder stage), for 20–50 year olds, is when you earn your living, marry and have a family. You should choose a job suitable to your class, and speak, eat and dress in a way befitting your calling.

Stage Three. Vāna Prastha literally means 'retirement as a hermit to search for the truth'. It begins with the birth of your first grandchild.

> When a householder sees his skin wrinkled and his hair white ... then he may resort to the forest .. Abandoning all food raised by cultivation, and all his belongings, he may depart into the forest, either committing his wife to his sons, or accompanied by her ... Let him wear a skin or tattered garment; let him bathe in the evening and in the morning, and let him always wear his hair in braids; the hair of his body, his beard, and his nails being unclipped ... and give alms (or water, roots, fruit) according to his ability ... Let him live without a fire, without a house, wholly silent, subsisting on roots and fruits. (Laws of Manu)

8. List what a hermit gives up.

9. Do Hindu children care for their hermit parents or not? If not, what would the hermit parents miss which elderly parents in the West expect from their children?

Stage Four. Sadhus, or sannyāsīns, are holy men. Reaching this stage involves becoming a wanderer possessing only a loin cloth, food bowl and water pot, but freed from worries and duties. Only a very few women become sadhus. Sadhus may shave their heads, to show they are no longer of this world and no longer wear the sacred thread.

> Take no thought of the future, and look in indifference upon the present. Departing from his house fully provided with the means of purification let him wander about absolutely silent and caring nothing for enjoyments that may be offered to him. Let him always wander along, without any companion, in order to attain final freedom ... he shall neither possess a fire, nor a dwelling, he may go into a village for his food, but be indifferent to everything ... concentrating his mind on Brahman. A potsherd in place of an alms bowl ... coarse worn-out garments, life in solitude and indifference towards everything, are the marks of one who has attained liberation ... let him bless when he is cursed ... sitting (i.e. in yoga position) ... entirely abstaining from enjoyment. (Laws of Manu)

A sadhu.

10. List the changes between the Third and Fourth stages.

11. What attitude to worldly things is a holy man required to have and why?

Bhakti Yoga (Path of Love and Devotion) is the second path, and it is the most popular of the four. Instead of using your brain to search for the truth, you use your emotions, your feelings. Parents should love their children, children their parents, and so on. God loves you, so you should love Him.

> All that you do, all that you eat, all that you offer and give away . . .
> should be done as an offering to Me. Thus you will be freed of all
> reactions to good and evil deeds; and by this principle of renunciation
> you will be liberated, and come to Me. Whoever renders service unto Me
> in devotion is a friend; and I am a Friend to him . . . Engage your mind
> always in thinking of Me, engage your body in My service; and
> surrender unto me . . . Completely absorbed in Me, surely you will
> come to Me. (For anyone devoting himself to Me) I am the swift deliverer
> from the ocean of birth and death . . . Just fix your mind upon Me, the
> Supreme Personality of Godhead . . thus you will live in me always.
> (Bhagavad Gītā)

12. Could a Christian follow this path to his God? Give your reasons for or against.

13. Would this path appeal to you or not? Why?

14. In what ways is this path easier to follow than Jnāna Veda Yoga?

Karma Yoga (Path of Works) is the third path. The more you do things without thought of gain for yourself, the less self-centred you will become. 'One to me is loss or gain, one to me is fame or shame, one to me is pleasure, pain.' What makes you work is your devotion to God, not your desire for more money or power. If you yourself do not count, you are freed from yourself. Work must be done as a sacrifice to the gods; otherwise it is selfish. Regular worship is essential. You must build up merit. The Laws of Manu lay down diets, home and public rituals and duties for each class, including those for birth, marriage and so on.

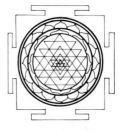

Yantra, wooden or metal pattern with four openings and sanctuaries for gods. Used by worshippers of Shakti. The triangles pointing down are female and those pointing up are male.

Each home has a shrine room or at least a god-shelf with a picture, symbol (pratika, or linga) or image (pratima) of a god or goddess. A yantra or mandala (see p. 74) may be used too. Before dawn the Hindu utters the sacred sound OM or AUM which symbolizes the whole world, past present and future. It is pronounced AA-OO-M; AA is the deepest note, produced in the chest; OO takes the vibration through the open mouth; M is pronounced softly with the lips together. If it is intoned properly he can feel his inner self withdrawn from his body. He also utters the name of his god and ties a coif of hair and marks his forehead with ash or paste. At dawn, midday and sunset he recites the most sacred of all Vedic verses, the Gāyatrī mantra, or Mother of the Vedas: 'Om, Let us meditate upon the most excellent light of the radiating sun [shavitri]; may he guide our minds.' There he sits bare-chested and bare-footed, facing east. He meditates, and touches his body at six points to express the presence of God in

his physical being. He bathes and at midday meditates again, offering flowers, food, and light to God. His final worship is in the evening. Each day he must honour his parents and ancestors, and give shelter to guests or alms to the poor as well as feeding animals, especially cows. Even a starving family will divide its food into three portions: for guests, animals and themselves. In fact a Hindu's whole life is an act of religion as he makes a ritual of the simplest acts of washing, working and praying. Temple worship (pūjā) is described on pp. 151–2. Temple attendance is a routine only for those who have chosen this way as their path.

15. *Why does a Hindu do good works?*

16. *How important do you think routine is to the followers of Karma Yoga?*

17. *Explain the meaning of OM for a Hindu.*

Raja Yoga (the 'kingly' Path of Psychological Exercises) is the fourth path. In life you get so swamped with things to do and problems on your mind that you cannot see where you are going or what you are like, so this path is the one designed to clear your head and calm your thoughts. There are eight steps to follow.

Step One. Yama (self-control) is 'abstaining from harming others, from falsehood, from theft . . .'

Step Two. Niyamas (observances, see p. 95) involves making your relations with others pure and devoted to God so that you gain supreme happiness.

Step Three. Āsanas consist of 86 body positions for meditation. The Lotus position involves keeping your eyes half open and focused on your nose or stomach. If you sit correctly you form an isosceles triangle with your legs and backbone at 90° angle. If you close your eyes you will daydream; if you keep looking around, your mind will wander. Cross your legs to numb their nerve ends and start to control your breathing for Step Four.

Step Four. Prānāyāma is controlled breathing, in which you aim to breathe in slowly (count 16 slowly), hold your breath (count 64) and then slowly let your breath out (count 32). Try this out for yourself by starting with numbers such as 6, 24 and 12 as you will find it very hard to do. When you get into the daily rhythm of quietly doing this you will be able to release your mind and think of nothing, no earthly thing, as the remaining steps show.

Step Five. Pratyahara is 'being alone', withdrawing your mind from things around you so that you have complete mastery over all your senses of smell, touch and hearing.

Step Six. Dharana is 'concentration', fixing the mind on some divine thing.

Step Seven. Dhyana is 'meditation', allowing your mind 'an unbroken flow of thought toward the object of your concentration', losing all sense of time and space.

A yoga position. What indicates his state of mind?

Step Eight. Samādhi is 'becoming absorbed into atta', perceiving 'the true nature of the object shining forth, not distorted by the mind of the perceiver' (Yoga Sūtras). Then you will find your real self, your atta, for you will have completely forgotten all your worries and hopes. You will have become detached from everything around you. You will have overcome the aches and pains of your body, the itches and fidgeting. Time stops, eternity is with you, as you hold your breath and almost stop living.

18. *Hindus keep their eyes half open when meditating; Christians close theirs when praying. What are the merits and weaknesses of these two methods?*

19. *Raja Yoga is designed to help you find reality, so how does it also help to make you cope with life more easily? What do local advertisements for yoga classes claim for those taking a course?*

20. *Why will this method involve years of practice to achieve success?*

21. *Which of the four yogas would you prefer to try and why? Put them in your order of preference and say what you would find particularly difficult when trying each.*

22. *St Paul talked of Christ living in him and the Holy Spirit working in him; a Hindu talks of god being in himself. What conclusion can you draw from these viewpoints?*

Pilgrimages. Their purpose is to remove sins, even those of past lives. Pilgrimages can be made to rivers, mountains, coasts, etc. Before setting off Ganesha will be worshipped as the god who controls the success of any venture. Vārānasī (originally Kāshi or Benares) is the most famous pilgrimage centre as it is situated on the holy river Ganges where it is joined by the river Varuna. Shiva is said to have lived there and two small white stone footprints of Vishnu are to be seen too. Rama is worhipped there and the annual Dussehra festival re-enacts the Rāmāyana story (see p. 76). To die in Benares and have one's ashes cast into the Ganges is the desire of all Hindus (see pp. 227-9).

On arrival you are met by a pandā (pilgrimage priest) who will arrange your accommodation and supervise your pilgrimage. You can spend five days doing the five mile (eight kilometre) circuit of the five river fords (tīrthas). At each the priests will say sankalpa (a statement of intention to worship) for you and then you will bathe. When you bathe at the ghāts (steps) of the Ganges your dry clothes will be looked after by the pandā or ghātiā (ghat priest) who sits under a large shade. You will give him a dāna (ritual gift) and a fee, and he will daub your forehead with a red tilaka spot to show you are blessed. There are a few cubicles for private changing. You may also arrange for special rites to be performed for relatives and then the priests will guide you through the procedure, calling for contributions at various stages. You will probably take a bottle of Ganges water home with you when you leave.

In February the Magh Mela pilgrimage festival camp of tents is put up at Allahabad where the muddy Ganges is joined by the clear river Yamuna or Jumna. People are rowed out to the meeting point and carefully supervised when bathing, to prevent them allowing themselves to be swept away into the

Benares on the River Ganges. Ghātiās sit under the shades and look after pilgrims' clothes. A temple's sikhara is on the left. People stand in the water to pray and immerse themselves completely. Notice the sacred thread worn by those on the right.

next life by the currents. Religious plays are performed and sermons preached on numerous stages, amidst the rows of stalls.

At Hardwar, where the Ganges enters the plains, pilgrims have to grip chains to prevent themselves being swept away by the cold current. Each evening the arti (light ceremony) is performed. While priests wave flaming dishes (camphor tablets are used), people launch leaf boats full of flowers and candles on to the water. Beggars, who have perhaps been deliberately maimed when young to provide them with this 'job', line the shore to exploit the pilgrims' generosity.

Rāmeswarum, in Tamil Nadu, is the southern pilgrimage centre for Shaivites and Vaishnavites as Rāma sanctified the spot by worshipping Shiva here after the battle of Sri Lanka.

23. (a) *What reason would a Hindu give for making a pilgrimage? How could he become a victim of commercialization?*
   (b) *Write a letter home telling a friend what to expect when visiting Varanasi on a pilgrimage.*

Āshrams. Hindus, and followers from the West, may spend a period of time in an āshram, a kind of retreat centre. There are hundreds of them. Some have gaudy statues of the gods and tend to exploit those who come to them, while others like the Divine Life Society Sivananda Āshram (started 1936) at Rishikesh are quite genuine. This āshram has 7000 visitors each year, and it brings together traditional and modern Hindu ideas. It publishes books and provides medical aid. When you arrive you are allocated a kutir (room). You can begin the day at 5.30 a.m. with one and a half hours of yoga exercises, such as standing on your head or being stretched with bound legs over two chairs. Breakfast is a cup of tea. Then you might attend a lecture or meditate. A swami (teacher) will supervise your time there. Lunch and supper are eaten sitting in rows on the floor in the dining hall. Mountain boys who have come for free education come round with brass buckets and dole out dhal (lentil soup), rice, vegetables, buttermilk and role (bread). You eat the food with your right hand and wash your bowl and mug at the tap outdoors. Any food left over is given to beggars at the gate. No meat, eggs, alcohol, smoking or radios are allowed in the āshram.

Lunchtime in an āshram.

In the Bhajan Hall, bhajans (songs of praise) are sung regularly. After supper the two hour satsanga (worship) takes place in the meditation hall. This includes solo singing, a lecture, the chanting of bhajans and kirtans (chorus singing repeating a god's name). Besides visitors there are permanent residents. There are sannyāsīns (addressed as 'swami') who have renounced everyday life; they wear orange robes. There are also brahma charyas who are studying the Vedas and doing Karma Yoga; they wear yellow robes. Finally, there are sadhakas, who are beginners doing karma and Bhakti Yogas. They wear white.

SHINTOISM

Standards of behaviour. Shintoists believe that people are born innocent of evil and so are essentially good. So too is the world as it is the kami-controlled world. Since the Shintoist does not have to root out inherited evil, he does not think a set of behaviour rules necessary. He argues that as he was born with the kami spirit in him he will know right from wrong in his heart. All he has to do is to follow his conscience. To have a set of behaviour rules would make him inferior to animals as they instinctively know what to do.

24. Why are parents and teachers likely to disagree with the idea that following your conscience is sufficient. Can you run (a) a school, (b) a religion, (c) a country, on the assumption that conscience is sufficient?

A Shintoist's religion does not set out to tell him whether his conduct is good or bad; instead it seeks to free him from his worries. He will not think of his attitudes or actions as sinful so much as shameful to his honour.

25. What is the difference between 'sinful' and 'shameful'?

To maintain his honour a Shintoist will observe high standards of behaviour. The way (michi) of the kami is vitally important to him. Michi is the essence of human life as it links him to the will of the kami and is the natural way to live. If he is to live an honourable life he must be sincere, honest, tolerant and generous. There are no real objections to drinking or indulging in sex. People's values are constantly changing, say Shintoists, and what may be the 'done thing' in one place or circumstance may not be elsewhere in different circumstances. A modern sect which broke from Shintoism, called Tenri-kyō, believes there are Eight Dusts which fall on the mirror of one's soul so that the mirror no longer reflects a true picture. The Dusts are covetousness, meanness, undisciplined love, hatred, revenge, anger, pride and selfishness. They are all to do with human relationships and they show that a follower may find it difficult to live up to his conscience. But he will not blame himself so much as the magatsuhi (evil spirits) as they are the cause of evil (maga). His soul is good, but his flesh and senses can fall victim to the magatsuhi. To solve the problem he has to wipe the Dusts off and the mirror will be pure again.

26. (a) Are there any other 'dusts' you could add to the Tenri list?
     (b) Compare the basic Shinto belief about being born with the knowledge of right and wrong with the Tenri belief about Man's nature. Which is more likely to be right in your opinion, and why?

Harai Purification.
The priest is using his haraigushi wand to purify the car.
He throws sand from the shrine on the car to purify and protect it. On Sundays and holidays cars queue for purification at shrines like Tsubaki in Yamamoto.

Purification. You can purify yourself by means of two ceremonies. These will cleanse you so that you do not have to feel personally sorry for your weaknesses, make a personal confession or ask for forgiveness. Notice the contrast here with the Christian who feels guilty if he has sinned in some way. Here are the two ceremonies.

Misogi (or Kessai). You must eat simple food in small quantities, avoiding meat, tea, coffee and alcohol, and take a cold bath or shower after a hot bath. For the best effect you should take your cold dip in a river, the sea or under a pounding waterfall, preferably naked or in a thin white robe. If no water is available, then you sit on a mountain top in a biting snowstorm. You should spend an hour each morning and evening in meditation sitting in an awkward position, with little or no clothing, even if your skin turns blue. Notice the sharp contrast to the Hindu's comfortable meditation position.

Harai (or Oharai). This involves a white-robed priest 'paying' offerings on your behalf while waving a purifying wand (nusa, or haraigushi) made of long paper streamers and a few flax ones. He will wave it over his shoulders, left, right and left again. He may carry out the purification rite for your new car or house to make them safer.

Both rites end with the same prayer:

> *Awe-inspiring, august Izanagi, when thou performed misogi-harai, facing the sun, in the plain covered with green trees at the mouth of a river, the great Kami of Purification, Haraedo-no-Kami, appeared. Give us purification for every kind of sin, blameable action or pollution. Cause the Heavenly Kami, the Earthly Kami and the august 80 myriads of Kami, all together, to give us purification. Please listen to me and augustly speak.*

27. *With Misogi, what connection do Shintoists assume between bodily punishment and purification?*

28. *With Harai, what must be the source of the priest's power to purify?*

Misogi Purification. 200 ft (60 m) Shasui Waterfall, Ashigara-kami County. What are the main differences between Hindu meditation and Shinto purification?

Daily Worship (matsuri). Every Shintoist has his local guardian kami and every house's living room, workshop or office has its kamidana (godshelf) made of plain white wood and fitted with beautiful brass fixings. Inside it will be shintai (god emblems) such as a mirror (see Amaterasu's mirror, p. 153). The kamidana honour the 'Kami of the World', the local kami and ancestors. For the first 33 years after a person's death he or she is venerated in the home's Buddhist butsudan (butsudō, the way of the Buddha) which is kept in the formal entertaining room. It is an expensive black and gold shrine, and its ornate design is in sharp contrast to the plain kamidana. By the end of the 33 years, after the last of a series of Buddhist rituals, the soul of the deceased is believed to have lost its individuality so joins the kami in the kamidana. Food and drink (rice, fish, saké

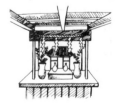

Kamidana. How does the Kamidana bring worship alive in a Shinto household?

and tea) are put out as if the deceased is still in residence. On the anniversary of a person's death his or her favourite food is put out. You can hang up ema (small wooden prayer tablets) on which you write your prayers – for example, 'I would like to find a nice girl to marry. I am fond of children so I think I can be a good father. Please help me.' There are four reasons for such daily actions:

(1) You must tell the kami what you have been doing – school-children will report their marks, even before telling their parents what they were.
(2) You must say your thanks for blessings received.
(3) You must offer praise to the kami.
(4) You must pray for the community and perhaps for yourself.

29.   *How does having a kamidana (a) at home, (b) in the office, help to bring Shintoism into daily life?*

Isé temple stamp.

Pilgrimages are very popular and there are pilgrim associations to help you visit as many as possible. It is almost a tourist industry. At the shrine you will throw a pebble to the komainu (dog statues) or torii (arch) (see pp. 152–3). Pilgrims like to collect the shrine's rubber-stamp seals in their 'stamp-books'. The seals state the temple's name and its kami's characteristics and the type of worship offered to him. The most famous shrine, at Isē, is described on p. 153. Every Shintoist is expected to make a pilgrimage there once in his life.

One hundred thousand visit Mount Fuji each year, doing the eight-hour climb in straw sandals (waraji). There are six routes, each with ten resting huts.

TAOISM

Yin and Yang. Taoists believe self-discipline is better than discipline imposed by a set of rules. Consequently there is no list to be kept.

The Way (Tao) the universe works is governed by the twin forces of Yin and Yang. Watching nature at work the Chinese concluded that all nature is busy – things happen as the seasons come and go. There is a rhythm behind it all. Nature is full of energy. The Book of Chuang Tzu (see p. 80) called the active energy Yang and the quiet energy Yin (literally the 'sunny side' and the 'dark side' of a hill). Yang is sometimes symbolized as a dragon, while Yin is a tiger, but the usual pattern (Tai Chi) resembles two tadpoles. Yang is shown in red or white and Yin in blue or black. They are the balancing powers in life. Yang can be seen as summer, Yin as winter; or Yang as masculine and Yin as feminine. Yang is represented by a unbroken line, while Yin is represented by a broken one; Yang exists wherever there is initiation, activation and development, and Yin where there is submission, decline and completion, and so on. They overlap each other as the diagram opposite shows. Each invades the other's hemisphere and establishes itself (the 'eye' dots) in the very centre of its opposite's territory. In everything there is the beginning of its opposite, for all is based on opposites. You cannot have light without darkness, for example. The message is that life is not clear-cut, a case of good or evil, right or wrong. Life is a mixture, a balance of good and evil. Yang is the power in life which produces all firm, solid, warm things; Yin, the power that gives soft, moist, changeable things. In life two powers are balanced, and life, like a wheel, rolls forwards and backwards. So sometimes nature and your life are governed by Yang, while sometimes Yin is in control. Where one or the other energy gets out of control they get 'out of balance'. However, everything comes of its own accord at the appointed time, so be patient is the message, for anxiety is unnecessary.

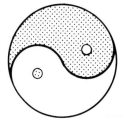

Yin and Yang.

This leads Taoists to argue that they cannot state what is fixedly good and evil as some religions bluntly do. Good and evil are relative to each other. A farmer's neighbour said he was sorry to hear the man's horse had run away. 'Who knows what is good or bad?' replied the farmer. Next day the horse returned bringing a drove of wild horses it had found. The neighbour congratulated the farmer on this luck. 'Who knows what is good or bad?' he replied. The next day the farmer's son broke his leg trying to ride one of the wild horses. The neighbour said he was sorry. 'Who knows what is good or bad?' the farmer replied. Then soldiers came to force all healthy young men into the army, but the son was not drafted because of his leg. Thus Yang and Yin alternate in life. 'The Way to do is to be.'

30. *Write a story, fictional or true, in which good and bad, happiness and misery keep alternating. At the end of each event put 'yang' or 'yin' in brackets to indicate which is in control at the time. Make sure one event follows on from the previous one as in the story above.*

31. *Some religions say man is born good but sinks into evil because of his own weaknesses and the corruptions surrounding him. Other religions hint that man is even born in sin, perhaps inheriting it.*
    (a) Are Taoists more honest and truthful in their assessment of a person's nature?
    (b) Is it better to say someone is born positively good or bad, or that he is born with a mixture of good or bad in him?

How can we cope with the Yin–Yang to-and-fro movement in life? Taoism split into two broad sects in its efforts to answer this problem. The Tao Chia or Philosophical Taoism (wise thinkers' way) says that we should harness ourselves to the movement of the Way (Tao) the universe moves. The Tao Chiao or Religious Taoist sect says you should call on priests to control the gods and so nature's effects with their rituals.

The Tao Chia method. Nature's energy is effortless; it flows rather than struggles. If we can use our energy as effortlessly as nature does, we will live naturally – as we are designed to do. So quieten yourself, your senses and your appetites and you will gain an inner vision of the Tao (the Way) which you are to follow.

> *I have three Treasures, Guard them and keep them safe. The First is Compassion. The second is Moderation. The Third is Humility. Because of compassion, one will have courage. Because of moderation, one will have power to spare. Because of humility, one can develop talent and let it grow.* (Tao Te Ching. Chap. 3)

32. *Are these three treasures sufficient to guide one through life? Why has Lao-Tse put them in this order?*

Just as Shintoists respect and hold nature in awe, so Taoists claim the Way is that of nature, or natural forces. If you want to become perfect you must not obstruct the ways of nature, but serve them. The way of life is called Wu-wei, meaning 'non-effort' or 'not overdoing', being receptive to life and what it brings and not resisting it. Life is a mystery but it has a rhythm to it. Your aim must be to be active as well as relaxed and free from tension. There is a Taoist saying, 'The longest journey starts with a single step.'

According to the Tao Chia method: 'One may move so well that a footprint never shows; speak so well that the tongue never slips, reckon so well that no counter is needed.' How can you be superactive and relaxed simultaneously? Taoists say water is the best example of Tao as it supports objects and carries them effortlessly. Its pattern is humility. Water behaves naturally. The Chinese for a swimmer is 'one who knows the nature of water'. A swimming instructor tells his pupils not to fight the water but to float on it. So one who knows that nature of the basic life force knows it will sustain him if he stops thrashing about and trusts it to buoy him up and carry him along:

> *Those who flow as life flows know*
> *They need no other force;*
> *They feel no wear, they feel no tear*
> *They need no mending, no repair.* (Chap. 15)

Water goes round obstacles, adapts itself to its surroundings and seeks the lowest levels; it is infinitely supple and yet incomparably strong:

> *Man at his best, like water*
> *Serves as he goes along;*
> *Like water he seeks his own level,*
> *The common level of life.* (Chap. 8)

'Muddy water let stand will clear.' So you should take life as it comes, be humble, oppose aggression. Do not over-assert yourself or be over-ambitious.

> *Standing on tiptoe a man loses balance,*
> *Admiring himself he does so alone . . .*
> *At no time in the world will a man who is sane*
> *Over-reach himself*
> *Over-spend himself*
> *Over-rate himself.* (Chaps. 24, 29)

While Westerners talk of 'conquering' nature, by climbing Everest or damming rivers, Taoists talk of 'befriending' it. Some religious people claim they are nearer God on the mountain tops, but Taoists seek ravines which receive all things in them. They build their temples to blend with nature, not to stand out provocatively. Some religions expect you to strive beyond your limits, but Taoism does not expect you to do so. Lao-Tse saw the futility of human effort and therefore advised the doctrine of 'doing nothing' as a saving of energy and a method of prolonging life. So a positive outlook on life became negative, in fact. Tao Chia argues that prayer is useless as nature cannot be influenced.

33. *Taoists see the wheel of life as one which rolls backwards and forwards rather than one which is propelled along to the end of the journey of life.*
(a) Do you think this means one can take life easily and not set out to achieve a definite goal?
(b) Should one take life as it comes or make something positive of it?

The Tao Chiao method. The aim of this Power (Te) is to achieve immortality and control the forces of Yang and Yin to one's advantage. It is claimed this can be done by alchemy in one of two ways. Wai Tan (External Elixir) involves the use of chemicals, drugs and metals. Nei Tan (Inner Elixir) works by priests controlling the spirit world so as to draw on the strength of the spirits. Alchemists claimed that special gold could be made, which, if eaten, would give you immortality. Long-life pills were another speciality. But the Nei Tan method of the Taoist master priest lives on today. Training in spirit control is a very long and complicated one. The priest must summon spirits out of his body (Fa-lu rites, meaning literally 'lighting the incense burner'). He can then unite himself with the Tao (Way) by his k'o-i, meditation rituals, and use this power (Te) over spirits of heaven, earth and the underworld, before returning them to his body.

Masters who specialize in the exorcism of evil spirits are not popular figures and their visits are always to do with sickness and death. Their training involves running and jumping with weights on their shoulders so as to be able to jump great heights without them during the rituals. They strengthen their wrists by hitting hard things as exorcism involves somersaults in mid-air and fighting demons with swords. A Master will have a large team to aid him so that if he is famous the cost of his services will be high.

The Master's closest secret is his list of the spirits' names, faces, clothes and weapons, without which his ritual to alter Nature would be useless. Among the six Chia demon spirits is Chia-tzu, who is 12 ft (3.6 m) tall, rat-faced, yellow-haired and bearded, and armed with a bow, sword and shield. He can move mountains, plug up the sea, and shrink or stretch the earth with his 100 000 spirit troops. Another demon spirit is the violent, merciless Chia-hsu, who is 9 ft (2.7 m) tall, with a man's face, snake's body, golden crown and yellow robe. He is armed with a spear made of eight snakes, stone and arrows; he commands 100 000 troops. If Chia-hsu draws a line on the ground a river appears; he can make cliffs, drill wells, invade cities, and so on. Offerings of wine, dried fruit and meat are made to all six demons in sacred areas. The Master draws the shapes of the spirits in the air, recites and makes sword strokes. Once in control he can get them to defeat enemies in battle, cure illness and exorcize spirits. He needs to be a strong-minded Master to cope with these demons and he expects to die young from the exhaustion of these rituals.

Thunder magic is a highly prized art and requires a high-ranking Master. It is a purification rite to deal with black magic. On the first day after the New Year when thunder occurs, he faces the thunder and breathes in the electrified atmosphere which circulates through him until it reaches his gall bladder where it will be stored for later use. To use it, he breathes through his nose and the vapours will mix with saliva which is swallowed and sent to the furnace of the belly. He repeats this until he stops breathing altogether in meditation. Thunderblocks (vajra) of carved datewood are used in the elaborate rituals for summoning the thunder power from the gall bladder. He uses the thunder power to cure illness and expel evil, as well as to control the sun's rays for exorcisms.

34. *Draw a picture of what you would imagine a Chia demon to look like.*

All traditional Chinese homes will have a god shelf facing the front door. On it is a picture of Tzau Wang, the kitchen god, his wife, horse, dog and chicken, with ancestral plaques and photographs on either side. Two candles, three wine cups, a basket of flowers, fruit and a small urn for joss sticks are on the shelf too. The New Year Festival connected with Tzau Wang is described on p. 188.

Followers of Tao Chia argue that Lao-Tse would not have accepted the Chiao way of priestly magic.

Tzau Wang, the kitchen god.

BUDDHISM

The Five Precepts. Buddhists try to practise five basic guidelines known as the Five Precepts (Pancha-shila, or Pans'il):

(1) Try not to kill humans or animals
(2) Try not to steal
(3) Refrain from improper sexual relations: monks to refrain completely
(4) Try not to lie
(5) Try not to drink intoxicants.

Monks have an additional five to make various points more precise:

(6) Eat before noon
(7) Try not to look at dancing, singing or drama
(8) Try not to use perfumes or ornaments
(9) Try not to use high beds or seats
(10) Try not to accept gifts of gold or silver.

Theravādins say one should observe 227 precepts in all.

35. *(a) Is it true to say that the Five Precepts deal with human weaknesses whereas the monks' precepts deal with luxuries?*
(b) Why do you think monks must obey additional precepts?
(c) Should people who set out to be religiously special have to obey such extra rules as part of their calling?
(d) What is the aim behind such rules and are they helpful?

36. *The Buddha argued that first we act, then we put into words what we have done and finally we think about the matter; in the West we say that we think of something, put it into words and finally act on it. For example, the Buddha would say, 'Root out killing and you will end hatred,' while a Westerner, influenced by Christianity, would say, 'Root out hatred and you will end killing.'*
(a) Which is more likely to be true in practice?
(b) Give other examples aimed at good behaviour and present them in a (i) Buddhist way, (ii) Western way.

It is important to realize that the Buddhist road does not lead to a Being in the sense of a creator God which other religions believe in. It does not start with the assumption that God exists, in fact it begins with the reverse. For Buddhists, life is not a preparation for eternity, but a way of living out your present life until you reach the highest good. The Buddha's teaching (dhamma, or dharma) works because it offers a solution to this life's problems and not because it taps supernatural resources to aid you. Freedom is your quest. Your aim is to develop yourself from an ordinary person into an extraordinary or enlightened person – the superior species.

He began with the Three Marks, or universal truths, Anicca, Dukkha and Anatta. Looking at life he concluded that everything was impermanent (anicca) for as soon as one is born one is heading towards death. Even mountains do not last for ever, as geologists can show. For the Buddha life was like an ever-rolling wheel with four segments – birth, growth, decay, death – with rebirth after rebirth following as it turned round and round. Ordinary life invariably involved some form of suffering (dukkha, see below). When one died there was no soul (anatta) to go to a heaven, only an impulse of energy to be reborn again (*see* p. 238). Thus everything in life is transient (anicca), has no substance (anatha) and is imperfect (dukkha). What then could one make of life?

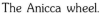

The Anicca wheel.

The Buddha argued that you had to know where you were going to start from before you could set off on life's road. He saw a person's chief problems as suffering and self-deception, and so he listed Four Noble Truths or sensible ideas, in the same way that Indians diagnosed illnesses.

First Noble Truth, Dukkha. Dukkha means 'unsatisfactoriness'; something which is not perfect or permanent, hence 'imperfection', 'impermanence'; 'ill-fare' as opposed to 'welfare'. The Buddha meant that we are all suffering from a kind of illness. For us all life is made up of unsatisfactoriness or suffering. He was not trying to frighten us, simply to alert us to the position we are in. There is no need for us to panic or get depressed, since the Buddha has a ready cure.

There are three kinds of dukkha:

(1)   Suffering – headaches, bereavements, etc. A mother giving birth suffers pain; being born is painful; a baby might be deformed; growing old is painful.
(2)   Unsatisfactoriness is part of pleasure as pleasures do not last, so in the end they are unsatisfactory.
(3)   Ordinary life is unsatisfactory until one becomes enlightened.

Dukkha is the symptom of life's disease. Just to exist seems dukkha, so do not get angry about it; instead hunt for its cause and cure. Like a doctor treating his patient, the Buddha went on to diagnose the disease.

37.   List examples of dukkha under headings (1) and (2) above.

Second Noble Truth, Samudaya. The Buddha saw the origin (Samudaya) of life being full of dukkha as being caused through ignorance (avijjā) of the Three Marks we crave (tanhā) and hate (dosa) things – our passionate greed for pleasures, power, wealth and our own opinions. These are the sorts of things which give rise to quarrels. They even cause countries to fight because of their greed for economic wealth, political power and social wellbeing. The Buddha claimed that we cannot blame a god for all this dukkha. The immediate problem is to cope with dukkha, and any attempt to define God can be left aside for the time being. He argued that people have made up two false ideas in their minds. To give them a feeling of safety they have conjured up the concept of a god, some great Being who protects people. Then to satisfy their worry that they will become totally extinct when they die, people have invented the idea of everyone having an immortal soul. These two false ideas simply console people in their fears and desires and show how ignorant they are. Thus he demolished the Hindus' two realities, Brahman and Atman, a devastating rejection.

If dukkha is not caused by some Being, then where does it come from? It must have a human cause. Eat too many cream buns and you will see. Admittedly you could suffer as a result of someone else's selfish action (e.g. a motorcyclist breaking the speed limit injures you) but mainly you are to blame because of your selfishness. Worldly life is wanting pleasure and prosperity and these things will not satisfy you in the end. To desire such things is not 'sinning' in the Christian sense of disobedience to God. It is just that you are ignorant about how you cause dukkha for yourself.

Our selfish craving even leads us to wanting to be reborn again and again so that we can continue to gratify our desires (see p. 238). The Buddha used the word karma in a different way to the brahmins, preferring the word 'kamma'. For him it did not mean that at rebirth a person was up- or down-graded according to how he had behaved for there is no divine judgement to face. Instead he meant that kamma is the theory of cause and effect. Our cravings cause the effect of our being reborn. So how can one stop this cycle? How can one cure this 'disease'?

38. Briefly say why the Buddha decided humans cause their own dukkha.

Third Noble Truth, Nirodha. The doctor's prognosis – the cure – is the Third Noble Truth. It involves overcoming selfishness and releasing yourself from your cravings. Dukkha disappears when you cease (Nirodha) wanting things. 'Deconstruct' your false assumptions that everything is permanent, substantial and perfect, and grasp that they are transient, lacking substance and are imperfect – the Three Marks of experience. If you continue to live on a worldly plane or level you will be dogged by the Five Mental Hindrances, which the Buddha likened to impure water.

(1) Greed, for food, sex, etc. – like water discoloured by bright colours
(2) Hatred – like boiling water
(3) Sloth, torpor, keeping your cravings for sensuous desires – like water choked with weeds
(4) Restlessness and worry – being unable to settle down to anything – like water whipped up into storm waves
(5) Doubt, indecision, a lack of faith or trust – like water full of mud.

Fourth Noble Truth, Magga. This is the Middle Way (Magga) of the Eightfold Path – a kind of moral and mental development scheme designed to raise you from the worldly to the spiritual plane of life. It is a Middle Way between craving and hatred as you do not have to follow the extreme of being a hermit or living an extravagant life. Instead of allowing your life to go on like a vicious circle (sleep-wake-sleep; love-hate-love) you can improve yourself and climb the spiral (the creative spiral) of life, going up and up as you go along. He insisted that you must test his theories for yourself, as you go along by following his meditation course so as to achieve 'understanding' (panná, wisdom). The Buddha stressed that *everyone* can do this, and so one should be realistic rather than optimistic or pessimistic, in the face of dukkha. It is like a mental disease which can be cured when the cause or secret of the illness is discovered and understood by the patient.

The Dhamma-chakra, the wheel of the law, has eight spokes for the eight steps involved in the course of treatment prescribed. No pill-taking is involved; you go into rigorous habit-forming training, but of a different kind to that which your games coach instils into you. The goal is enlightenment, rather than winning a race, but the specialist training to climb the spiral is just as essential. Piti (joy) is one of the essential qualities to be cultivated to reach Nibbana.

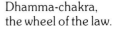

Dhamma-chakra, the wheel of the law.

39. (a) Do you think the Buddha is right in seeing suffering as the starting point of the journey? What alternatives are there?
    (b) What do you think of his diagnosis and prescription? Give your reasons.
    (c) Give examples of how you have suffered
        (i) Because of actions of others
        (ii) Because of your own actions
        (iii) Because of non human-causes.

Eightfold Path. Although the steps are numbered you do not necessarily have to climb them in that order as they are linked and so you can tackle them together. The object is to enable you to break away from the worldly plane of unwholesome thinking (akusala) and set off for the spiritual plane of wholesome thinking (kusala). Then you will be able to stop your cravings and so stop being reborn. With your cravings and hatreds gone you will be enlightened, free from the kamma force which has kept you going round and round. You will find Nibbana when you will be free from all worries, obsessions, complexes, etc. Your 'mental health' will then be perfect. You do not have to wait until you are dead to 'attain' the bliss of Nibbana as you can find it in this life. Notice this contrast with other religions which say you cannot reach heaven until you have died. As we shall see, Nibbana and heaven are rather different.

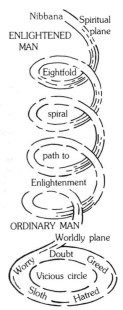

The Eightfold Path to Enlightenment.

As you follow the path you experience the Three Marks by observation, and so cover three essential things:
(1) Good or moral behaviour (Sīla) – steps 3, 4 and 5
(2) Mind control or mental discipline (Samādhi) – steps 6, 7 and 8
(3) Wisdom (Pannā) – steps 1 and 2.

Notice as you go through them that they do not include prayer, worship or ceremony, which religions normally include (although worship and ceremony do have their place in Buddhism). This is because Buddhists do not believe in God. With no God, you can have no outside help along the path – it is all up to you.

Step 1: Right/perfect viewpoint. Be wise and start by believing the training scheme is the right one to cure you. In other words, accept the Four Noble Truths; accept that life is painful and unsatisfactory, and that something better is possible. You need a vision of what you might become. Then you will see things as they really are, and have a penetrating understanding of life.

Step 2: Right/perfect attitude or purpose. Be wise by being determined to succeed; having your heart in the task; setting out unselfishly. True wisdom requires some noble qualities in you.

Step 3: Right/perfect speech. The language you use matters. Unwholesome words are harsh and false ones; wholesome words are true and helpful.

Step 4: Right/perfect behaviour or action. Obey the Buddhist directives – the Five Precepts. Live an unselfish, charitable life; keep regular hours; help the sick; and so on.

Step 5: Right/perfect livelihood. Choose your job carefully for the more it helps others the more it will raise you to the spiritual plane. Butchers are frowned on because they destroy life. Change your environment for this will change your level of consciousness. For example, a mountain holiday will enlarge your vision of the greatness of creation.

Thus Steps 3, 4 and 5 are aimed at making you a better person for you will not be able to climb higher unless you behave well. Next come the mental, mind-training steps.

Step 6: Right/perfect effort. Use your willpower to stick to your moral standards and make a right use of your energies to produce good and not evil states of mind. One way to help yourself is Mettā Bhāvanā ('bringing love into being'):

(1)   Think about yourself – remember happy times; wish yourself well
(2)   Think of a good friend of the same sex and age – wish him/her well
(3)   Think of a neutral person – the postman, ticket collectors – wish him/her well
(4)   Concentrate on an enemy or someone you do not get on with well – wish him/her well
(5)   Concentrate on all four – then all in the room – the town – the country – overseas . . .

So you will expand and radiate the warmth of your love. Besides Mettā Bhāvana there are three other meditations which collectively are known as Brahma Vihāra (Four Sublime States). The others are:

(1)   Karuna (having compassion), understanding the suffering of others and making plans to help
(2)   Muditā (having sympathetic joy), feeling happy about the joys of others
(3)   Upekkhā (being well balanced), having a balanced, steady mind without tempers or depressions or over-excitements.

But this meditation will only help you live happily in this world. It will not give you complete freedom or insight into the truth. So you must take another step.

Step 7: Right/perfect awareness of mindfulness. This step requires you to eliminate thoughts from your mind, especially many unwholesome ones or mindfulness the Five Mental Hindrances kind. You need to stand outside yourself and see yourself as you really are, for then you can cope with all your cravings. The aim of this step is to improve yourself by working directly on controlling your mind through meditation.

Step 8: Right/perfect absorption, enjoyment or meditation. Now meditation reaches its peak and you will become 'absorbed' – just as soap (powdered) is absorbed in water, said the Buddha. You will find bliss and ecstasy. You will discard all desires, worried thoughts, etc. and find Nibbana, or Nirvana. You will see everything in its true place and realize that all earthly things are unsatisfactory and impermanent. Nibbana will give you release from the limitations of your human self. Nibbana means literally the 'going out' or 'cooling off' of a flame. Thus your earthliness is 'extinguished' as you reach the 'incomprehensible, indescribable, inconceivable, unutterable' states of Nibbana:

> If you ask, 'How is Nibbana to be known?', it is by freedom from distress and danger, by confidence, by peace, by calm, by bliss, by happiness, by delicacy, by purity, by freshness. (Milanda Panha)

You can reach this state in this life and continue in it when your human self dies (see also p. 238). A person who has reached Nibbana is called an Arhat, or Arahat.

Meditation (Bhāvanā, mental culture). Meditation involves mind-training and it cleanses your mind of all unwholesome thoughts, worries and lusts, etc. and cultivates wholesome thoughts, joy and peace of mind. Mindfulness (sati) is the vital stage of alert analysis you must achieve before doing Samatha meditation. As you take a drink be *mindful* of first touching the cup, then noticing the tea's temperature and finally its taste. Then add *clear comprehension* (*noticing the reason* behind your actions) to quench your thirst. This will quieten your mind. Be *mindful* of your *feelings* (pleasant, unpleasant, neutral). Meditation is not getting away from things, but *seeing them for what they are.*

Samatha is one form of meditation which the Buddha adopted and so it is used today. It is simply designed to help you to concentrate your mind, not an easy thing as you must have discovered when your teacher has told you off for inattention. It takes about 20 minutes and involves sitting comfortably on cushions. It calms your restless mind by fixing it on an object (kasina) – for example, your breathing. The aim is to pull yourself together. Each of us is made up of a number of part-selves – the dutiful self (we do our work), the disobedient self (we are lazy), and so on. We hardly know which of these selves we really are. In fact, we have got to bring our real self into being by mind control. You divide the time between these four stages:

(1) Concentrate on your breath as it moves through your nose
(2) Relax, breathe quietly; count after each breath: in . . . out . . . one; in . . . out . . . two – to ten, then returning to one
(3) Count as in (2) but before each breath
(4) Observe the breath without counting.

Anapanasati (anussati, anusmrti) is the term for the mindfulness involved in this in-and-out breathing. Samādhi is the term used to describe the state you are in when you have done Samatha. It is used in Step 8. This concentration of the mind (upacāra-samādhi, 'access concentration'), together with the peace it brings, enables you to see how your mind wanders over the Five Mental

Hindrances, stop this wandering and get things really in focus. For example, to deal with sloth, get out in the open air more – this will help you concentrate on resolving this Hindrance. Then you are ready for Vipassanā meditation, Buddhism's unique meditation.

Vipassanā or 'insight' meditation can be used in Step 7. When Samatha's mind-control has calmed your mind, Vipassanā's detached observation will enable you to observe and examine things, emotions and people in a calm, detached way. Suppose you want to meditate on why you are very angry and filled with hatred. You must not keep thinking of 'my angry mind' but imagine you are outside yourself looking at 'an angry mind' in action. Have you noticed that someone who is angry is not mindful of his anger until the moment he becomes aware he is angry – then his anger subsides as he has grasped what is happening to him and can master it.

At the Vipassanā Meditation Centre, Kanduboda, Sri Lanka, for example, you can take a ten-day free course. Men and women are kept in separate sections and silence is observed. You wear a white sarong and shirt and as a trainee are called a yogi. You sleep on the floor under a mosquito net in a 'cell' called a kutiya or Kitu. The daily routine is: 3–5.30 a.m., meditation in kutiya; 5.30 a.m., cup of gruel (lentil soup); 6.30 a.m., breakfast; 7–8 a.m., a cup of 'juice of king coconut'; 8.45–11 a.m., private study, meditation or seeing your tutor-monk; 11 a.m., lunch; 12.15–1.15 p.m., group meditation; afternoon for washing clothes and yourself with a bucket at the well, study, meditation; 6.30 p.m., optional pūjā; 7 p.m., small cup of tea; 7.15–8.15 p.m., group meditation; 10 p.m., lights out.

You and the monks are fed by villagers from all over Sri Lanka who come and stay for 24 hours at a time. They can gain the merit of self-denial by caring for the monks, for their chief aim in life is not to find Nibbana like the monks, but to ensure a more prosperous rebirth for themselves by such merit-gaining. They feel Nibbana is beyond their reach and in any case they would like to live a well-off life first (see Pure Land Buddhism as a contrast, pp. 45–6). When they come round to your kutiya with your drink they kneel before you in homage, but you must not thank them, as that spoils the merit-gaining. At breakfast and lunch you will follow the monks carrying your bowl and mug to the dining hall. The villagers will serve you liberally with numerous curries, rice, curd and fruit and may give you soap or a native stalk-like toothbrush. Each year monks will be given a new robe.

Once Samatha's walking meditation has relaxed and concentrated your mind, Vipassanā's observation can begin. You walk slowly up and down thinking 'left, right, left' as you go; then you go more slowly, thinking 'up, forward, down' as you move each foot. If you try it carefully and long enough you will find that you do calm down and forget other things.

Then comes sitting meditation, preferably in a lotus position. With Samatha mind-control, you concentrate on the rise and fall of your stomach, making a mental note of the movements, thus – 'rising', 'falling', 'rising', at the outset. Now if any thought comes into your mind, your Vipassanā detached observation will enable you to make a mental note of its appearance and disappearance. But you must not start developing that thought or having any emotional reaction to it. For

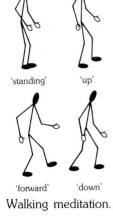

'standing'   'up'

'forward'   'down'

Walking meditation.

example, if you suddenly remember you have an important interview tomorrow, you must note the fact that you have remembered it with one word 'remembering' but not allow yourself to think about what the outcome will be or get into a panic about it. See it as an inevitable event that will come but will also go by. Gradually this will lead you to realize that everything, every thought, is impermanent and so unsatisfactory, and that you do not have to be overwhelmed by it. You can remain detached and relaxed, letting it flow by. You can get things and people in perspective. Life flows by – thoughts, events, people come and go – births, marriages, deaths happen, but they need not overwhelm you for you will take them in your stride as part of the flow of life.

Whereas Samatha meditation seems to produce excellent results by way of relaxing you, in fact its effect on the Five Mental Hindrances is temporary, as your problems will return when you stop, for you have simply kept them at bay. But Vipassanā enables you to remove permanently the Hindrances by observing things clearly for what they are, as characterized by the Three Marks. Thus it teaches you to be detached in all your daily life. Ultimately all that Buddhism aims to do is to see things as they are, thereby removing ignorance. With practice you can do Vipassanā meditation without having done Samatha first.

It is almost essential to have tuition from a practising meditator as each individual faces problems in coping with the mind's alertness.

40. (a) Give brief descriptions of (i) Samatha, (ii) Vipassanā meditations. (b) What is the aim of each?

41. Is mind-training really the way or should one try and find the truth elsewhere and by other means?

42. What problems would you face trying to follow the Eightfold Path? Give examples.

The two types of vehicle. All Buddhists talk of coping with the river of life – the great river of self-desire – by means of vehicles (yāna). They leave the shore of death and reincarnation, fear and peril for the land of Nibbana. The Southern Buddhists are sometimes known by the word Hinayāna, meaning small vehicle, as they see the craft as one designed to get an individual to Nibbana by his own efforts in contrast to the Northern Buddhists' Mahāyāna, a big vehicle which carries many at one time. The difference between the two ways is illustrated in the story of four men, who, crossing a desert, came upon a high-walled compound. One, determined to find out what was inside, scaled the wall, shouted for joy and jumped over. The second and the third did likewise, but when the fourth got to the top and saw the garden with sparkling streams and delicious fruit, he resisted the temptation to jump down, remembering the other wayfarers in the desert. He climbed back down and devoted his life to directing others to the oasis. The first three were Southern Buddhists and the fourth a Northern one.

Theravāda Monks. Southern Buddhists aim to become arhats, to attain Nibbana, by meditation and wisdom while caring little about helping others to find Nibbana. The wisdom route tends to be for monks. Children can become novices (sāmanera) at the age of seven. In Thailand and Burma they will be fully

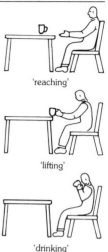

'reaching'

'lifting'

'drinking'

Being aware of what one does by carrying on the Vipassanā noting-process in everyday life.

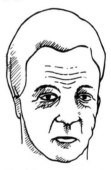

The cluttered head full of thoughts of personal problems and anxieties.

Clear head.

ordained as monks (bhikkhu) at the age of 20 years and may resign from the monastery when they wish, as it is believed that merit can be obtained from being ordained for a matter of weeks or months. In Burma people take their holidays in meditation centres. But in Sri Lanka men entering monasteries usually stay as novices for all their lives, for novices have to keep 75 introductory rules (e.g. eating quietly without blowing out their cheeks) whereas bhikkhus keep 227 rules covering everything. Nuns (chees) have 500 rules; for example, elderly nuns must obey the youngest monks; nuns cannot correct a monk but a monk can correct them. Heads are shaved and robes donned as part of the ordination ceremony.

Monks rise before sunrise, and after meditation they wash, sweep the monastery and the garden. They filter their drinking water to ensure that no insects are killed accidentally. Then they set off in a line to collect food from householders. The donors thank the monks for accepting their food offerings. If the monks thanked the donors they would rob them of their due merit. It is better to give than to receive. The monks eat twice a day, both meals being before mid-day because after then they may only drink. They study and pray, receive friends, and may sometimes be allowed to give people advice. The brotherhood of monks is called the Sangha. There are Sanghas for nuns too. In Thailand there are 150 000 bhikkhus, 90 000 sāmaneras and 2000 chees. There are 120 000 dekwats (temple boys), who live in monasteries and perform serving duties.

Monks wear yellow in Burma, red in Tibet and grey in Korea. The robes are often deliberately made of cut-up and sewn-together material to suggest they are made from rags.

About 10 per cent of monks meditate regularly while the rest study, teach and carry out ceremonies. Becoming a monk can be a way of opting out of ordinary

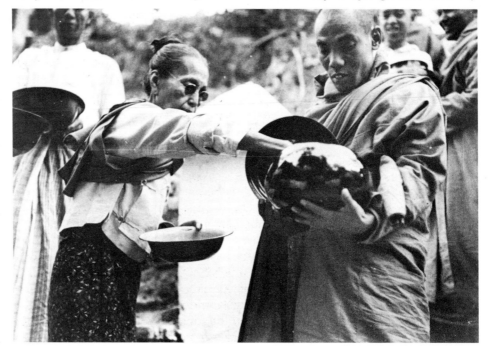

Burmese Buddhist monks with their begging bowls. Why do the donors thank the monks and not the monks the donors?

life and being supported by society as they are given their food, robes, soap and toothbrushes, etc. Remember, monks are not priests as they do not administer sacraments or pardon people. In Mahāyāna Buddhism we shall see there are priests.

43.   (a) What benefits do you think you would get from being a temporary Buddhist monk (i) in your teens, (ii) in later life?
(b) Do you think all people would benefit from some kind of monastic life for short periods in their lives? If so, why?

Northern Buddhism. Mahāyāna Buddhism began just before Christianity was preached. It stressed love of others and putting oneself last. Anyone can become a buddha as the Buddha is the mind which is enlightened. Thus it is essentially Buddhism for the layman rather than for the monk. Its message is that ordinary people can be saved in the midst of their daily lives and they do not need the benefits of becoming monks or nuns. In Japan this has led to priests marrying and living normal daily lives (see p. 48). Mahāyāna has adapted itself to Confucianism, Taoism, and Shintoism to fit the settings into which it has spread. In Japan it is known as Butsudō (The Way of the Buddha) to complement Shinto (The Way of the Kami). Finding the doctrines of kamma and reincarnation not congenial to the Japanese with their concern for ancestral spirits, Mahāyāna had to develop a simplified route to enlightenment which it made more readily available, while concerning itself with funerals as a means of income. At the funeral the priest initiates the deceased into immediate buddhahood by giving a posthumous name (kaimyō) to the deceased. Similarly priests were allowed to marry so as to perpetuate the family in the Japanese family tradition.

A Mahāyāna Bodhisatta (one who has the desire, sattva, for enlightenment, bodhi, see p. 44) is a saint who gives up his own hope of reaching Nibbana for the sake of others. So you can pray to a Bodhisatta for help to find the way to Nibbana. This intermediary help from a Bodhisatta has the effect of reducing the role of the priest and so lessens the distinction between priests and layfolk. This in turn gives rise to the new lay Buddhist sects such as Risshō Kōsekai (see pp. 40, 48).

44.   Which is better, to be an arhat content with having found Nibbana for oneself, or a Bodhisatta showing others the way? Give reasons for your answer.

Pure Land Buddhism. There are two sects under this heading, the Jōdo and the Shin sects (shū). All you have to do, they claim, is to trust Amida or Amitabha, Lord of the Western Paradise or Pure Land, and you will reach there because of his merit, not your own. Enlightenment is by faith in him alone and this will enable you to bypass kamma's effect of rebirth (see p. 239).

Zen. One branch of Mahāyāna Buddhism is called Zen (Ch'an in Chinese). 'Zen' is a Japanese word which today implies a belief in the suddenness and directness of enlightenment. There are two main Zen sects. The Rinzai sect believes enlightenment comes in a sudden flash while the Sōtō sect believes in a slower enlightenment. Young men who are going to succeed their fathers as temple priests will choose a monastery where there is a good rōshi (Zen master) and go

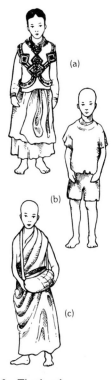

In Thailand, Buddhist boys and young men go through changes of clothes to make them realize that the Buddha was once a prince (a), gave up all to become a holy man (b), and favoured the middle way of a monk (c).

Keisaku in use.

Rodin's Thinker who sits in a position given over to delusion and tenseness. Notice the bent position of his body.

there for a year. In such monasteries men and women sleep, eat and meditate on their small area governed by a tatami mat (1 m × 2 m) on the raised 'tan' floor (1 m off the ground) in two rows down the zendō (meditating hall) which measures 10 m × 20 m for 30 people. When meditating they face the wall and stow their bedding away on shelves. The rail on the edge of the tan serves as a food table and pillow. The senior monk lights an incense stick to mark the 45 minute meditation period (zazen). His deputy will patrol the hall with a keisaku ('encouraging stick', shaped like a 'flat' sword; originally a sword was used). If any meditator feels he is dozing off or getting stiff, he will signal to the deputy and incline his head before him. The deputy will bow and then strike him very hard three times on each shoulder. Not only will this jolt the meditator, it will also loosen the shoulder muscles which can get over-tense in meditation. The Rinzai sect administers this encouragement without waiting for the meditator to ask for it.

When 45 minutes are up the monks and nuns perform walking meditation round the hall before starting another 45 minutes. This will go on for three hours at a time. In the Rinzai sect the monks have a daily sanzen, an interview with their rōshi, in which they are asked how they are getting on with solving their 'kōans' (lit. 'legal precedents', problems, riddles or puzzles). The monk bows before his master as bells are rung and then the question-and-answer session begins. Here are some examples:

(1) When a man comes to you with nothing, what would you advise? *Answer:* Throw it away.
(2) What did your face look like before your parents begot you?
(3) A fable says, 'A cow passes by a window. Its head, horns and four legs all pass by. Why did not the tail pass by?'
(4) We all know what two hands clapping sound like. What is the sound of one hand clapping?
(5) A long time ago a man kept a goose in a bottle. It grew larger and larger until it could not get out any more. He did not want to break the bottle, nor did he wish to hurt the goose; how would you get it out? 'There, it's out,' was the reply. In this story the goose represents the man, and the bottle the circumstances in which he lives. Either he must abandon the world or be crushed by it – a suicidal dilemma. But the moment he finds a way through he has a flash of satori (instinctive experience of enlightenment) and the goose is out of the unbroken bottle. He has escaped from his imaginary prison which consisted of the rigid way of life he had created for himself over the years.

The object of setting these topsy-turvy problems is to show you that your intellect, your brain power, is insufficient. The problems lead you into a cul-de-sac, for the ordinary thinking mind can find no way out. The problems destroy your usual thinking process in order to make you see beyond what the mind can think of. To see beyond, you must first exhaust your thinking process and then break out of the cul-de-sac. You abandon your thinking for intuition – a flash of sudden insight and revelation – which enables you to bridge the gap. The mind is then freed; you have had a mystical experience, a heightened sense of reality, so that you now view things from an entirely different angle. There are 1800 Rinzai kōans and one must solve them all to become a rōshi. This takes at least 10–15 years.

45. *What is meant when one says, 'She grasped the point intuitively (instinctively) without pausing to think'? Is this an example of solving a kōan?*

46. *Try to solve a kōan set for you by someone else.*
    (a) Why is it difficult to solve?
    (b) If you spend two hours a day for a month trying to solve it, what effect might it have on you?
    (c) What do all kōans have in common?

47. *How might a satori experience alter a person's life? Can a satori be taught or only experienced?*

48. *Is there knowledge to be discovered in ways which are beyond Man's thinking mind to find?*

Zazen forms only part of a monk's life for he must work hard too. Periodically he may be sent on a three-hour walk to beg for food, which teaches him the merit of self-denial. The monk bows on receiving a donation (notice the contrast here with Theravāda monks, see pp. 117–18). Bathing in the communal Japanese-style bath emphasizes purity. Monks shave each other's heads every fifth day. Twice a year there are sesshins (lit. 'gathering one's thoughts') lasting a week, which consist of concentrated zazen and lectures. The year is divided into three-monthly sections, two for retreat and two for pilgrimages, during which a monk will return to his home temple to help in its maintenance. On pilgrimage a monk carries two bags, in the front one a spare set of robes and a kimono, with scriptures, bowl and razor, and in the back one a raincoat. He will wear a large straw hat which will prevent him seeing too much of the world around him.

Student monk at chōka service.

The daily routine in a Rinzai monastery is as follows: A bell wakes the monks at 3.20 a.m. in summer and 4.30 a.m. in winter. A half-hour service (chōka) in the hondō (main hall), then chanting and zazen in the zendō for two hours begin the day. 7 a.m. breakfast consists of three bowls of rice, pickled plums and vegetables and 12 p.m. lunch is a bowl of mixed rice soup, vegetables and pickles, while supper is lunch's left-overs. The afternoon is spent on work projects, for example, gardening. Periodically the toilets are cleaned and the contents used to manure the vegetable garden. Evening service and floor scrubbing follows. Bed time is 9 p.m. but 'voluntary', virtually compulsory, zazen may continue until midnight. Calligraphy, the art of Japanese writing, is an important part of a monk's training.

Pilgrimages are not essential for Buddhists as the Buddha said it was more important to visit a good teacher than a place. However, he did mention four places which were important in his life. His birthplace, Lumbini Grove (Nepal); his enlightenment spot, Bodh Gaya (Bihar); his first sermon venue, the Deer Park, Sarnarth (near Benares); Kushinara (Uttar Pradesh) where he died. Bodh Gaya is the most sacred of these. There a descendant of the Bo tree he sat under flourishes today. Followers believe they will gain merit by walking round it clockwise as they will then show respect to the site. They will make flower offerings and hang sacred text prayer flags on the tree before sitting beneath it in meditation. Nearby stands the Great Enlightenment Temple, Mahabodhi, where they will make offerings of flowers, incense and light.

The Commandments — Decalogue.

The Commandments — Decalogue. When Moses was having a difficult time leading the Jews away from slavery to a new freedom, he needed a basic set of minimum rules to control them. These Ten Statements or Commandments he secured from God as a result of consulting Him on Mount Sinai (Exod. 19–20; Deut. 5:6–21). They made it plain that religion and moral behaviour depend on one another.

(1) I am the Lord your God.

(2) You may worship no other god but me. You shall not make yourselves any idols; any images resembling animals, birds or fish. You must never bow to any image or worship it in any way; for I, the Lord your God, am very possessive; I will not share your affection with any other god.

(3) You shall not take the name of God irreverently, nor use it to swear to a falsehood.

(4) Remember to observe the Sabbath as a holy day. Six days a week are for your daily duties and your regular work, but the seventh day is a day of rest and on that day you shall do no work . . . for in six days the Lord made heaven, earth and sea and everything in them and rested on the seventh day.

(5) Honour your father and mother.

(6) Do not murder.

(7) Do not commit adultery.

(8) Do not steal.

(9) Do not lie.

(10) Do not be envious of other people's property or circumstances.

49. *(a) How does this set of rules show how important God is in the Jewish life?*
    (b) What picture of God do they conjure up in your mind?

50. *Some argue these rules were designed to cope with a crisis period in Jewish history. Do they show this or are they suited to any conditions?*

51. *The Ten Commandments have been used as the basis of many of the world's sets of moral and legal rules. Find out what item worn by judges, barristers and clergymen in England shows this and explain how.*

These Ten Commandments are just a few of the 613 in, for example, Exod. 21–23, 34; Lev. 1–27 and Deut. 5–31. These chapters give precise directions on how Jews were to behave. The Jews' delight in keeping their rules comes from a sense of obeying God's will if they do so. Six fundamental human rights are laid out in the Torah: right to life, to possessions, to clothing, to shelter, to work and to liberty.

52. *Examine the examples of Exod. 21:16, 18–19, 22–24, 33. Summarize them briefly and give your opinion on them.*

53. *Leviticus deals with sacrifices to God as well as health hazards such as leprosy.*
    (a) Read chapters 1–3. Why are the rituals so clearly stated?
    (b) Read chapters 13–14 on leprosy. List (i) the priest's duties, (ii) what the leper is to do when he gets leprosy and when he is cured, (iii) what is to be done with affected clothing.

54. *Lev. 11:2–23 and Deut. 14:3–21 give details of what you may or may not eat. Make a list of (a) permitted, (b) forbidden beasts. Dietary rules are part of Jewish worship (see pp. 124–5).*

55. *(a) Read Deut. 22:22–27. Is this a fair law for women in the two cases?*
    (b) Read Deut. 24:5. How long is the honeymoon period granted?
    (c) Does Deuteronomy combine gentleness with being severe?

The Hindus believe the world we live in is an illusion (maya) and that we have to escape from it to find life in eternity. But for the Jews there is no such illusion in life; life is *real* life, leading to another real life after death. The Jews see God controlling history, ensuring His Chosen People win their battles when they deserve to and lose them when they need to be punished for their poor behaviour. For the Jews, God is righteous and just. He is not unfair or unreasonable. He also shows loving-kindness, so He treats people like His children, praising or telling them off as necessary.

The Sabbath, Shabbat ('rest'). If the Jews are to secure God's favour they must keep His commandments and observe the Jewish way of life as He chose them to do just that. Strict or Orthodox Jews will observe the Sabbath (Friday evening to Saturday evening) by not doing any work (see the Fourth Commandment). They will not travel, use electricity or write on the Sabbath and may even not put up an umbrella as that is like putting up a tent. Some Jews will use interleaved toilet paper so as not to work by tearing off a sheet. Jews feel that each age reveals a new significance and value in Sabbath-keeping. For example not using the telephone on the Sabbath is a joy for an office-bound Jew. The pressures of the twentieth century are kept at bay for better things such as family life and worship. Many Reform Jews will allow the use of transport to the synagogue but nowhere else on the Sabbath, while Orthodox Jews insist on walking there. In an emergency one can break the Sabbath so long as murder, idolatry or adultery are not committed.

Daily prayers are said at home as much as at the synagogue and especially on the Sabbath. An Orthodox or Reform Jew puts on a cappel, kipa, yamulkah or yarmulke (small round cap) and straps on tefillin (tephilin) or phylacteries, one to his forehead to remind his brain to think and another to his left arm (left-handers put it on their right arm) to encourage him to take action about his beliefs as it is near his heart. Tefillin are small black leather cubes (with each side 25–50 mm) containing four little parchment squares called the Shema (Hear), stating what Jews believe about God and His care for them (see Exod. 13:1–10, 11–16; Deut. 6:4–9; 11:13–21). They are put on as a sign of God's covenant with Israel, but are not worn on the Sabbath or festivals since these days are themselves such signs. They are sometimes referred to as the 'bridal garment' as they stress the devotion between God and Israel. When praying, Jewish men wear a tallith (silk or wool prayer shawl) round their shoulders (Deut. 22:12; Num. 15:38–40). In 1982 a pair of tefillin cost £200 and a tallith £20. Jews regard the day as starting at dusk so the Sabbath begins on Friday evening when the mother lights the Sabbath candles, saying, 'Blessed are you, O Lord our God, who has sanctified us by your commandments and has commanded us to light the Sabbath lights.' A clean cloth is put on the table. The father sits at the

A tallith, or tallit. The fringes (tzitzit) remind the wearer of the Ten Commandments.

head of the table with two loaves representing the double portion of manna (possibly plant lice or gum resin) which the Israelites were allowed to gather on their desert journey 3000 years ago (see Exod. 16; Num. 11:4–35). He takes a cup of wine and recites the Kiddush (Sanctification) and the Genesis verses on the creation and the need to rest on the Sabbath. He reads Proverbs 31:10–13 on the 'perfect housewife'. All drink from the cup, hands are washed, and the bred (challah) is broken.

56. *Why do you think the mother and not the father initiates the Sabbath ceremonies?*

57. *(a) What is your opinion of the Sabbath ceremonies beginning in the home rather than in the synagogue?*
(b) Would all religions benefit by having a regular weekly ceremonial meal at home?

The main service is on Friday evening (see pp. 161–2).

Boy wearing a tefillin. What has he got on his head? What effect is the lengthy task of putting on the tefillin likely to have on him?

The Jewish kitchen plays a vital part in religious life at home, as several Torah laws (kashrut) refer to diet. For example, you cannot serve pork, or meat from the hindquarters of any animal. A full list of permitted (kosher, or kasher) and forbidden (treyfah) foods is given in Leviticus, chapter 11. Parev, or parve, foods are neutral uncooked ones. As blood is the vital ingredient of life, it must be drained from meat before it can be eaten. After Noah had survived the Flood, God told him that people could kill animals for food provided they did not consume their blood, which was life-essence, as that would imply they were trying to absorb the animals' strength in a magical way. So meat is bought from a kosher butcher, called a shohet, who slaughters animals according to the slaughter laws (shehitah). Meat is soaked in cold water for half an hour, rinsed and sprinkled with salt to extract the remaining blood. This process is called kasher. An hour later it is washed before being cooked. In fact it will not taste different from normally prepared meat. Meat and milk may not be cooked or eaten together so rice pudding cannot follow a meat course, nor can you have butter on a chicken sandwich. White coffee after chicken and chips is also banned. A long gap after eating must occur before milk can be consumed. Housewives have to have two sets of saucepans, cutlery, cloths and two washbasins to keep these foods separate. Many use red pots and pans for meat, and blue ones for milk dishes so they do not make mistakes.

The Messiah. From what has been said we can see that Jews consider duty and tradition to be extremely important. In the synagogue one prayer always said is the Alenu, beginning 'It is our duty to praise the Lord of all things, to ascribe greatness to Him who formed the world.' The ritual of the kitchen and the meal table and numerous annual festivals (see pp. 191–6) commemorating historic events in Jewish history, are the aids which keep them on the road of faith. Notice that they do not usually do anything similar to Eastern meditation as training the mind is not so important to them as doing their duty. Strict Jews look to the future when a 'Messiah' will come to set up God's Kingdom on earth. This Messiah is seen as a human being who is specially gifted with leadership and wisdom. Reform Jews have reinterpreted the Messiah belief into meaning that society, not a single person, will eventually usher in the Kingdom by its goodness. Bible references to this are: Isa. 2:4; 11:1–10; Zech. 14:9.

58. *The Hindus argue that you must escape from the life of illusion here to the real world of eternity; the Jews see God's control of this life and the final coming of the Messiah as showing that life now is real. Compare the two opinions and say why you prefer one of them to the other.*

59. *Can God show His care and love, or His justice and judgement, unless He intervenes in the events of history?*

60. *Do you think doing things in a traditional ritual way helps you to worship and understand God better?*

61. *Why do you think some Jews are so very strict about the Fourth Commandment? Try to defend them in your answer.*

The Western (or Wailing) Wall in Jerusalem.

Pilgrimages. Jews have not been expected to go on any pilgrimages since the destruction of the Temple in 70 CE. The Wailing or Western Wall (the Temple Mount's retaining wall; the only part to survive the Romans' sack of the city) is a special place of prayer, however. It is all that remains of the Temple built by Herod the Great and others on the site of Solomon's Temple. Some kiss the stones as they pray and many weep openly. Some push papers with prayers on into the cracks.

In recent years Jews have taken to visiting Yad Vashem in Jerusalem where there is a memorial to six million Jews who died in the Holocaust of Hitler's extermination campaign. Yad Vashem means 'A Place and a Name' (quoted from Isa. 56:5). The place is a bare room lit by candle, with the names of the concentration camps inscribed on the floor. The Holocaust Museum is nearby.

CHRISTIANITY

The Commands of Jesus. Christians accept not only the Jewish Ten Commandments but also Christ's summary of them:

> *Love the Lord your God with all your heart, soul and mind. This is the first and great commandment. The second most important is similar, Love your neighbour as much as you love yourself. All the other commandments, and all the demands of the prophets stem from these two laws and are fufilled if you obey them. Keep only these and you will find that you are obeying all the others.* (Matt. 22:37–40)

62. *(a) Is Jesus right in saying if you keep those two important commandments the others will all be obeyed?*
   (b) Is it better to have just two all-embracing directions than a lengthy set of detailed rules?
   (c) Would this work if applied to your school?

63. *Notice how Jesus takes it for granted that people's thoughts and attitudes lead them to do things. Which religion held the opposite view? We looked at it earlier in this chapter.*

In fact, Jesus did explain and elaborate on his basic rules. (Note – Jews argue that Jesus misinterpreted the Torah.) For example he said:

> *You have heard it was said, 'Do not commit adultery'. But now I tell you; anyone who looks at a woman and wants to possess her is guilty of adultery with her in his heart. (Matt. 5:27–28)*

> *You have heard that it was said, 'An eye for an eye, and a tooth for a tooth'. But now I tell you: do not take revenge on someone who does you wrong. If anyone slaps you on the right cheek, let him slap your left cheek too . . . When someone asks for something, give it to him. (Matt. 5:38–42)*

> *You have heard that it was said, 'Love your friends and hate your enemies'. But now I tell you: Love your enemies and pray for those who mistreat you. (Matt. 5:43–44)*

There are other points in Matt. 5:5–7, 9, 21–24; 6:1–4; 18:1–5.

64. (a) *Think about all these teachings of Jesus and then say why Christianity is a very tough religion to follow.*
    (b) *Is Jesus really demanding too much of his followers?*
    (c) *What effect would living by his standards have on your character?*

Modern Ideas. Over the centuries the churches have brought out more detailed sets of rules for themselves. The Society of Friends (Quakers) will not fight under any circumstances. Their Peace Testimony proclaims:

> *We utterly deny all outward wars and strife, and fightings with outward weapons, for any end, or under any pretence whatever; this our testimony to the whole world . . . we certainly know . . . that the Spirit of Christ . . . will never move us to fight and war against any man with outward weapons. (Declarations from the Harmless and Innocent People of God, presented to Charles II, 1660)*

65. (a) *Should all Christians never fight in any circumstances?*
    (b) *In what circumstances do you think they should fight?*
    (c) *How would you explain to a non-Christian that Christians have often fought Christians in the last 2000 years?*

66. *Quakers also refuse to take oaths as that involves taking the name of God 'in vain'. What do they do when required to tell the truth in court today?*

The Salvation Army is firmly against drinking alcohol as its members daily come up against the effects of over-drinking in the people they seek to save. In 1980 they were running 52 homes and centres for the treatment of alcoholics.

67. *The Salvation Army believes that you must practise what you preach. Should other Christian churches stop members drinking?*

Salvation. Christianity is based on the belief that Jesus is part of the Godhead, not just a great human being. Other religions see their founders as outstanding humans. Christians argue that God appeared on earth in the form of a human being to demonstrate His love by sacrificing Himself for the failings of people, so following the Christian road involved believing at the outset in who Jesus is and what he did on earth.

The Christian has to find his way to salvation although it is equally true to say God may seek to find him. He wants to be saved from his sins, his weaknesses and from himself. He hopes he will then be received into heaven when he dies. He does not believe in reincarnation, so there is a sense of urgency about being 'saved' as he does not know when he will die. Jesus had a number of things to say about salvation:

> *Not every person who calls me 'Lord, Lord', will enter the Kingdom of Heaven, but only those who do what my Father in heaven wants them to do.* (Matt. 7:21)

> *Remember this, unless you change and become like children you will never enter the Kingdom of Heaven. The greatest in the Kingdom . . . is the one who humbles himself and becomes like this child.* (Matt: 18:1-5)

> *I am the resurrection and the life. Whoever believes in me will live, even though he dies.* (John 11:25–26)

> *I am the way, the truth and the life; no one goes to the Father except by me.* (John 14:6)

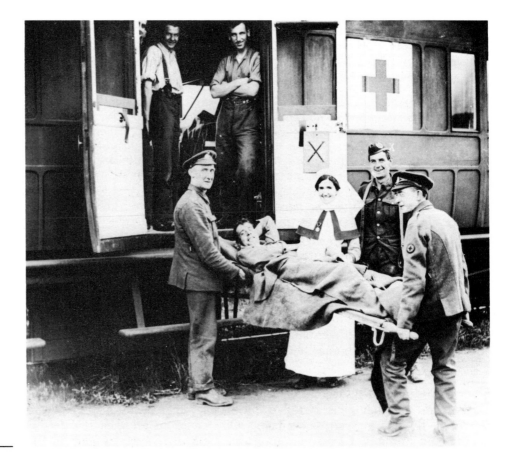

Quakers in action during the First World War.

68. *Summarize Jesus' teaching on salvation and how a person can achieve it (see Matt. 7:21; 18:1–5; John 5:21–24; 6:48–51; 11:25–26; 14:6). Which Hindu yoga is the closest to the Christian road to salvation?*

69. *Jesus told his followers how they should behave (see Matt. 5:5–9, 38–47; 6:24–33; 7:1–5, 12).*
    (a) Which points do you think you could succeed in following and which do you feel are beyond you? Give your reasons.
    (b) If a community followed these directions would it live in peace and happiness?
    (c) Do you think people could follow such directions without being religiously minded?

70. *Why does the Christian have to consider his life and beliefs with some urgency compared to the Hindu?*

The Christian argues that by praising God, loving Jesus and allowing yourself to be guided by the Holy Spirit in you, you will be freed from fear, even fear of death, and released from any sense of guilt or sin. You will be free to serve others in love. You will be 'born again' when you accept what Christ did for you and turn to follow him. For example, John Wesley, the eighteenth-century founder of Methodism, called on people to accept Christ as their Saviour. William Clowes wrote what it was like to be converted.

> *The power of Heaven came down upon me and I cried for help to Him who is mighty to save . . . I felt my head splitting and when the change was taking place, I thought within myself, What is this? This, I said, is what the Methodists mean by being converted. Yes, God is converting my soul. In an agony of prayer I believed He would save me. Then I believed He was saving me. Then I believed He had saved me. And it was so.*

Some Christians will tell you that they were brought to this point by Jesus seeking them rather than their turning to him.

The 'evangelical' or 'low church' branch of Christianity emphasizes that Christ died for your sins, and if you really believe this you will have a place in heaven because of his merciful sacrifice, and not because of your own efforts to be good. You are 'saved' when you accept Christ as your Saviour, and it is then your duty to show this by living a Christian life. The 'catholic' or 'high church' branch argues that you must humbly live out the good Christian life in the hope that his death together with your own efforts will ensure a place for you in heaven.

Contact between God and a Christian can occur in various ways. Some people use their reason to try to work out whether Christianity is true. Others see glimpses of God through beauty and love of others. Sometimes, though, people experience the Christian faith through suffering or feelings of their own inadequacy as these hymn verses show:

> *Abide with me; fast falls the eventide*
> *The darkness deepens; Lord with me abide!*
> *When other helpers fail and comforts flee,*
> *Help of the helpless, O abide with me.*

(H F Lyte, 1793–1847)

Just as I am, though tossed about
With many a conflict, many a doubt,
Fightings within, and fears without,
O Lamb of God, I come

Just as I am, thou wilt receive,
Wilt welcome, pardon, cleanse, relieve;
Because thy promise I believe,
O Lamb of God, I come.

(Charlotte Elliot, 1789–1871)

The Lamb of God is Jesus and many Christians have found strength through meditating on His cross.

When I survey the wondrous Cross,
On which the Prince of glory died,
My richest gain I count but loss,
And pour contempt on all my pride.

See from his head, his hands, his feet,
Sorrow and love flow mingled down;
Did e'er such love and sorrow meet,
Or thorns compose so rich a crown?

Were the whole realm of nature mine,
That were an offering far too small;
Love so amazing, so divine,
Demands my soul, my life, my all.

(I Watts, 1674–1748)

Christians also see God as their Father too:

No earthly father loves like thee,
No mother e'er so mild,
Bears and forbears as thou hast done
With me thy sinful child.

Father of Jesus, love's reward,
What raptures will it be
Prostrate before thy throne to lie,
And gaze and gaze on thee.

(F W Faber, 1814–1863)

71. The idea of Jesus being a slaughtered 'lamb' on a 'cross' seems very gory. Why are Christians drawn to it?

72. What does the writer F W Faber long for and why?

Fellowship with other Christians is very important too. Jesus said that if two or three were gathered together in His name He would be there with them (Matt. 18:19–20). Together they can create an atmosphere which helps them to find God.

Prayer is essential for the Christian although no set times or positions are laid down. Reading the Bible can take up part of his or her devotional time. Prayer can take many forms and may be spoken out loud or silent:
Praise – telling God that you appreciate His greatness.

Thanksgiving – for all the good things of life, for God, for Jesus, and all blessings received.

Penitence – saying sorry to God for wrong doing.

Intercession – prayer for other people, especially those in need or who are sick, or for ourselves.

Prayer is not only about talking, though, but about listening to God. Silent contemplation has always been regarded as important: 'Be still and know that I am God' (Ps. 46:10).

Contemplation includes meditation. The Christian quietens his brain and imagination to find an inner peace. He may find it helpful to repeat a phrase such as 'Lord Jesus Christ, Son of the Living God, have mercy upon me, a sinner', or 'My God I want thee; help me to want thee more'.

Hands in prayer.

73.   What other religion(s) involve the repeating of a 'mantra' (phrase)?

74.   Look up Ps. 46:10. How does this express contemplation?

Some Christian saints have become so engrossed in contemplation that they have seemed to enter a 'void' when God is absent. St John of the Cross called this the Dark Night of the Soul.

75.   Does the experience of a 'void' in prayer remind you of another religion?

Beyond this painful experience, some saints have felt a release into love and ecstasy, a feeling of God himself.

The training of church leaders in Africa.

The Virgin and Child – a sculpture which many Roman Catholics would find helpful.

Variety in Christianity. For the Roman Catholic, God's presence today is brought out by the splendour of candles, incense and processions, while the Quakers believe that worship should concentrate on the Holy Spirit, which, they claim, can best be found in a plain room in the midst of a quietly praying congregation. Between these two extremes the various churches offer a variety of ways.

The Roman Catholic Church also requires you to make regular confessions of your failings to a priest, whereas such confessions in the Church of England are voluntary and rare. The priests and penitent (sorry person) usually sit in two halves of a 'confessional'. This is a cubicle divided by a wall in which there is a screened grille through which they talk. Alternatively, face-to-face confessions are done today. The priests must never tell anyone what he hears in confessions and he will tell the penitent what penances he should do. Penances might involve saying certain prayers or putting a wrong right. Contrition, the act of confession and penance, is one of the seven Roman Catholic sacraments. Rosaries are used to count the prayers. A full rosary has 15 sets of ten beads, with single larger beads between sets, and a crucifix (a cross with Jesus on it); a lesser rosary has five sets. The Creed (statement of beliefs) is on the crucifix; 'Our Father' (Lord's Prayer: Matt. 6:9–13) on the larger beads; 'Hail Mary full of grace' (to Jesus' mother) on each of the small beads; and the Gloria ('Glory be to the Father . . .') on the chain.

Some Christians recall Jesus' sacrifice by making the sign of the Cross on their chests as they enter a church or when praying. An Orthodox Christian puts his thumb and two fingers together for the three Persons in one Godhead, and bends the others into his palm (Christ with God and Man). Then he touches his forehead, chest and right and left shoulders with the three fingers as the head is the centre of his mind, the chest his feelings and inner self, and the shoulders his physical strength.

The Salvation Army sees the Christian's duty as a 'military' operation in which 'soldiers' march behind the flag to take Christianity on to the streets and particularly to deprived areas. Their vocabulary is military: 'knee drill' for a prayer meeting, 'cartridge' for a donation. Its full-time leaders have officers' ranks and they and all its members buy uniforms to wear. Officers only stay at a citadel (i.e. a 'fort') for three to four years before being posted elsewhere so as to keep them fresh on the job. Members are expected to devote most of their free time to 'fighting the battle' for Christ. Care of tramps, drunks and drug addicts, unmarried mothers, runaways and so on is uppermost in their efforts. If someone comes forward to the penitent's form or mercy seat (bench in front of the congregation) during a service in the citadel, the whole congregation will stay there for however long it takes for that person in need to find help in Christ. That person's soul is considered so precious that the pattern of the service must be changed to one of care and help.

76. The Salvation Army is against alcohol and the Quakers are flatly against fighting.
    (a) Why do they think it vital to be so rigid on these points?
    (b) Should Christian groups all take firm stands on such matters? If not, why not?

Wesley's 'method' involved doing three things each day: prayer, Bible study and a charitable deed. He saw the need for Christians to be methodical in their lives. Bible study is a basic part of the Christian's life as is daily private prayer. There are no rules on washing or praying in a precise position or at a definite time. Praying morning and evening is simply suggested. Some churches have 'house groups', small groups meeting in private houses for Bible study, discussions and prayer.

77. *Is Methodism's 'methodical' approach helpful in keeping one's faith alive?*

Christians may serve others through their church, at work or at home, as well as through welfare organizations. They may see evil in the world but often want to transform the world with God's help. As God loves them and forgives them, so they can love and forgive others.

78. *In what ways could a Christian serve God and other people (a) at home, (b) at work?*

79. *Name any Christian organizations that help the needy.*

Some Christians find it helpful to go on a retreat – that is, a quiet weekend or longer at a centre where they can receive instruction and fellowship with others of like mind. Usually quiet is observed for much of the day to allow for personal reflection and prayer. Christians find the experience very refreshing.

Some Christians concentrate on worship in a particularly solemn and humble way, while others stress the joy of their faith. So worship ranges from that provided by the cathedral choirs to pop groups and guitars. You can express your worship by reciting set prayers and attending elaborate services or you can make your own prayers with others or alone.

Monasteries and nunneries are places of worship, contemplation, study and work where people called monks and nuns, who have committed themselves totally to God, live. There are several different orders (sects) with varying rules and purposes. Poverty, chastity and obedience are their basic vows. Also there are friars who perform a more missionary function out in the world while also taking the three vows.

Nun.

Life in a Benedictine monastery in Britain today depends on whether it runs a large school, as Ampleforth and Downside do, or whether it does not. Those with schools have to adjust their religious timetables to fit in with the school day, while those without can concentrate more on the worship of God.

At Prinknash in Gloucestershire some 35 monks are woken by a 4.40 a.m. buzzer. Each monk has a centrally heated study-bedroom, crammed full of his books, robes and working clothes. At 5 a.m. he will attend two services before 6.30 a.m. breakfast of tea and toast. Then he washes, shaves and has time for private prayer and study. A short five-minute service follows at 8.15 a.m. before work which lasts until 11 a.m. Work could be study, administration of the estate, running a retreat for visitors, working in the incense factory or supervising the abbey's successful pottery works. Sung mass is from 11.30 a.m. to 12.15 p.m. and is followed by a three-course lunch during which a thought-provoking book is read. The monks sit at three long tables in the refectory.

Monk.

After half an hour's rest and a short service, it is back to work until 5 p.m. Normally dressed in flowing white robes, Prinknash monks put on rough patched trousers and smocks for tasks on the estate. After a 6 p.m. service, supper follows during which parts of the Rules of St Benedict are read out. Afterwards there is half an hour for a general chat in the common room. At 8 p.m. the monks gather for a 'chapter house' meeting so that the abbot can give out notices, etc. The Compline service ends the day at 8.10 p.m. Silence is expected for much of the day. About a third of the monks are priests and are called 'fathers', while the rest are called 'brothers'. Sometimes fathers go out to Catholic churches to stand in for sick or absent clergy.

Pilgrimages are not essential although 'high-church' followers favour them. Ancient holy wells have become 'christianized' in some cases, but most sites are those where some historic event occurred. Pilgrimages have come to be centred on places where visions of the Virgin Mary have been seen and miracles recorded. Knock, a village in County Mayo, Ireland, was the place where two women saw her in 1879. Since then cures have occurred there. Lourdes in France has been the centre for cures since Bernadette Soubirous saw Mary in 1858 on 18 occasions. Her visions were very vivid ones. She was made a saint by the Pope in 1933. About a million people go there each year and most are seriously ill or handicapped. For most of the year two 'jumbulances' carrying 24 pilgrims, including a doctor and nurses, regularly leave Britain for Lourdes.

In England half a million people make their pilgrimage each year to the tiny Norfolk village of Walsingham. About half of them are Roman Catholics and half Church of England, and they go to visit their respective shrines to 'Our Lady of Walsingham'. In was in 1061 that Richeldis de Faverches, Lady of the Manor, had three visions of the Virgin Mary and in each she seemed transported to a house in Nazareth where Mary was told by the angel that she would have a son. So Richeldis ordered a wooden replica Holy House to be built at Walsingham. Within a century it was one of the four great Christian pilgrimage centres, the others being Rome, Jerusalem and Compostella. Henry VIII, once a barefoot pilgrim himself, ordered its destruction in 1538. But in 1897 it was reopened as the Slipper Chapel for Catholics – probably so called because pilgrims removed their shoes.

In 1931 the Church of England vicar of Walsingham had a new Holy House built for Anglicans and Orthodox Christians. So today Walsingham stands for the root of Christian belief, namely that God became man – the Incarnation – and that in honouring Mary, Jesus' identity is guaranteed.

Apart from special annual National Pilgrimages and Pilgrimages for the Sick and for Young People, there is a regular arrival of coach-loads of pilgrims organized by parishes. Hostel accommodation is available.

As a Catholic pilgrim you would probably say your confession to a priest (see p. 132) and attend mass and possibly join in a procession through the village, while Anglicans will take communion, drink holy water from a well and light candles at a 6 p.m. service to remember particular people in prayer. Both centres have rows of crosses called the Stations of the Cross to mark the last events of Jesus' crucifixion day. Pilgrims pause in front of each cross to recall those events.

One of the Catholic prayers used is:

> O Alone of all women, Mother and Virgin, Mother most happy, Virgin most pure, now we sinful as we are, come to see thee who are all pure, we salute thee, we honour thee as how we may with our humble offerings; may thy Son grant us, that imitating thy most holy manners, we also, by the grace of the Holy Ghost may deserve spiritually to conceive the Lord Jesus in our inmost soul, and once conceived never to lose him. Amen.

80. It has been said that 'A visit to a holy place to reflect on one's life and faith is seen as a microcosm of the journey of life itself.' Discuss what you think the writer means. Do you agree with him or not?

81. Walsingham, Lourdes, Knock were never visited by the Virgin Mary while she was alive on earth. How did they come to be places of pilgrimage and what significance should be attached to visions?

82. Some Christians put a lot of trust in repeating set prayers, possibly using a rosary, while others prefer to make up their own prayers spontaneously. Give reasons for and against each way and then say which you would prefer.

83. Is the main purpose of prayer to praise God or to petition Him?

84. Does the strength and weakness of Christianity lie in the wide range of approaches its offers to its followers? List points which provide (a) strength, (b) weakness.

85. (a) What makes a place into a centre of Christian pilgrimage? Give examples.
(b) Have pilgrimages a value today?

ISLAM

Obedience to Allah. Islam agrees with Judaism and Christianity in seeing God's role as one of ruling while Man's is one of obeying. God has given Man command over nature, but expects to be served in return. This does not make Man a slave of God, but gives him the dignity of being above all other creatures on earth. In all three religions Man is God's tenant controller of the world on God's behalf. Like a tenant farmer he can farm the land provided he pays his due to his overlord. So Man must act in a responsible way and must ask himself if he should 'misuse' nature by making nuclear bombs, or allowing abortion except for medical reasons. The Qur'ān (Surah 2) points out that the angels thought God was taking a big gamble in setting Man over the world. They thought they ought to rule it. However, God got all of them to change their minds except Satan (Shaytan). Man's task is to prove God was sensible in giving them power. Satan spends his time in trying to prove he is right by making people not act responsibly. It follows that for Muslims it is essential that they keep Allah's laws if they are to live up to God's requirements for human beings. It also follows that if there is *one* God, all people belong to a *single* tribe of humanity. So Islam claims to have invented the first plural society (i.e. all races) with one God.

Muslims and Christians disagree on one important point. While Christians argue that all people have sinned and need to be 'saved' by God's grace, Muslims say that people have not 'fallen' and so do not need a 'saviour' to 'save' them.

A Muslim will point out that you are born innocent – free from sin – and you are just as inclined by your human nature to do good or evil. This is because you are free to obey God or not as you like. You are not compelled like a puppet to do either good or evil. You are capable of being *both*. You have the chance to prove yourself by worship and good deeds. You are entitled to take pride in doing so. But if you deliberately reject Allah's call, you do evil and do deserve punishment. Only Allah is self-sufficent. This means you are insufficient on your own and need to serve Allah.

Rather than upset you by saying you are born with inescapable sin, Islam reassures you. You are born with eyes and ears, an active mind and a heart – all of which will aid you to learn of Allah and serve Him. It is stressed that good can be achieved in this world and, as a Muslim, it is your duty to see to this. The 'other world' after death will be one of reward or punishment depending on what you have done in this life. If you serve Allah you will have happiness here and hereafter. You must remember that you are God's tenant controller or manager (khalifah) on earth and have a responsibility towards Him. The rules of Islam must be understood in this context.

Coming after Judaism and Christianity, Islam could draw on their commandments. Among the 6239 verses of the Qur'ān can be found Nos. 1 and 5–10 of the Ten Commandments, with different wordings. For example:

> *Thy Lord has commanded that you shall not serve any but Him and that you do goodness to your parents . . . Do not kill your children for fear of poverty. And go not nigh to fornication, for it is an indecency . . . And do not kill anyone whom God has forbidden except for a just cause . . . Do not say, if people do good to us, we will do good to them, and if people oppress us, we will oppress them, but resolve that if people do good to you, you will do good to them, and if they oppress you, do not oppress them in return . . . Repel evil with that which is better.*
> (Surah 17: also Surah 6: 151–3)

The Shar'ia, or Shari'ah (The Clear Path, Islamic law) tells Muslims how to lead their lives. It lays down how to apply the points made in the Qur'ān and the Sunnah (Muhammad's practices and thus recommendations) of the Hadith in daily life (see pp. 90–1). There are five grades of Fard (obligations) to be followed, namely; (1) binding, (2) recommended (mustahab), (3) indifferent, (4) disapproved of (makruh), (5) forbidden. The first four are called Halal (permitted) while the fifth is Haram (forbidden). Among the Fard are the Five Pillars (see pp. 137–45) as well as some on trade and political matters, even one on how to cut your nails. A recent leaflet on the Shar'ia's rules on dress says, 'Do not ape the trends set by money-making non-believers in Paris and London', arguing that it is wrong to 'mould one's social life according to that of non-believers', and calling on Muslim parents to 'stop this total imitation of western attire and vulgarity'. Eating is governed by such laws as: eat with the right hand, using the thumb, index and middle fingers, the fourth finger being used if the food is very soft. One may not blow on hot food, or express one's dislike of any food. In other words, have good table manners. Wrong doing is called zulm.

Harsh punishments are set down to deter people and to emphasize a criminal's lack of compassion for his victim. These were felt to be better than imprisoning people as that would deprive them of their God-given freedom. 'The man who steals and the woman who steals, cut off their hands as a punishment' (Surah 5:38) for burglary, not impulse theft. But the verse goes on to suggest that it is only habitual thieves who are to lose a hand; the first offender who is repentant is forgiven. If one steals for the sake of one's starving family one would not be punished. The point is that if there is a social security scheme for all there is no excuse for theft. Where there is no scheme, there may be an excuse. Another harsh punishment recommended in the Qur'ān (Surah 24:1) is this: 'The adulteress and the adulterer, flog each of them a hundred stripes.' This is not necessarily put into practice. In fact four male witnesses to the fact that adultery has taken place, or four voluntary confessions by those concerned, are needed first. This is in contrast to the Jewish Torah's requirement of two witnesses. Thus some Muslims argue that their laws are less harsh than those of the Jews, for example.

The Shar'ia affects the business world too. Honest trading is insisted upon and this means that investing money solely for the sake of getting interest (riba) is not allowed, as it does not involve trading or earning by work. Muslim partnerships are acceptable. Insurance against fire, flood and accidents has to be in the form of a *donation* upon *condition* of compensation. Islam in fact is against the Western *means* and *methods* of insurance, rather than against insurance as such. Life insurance is seen as unfair trading as it is a form of gambling on life. Lotteries and gambling are haram.

Muhammad believed that Christians were wrong to think Jesus was the Son of God. He saw Jesus as just a prophet. He stressed that Allah (God) was almighty ('Allahu Akbar' – 'God is the most great', i.e. nothing can be compared to him), and that people were His slaves. 'Muslim' means a 'surrendered person', just as 'Islam' means 'submission' to God. God is set apart from people, and not to be seen in quite such a personal way as Christians see God. So you should humbly plead for mercy, forgiveness and guidance. Allah will be merciful to those who humble themselves before Him.

> O My Lord ! If I worship thee from fear of hell, burn me in hell; and if I worship thee from hope of paradise, exclude me thence; but if I worship thee for thine own sake, then withhold not from me thine eternal beauty. (Rabi'a, female poet and mystic)

The Five Pillars. Islam lays down a clear straightforward road for its followers, namely do your duty (dīn or deen, which can also mean religion or divine judgement). There are five requirements called the Five Pillars of Islam. In diagram form the four minarets (towers) and the dome of the mosque (place of worship) emphasize this. Not all these pillars are of equal importance. The first is the vital one, the second of great importance and the others should be followed if at all possible.

The First Pillar: Shahādah, Shahāda or *Kalimah* (declaration of truth). You must accept that 'There is no god but Allah, and Muhammad is His Prophet'. This will make you aware of what the universe stands for and how you fit into it as Allah's servant – 'La ilaha illal lah Muhammadur rasulul lah'. (There is no god except Allah, Muhammad is Allah's prophet.)

The Second Pillar: Salāt, salah (regular worship). This consists of rakats (rak'ahs) (prayer sequences) five times a day, as follows:
At daybreak (fajr): two rakats. At midday (zuhr): four rakats.
In the afternoon ('asr): four rakats. In the evening (maghrib): three rataks.
At night ('isha): four rakats.

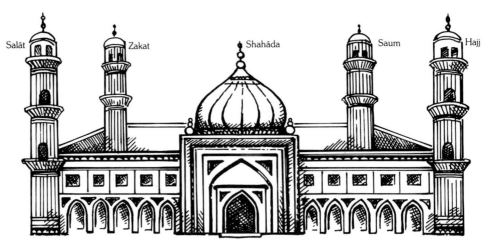

Salāt   Zakat   Shahāda   Saum   Hajj

The Five Pillars of Islam in diagram form. List the meanings of the Five Pillars in English.

The aim of this regular prayer is to strengthen the Muslim's ties to Allah and develop his love for Allah so as to appreciate His Mercy, Power and Glory. Worship is time- and direction-based. It does not matter where you are, so long as you pray at the right time and facing Makkah. This procedure stresses the unity of Allah, the universe and humanity. Muslims thus worship in *one* direction at *one* time. The Muslim's life revolves round prayers. It is a natural expression of his need to worship.

The muezzin (caller) calls the faithful to prayer (azzan or adhān, 'call to prayer') from the top of the minaret by shouting, 'God is the greatest. I bear witness that there is no God but Allah. I bear witness that Muhammad is the messenger of Allah. Come to prayer. Come to security. God is the greatest'. Each time, a Muslim must carry out different acts of devotion, each with a set prayer and position to take up. The illustrations make these clear. If you are a Muslim, this is what you do.

A muezzin calls the faithful to prayer.

Before you can begin, you must make yourself thoroughly clean. This procedure (wudu) removes dirt and also purifies you from any defilements as well as helping you to concentrate on Allah. First, you wash your hands, then your mouth and nose, before the whole of your face. After that you wash the right hand and forearm, then the left, before wiping your head with your hand; finally, your ears and feet. Parts are repeated three times. 'Believers, when you rise to pray, wash your faces and your hands as far as the elbows and wipe your heads and your feet to the ankle', says the Qur'ān (Surah 5:6). Men put on a topi (small cap) and women a burka (shawl).

1 Wash hands and between fingers three times.

2 Wash mouth thoroughly three times.

3 Clean teeth with fingertips.

4 Wash and blow nose three times.

5 Wash the whole face three times.

6 Wash up to each elbow three times.

7 Wipe the whole head with water.

8 Wash the ears inside and out.

9 Wash each foot up to the ankle.

The wudu procedure.

Next you face Makkah, the direction of which can be found by looking for the mihrab (niche) on the qibla (direction) wall of the mosque. You can buy special compasses which enable you to work out the direction from anywhere in the world. You lay out your musulta (prayer mat). Each rakat is then performed using

1 Face Mecca; raise hands and say 'Allahu Akbar'.

2 Put right hand over left to show humbleness and recite part of the Qur'ān.

3 Raise hands and say 'Allahu Akbar'.

4 Bow from the hips placing hands on knees and saying in Arabic 'Glory be to my Lord, the Great'.

5 Straighten up, raise hands and say 'Allah listens to whoever thanks Him'.

6 Prostrate yourself twice, nose touching the ground.

The rakat sequence.

7 Straddle your hands and thighs while prostrate, and say 'Glory be to my Lord, the Highest'.

8 Sit upright between the two prostrations, with hands on thighs, saying 'Allahu Akbar'.

9 Turn the head to the right and left, saying 'Peace be on you and Allah's blessings'.

the following sequence. You raise your hands beside your face and say, 'Allahu Akbar'; you then put your right hand over your left at waist level and recite part of the Qur'ān before raising your hands again as you say, 'Allahu Akbar'. The act of saying these words is called takbīr. You bow from the hips, placing your hands on your knees saying, 'Glory be to my Lord, the Great'. Straighten up and with your hands beside your face say, 'Allah listens to whoever thanks Him. Our Lord, thanks be to Thee'. Then you prostrate yourself twice with your face and palms to the ground, sitting back between each prostration. When prostrate, you say three times, 'Glory be to my Lord, the Most High'. You then sit back on your heels and say, 'I bear witness that there is no god except Allah'. Finally you turn your head to the right and left to give God's peace to those on either side of you, saying 'Peace be on you and Allah's blessing'. (Compare the Christian giving of the Peace in the Communion service, p. 167.)

In this set pattern you show your complete humbleness before Almighty God, from whom you expect nothing in return except what you deserve, which in turn is determined by how you have behaved. Du'a (the cry-of-the-heart or voluntary prayer) follows next. You stay kneeling with palms upwards level to your chin and petition God in your own words as well as quoting the Qur'ān. You end by wiping your hands over your face to show your receipt of God's blessing.

86. *What is the purpose of this cleaning rite, wudu, before praying? Describe the rite with illustrations.*

87. *What is the relationship between Allah and the person praying as suggested by the form the Salāt ritual of rakats takes?*

88. *Draw the rakat sequence, explaining each picture.*

89. *What influence is regular prayer several times a day likely to have on Muslims and the maintenance of Islam?*

90. *(a) If one believes it is a man's duty to worship humbly an Almighty God, is this best done by having a strict routine to follow?*
(b) Is spontaneous worship more genuine?
(c) Which will have a more lasting effect and be better maintained by the worshipper?

The Third Pillar: Zakat, zakah (purification) or *sadaqah, sadaqat* (charity payment). Charity can purify you because giving your possessions to those less fortunate than yourself will make you more generous and friendly. It will help to build up a community sense, free of class distinctions and rivalries.

> *Alms (sadaqa) shall be used only for the advancement of Allah's cause, for the ransom of captives, debtors, and for the distribution among the poor, the destitute, the wayfarers, those that are employed in collecting alms, and those that are converted to the faith. This is a duty enjoined by Allah. He is wise and all knowing. (Surah 9:60)*

It is fixed at 2½ per cent or one-fortieth of your savings. However, certain deductions to your income can be made before you calculate what Zakat you must pay. Rent from houses you let, debts, household goods, clothes, car and travel money can be subtracted, for example. Your should give Zakat to relatives if they are in need. You can also give it to poor or needy people, but if such people cannot be found you can give Zakat to any organization serving Islam. It is entirely up to you to arrange how to give Zakat. You are put on your honour to do so; after all, if you do not give it you will get what you deserve on the Day of Judgement.

Muslims prostrate in London's Hyde Park. The Regent Street Mosque has recently been built there on a site donated by King George VI in gratitude for Muslims' service in World War II.

The Fourth Pillar: Saum, sawm or Siyam (fasting). You must observe the holy month of Ramadan by fasting. Ramadan is the ninth month of the Islamic year, which consist of 12 lunar months, so it comes at different times of the (solar) year. Because of this Muslims all over the world get a fair share of different climatic conditions when coping with the strain. Ramadan marks the time when Muhammad received Allah's first revelation of the Qur'ān. You must fast from daybreak until sunset or during the hours when a white thread can be distinguished from a black one. So you must get up before dawn and eat a large breakfast and then another large meal after sunset. Calendars are printed giving local sunrise and sunset times so there can be no error. For example:

Date	London		Birmingham		Sheffield	
	begin	end	begin	end	begin	end
Oct 31	6.34	5.36	6.41	5.32	6.42	5.36
Nov 1	6.35	5.34	6.43	5.34	6.43	5.34
Nov 2	6.37	5.32	6.44	5.36	6.44	5.32

Young children and pregnant women are exempt. If you deliberately break the fast without a good reason, you must give a meal for 60 people or fast 60 further days. Those who are sick or travelling must make up any days they miss later on. No smoking is allowed in the daytime as swallowing any smoke would break the fast; likewise no toothpaste is allowed. You must behave extra well during this self-disciplining month and not talk in a vulgar way or refer to anyone behind their back.

So far as food is concerned, certain animals such as the pig are forbidden (haram) although the skin, bones and hair can be used. Tanning removes impurity. Beasts of prey are detestable (makruh). Farm animals must have their throats cut, in the name of Allah, so that they bleed, and wild animals must be killed as nearly as possible in the same way. There are four broad haram categories and six more detailed categories: (1) Animals which die naturally, (2) Flowing blood, as it is repugnant and dangerous, (3) Pork, as pigs eat offal and carry parasites, (4) Any animals slaughtered in the name of an idol, (5)–(9). Animals which have been strangled, beaten, fallen into gulleys, etc., gored, partially eaten by beasts – unless they are killed correctly before they die, (10) Animals sacrificed to idols. All fish are halal, as the sea cleans them. Intoxicating drinks (khamr) and drugs (except for medical purposes) are haram. The punishment for consuming them is 40–80 lashes.

Hajj statistics
1929: 1 Muslim in 4000 went (82 600). There were then 330 million Muslims.
1977: 1 Muslim in 1000 went (1 489 319). There were then 850 million.

91. *Is a period of fasting a good aid to humility? Why do Muslims succeed in keeping Ramadan better than Christians keep their Lent (period before Good Friday)?*

The Fifth Pillar: Hajj or Hadj (pilgrimage). Hajj literally means 'setting out for a definite purpose' and the place 'set out for' is Makkah. This is designed to purify you from your pride and prejudices and make you realize that everyone will be equal at the Day of Judgement. It is hoped that the spirit of companionship you will experience will be carried over into your daily life:

> *Make the pilgrimage and visit the Sacred House for His sake . . . Make the pilgrimage in the appointed month. He that intends to perform it in those months must abstain from sexual intercourse, obscene language, and bitter disputes while on the pilgrimage. Allah is aware of whatever good you do. Provide yourselves well; the best provision is piety.*
> (Surah 2:196)

You should go once in your life if you can afford it, and each year one to two million camp at Makkah in the twelfth month. Men and women wear special clothes to show that they are living in a consecrated state (ihram) of self-denial and total submission to Allah. Sixteen kilometres from Makkah, men must shave their heads and put on two white sheet-like garments, one around the waist and the other over the left shoulder. A woman may go only if accompanied by a male relative, and she wears a covering white garment.

92. *How does wearing special clothes help to fulfil the purpose of Hajj? Clue: Think of colour, class status, nationality.*

As you approach you call out 'Labbayk' ('I am here [God] at your service'). This greeting acts likes a password. After camping in the colossal pilgrim camp, the first thing to do is the tawaf (walk three times quickly and four times slowly) round the Ka'ba. This is a cube 15 m (48 ft) long, 10 m (32 ft) wide and 14 m (45 ft) high, and also known as the Bait-ul-lah, the House of God. It is said to be the first man-made structure built solely to worship one God. It is covered in a black cotton and silk cloth (kiswa) with the Qur'ān embroidered on it. This is renewed annually and pieces of the old cloth are given to distinguished guests. The Black Stone (Hajri Aswad), an oval of 18 cm (5 in) in diameter, mounted in the south-east corner, is traditionally said to have been received by Ishmael, or Ismāil, Ibrāhīm's son, from the angel Gabriel. Said to have once been on Adam's grave, it may be an ancient aerolite. It is said to have been white originally to guide pilgrims, but to have turned black owing to their sins. Every Muslim's ambition is to be part of the big ummah, or umma (the whole Muslim community), and to kiss the stone. Only special visitors are allowed inside the Ka'ba on one day a year. A recent pilgrim said that when he saw the Ka'ba he felt he was not on earth at all but on a different planet, so vivid was the experience of his pilgrimage to him.

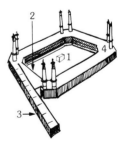

1. Ka'ba
2. Well of Zamzam
3. Covered way linking Safa and Marwa
4. Mosque

The hajj: above, a small part of the pilgrim camp; below, the Ka'ba. Each pilgrim is assigned to a mutawwif (courier), who has been allocated a block of tents in the tent city which fills the valley. All the 'streets' in the camp are numbered.

Stoning the devil.

The next thing you must do is to walk and jog 420 m seven times between the two little hills, Safa and Marwa, along one of the levels of the new double-deck covered way adjoining the mosque. The walkway includes a wheel-chair passageway. This is where Ishmael's mother, Hagar, had once run to and fro looking for water, only to find on return that her dying son had dug his toes in the sand and found water (the Well of Zamzam). The running is called the Sa'y. You go on to 21 km to Mount Arafat, the Mount of Mercy, where you meditate from noon to sunset. You stay overnight in the open at Muzdalifah and then return to Mina, a village east of Makkah, collecting 49 pebbles the size of peas on the way. At Mina you stone the devil (Jamrat, or Iblīs) by throwing them at the stone-pillars where the devil tempted Ishmael to disobey his father. It is believed that Ishmael threw stones then.

After this there is the Eid ul-Adha (Great Festival of Sacrifice) lasting four days. This is a thanksgiving feast in which sheep are sacrificed as Ibrāhīm sacrificed a sheep instead of his son (Gen. 22; Surah 37:100–111). Note that Muslims think it was Ishmael not Isaac who was to die (see p. 199).

Finally, you walk round the Ka'ba seven more times. Some men dye their beards red after the pilgrimage, and all can call themselves Hajjis (people who have made the pilgrimage). If you cannot afford to go, you give contributions for a substitute to go. He will bring merit to you for making his journey possible.

93. *Should Christians be encouraged to make a pilgrimage to Jerusalem once in their lives in the same way that Muslims go on the Hajj?*

94. *'You get what you deserve.'*
(a) Is this a just and loving way for God to treat you?
(b) What alternative rule could God apply to people's lives?
(c) Does 'You get what you deserve' help to ensure that Muslims take care to follow their faith properly every day of their lives?

95. *Draw a picture of the Ka'ba and underneath say where it is to be found and why it is so important to the Muslims.*

Clothing rules forbid men to wear gold (rings, watches, etc.) or silk, which are permitted for women. Women may not wear transparent or clinging clothes. Men may grow beards as they emphasize their manliness.

If you go to Makkah at any other time of the year, it is called a 'lesser pilgrimage', Umrah.

SIKHISM

Commandments. Guru Nanak's teachings included these points:
(1) There is only one God. Worship and pray to Him and no others
(2) Remember God, work hard and help others
(3) God is pleased with honest work and truthful living
(4) There is no rich, no poor, no black and no white, before God. It is your actions which make you good or bad
(5) Men and women are all equal before God
(6) Love everyone and pray for the good of all
(7) Be kind to people, animals and birds
(8) Fear not, frighten not
(9) Always speak the truth
(10) Be simple in your food, dress and habits
(11) God alone can measure His own greatness; what He gives we must treasure.

These are enlarged upon in Sikh holy writings to include other commandments. For example, idol worship is not allowed. Also forbidden is the caste structure, though this may be allowed in practice. Sikhs forbid anything superstitious such as black magic or omens, ancestor worship and the wearing of sacred thread (see pp. 202–4). These points show the Sikh's criticism of Hinduism. Sikhs may not cut their hair, partake of alcohol, tobacco or drugs, gamble or steal, or commit adultery.

Burn egoism, selfishness and avarice; remove impurity with the help of God's word; burn attachment, grind it down into ink powder. Wash the mind into clean papers ... Make God's love your pen, let your consciousness be the scribe ... All beings are born from the same light, how can some be good and some bad?

No Sikh is allowed to retire from life to become a hermit or monk. He follows Sahaj Yoga, the gradual process of union with God. He should meet the demands of family life. He should not criticize others for following their religions sincerely, as there is goodness in all religions: 'Words do not the saint or sinner make, action alone is written in the book of fate'.

96. *List any points you can find in the Sikh rules which suggest a particularly modern outlook.*

97. *What examples of (a) tolerance, (b) intolerance of other religions can you find?*

98. *Which are the Sikh rules designed to cope with the usual human weaknesses?*

99. *Do any Sikh rules particularly impress you? Give your reasons.*

Guru Nanak drew on what he saw was best in Hinduism and Islam, ruthlessly sweeping aside what he thought they had got wrong. Sikhs reject the Hindu meaning of maya (see p. 97). For them it is not the world which is maya (illusion), as it is God's creation. The illusion is that people can be self-centred whereas they need to be God-centred. The worst thing is to be too self-reliant, and this weakness is called haumai. Maya separates people from God and so is a trap for the soul. It makes people over-proud, seekers of pleasure and wealth. The dirt of maya accumulates through many births and isolates people from God. Religion is the real happiness, producing harmony with God and within oneself. If you are a self-centred person, you are manmukh; if a guru has enlightened you, so you are God-centred, you are gurmukh, or a jivan mukt.

You suffer in this life for two reasons. First, you have either not appreciated what God has created around you or you have forgotten his existence. Second, your mind is not under proper control and you allow yourself to keep thinking of worldly pleasures. So if you want to please God and obtain salvation, you will have to live in brotherhood with other Sikhs and be humble and tolerant. Just believing in God is not enough; you must prove it by your life. You must be prepared to die for your faith if need be. There are two paths open to you: that of Simran, concentration on God's name; and that of Seva (or Sewa), service to humanity.

You have to realize that the effects of your actions on earth will follow your soul like a shadow. The five main sins you must overcome are Kam (lust), Krodh (anger), Lobh (greed), Ahankar (pride), and Moh (over-attachment to people or things). 'My adversaries are five, and I am but one. How shall I defend my house, O Soul?' In fact you were once good, but evil has overshadowed your basic goodness. However, God's mercy will enable you to find your true self and overcome these problems provided you prove your devotion to God and do good.

Daily Worship. You are expected to get up early, wash and meditate on God. You must also recite the 38 verses of the Japji (a Guru Nanak hymn) and the Ardas (prayer recalling the lives of the gurus and those who died for Sikhism): 'beaten . . . shot, cut up or burnt alive with kerosene oil, but did not make any resistance . . . think of their patient faith . . .' The Ardas calls on God to aid them, to unite and humble them:

> May [Sikhism] find a loving place in our hearts and serve to draw our souls towards Thee. Save us, O Father, from lust, wrath, greed, undue attachment and pride . . . Grant . . . the gift of faith, the gift of confidence in Thee . . . grant that we may according to Thy will do what is right. Give us light, give us understanding . . . Forgive us our sins . . . Help us in keeping ourselves pure . . Through Nanak may Thy name forever be on the increase . . . Hail Khalsa of the Wonderful Lord who is always victorious.

This prayer performs the same role as the Jewish Shema and the Lord's Prayer in Christianity. You may use a woollen mala (rosary) to aid you in the meditation (Nam Simran, 'Calling God to mind'), saying 'Waheguru' ('Wonderful Lord') at each knot. In the evening you use the Rahiras (True Path or Evening Prayer) and at bedtime the Sohila Prayer (see p. 244). If you have a copy of the Guru Granth Sahib, you open it anywhere. A family facing problems will read the Guru Granth Sahib right through non-stop, reading in relays for 48 hours. Such a reading is called an Akhand Path.

A three-fold service, physical (tan), spiritual (man) and material (dhan), is required of you. Kirt (Kirat) karna is the term for the hard and honest physical work you must do. Your practical training will be sweeping the temple (gurdwara) floor, cleaning the utensils, and so on. Then you must help those in need and defend the weak. 'Useless the hands and the feet if they will not serve humanity.' Nam Japna (the remembrance of God's Name) requires you to serve others spiritually by telling them about God. So you must study the Guru Granth Sahib and read it completely every month or so. Praying for others is a spiritual service too. Materially you must give 10 per cent of your income in charity, bringing it to the gurdwara. This is called Wand Chakna (sharing your earnings). It will be used for communal means, hospitals, the poor, and so on. These three services will enable you to surrender your 'I-hood', yourself, to God's will. The Sikh Code of Discipline is called Rehat Maryada.

Pilgrimages. Sikhs do not believe in miracles or animal sacrifices, and they see no merit in fasting. They have no pilgrimage like the Islamic Hajj, but many go to visit the Golden Temple at Amritsar (see pp. 179–80). They will bathe there and file past the Guru Granth Sahib while hymns are sung from dawn until late at night.

100. *Sikhs believe all religions began with good intentions and are like different roads leading to the same destination. Do you agree with them now that you have followed these different routes in this chapter?*

101. *Sikhs welcome people of other religions to their services.*
     (a) Do other religions do this?
     (b) Should they do so?
     (c) Why might they not do so?

102. Guru Nanak voiced his criticism of Islam thus: 'The path of the true Yoga is found by dwelling in God while yet living in the midst of the world's temptations. Make mercy your mosque, faith your prayer mat, and righteousness your Qur'ān. Make humility your circumcision, uprightness your fasting and so you will be a Muslim.' Why do you think he said this and what is he trying to say? Do you agree with him?

103. Construct a road to find God by drawing on all you think is best in the various roads you have read about in this chapter. When you have done so, consider whether you have learnt more about (a) God and (b) yourself, your strengths and weaknesses, in doing so.

104. Tabulate the different religions under these headings: (a) Daily set prayers, (b) Ritual washing, (c) Pilgrimage, (d) Fasting, (e) Meditation, (f) Confessions, (g) Penances, (h) Sacrifices, (i) Communal meals.

105. Tabulate the rules given in this chapter by religions. Tick in the appropriate columns below:

God	Hindu	Shinto	Taoist	Buddhist	Judaic	Christian	Islamic	Sikh
One God								
Greatness of God								
No images								
No oath-taking								
Man's duties	**Hindu**	**Shinto**	**Taoist**	**Buddhist**	**Judaic**	**Christian**	**Islamic**	**Sikh**
Work hard								
Do not steal								
Do not covet								
Do not lie								
Do not kill								
Do not harm animals								
Do not drink alcohol								
Honour parents								
Treat all equally								
Love all								

Comment on anything striking or interesting in the result of this table.

106. Draw up your own set of rules on the assumption that you are a religious leader. Comment at the end on why you have chosen to insert some rules and leave out other possible ones.
    (a) Is 'being good' essential if you're to follow any religions?
    (b) How is 'being good' related to God?
    (c) Is it obedience or love which (i) does, (ii) should make you serve God by 'being good'?

107. *'One of the main consequences of pilgrimage for many people is a sense of urgency to do something more with their lives than they have done so far'* (Prof. J. Bowker). *Explain what the writer means and use examples of pilgrimages of different religions to support this viewpoint. Before you start your answer, consider how some places can fill one with a sense of peace, love and respect.*

6
WHERE AND HOW TO WORSHIP

If we study the structure of places of worship carefully we should be able to find out how they have been designed to serve their religion. Do they point to heaven in the sky? Do they stand out for miles around or merge into the natural background? Do they face a particular direction? Are they designed for worshippers to be mere spectators to a ritual performed by priests, or are they laid out for the congregation to play an active part? Do they make provision for sacrifices, or are they primarily places for preaching sermons? Are they meant to be places for gods to live in? Are they decorated to encourage and aid worship or plain so that worshippers are not distracted? What is the focal point in the building – an altar, a pulpit or a holy book? Remember these questions as you read on.

HINDUISM

The Hindu temple is called a mandir ('place of worship'). It may be of any size but is built to a definite plan so as to face the rising sun. Temples stand within a walled enclosure. As you enter with your back to the sun, the first thing you will meet is a large stone statue of the creature which is said to convey the temple's god around. For example you may see a lion for Durga to ride or a bull for Shiva. Then you go up some steps to the vimana (central sanctuary) and under the torana (entrance gateway) into the ardhamandapa (porch) before arriving at the mahamandapa or mandapa (corresponding to the nave). There you can sit on the floor to worship. Beyond is the adytum or garbagriha (the sanctuary or shrine room, also called the cella) where the god's image (murti) is kept. This is a smaller, dark room. It is normally kept shut and only priests may enter there to wash and dress the image, presenting it with flowers, incense, fruit, jewels or other offerings. It is believed that the god is in the image, as a ceremony to put his breath in it took place when it was set up. The image will be dressed in rich garments and have a golden crown on festival days. Above the shrine is the sikhara (pyramid tower) which represents a mountain, always considered a holy place. A pradakshina (processional passage) goes round the garbagriha, and worship may involve walking round and round the shrine. There will also be a large pool for worshippers to descend into for ritual washing. Gopurams (watch-tower gateways) are set in the outer wall and are decorated with scenes from Hindu stories.

If the temple is made of hard crystalline rock it will have little carving on it, but if it is made of soft stone it will be covered with countless figures. The climate too, affects the design. Sloping tiled roofs are needed for heavy rain areas in the west, while Himalayan temples have sloped wooden roofs to cope with snow. The hotter and drier the climate the flatter the roof.

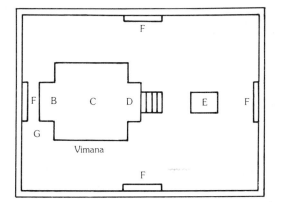

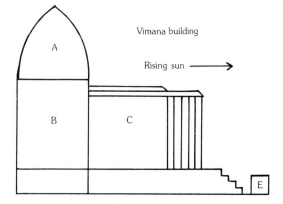

Hindu Temple or Mandir. Vertically, the temple represents the god's body with the sikhara as head and garbagriha as neck, mandapa as body and gopuram as feet. Write down the uses or meanings of the different parts.

Worship starts at dawn when the priests (pūjarīs) greet the awakening of the god, providing for his washing and refreshment before clothing him ready to receive worshippers. Marigolds and jasmin, fruit and incense will be presented. Music follows to entertain the god and then the worshippers come to offer their bhakti (devotion), by lighting a candle and saying prayers. Anjali, the putting of hands together and raising them to the forehead or chest, is done. As they leave, they are given prasad (sacred food) which has been offered to the god earlier in the day. In the evening, food and retiring-to-bed ceremonies are performed by the priests to the sound of bells and drums, and the image is bathed again.

Congregational acts of worship (pūjā) consist of three parts. Havan (offering of fire) involves the priest kindling a sacred fire on a portable fire-altar, called a havan kund. Wood, camphor and ghee (melted butter) are used. Sections of the Vedas are recited. ('Let us meditate upon the most excellent light of the radiant sun; may he guide our minds.') The fire represents the mouth of the god devouring the offerings in the smoke. Prayers for purity follow and the priest ceremonially washes himself by touching each part of his body as he says, 'Let my tongue have speaking power, ears have the power of hearing, the nose inhaling power and the eyes seeing power. May the arms and thighs have strength and all the limbs be full of energy'. The worshippers copy him. Arti (the worship of light) involves the use of a flat tray with five candles on it representing the elements (see pp. 157, 159, 187, 207). It is waved in front of the shrine. At the same time, incense and flowers representing the earth are presented, a fan is waved to represent the air, and a conch shell is sounded to stand for ether. Another element, water, is contained in the shell. A spot of red paste is put on the foreheads of the statues of the gods before the arti dish is passed round for

A linga (image) representing Shiva. Water is poured over it, flowers are draped round it. The base is called a yoni.

people to pass their hands over the flames and then over their heads. This enables them to receive the gods' blessing and power. Prasad is then given out. It means 'favour', as the god has favoured worshippers by allowing them to eat his left-over food. It gives peace, and destroys pain and sins. It is the antidote for misery and anxiety provided you have faith. Finally, the singing of bhajans (hymns) follows. Bells, tambourines, triangles and other instruments will be used and people clap too. Dancing is another form of worship which may be used. There will be readings from the Gītā, called Gītā Path. The prayer for peace, 'OM, O God, let there be peace, peace, peace', ends the service. You must remember that Hindus consider that a ritual properly performed has tremendous creative power, whereas if a flow or mistake is made that power may backlash and make everything go wrong. A Hindu uses a japa mala, a rosary of 108 beads. It is calculated that a person breathes 21 600 times a day, equivalent to saying a rosary 200 times, each bead being one breath or repetition of the Mother of the Vedas.

Temple attendance in India is not expected of every Hindu, only those who have chosen such attendance as their path. They may go to have darshana (sight) of the god in his image. But in Britain the temple has taken on a new role, for it has become the focal point for the community and a social centre too. The bhajan mandal, a kind of 'rock mass' of singing and praying, has put new life into temple worship, as well as a fresh focus on the cult of gurus. Sunday is now the day for attendance.

1. Draw a plan of a Hindu temple, naming the parts.

2. What does the daily ritual care of the god's image suggest is the Hindu belief about a god's life?

SHINTOISM

The Shinto shrine is called a jinja (literally 'kami house'). They are erected on sites chosen by the kami, that is, places that give a clear sense of the sacred. The shrine is put up to enshrine the kami. Compare Jacob's stone in the Bible, Genesis 28. Notice the difference compared to Christian churches, named after saints who are *not* believed to live in them.

Jinjas are often tiny huts beside a road or a factory or even on top of a large building and they look like little houses. The larger ones are set in the midst of trees, near the sea or on a hill. The aim is to blend them with the landscape. They usually face east (never north, as that is death's side). An avenue of trees leads up to the haiden (hall of worship) which is large and open on all sides to receive worshippers. Along the avenue will be one or more arches called torii (literally 'bird perches'). These have praises to the god on them, and are usually made of wood but sometimes of stone, bronze or concrete. Worshippers bow and salute them as they pass. Across them are hung shimenawa (sacred twisted rice-straw ropes). Toro (stone lanterns) also mark the route. Komainu (Korean dogs) and karashishi (Chinese lions) guard the god-house. The washing pavilion (temizuya) has a stone basin and wooden dippers for worshippers to rinse their mouths and pour water over their fingers.

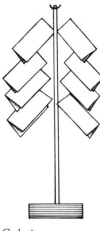

Komainu.

Gohei.

In the haiden Shintoists put gohei, which are small poles with strips of white, gold, silver, red or blue paper, metal or cloth folded into a plait design to the gods. In the heiden (hall of offering) the priests say prayers and make their offerings. The principal shrine is called the honden; it has a small upstairs room where the god lives. Only priests may enter the honden where the mitama-shiro (spirit substitute), a mirror or cloth representing the god, is kept. A mirror symbolizes brightness and purity. The room is otherwise bare except for curtains, branches of the holy sakaki tree, vessels for gifts, and a mat for the priest to sit on. The jinja will also have space for ceremonial dances to be performed, called a kagura-den. Shimenawa ropes mark off every sanctified object or piece of holy ground within the jinja to keep away evil spirits. Pieces of paper hang from these ropes.

Futaarasan Jinja, Nikko. Draw a sketch of this picture and name (a) Torii, (b) Shimenawa, (c) Toro.

The most famous shrine is that to Amaterasu, the sun goddess, at Isé. It is rebuilt every 20 years, the next renewal being due in 1993. In 1973 the eight-year task was completed by 200 000 craftsmen using 13 600 cypress trees and 12 000 bamboo poles at a cost of £7½ million. No nails are used. Renewal is necessary to preserve its purification. It contains a sacred mirror sent to earth by the goddess's grandson. Amaterasu is regarded as the ancestress of the Japanese imperial family. An outer shrine (geku) is dedicated to Inari, the food god. It is set in 200 acres of cedars. This shrine and its torii are painted bright red. Stone and wooden foxes, with keys, or texts, in their mouths, are everywhere, since they act as the god's messengers. The prime minister and cabinet visit Isé once a year and after the formation of a new government.

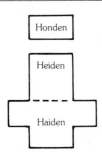

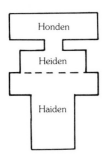

Jinja designs.

Shinto priest. What is he holding in his hand?

3. *Japanese shrines are rebuilt even though they physically do not need to be rebuilt. In England people preserve the crumbling stones of Norman churches. What lies behind these different approaches to places of worship?*

At the Fushimi-inari shrine to Inari at Kyoto there are 10 000 torii, many 3 m high, donated by worshippers hoping to get rich from this agricultural and business god. Worshippers pay for young girls (miko) to dance for the god. The Meiji shrine at Tokyo is set among 120 000 trees, and honours the Emperor Meiji (1867–1912).

Since the government ceased to supervise the shrines in 1945, many have opened community centres, with playground facilities. They also offer social welfare help for worshippers if asked.

There are 21 000 priests, of whom 480 are women, in charge of 16 674 jinjas. Most of them are part-timers. Their main function is to worship and serve the kami so as to keep the world on good relations with them. They provide divine protection for people and objects by means of harai purification (see p. 104). They do not preach. They are expected to marry and have children. High priests are called guji and their assistants are negi, while juniors are shuten. Women priests were introduced in World War II, when as priests' wives they often had to care for the jinjas. Priests carry wooden sceptres called shaku, or shaken, which are purely ornamental. Their kari ginu robes (literally 'hunting robes') vary in colour according to their age and the season of the year. They wear huge black clogs.

Miko are girl attendants who serve the shrine for five years on leaving school. They work long hours for little pay as dancers, musicians, secretaries and servants. They are usually priests' daughters. They wear white surplice-style kimonos and vermilion divided skirts and carry cypress fans.

Daily worship (nikku) involves the white-robed priests renewing the sakaki branches, making offerings as they perform their ritual with handclappings to arouse the kami. Otherwise all is quiet as Shintoists believe rituals should be quiet and solemn – in sharp contrast to the performance of lively songs and dances about myths for the lay worshippers in their part of the jinjas.

There is no congregational worship. Individual worshippers stand in front of a shrine, pull a white cord to ring a bell to get the kami's attention, and throw 'homage' coins into a box. They clap their hands (kashiwade) twice to alert the kami and then bow to pray. They can purchase wooden ema (see pp. 102, 150) on which to write their prayers before hanging them up with hundreds of others. They can give offerings too. They can buy charms to drive off evil spirits, or to ensure good harvests or successful business deals. They can shake a box of sticks, pull one out, check its number and collect a printed sheet (o-mikuji) with predictions and warnings on it. It is customary to knot the paper round a twig. A 1970 survey showed that 66 per cent of men and 75 per cent of women got a feeling of inner renewal after visiting a shrine.

4. *Draw a plan of a jinja and its avenue, naming the parts.*

5. *Draw (a) a tori, (b) a toro, (c) a komainu.*

6. *Jinjas are deliberately designed to blend with their natural surroundings*

rather than stand out, and they are modestly constructed of wood. Why do you think Shintoists prefer shrines of this kind?

7. *What is the value of charms? Do you or your friends carry any? What are they and why do you trust them?*

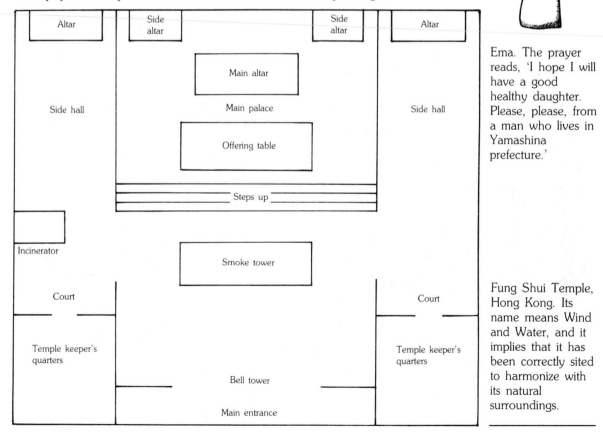

TAOISM

The Taoist temple is called a kuan ('to look') if it is a small one with one priest, and a kung ('palace') if it contains a community of priests under an abbot. A wall keeps evil spirits from the Pai lou (portal of honour) and the marble entrance which opens out into the first courtyard. On both sides are towers or pavilions, one with a bell, struck at 6 a.m., and the other a huge drum, struck at 6 p.m.

In the two opposite corners are two more pavilions with inscribed pillars which stand on turtle or dragon statues. Through a large gateway guarded by gigantic lion statues, you come to another courtyard, followed by several more. Each courtyard is enclosed on its north side by a temple dedicated to a god or holy man. Courtyards also contain huge bronze bowls and incense burners on tripods. Long spirals of incense, looking like bed springs, hang down above the worshippers' heads. The spiral of incense takes two weeks to burn and you tie your prayers on to it when you purchase it. Libraries, refectories and dormitories for priests complete the building. The temple-keeper's shop will sell joss sticks and paper money and he will tell fortunes and interpret signs.

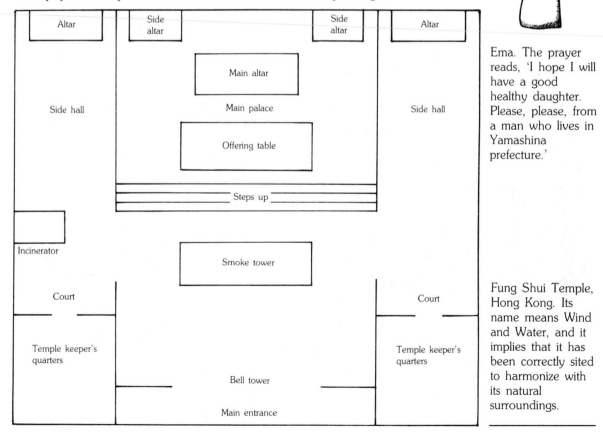

Ema. The prayer reads, 'I hope I will have a good healthy daughter. Please, please, from a man who lives in Yamashina prefecture.'

Fung Shui Temple, Hong Kong. Its name means Wind and Water, and it implies that it has been correctly sited to harmonize with its natural surroundings.

155

Incense spiral.

The Ching Chung Koon temple in Hong Kong has a clinic, accommodation for the elderly and schools attached. It organizes flower competitions and has a popular restaurant to help cover its running costs. In some rooms there are rows of cremation urns, but the latest procedure is to put the ashes in small lockers in the wall and have a photograph of the deceased on the locker's door (see pp. 234–5).

The village temple (miao) in Taiwan is a social and cultural as well as a religious centre. It is run by a lay committee who employ priests to perform the rituals. The most famous temple is the Temple of Heaven at Peking, where the emperor used to offer sacrifices. It is different from other kuans and its double red wall encloses 5000 cypresses. It is divided into the Hall of Annual Prayers for Good Harvests, the Hall of the God of the Universe and the Altar of Heaven. The Hall of Prayer has a three-tiered roof of blue tiles; here the emperor spent one night a year in fasting and prayer. The Altar of Heaven is approached by three terraces – for man, earth and heaven. Incense was burnt and an ox sacrificed while the emperor, the 'Son of Heaven', stood in holy ecstasy.

A Taoist kuan.

Worship. People go to kuans to burn incense and candles and offer prayers. They bring bananas or a chicken and purchase paper money to burn for ancestors, and joss sticks for their own devotion. They hold the burning sticks in both hands and bow to the altar, and shake the sticks before placing them in an urn. If they want some question about marriage or business answered, for example, they cast divining blocks on the floor. Each block is convex (yang) on one side and flat (yin) on the other. If one falls with the convex side upwards and the other with the flat side upwards, the answer is 'yes'. How these fall indicates what the worshippers should do – this is an example of divination. Divination is also performed as well as exorcism. Beggars sleep in the courtyard as it is thought a good thing to die in a god's presence. Temples also serve as schools and relief distribution centres.

On a god's birthday the temple is crowded. Many candles are lit and incense is burnt. Drums, gongs and crackers sound, and the images of the god are carried in palanquins (god-carriages) in processions. There is so much firecracker smoke that a man with a small bellows follows each palanquin.

8. Draw a plan of a Taoist temple.

9. Compare Shinto and Taoist temple construction and the uses made of them.

Buddhist temples vary in design from one country to another. They are usually built to symbolize the Five Elements.

Theravāda temples. In India temples are called stūpas (mounds). They were originally relic chambers, housing bones, hair or clothing of the Buddha or his leading followers. In Sri Lanka they are called dāgobas (relic chambers). They are bell-shaped and still contain relics of the Buddha or his followers, but are otherwise solid. Their three rings represent the Three Refuges and the dome the Buddha's teaching, while above is a four-sided enclosure for the Four Noble Truths and an eight-ringed spire for the Eightfold Path and a conical pin for Nibbana. They can be enormous, 70 m (230 ft) high for example. The Abhoyagiriya Dāgoba has enough bricks to build a wall 3 m (9.8 ft) high from London to Edinburgh.

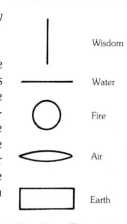

The Five Elements.

In Thailand temples are called chedis or wats (worship centres). There are 23 700 of them, varying in size from single rooms to great monasteries. The people give about a tenth of their incomes to support them so no fund-raising is needed. They are built and maintained by voluntary labour. Their courtyards are covered with sand brought in by locals as a form of merit-making. This ensures that they remain above flood level in a land of floods. The main hall usually faces east as the Buddha faced east when he sat under the bodhi tree, and a big bodhi tree grows in the wat. If possible it is from a sapling of the original tree. Some chedis have huge dome-topped towers, prangs, dedicated to the Hindu Shiva.

1 Stūpa in India.

2 Dāgoba in Sri Lanka.

3 Wat in Thailand.

4 Pagoda in Burma.

Theravāda Buddhist places of worship. What is the difference between a stūpa and a dāgoba? What are the meanings of wat and pagoda?
(a) 'umbrellas', symbols of honour, (b) relic put inside here, (c) terrace for walking round in homage.

Burmese temples are called pagodas (relic chambers), and they vary in size. They often are white-washed conical buildings. The Golden Pagoda in Rangoon is 61 m (200 ft) high, taller than St Paul's Cathedral, London. It is covered with gold leaf and has 25 tonnes of pure gold statues. It has four main entrances leading to long flights of stairs to chapels, each containing pure gold Buddhas. Large courtyards and small chapels contain countless other Buddhas, many of which are the property of families. The hairs of the Buddha, a sandal and robes of previous Buddhas are kept in a barred basement. In the town of Pagān there are 5000 pagodas.

Theravāda devotion. In the temples there is a steady stream of worshippers. Flowers, paper lamps and incense are everywhere. Pagodas and wats are surrounded by stalls selling paper umbrellas, flowers, joss sticks, images, rosaries, and flat bells. The bells are sounded when gifts are presented. Worshippers remove their shoes, bow, kneel and prostrate themselves with the palms of their hands together in front of their foreheads, and say the Three Refuges. Gifts are brought to the Three Jewels, namely the Buddha, Dhamma (the vehicle representing teaching of the Buddha) and the Sangha (the community of monks). In some cases worshippers throw two horseshoe-shaped pieces of red wood to see which way they will fall and then pull a spill from a wooden box and look at the number of it. The official gives them a printed sheet from a drawer with the same number on it, and this has the answer to the question about the future which they sought – or worshippers may rattle a vase of sticks and pull one out. Alternatively, worshippers may spin the golden wheel of life with its 28 sections and take the paper from the drawer below where it stops.

Worship is individual and not congregational, although there is the exception of great temples like the Temple of the Sacred Tooth of the Buddha, Kandy, Sri Lanka, which do have daily pūjā, communal worship. Drummers make deafening noises and trumpets are sounded. Yellow and white flowers are given to monks who place them on a silver altar containing the tooth.

Mahāyāna temples. Chinese pagodas, 9–13 floors high, are often on sites determined by omens. They are not places of regular worship, and are separate from monasteries with their temples (szes). These buildings have halls with alcoves for Bodhisattas with tables of flowers and incense before them. The first hall might contain the Four Lords of Heaven, huge bright colourful images. Metteyya, or Maitreya ('the Buddha-to-come') holds in one hand a bag of fortune and in the other a rosary, each bead of which represents 1000 years which he spent doing good in previous lives. The Golden Hall will contain the Buddhist triad ('three precious ones'): Shakyamuni (a title for Gotama, meaning, sage of the Shākya tribe), Amida or O-Mi-T'o-Fu (Lord of the Western Paradise) and Wen-shu (Lord of Knowledge and Meditation).

Pagoda in China. A Japanese or Chinese pagoda's structure balances from a central axis from the top, instead of being built up from the stone base. This enables it to withstand typhoons and earthquakes.

10.   Draw a stūpa, a dāgoba, a wat and a Chinese pagoda.

The szes are always aligned south to north, and their layout is similar to Taoist ones but with an extra 'the Buddha Comes' room in the main courtyard. Monks' quarters are included. Pagodas in Japan and China are only part of a temple's complex. Scenes of the Buddha's life can be seen through the windows but the pagoda cannot be entered.

In Tibet, pagodas are called chortens (funeral pyres). They are situated in monasteries, beside roads and on hilltops. They may contain a relic or a memorial to a saint. On a plinth representing earth stands a solid dome for water, crowned by a spire for fire, a crescent for air, and a solar disc as space. Chortens may have two eyes painted on the base if they guard gateways.

11. Draw a chorten and label the Five Elements on it.

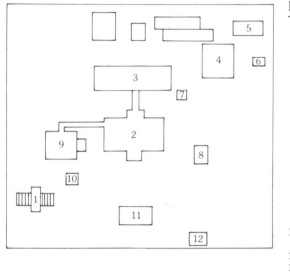

Plan of Chion-in Pure Land Temple, Kyoto, Japan.

1. Sanmon - main gate 27 m (90 ft) wide, 1619
2. Miedō - Memorial hall to Hōnen, 53 m × 42 m (174 × 140 ft), 1639
3. Shūedo - Assembly hall, 23.7 m × 44.5 m (78 × 146 ft), 1639
4. Ohōjō - Guesthouse, 36.5 m × 26.5 m (120 × 87 ft), 1639
5. Kohojo - Guesthouse, 24 m × 21 m (79 × 69 ft), 1639
6. Seishido - Bodhisatta hall, 1530
7. Bussokuseki - Marble stone imprinted, with the Buddha's soles
8. Kyozo - Library with 5600 books, 1619
9. Amidado - Amida Hall, 1910
10. Rēto pagoda to 7½ million spirits, 1959
11. Taiheitei - Peace Hall, 1958
12. Daishō - Bell tower with 67½-tonne bell cast in 1633

Chion-in's archbishop Jitsuo Fujii in golden robes.

Mahāyāna devotion. In Tibet worshippers can gain merit by walking round a chorten clockwise and chanting texts. Prayer wheels are everywhere, ranging from small hand ones for use as you walk, to huge ones 2 m (6.5 ft) high. The large ones have bells on them. Paper prayer wheels turn slowly over candle flames in the temple. They are inscribed with texts. Prayer walls and prayer flags have texts and pictures of gods.

Buddhist prayer wheels in Nepal. In Birmingham, the Karma Ling sect have made a unique electric-powered prayer wheel.

Chorten in Tibet.

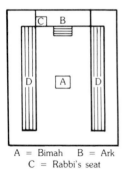

A = Bimah   B = Ark
C = Rabbi's seat
D = Congregation

Synagogue plan.

Monks maintain daily rituals, and people join in by lighting joss sticks, setting the prayer wheels going, and walking round the shrines. Gongs are sounded as they make their offerings. Large rosaries with 108 beads for 108 worldly passions or 54 for the steps to becoming a Bodhisatta (twice 54 as a large bead in the middle represents the Buddha) are used by monks and smaller ones by lay people.

12. *Comment on the form of worship which goes on in Buddhist temples. What is the point behind the different things which are done?*

JUDAISM

Synagogues. Jews worship in synagogues ('synagogue' means 'bringing together'), which were originally called beth ha knesset ('house of assembly'). The library section is known as shul (shool), or the bet ha midrash ('house of study'). At one time it would have been a separate building. Synagogues can be of any shape – for example, oblong, round or octagonal – and seats may face the ark or inwards. The holy ark is at the end facing towards Jerusalem. It is a cupboard (Aron Hakodesh – Holy Ark) containing the Torah on a scroll, with a curtain (parochet) in front (Exod. 26:31–34). Above the Ark are two tablets with the first two words of each of the Ten Commandments on them. At the central point of the service the Torah scroll will be carried in procession to the bimah (reading desk) so that it can be read (Neh. 8:2–8). The scroll is mounted on two wooden rollers ('trees of life') with silver heads and bells on the crown which represent God's sovereignty. It is wrapped in velvet with a breast plate to represent the High Priest's breastplate. The Torah is handwritten in Hebrew. As it is taken from the Ark the words, 'This is the Law of Moses set before the Children of Israel,' are said, and, when it is returned, 'It is a tree of life to them that grasp it'. Torah scrolls which become too worn for further use are buried. In front of the Ark is the ner tamid (lamp of perpetual light: Exod. 27:20–21) which burns continually to represent the continuity of Jewish tradition and God's presence.

In Orthodox synagogues men and women sit separately and singing is unaccompanied in a seated position. Jews stand for prayers as humans are created in God's image and have superiority over animals. It would be unthinkable for God to kneel. Chasidim Jews rock and shake as they pray to interpret the Scripture passage, 'Love your God with all your heart and all your might'. The lockers under the men's seats are for Orthodox Jews' talliths, so they do not have to 'work' in carrying them on the Sabbath. Services are in Hebrew.

In Liberal synagogues both sexes sit together and an organ accompanies the singing. Tefillin and talliths are not usually worn in Liberal synagogues. Their main service, held in English, is on Friday evenings, and its highlight is a sermon. Reform Jews sometimes have family seating and an organ, but not always. They may have a sermon or a Torah discussion, but their service is mainly in Hebrew.

Worship. The rabbi is the Law expert. He is not a priest but a community teacher, so he will preach but not necessarily lead the service. He should marry and have children, as an example to others. There may be a cantor, chazan, or hazan (a musical and ritual expert) to lead the singing. This is particularly important in Orthodox synagogues as they have no organs. For a service to take place there must be a minimum (minyan) ten adult males present. These represent (among other things) the Ten Commandments, ten plagues, ten days of penitence, and Abraham's ten tests. Worshippers on entering say, 'As for me, in the abundance of thy loving kindness will I come unto thy house'. Men wear hats or kipa (skull caps) in reverence, as well as their talliths.

The weekly Sabbath service lasts two hours. The siddur (prayer book) service opens with the reading of psalms, before the cantor sings about God's help for the Jews in the past (e.g. deliverance from Egyptian slavery). He then sings God's blessing before the climax is reached with the Shema ('hear') from Deut. 6:4–9, 'Hear, O Israel, the Lord your God, the Lord is One . . .' which is the Jewish statement of belief.

The Amidah ('standing') prayer follows with people standing facing the Ark. On the Sabbath this prayer is one of praise, but on weekdays it recalls the Eighteen Blessings, such as knowledge, forgiveness, good crops, punishing the wicked and rebuilding Jerusalem. When the Third Blessing, Kedusha, is said some Jews

The Sefer or Sepher Torah is carried to the Bimah in Djerba Sem synagogue. The Torah is an oriental style one in a wooden case. Notice the crowns and bells and the men's talliths. What is the mood of the congregation?

161

rise on their toes, as it hallows God's name. The doors of the Ark are opened and the Torah is carried from it. Men touch it with their talliths and then kiss them. Members of the congregation are called to the reading of the Torah. They stand beside the reader who points to the place with a special silver or ivory pointer (yad) as he reads. The whole Torah will be read through a year of Sabbath services. The cantor will then read a matching portion from the Haftarah ('conclusion', 'completion'), which is a selection of the Prophets. Further prayers are said before the scrolls are returned to the Ark. At this point the rabbi may preach a sermon. Another Amidah is said and the Kaddish (sanctification) prayer follows, beginning 'Magnified and sanctified be His great Name in the world which He hath created according to His will. May He establish His kingdom during your life . . .' To this the people reply, 'Let His name be blessed for ever and for all eternity'. Sabbaths and festivals end with the Havdalah (differentiation) ceremony marking God's distinguishing of holy and profane, Israel and other lands, the Sabbath and the six days of creation. It is a prayer recited over wine, spices and candles.

Several rabbis may unite to form a beth din, which is a house of law or court. It licenses kosher butchers after inspecting their premises and issues a certificate for them to display. It also issues divorce documents ('gets') if a marriage really breaks down.

13.   Draw a plan of a synagogue.

14.   Why is the Torah held in so much reverence?

15.   A rabbi must marry and have a family; a Roman Catholic priest must stay single. Give arguments for and against both rules, and say why you prefer one of them.

16.   Explain how the actions of worship in the synagogue may help to remind Jews of the importance of the Torah.

CHRISTIANITY

Orthodox churches. The plan is basically that of a cross with a dome above the centre. There are usually no chairs in the nave (congregational area) as the worshippers stand to pray. The choir is out of sight in the transepts (side arms of the cross). Round the walls and on the iconostasis (screen of wood, stone) are icons which are paintings of Jesus, the apostles and saints done in bright colours. There are no statues as they might be taken as idols. The icons on the iconostasis may have a message depicted, such as God rescuing Man from sin. The icon on the left of the royal doors in the centre will show the incarnation (Jesus born of Mary on earth) while the one on the right side will show the promised second coming of Christ to earth in glory and power. This means that when the communion bread and wine are brought through the doors to the congregation the fact that Christ *is* in the Church in the communion elements is stressed, so linking the two icons on either side of the doors.

At certain times during the service the scarlet curtain (symbol of the Jerusalem Temple curtain) is pulled back and the door opened to show that God has opened the way for man to be united with Him. Behind the doors is the holy table or throne, a sign of God's presence. Beyond this is the bishop's seat. Only priests may enter this part of the building.

The main service is the liturgy which means 'people's work of thanks to God'. When a worshipper arrives he will buy a candle, and put it before an icon, which he kisses, before crossing himself. The icons will help him to concentrate on his prayers. The choir sings unaccompanied. The first part of the liturgy is the liturgy of the word and it consists of prayers and Bible readings. The climax comes with a priest carrying the Book of the Gospels (stories of Jesus' life) raised high above his head as he comes through the royal doors to the nave. He then reads passages before returning through the screen. The second part, the liturgy of the

Worship in an Orthodox church. The patriarch is facing the congregation. Where is the iconostasis?

163

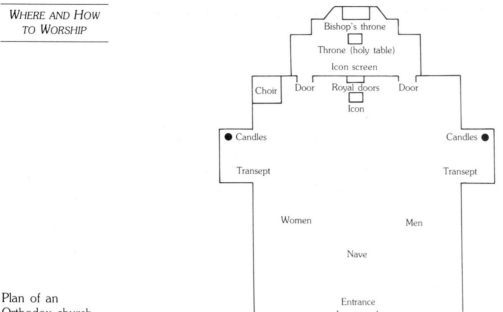

Plan of an
Orthodox church.

faithful, is the preparation of the bread and wine for Communion at the holy table behind the closed royal doors. After the bread and wine are blessed he comes through the doors to give a portion of bread dipped in wine to the communicants.

17. Draw a plan of an Orthodox church and name the parts.

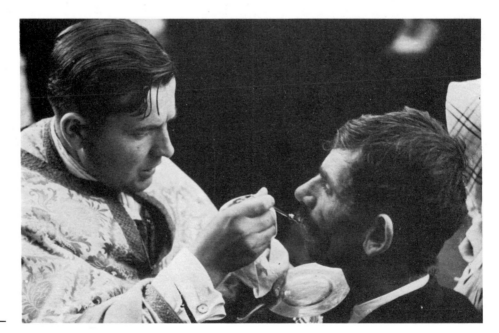

Communion in an
Orthodox church.

18. *Why do you think the blessing of the bread and wine takes place behind the screen?*

19. *Are icons likely to be a better aid to worship and meditation than statues?*

A censer.

Roman Catholic churches. The church is usually in the shape of a cross or an oblong. At the centre of the east end will be the High Altar with cross and candlesticks on it. The choir stalls will probably be near it and so too will be the lectern, an elaborate stand for the Bible, and the pulpit, where the priest stands when he delivers the sermon. An organ will accompany the singing. Round the building will be a number of side chapels, one of which will be dedicated to the Blessed Virgin Mary, Jesus' mother. All priests must say Mass (Communion) daily. Confession cubicles will be placed in convenient places. A font for baptizing new members will stand near the entrance. On the walls will be pictures or carved scenes showing the 14 stages of Jesus' last hours until the crucifixion. Statues of Mary and saints will be surrounded by candles lit by the faithful who have asked their help. A tabernacle (cupboard) behind the altar or in a side chapel will contain the Blessed Sacrament (consecrated bread) to mark Jesus' presence. A light will always be kept burning in front of it.

When a worshipper enters he will cross himself with holy water from a stoup (basin) and genuflect (bend one knee to the floor and bow) towards the altar. He will kneel in prayer. The priest will stand behind the altar facing the congregation

Two styles of Roman Catholic church:
(a) traditional,
(b) modern 'round' at Clifton, Bristol.

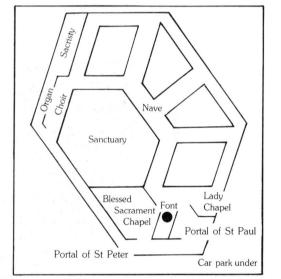

P = Pulpit
L = Sanctuary light indicating presence of Blessed Sacrament
S = Stoup containing holy water
F = Font
T = Tabernacle for consecrated bread

Priest breaking the Host while recalling the events of the Last Supper.

to say Mass. All confess their sins using a set prayer before the priest pardons them. Chants such as 'Glory to God in the highest' are sung and there are readings from the Old Testament, an Epistle (letter from an apostle to be found in the New Testament) and the Gospel ('good news' from Jesus' life on earth). A homily (helpful talk) is given and the Nicene Creed (statement of beliefs) is recited. The offertory (bread, water, wine) is presented at the altar. As the Host (bread or wafer) and the wine are blessed a bell is rung three times. Catholics believe that the bread and wine are mystically transformed into the Body and Blood of Christ. This belief is called transubstantiation, as the substances (bread and wine) are transformed. (In contrast, Protestants believe the bread and wine simply represent Christ. This is known as consubstantiation.) The celebrant (priest) consumes some himself before the Host (and sometimes the wine too) is given to those who come forward to the altar. All Catholics must attend Mass on Sundays. The Catholic prayer book is called the Missal.

20. *Draw a plan of a cruciform (in the shape of a cross) Roman Catholic church.*

21. *Why do you think the church has statues to saints and scenes of Jesus' crucifixion story? Can you see why some people would find this helpful whereas others would not?*

22. *Bishops in the Orthodox Church and priests in the Roman Catholic Church are not allowed to marry. Do you think this rule makes sense today?*

In recent years round buildings have been introduced – for example, the cathedrals in Liverpool and Bristol. These emphasize the family of Christ gathering round the altar.

Church of England. Churches are usually in the shape of a cross or oblong, but some are round, like modern Roman Catholic churches. Most churches have a stone altar at the east end with choir stalls between it and the congregation. New layouts often involve a wooden Communion table in the centre, so emphasizing a change of attitude towards the Communion service from one of humble offering to one of communal meal. A lectern, pulpit, font and organ complete the essential features of the building. There may be one or two side chapels. The windows may contain stained glass scenes from the Bible or of worthy Christians. Memorial tablets to the dead may cover the walls but these are not the objects of worship.

The worshipper kneels for a few moments on entering. There are three basic services: Communion (at 8 a.m., or mid-morning when it is called 'Parish Communion'), Matins (morning service) and Evensong (evening service). These services include Bible readings as laid down in lectionary (list of readings for the Christian year) and usually a sermon. Communal singing and saying prayers may form a prominent part of all these, with a robed choir giving a lead. Sometimes Matins is replaced by a family service in which children participate.

The Communion service is in many ways similar to the Catholic one except that incense and bells are rarely used and all communicants receive the wine as well as the bread. Whereas the 1662 *Book of Common Prayer* Communion consecration prayer (when the bread and wine are blessed to mark Jesus' body and blood sacrifice) stressed the suffering of Jesus on the cross and the individual's personal, humble approach to God when receiving the bread and wine, the new *Alternative Service Book* (the ASB) returned to the original teaching with its Third Eucharastic Prayer of 215 CE. This stresses the importance of God's creation and Christ's resurrection, and the need for all Christians to join in a community meal. In turn, this suggests 'spiritual food' is given for members in their life's task of proclaiming the Gospel. This restoration of the community atmosphere of 'being a Christian' is also brought out by the 'Giving of the Peace', involving people clasping each other by both hands and saying, 'The peace of the Lord be with you'. (Compare the Islamic giving of the peace at the end of each rakat, p. 141.)

People come forward to kneel at the chancel rail before the altar, where the priest has blessed the bread and wine. When they receive them the priest may say 'The Body of our Lord Jesus Christ' and 'The Blood of our Lord Jesus Christ'. Some members accept the Catholic belief about the bread and the wine, whereas others believe that the service primarily commemorates the Last Supper and no miraculous change occurs. For most believers, the bread and wine have a special significance, just as a wedding ring signifies not just a gold ring, but the love and care of one's spouse. Some take Communion weekly, others less frequently, and a few daily. Services end with the benediction, a blessing by the priest in the name of God, the Father, Son and Holy Spirit.

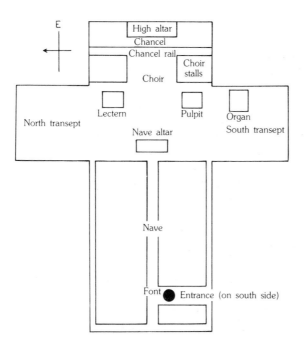

Church of England plan. Why is the font near the door? Who sits in the nave?

THE CHURCH OF ENGLAND'S CLOTHES – THE VESTMENTS

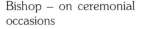

Bishop – on ceremonial
occasions

Bishop – for everyday
services

1   ALB – long white linen garment reaching to the ankles, from ancient tunic.

2   AMICE – a linen square worn round the neck to protect the other vestments. Often decorated.

3   APPARELS – ornamental panels at the foot of the alb, front and back, and on amice.

4   CASSOCK – the long black gown worn under other vestments. It used to be the day-to-day working clothes of the clergy. A bishop's cassock is purple.

5   CHASUBLE – worn by priests when celebrating the Holy Communion.

6   CHIMERE – of black or scarlet, open in front, worn by bishops over the rochet.

7   COPE – a long cloak, worn by bishops on occasions such as Confirmations or Ordinations, and by priests in processions on Festivals, etc.

8   CROZIER – shepherd's crook, as Jesus is the Good Shepherd.

9   GIRDLE – a cord used to secure the alb or cassock round the waist.

10   HOOD — worn by clergy at choir offices (Matins and Evensong, etc.) worn hanging down the back. It denotes an academic degree.

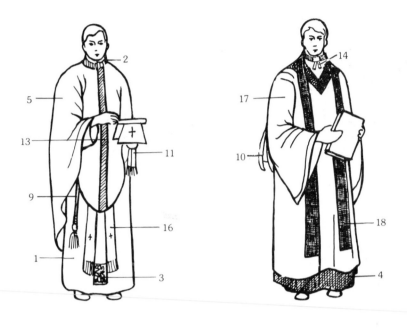

Priest – taking the Eucharist

Priest – taking morning or
evening services

11 MANIPLE – originally a napkin. It is worn over the left arm by bishops, priests and deacons at the Eucharist. Used to cleanse the vessels after the stole had developed as described below.

12 MITRE – the head-dress of a bishop. Mitres are tongue-shaped because of the tongues of fire which lighted on the Apostles at Pentecost.

13 ORPHREYS – the embroidered strips, usually cross-shaped, on a chasuble.

14 PREACHING BANDS – two white linen tabs represent the Ten Commandments.

15 ROCHET – worn by bishops. It is like an alb, but is used without girdle or apparels.

16 STOLE – was once a napkin or towel carried by servants on the left shoulder. It became folded and narrow. As the deacon's duty was to cleanse the sacred vessels they wear it over the left shoulder. Priests wear the stole over both shoulders.

17 SURPLICE – of white linen reaching to the knees. It is worn by choir and servers as well as clergy.

18 TIPPET – the black scarf worn with the hood for morning and evening services.

Church of England
Sunday sermon.

In cathedrals (main churches where a bishop is based) the choir sings the services daily and the ritual is more elaborate.

23. *Draw a plan of a Church of England church.*

24. *List the things which are not in a Church of England church but which are in a Roman Catholic one. Comment on the list.*

25. *The communion service is now much less of a 'spectator' service for the congregation and more of a communal one.*
    (a) Why do you think this change has been made and what advantages are there?
    (b) What difference does it make to the relationship of the priest to the people?

Baptist chapel. A chapel's shape will vary, but a large pulpit will dominate one end from which the minister (clergyman) or deacon (lay helper) will conduct the service. A wooden table will have a Bible on it. The baptismal water tank (baptistry) will be in the floor nearby, and it will be uncovered when needed (see pp. 213–14). An unrobed choir will lead the singing to the accompaniment of an organ. The chapel will be part of the whole building, which will contain offices, teaching and recreation rooms.

Worshippers sit to pray. Their Lord's Supper (Communion) is usually held fortnightly; other services are devised by the minister and his congregation. During Communion people remain in their seats. One custom is for each person to break a piece of bread from the loaf passed round. It is eaten as soon as it is taken, to show that Christ died for individuals. The wine is served in tiny glasses brought round on slotted trays. When everyone is served they all drink together to show the unity of the church. The glasses are then put into slots in the chair backs for later collection.

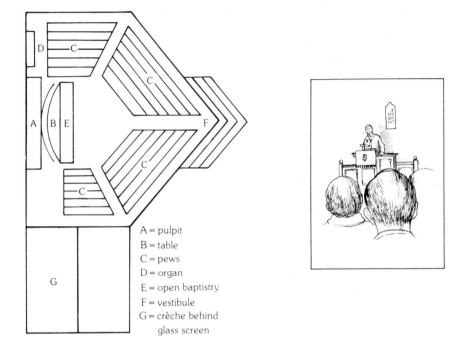

A = pulpit
B = table
C = pews
D = organ
E = open baptistry
F = vestibule
G = crèche behind
   glass screen

(left)
A modern Baptist chapel plan. Compare its layout with that of the Church of England church.

(right)
Baptist chapel interior.

26. *Draw a plan of a Baptist chapel.*

27. *List things which are in a Church of England church but not in a Baptist chapel. Comment on the list.*

28. *Why does the pulpit rather than the Communion table, dominate the chapel?*

29. *In what ways are 'home-made' services (a) better, (b) worse than set services? Which would you prefer and why?*

Salvation Army citadel. (The word 'citadel' means 'fort'.) The main hall for worship will be part of a building containing offices, teaching and recreation rooms. The hall will be divided into two sections. The upper one, or rostrum, is where the band (of perhaps 30) will sit. In front of this is a reading desk from which the officer can conduct the service. The lower section is for the congregation. The mercy seat or penitent's form (a long bench) will be at the front of the congregation, where anyone can come forward to ask God's mercy or for help. On it will be cards which the penitent can sign to say he or she accepts Christ as Saviour. The choir of songsters with their tambourines will play a prominent role and their corps' flag will be on display (see p. 214). They do not celebrate the sacraments.

The services are varied and will immediately change in nature and length if anyone is at the mercy seat in need of help. Someone will attend to that person while the rest will stay and pray and sing until the person's needs are met. The services are designed to appeal to the hearts of lost souls as well as to praise God in joyful popular songs. Preaching plays a big role too. Salvationists see

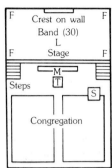

Around the main hall
are rooms for children,
social rooms, offices, band
practice rooms etc.
S = 30 songsters
L = Lectern F = Flags
M = Mercy seat
T = Table

Salvation Army
Citadel plan.

Yesterday . . .

themselves as soldiers fighting evil for Christ (1 Tim. 1:18; 2 Tim. 2:3–4; Eph. 6:14–17). Half the services should be held out of doors in a public place to attract people by taking the Gospel to them.

30. *Draw a citadel plan and name its parts.*

31. *List things (a) which are in a citadel but not found in other churches, (b) which you might expect to find in a citadel but which are not in fact there. Comment on your list.*

32. *Compare the different effects of having (a) an organ, (b) a band to lead singing. Which would aid you more in worship and why?*

33. *In the Orthodox and Catholic churches the emphasis in the services is on the humble congregation worshipping Almighty God, whereas the Salvation Army makes a point of concentrating on someone kneeling at the mercy seat. Explain why both approaches are right in their ways.*

34. *Should worship contain joyful popular songs sung to guitars, tambourines, etc? What are the arguments for and against?*

35. *Should all churches follow the Salvation Army's example of holding regular out of doors services? In what ways is the Salvation Army better equipped to do this than the other churches?*

... and today.

Society of Friend's (Quakers') meeting house. A room with a Bible on the table and chairs gathered round is all that is needed for this 'do-it-yourself' religion! There are no priests, no music, no ritual, no 'usual aids' in the form of pictures or statues. The meeting begins as soon as the first person arrives and sits down to pray and meditate in silence. Peaceful silence pervades the atmosphere and aids the worshippers who have come in from the busy world outside. Because all are there for the same purpose the silence is quite positive in its effect. It gives the worshippers a chance to review the past week and the future in their minds. During the hour someone may read from the Bible or another book which has impressed him, or he may share some experience which has a Christian significance. Perhaps three or four will speak during the hour. Two Friends chosen to be in charge of the meeting will signify its end by shaking hands.

During their meeting Quakers find *Advices and Queries* a help. This is a booklet containing questions such as: 'Do you seek to follow Jesus?', 'Is your religion rooted in personal experience of God?', 'How does it find expression in your life?', 'Do you *try* to make your home a place of friendliness, refreshment and peace, where God becomes more real to all who live there and those who visit it?'

36. *What do Friends (a) gain, (b) lose by their method of worship compared with that of other Christian churches?*

37. *Other churches see the Communion service as the main service, yet Quakers have no such sacrament. Why do you think this is?*

38. *'Instead of spending days on their knees praying, Christians should be helping the poor and needy.' How far do you agree with this comment?*

ISLAM

Mosques. Muslims worship in a mosque ('masjid,' 'a place of prostration'). It is usually square with a courtyard at the end. This contains water for ritual washing before prayer. Its outline of a dome (symbolizing the universe) and four minarets (towers) at the corners is reminiscent of the Arkan (Five Pillars of Faith, see pp. 137–45: Īmān (dome of faith), Salāt (prayer), Zakat (almsgiving), Saum (fasting) and Hajj (Makkah pilgrimage). The number of minarets is not fixed.

The building faces Makkah and the mihrab (niche) in the qibla ('direction wall') of the hall indicates the direction. There are no sculptures or pictures of humans or Allah, but the walls and ceilings may be adorned with tiles or geometrical patterns and lettering in a blaze of colour, particularly green. The minbar, or mimbar, (pulpit) is a desk or crowned structure up three steps (sometimes five – one for Muhammad, four for the first four kalifs, although this is purely a custom, as there is no rule), from which the Friday khutba (sermon) is given by the khatib (preacher). The leader (imam) chosen by the community performs this function. The khutba is in two parts: the first deals with the problems of today that must be faced; the second gives an explanation of the Qur'ān or religious practices. Birmingham Central Mosque has a room downstairs where bodies can be washed for burial and where there are refrigeration facilities for bodies awaiting transhipment back to their homelands. In England it is common to have indoor facilities for wudu (see pp. 138–9).

A large mosque.

Worship (Ibādah). From the top of the minaret the muezzin calls the faithful to prayer five times a day: 'Allahu Akbar . . .' – 'God is the most great, God is the most great. I bear witness that there is no god but God . . .' (see p. 138). The imam leads the prayers. None of the officials are priests as no sacramental duties have to be performed. There is chanting but no other music. There are no seats, but prayer mats are provided on the floor. Muslims must remove their shoes before entering a mosque, as a sign of reverence to Allah.

The rakat procedure has ready been described on pp. 140–1. All males must be present for Friday midday prayer, Jumma, Jum'a or Jum'ah, consisting basically of two salāts and a sermon. Women *may* go to the mosque, especially on these days. Friday is not a rest day like the Sabbath or Sunday, as Allah is said never to need a rest. Prayer beads (subha) may be used when reciting the 99 'Beautiful Names' of Allah. To recite Allah's Names is called dhikr, or zikr. A mosque is used as an evening school for Islamic education and as a community centre. Ummah (the community) has both a local and international meaning. Muslims will care for each other locally and regard themselves as a worldwide fellowship.

39. *Draw a view of the mosque and name the Arkan parts symbolized by the building.*

40. *Draw a plan and name the parts.*

41. *The emphasis of the worship is on the greatness of God and the sinfulness of humble humans.*
    (a) How does Islamic worship compare with Christian worship?
    (b) What different ideas about God and His relations with mankind are shown by these different types of worship?

42. *Explain the terms (a) mihrab, (b) minbar, (c) qibla, (d) khutba, (e) khatib.*

43. *In what different ways can a mosque be described as the centre of life in a Muslim community?*

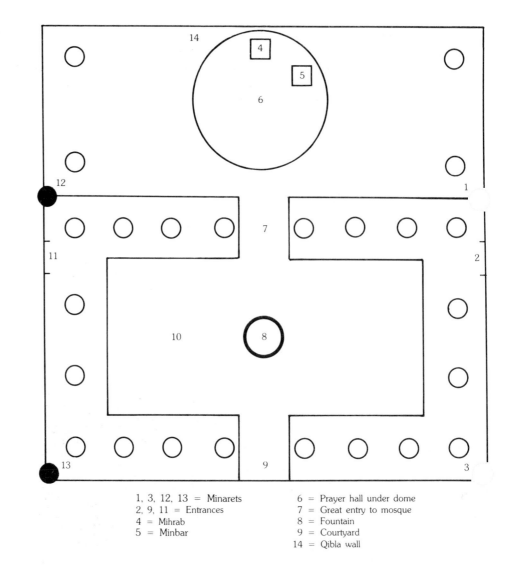

Mosque plan at
Edirne, Turkey.

1, 3, 12, 13 = Minarets
2, 9, 11 = Entrances
4 = Mihrab
5 = Minbar

6 = Prayer hall under dome
7 = Great entry to mosque
8 = Fountain
9 = Courtyard
14 = Qibla wall

SIKHISM

Gurdwaras. Sikhs worship in a Gurdwara, or Gurudwara ('Guru's door'). It is not only a temple but a community and action centre. A Sikh community is called a panth. In fact, any building containing the Guru Granth Sahib is a gurdwara. The following description is of a purpose-built one. Above the building is the nishan sahib (flag) with two swords (kirpans), a two-edged sword (khanda, indicating that one should fight with both spiritual and physical force), and a circle (chakra, showing the oneness of God and Sikhs as well as the continuity of life and the equality of all). The centrepiece is the takht (literally a 'throne'). This is a dais for the Guru Granth Sahib, which is ceremonially opened beneath a canopy (palki) supported by four poles. The gurdwara is decorated with streamers and lights.

Ten out of the eleven gurdwaras in Birmingham serving 40 000 Sikhs are ex-Christian churches. Those which have been purpose-built are differently designed from those of the homeland, owing to the colder climate and cost of labour. Instead of outdoor marble floors and a small park setting, they have all their facilities indoors and a car park outside.

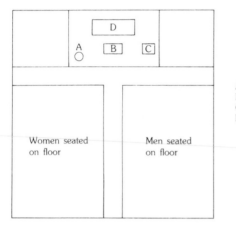

The Ik (or Ek) 'Oankar' symbol, which means 'God is one Being' in Punjabi. This symbol may be put on the outside wall of the gurdwara. It consists of two Punjabi letters.

A = Karah parshad in basin
B = Milk, fruit, etc., offerings
C = Ragis (musicians)
D = Palki, or chanani (canopy) on takht (platform) below which is the Guru Granth Sahib placed on Manji Sahib (stool). The Granthi (reader) sits behind the waving chauri as he reads.

A gurdwara plan.

'School' for Sikh children on Sunday. What are the boys wearing on their heads, and why? (See p. 222.)

Sikh gurdwara,
Rishikesh, India.

Worship. Worshippers take their shoes off, and bow low before the Guru Granth Sahib when they enter. They also give their alms money, food or a romalla (silk cloth to cover the Guru Granth Sahib) if they particularly wish to do so. Men wear turbans or scarves and women pull their dupattas (silk scarves) over their heads. No statues or bells are allowed and no one may bring tobacco or alcohol inside. The service lasts from one to five hours as people come and go. The Guru Granth Sahib is kept covered except when it is used, then the granthi (reader) carries it out on his head to place it on the takht. As the final Guru, the Guru Granth Sahib has a human quality and is put to bed at night, as it were.

The sangat (holy congregation) sit cross-legged on the floor, men on one side and women on the other. A Sikh will sit behind the Guru Granth Sahib, facing the sangat, and wave a chauri (silver sceptre with animal hairs; originally a bunch of peacocks' feathers was used, and still is in some gurdwaras) over the Guru Granth Sahib as a sign of the book's authority and to keep flies away. Kirtan (hymn-singing) is very important and the music is played on sitars and a tabla (drum). Anyone may conduct the service and men and women are treated equally in this. A sermon is given, followed by unaccompanied singing. Everyone stands and faces the Guru Granth Sahib and responds with

The granthi reading
the Guru Granth
Sahib. What are
the names of (a)
the canopy. (b) the
sceptre?

Waheguru ('Wonderful Lord') to the verses of the Ardas (common prayer). Its three parts are concerned with: (1) remembrance of God and the ten gurus, (2) keeping the Guru Granth Sahib's teachings, (3) asking God's blessing on their community and all mankind. For example:

> O true King, O beloved Father, we have sung Thy sweet hymns, heard Thy
> life-giving Word ... May these things find a loving place in our hearts
> and serve to draw our souls towards Thee. Save us, O Father, from lust,
> wrath, greed, undue attachment and pride ... Give us light, give us
> understanding, so that we may know what pleases Thee ... Forgive us
> our sins ...

Specific prayers for newly-weds, the sick or the dead may be inserted.

The Guru Granth Sahib is then read by a man or woman. Sikhs have no priests, as all are equal. At the end a Sikh will stir the karah parshad (mixture of flour and semolina, butter and sugar) with his kirpan (dagger), and then portions the size of golfballs are given to all to eat to show all are equal and united. It is consecrated by reading the Anand ('The True Name is my support; it is my food and drink...'). Parshad is sweet-tasting to stress God's kindness to mankind. Afterwards worshippers join in the langar (free food) served in another room, sitting in pangats (rows). This is designed to bring everyone together and break down any barriers.

Amritsar. The name of this Punjabi city means 'a lake of amrit' and refers to the 172 m × 172 m × 5.4 m (550 ft × 550 ft × 18 ft) deep lake in which the Golden Temple (Hari Mandir) is situated. In turn it gives its name to amrit, the sweetened water used in initiation. The temple stands on pillars which in turn rest on an underwater building. Its entire upper part is covered with gold which is reflected

Stirring and distributing the karah parshad.

The langar. In Britain, unemployed non-Sikhs come to this free meal in the same way as they could go to the Salvation Army for similar help.

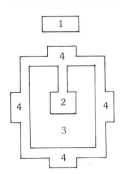

1 = Akal Takht
2 = Golden Temple
3 = The Lake
4 = Gateways

in the surrounding lake. It has four doors, one on each side, to show that it is open to everyone, and to emphasize that it does not point in one direction as mosques do. The Guru Granth Sahib is guarded by sentries with kirpans at night and brought in at 5 a.m. in a large silver palanquin. A trumpeter walks backwards before it blowing on his silver curved horn. It is put away at 10 p.m. Pilgrims leave shoes and socks at one of the gates, wash their feet and then walk round the lake before crossing the causeway to the Temple. Once inside, they will behave as they would in any gurdwara. But before leaving some will sip some of the lake's water and sprinkle it over their eyes. Nearby is the Akal Takht temple, meaning 'throne of the timeless one'. It is from here that Sikh edicts are issued and in 1984 determined defenders held out when the Indian government attacked the temple complex.

44. *Draw the Guru Granth Sahib underneath the canopy with the Sikh waving the chauri.*

45. *What does the treatment of the Guru Granth Sahib suggest about its importance to Sikhs?*

46. *What is the difference between Christian communion bread and wine and Sikh parshad so far as its significance and meaning are concerned?*

47. *Would all religions benefit from holding langars after services? Find out which other religions do something similar regularly.*

48. *How important is it, in each religion, for an individual to join with others in worship or meditation as a community?*

49. *How important do you think it is that members of a religion have special buildings to worship in?*

50. *Jews ceremonially bring the Torah to the reading desk as Sikhs bring out the Guru Granth Sahib.*
   (a) Why do these religions show such respect for their holy books?
   (b) Would the Bible be regarded differently if it were ceremonially taken from a special cupboard and carried in procession to the lectern in Christian churches, or is it better to have it there the whole time for anyone to read?

51. *What important religious beliefs are suggested by the name (a) mosque, (b) sanctuary, (c) ark, (d) palki, (e) bimah?*

52. *Hindu temples vary considerably in design. What are the essential parts of a temple?*

53. *Name the different styles of Theravāda temple. What might they contain? What unusual form of prayer devices are used by Mahāyāna Buddhists?*

7
HOLDING FESTIVALS

A festival is an occasion which provides an opportunity for people to give special recognition to an event. It can bring the past into the present so that an event can be commemorated by being brought alive again. Jesus' death on the cross is marked by Good Friday, while the Jews have their Pentecost to commemorate God's gift of the Ten Commandments. Most festivals are held annually. Some are solemn because of the sad events they record, while others are joyous occasions. The believer's faith is helped by the stories told and the customs observed.

HINDUISM

Hinduism has many festivals and there is space to mention only a few. Every temple has an annual festival to honour its principal god. The main item is the public procession of the image, which may be carried on an elephant or in a huge wooden carriage. The image is taken to the river to be bathed. The throwing away of the image at the end of festivals underlines the fact that it is not worshipped as an idol, but treated simply as an image.

Mahāshivrati, Shiva Ratri (Night sacred to Shiva), Shiva's Dance Festival in January or February on the day before the full moon, marks Shiva's teaching people to dance. He is called Nataraja, Lord of the Dance, and statues show him dancing in a ring of fire. During the night singing and dancing take place and milk, honey and ghee are poured over Shiva's linga pillar. People fast until 4 p.m. when pūjā is done, then sweet potatoes and cucumbers are eaten. Unmarried girls keep a night's vigil so that Shiva will help them find a husband.

Holi is the spring festival which lasts three to five days in February or March, at the time of the spring harvest. It is connected with Kama, the god of love, and Krishna. It used to be a fertility festival. It involves a recreation of Shiva's marriage procession in which people throw coloured water and powder at each other in a riotous way, just as cowherds and milkmaids used to do and as Krishna teased the milkmaids. Normal ranks in society mean nothing on this day. Balloons full of red, blue, pink and green gulal powder – made of rice flour and tumeric – are thrown, while children use homemade bamboo syringes with stick 'pistons'. Fortunately it all washes out. At noon the throwing stops and people visit their friends and make amends for any misunderstanding during the past year. They put dry red powder on each other's foreheads and wish each other a

Happy Holi. Community fires are lit by priests and effigies of demons are burnt. Everyone takes a bit of charred wood home for the year to keep illnesses at bay.

Krishna Janamashtami (or Krishna Jayanti, or Janamashtami) is the August birthday of Krishna. It begins with a fast the day before and a night vigil. Then at midnight the singing and dancing begin. Sweet foods are shared around in the temples as gifts to a new-born baby and sometimes an image of Krishna is put in a cradle. The day is kept as a fast but an evening feast concludes it.

Raksha Bandham takes place in July or August at the full moon. Raksha means 'to protect' and Bandham 'to tie'. Girls sit in front of their brothers (or if they have none, men who become their protectors and virtual brothers) and daub their foreheads with vermilion, saffron and rice powder before tying a rakhi, a brightly coloured thread with gold trimming, round their wrists, wishing them health and prosperity. They stuff sweetmeats in their mouths too. In return, brothers give sisters a rupee and promise to protect them. They wear the rakhi for the day. This dates back to the story that the god Indra's wife was given a rakhi by Vishnu to tie round her husband's wrist to protect him from the demon-king Bali.

Ratha Yatra is held in honour of Jagannatha, Lord of the Universe, a title usually applied to Vishnu or Krishna. At the Jagannatha temple three huge images of Krishna and his brother and sister are taken out to be bathed. They are carried in chariots called rathas. Such is the excitement that pilgims have been known to throw themselves beneath the wheels and get crushed to death. Hence the word juggernaut for a large, menacing lorry.

Navaratri in September or October is a nine-day event for Durga, motherhood goddess, with its climax on Dashara amidst blazing lights and music. Navaratri means 'nine nights' so the festival takes place in the evenings with major events in the Rāmāyana story (see p. 76) being enacted. Folk-dancing round a Durga shrine is all important. Newly-weds return to see their parents. It recalls Rāma's worship of Durga when he needed help to rescue Sita. It is a time to celebrate the triumph of good over evil. 'Pūjā Numbers' of magazines appear with stories, poems and plays.

Dashara (or Da Sera or Dussehra or Vijaya Dashami or Festival of Warriors). 'Das' means the tenth day as it follows the end of Navaratri's nine days. On this day Durga's spirit departs from the clay statue of Durga which has been worshipped for those nine days. The statue is put into the river. If it floats, it is a good sign as it will take away all unhappiness. Originally Dashara was a war festival; now it represents the fight of the hero Rāma against the demon Rāva or Rāvana. It refers to the cutting off of Rāvana's ten heads and so the festival alerts people to cut out the ten demons within them, namely, passion, pride, anger, greed, infatuation, lust, hatred, jealousy, selfishness and crookedness. The climax is a mighty war-dance with crackers and the explosive disposal of enemy effigies when fiery arrows are shot into the explosives inside them. At New Delhi a 30 m (98 ft) high statue of Rāvana is the centre of attraction.

Dashara, Festival of the Warriors. 40 to 50 m-tall figures of Rāvana, his son Maghnath and his brother Kumbh-karna, filled with firecrackers, about to be burnt at Cawnpore.

Ganesha Chaturthi takes place in August or September and marks the end of the Indian monsoon. Remember, Ganesha's head once belonged to the rain god's elephant (see p. 10). Schools are closed and children persuade their fathers to buy gaudy images of Ganesha in the market. The image is fastened to a plank which the adults carry as their children bang cymbals on the way home. Then rice flour, coconut and dried fruit are offered to it and the children hang streamers and coloured lights over it. The image will remain there for anything from two to nine days during which prayers and arti (see pp. 151–2) will be performed daily before it. In this way it is hoped that this god of wisdom will remove all difficulties and grant success to the worshippers' endeavours. Community large-scale images 6 m (19.6 ft) high are paraded too. Sometimes they are shown in new positions, such as blessing Sherpa Tenzing conquering Mount Everest. Poetry readings, plays and musical items are performed and children in uniforms parade, singing patriotic songs. Servants dance from house to house, collecting money for their musical instruments. To end the festival the images are taken in procession to be immersed in a river or lake. People throw coloured powder on those in the procession.

Dīvālī (or Dīpavali or Festival of Lights) occurs in October or November, when the monsoon starts. It is the five-day new year festival in which Vishnu and his bride, Lakshmi, the goddess of prosperity and happiness, are welcomed into every house. Alternatively, it is held to be connected with Rāma overcoming Rāvana. Boys are told to be like Rāma and girls like Sita, Rāma's wife. Family vows are renewed. Husbands and wives remember their duties to each other; likewise children to their parents, and vice versa. Houses are cleaned, clay oil lamps lit to welcome Lakshmi, and gifts are exchanged. Dīvālī means 'cluster of lights'. Roof tops and window sills are lit up with earthenware oil lamps as they are regarded as pure lights. Lamps in clay dishes are floated down rivers. Firecrackers scare away evil spirits. Thus light or good overcomes darkness or evil. There is a lot of music and dancing. Festival floats carry scenes from the lives of the gods. Papier-mâché tigers and cows are on sale. Sweets made of thickened milk and sugar or coconut and sugar are distributed. Businessmen celebrate by opening new account books with prayers to Lakshmi for success in the coming year.

Hindu dancing is used to tell stories about the gods. Shiva is called the Lord of the Dance, and it is claimed that the art originated among the gods before it was passed down to earth. At one time only female temple dancers were allowed to perform the dances. Each movement has a meaning so as to tell the legend. Hand positions mean 'wind', 'holding a sword', 'a year', and so on. Brahmins must have white faces, female demons wear black robes, and goddesses wear green, with pearls. Dancers' faces indicate whether they are afraid, happy or angry. Guitars, cymbals, drums and sitars are played.

1. *What things can you find in common in these festivals?*

2. *Explain how the celebration of festivals may help to strengthen a Hindu's religious beliefs.*

SHINTOISM

Matsuri. Each year shrines hold a major Matsuri (worship festival). The purpose may be to bless the crop or the year's fishing or, alternatively, purify the parishioners, or possibly mark a local kami event. The priests will prepare themselves by washing their hair, trimming their nails and dieting. Solemn chanting of prayers (norito) summons the kami before the cooked or uncooked food offerings (shinsen) are made. Shinsen always includes saké and 'happy presents' of birds, vegetables and fish as these have all been obtained by the grace of the kami. Shinsen rice is grown in a special paddy field and cultivated by hand. Miki (sacred rice wine) is offered too. The ceremony is a grand one and involves the priests praising the offerings from one to another from the shinsen-den (food room) to the heiden (hall of offering). After presentation it is passed back again and eaten by the priests and leading figures at the Naorai. This is a kind of communion meal, which gives the participants the 'prestige' (mi-itsu) of the kami. Much wine is consumed at what can be a jolly meal. Ordinary worshippers are given a sip of rice wine by the priests or miko.

Ceremonial music is played on traditional drums and wailing bamboo flutes and sacred (kagura) and classical (bugaku) dances are performed. There are 35 dance-dramas which depict the myths of Shintoism. The Lion's Dance (shishi-mai) involves two men impersonating a lion which goes round from door to door at New Year casting out evil.

Sports and processions conclude the Matsuri. Japanese wrestling, archery on horseback and boat races are popular. The horseback archery (yabusame) is used to divine the likelihood of a good harvest from the arrows' angle. Alternatively, a deer's shoulder-blade is heated in a fire and the crack pattern studied. Many other techniques are used. Processions involve taking the kami (shinkyo, or gohei) on a journey in an ornate, gilded palanquin (mikoshi). The mikoshi is carried on the shoulders of young men who consider it a great honour. They zigzag up and down with it shouting 'Wasshoi', which the kami is said to enjoy, although a horse follows in case the kami would prefer to ride. The purpose of the procession can be to welcome a kami coming from afar or an occasion for the kami to bless the parish, or to mark some historic event connected with the kami.

Shinto festival. What is in the priest's right hand? Notice the two mikosi in which the kami are carried joyfully round the town.

Rice-cultivation Matsuri concerned with Inari, the rice kami, occur at different times of the growing season and vary locally too. They can cover water examination, seed selecting, ploughing, weeding, manuring, sowing, etc. The Ta-Asobi-Matsuri (rice-field play festival) at New Year covers the whole rice growing process. A 'soot and cobweb' (susuharai) to clear evil out is done at New Year too. The god shelf is renewed to ensure good luck and all bills are paid. Decorations of bamboo and cut-out flowers are everywhere and priests wear blue, purple and scarlet sashes over their white kimonos.

Setsubun. This February festival celebrates the change of season, from winter to spring. It is held as the main purification Matsuri. On that day holly branches and sardine heads are hung outside houses while toasted soya beans are thrown out into the garden to the shout of, 'Come in, good fortune' and 'Devil get out'. During the matsuri ceremony at the shrine, people impersonating devils (oni) attempt to break in, only to be driven back by the priests with bows and arrows.

Bon (or Obon). This festival of the dead, in July or August, is designed to console the spirits of the dead. Welcoming fires (mukaebi) are lit in front of each house and offerings put on the kamidana's (god shelf) food tray (bon). Afterwards the 'sending off' fire (okuri-bi) speeds them on their way. Sometimes they are accompanied by tiny boats with lanterns and food aboard. This festival has been influenced by Buddhism to some extent, and provides a chance to consult the dead on matters such as a marriage or changing one's job.

Hoko, an ornamental float, weighing 12 tons, pulled through the streets of Kyoto during Matsuri commemorating an epidemic in 876 CE.

3. *(a) Name three reasons for holding a Matsuri.*
   (b) Summarize the main events of a Matsuri, giving the reasons for the events you describe.

TAOISM

Chiao Rites of Union (or Cosmic Renewal Festival). The Taoist masters of the Tao Chiao (Religious Taoism) hold these rites in most Taiwan and Hong Kong villages every 3, 5, 12 or 60 years. The event is a very exciting one lasting three to nine days or more. Years of preparation are involved, for the purpose of the rite is to restore the balance of Yin and Yang, free souls from hell, cure the sick and help those in need. The local temple will be repaired and the people will perform acts of purification and penitence for a month. Kind deeds are done and debts repaid. A host of gods and goddesses are invited, including buddhas and Bodhisattas, and of course the Jade Emperor. Shrines are set up for them. Ancestors and souls from the underworld are welcome, as their coming will release them from bondage.

A Taoist Master and his assistant, wearing elaborate red vestments, will lead the rituals. One assistant represents Yang and another Yin, and they approach the purified sacred ground from either side of the Master. They sing alternately just as Yang and Yin dominate nature in turn.

On the first day the gods are welcomed and evil spirits driven away. The Master recites lengthy prayers to ensure merit and repentance to release souls from hell. Then the meditation rites begin with Fa-lu (see p. 109). Noisy instruments sound as the Master enters the sacred area through the Gate of Heaven in the north-west corner and his entourage through the Gate of Earth on the south-west side. The Master first unites himself with the Tao by his k'o-i ritual and then uses the supernatural power (Te) to save others. As he starts, the ritual vapours of the five talismans or elements (see p. 207) are burnt: green, red, yellow, white and black. The drum is struck 24 times and he grinds different parts of his jaw on each blow, swallowing his saliva while reciting a spell. Then he kneels to summon out the spirits.

On the third day the Jade Emperor arrives and contact is made with the Three Pure Ones (see pp. 14–15). The Grand Memorial petition naming all the villagers present and their petitions is presented to them. Souls from the underworld are feasted and the Nine Hells Litany of Repentance is said to release all souls from hell. At least 31 ceremonies are included during the festival and noonday offerings are regularly made. The additional rites of 'climbing the 36 sword ladder', something of a competition because of their sharpness and the ladder's height, may take place before the gods are thanked and sent home. Each family gets yellow documents to put over the family altar to tell the gods and men for whom the trial took place that the family was present.

Birthday of Matzu, Queen of Heaven is celebrated with a colourful float procession (see p. 14). Palanquins (god-carriages) are carried by men as fire-crackers burst. Each contains an image of Matzu, who honours every home that is passed. The air gets so thick with smoke that a man with bellows follows each palanquin. Near the temple one may see women in trances, and men with weighted brass skewers piercing their backs, but feeling no pain because of their trance. Joss sticks are offered. In effect the Matzu images from village temples are being taken to the main Matzu shrine to be 're-charged' with power for the year ahead.

The other festivals, described below, are primarily Chinese rather than exclusively Taoist.

Hsin Nien is the New Year festival, a great occasion when all the gods have to report to the Jade Emperor, Yu Huang, the highest god. This means that Tzau Wang, the kitchen god on everyone's god shelf must report on the household's year. A small image of him with a paper horse is burnt symbolically to send him off to the Palace of Heaven. A piece of t'ang kwa (rice sweetmeat) is thrown into the fire so that he may make a sweet report. Sometimes sticky candy, opium or wine is put on his lips so that he will not speak clearly. As he will be away for seven days the house is cleaned in his absence (see p. 110).

On the last day of the old year, strips of red paper with prayers for peace and prosperity are put around doors to prevent luck leaving. Everyone stays up at night to await Tzau Wang's return. At 2 a.m. a meal of chu po po (meat dumplings) and nien kao (sticky cake or 'high' made of sticky rice flour, dates and bean flour) is put out. The hope is that each year will be 'higher' than the previous one, that is, more prosperous. His return is marked by a new picture or image of him being placed on the god shelf, amidst firecrackers and incense.

Taoist dragon.

A sacrifice of a pig, sheep, fish or fowl is made and a cup of blazing wine offered to the god. When the incense has burnt out, the food offering is prepared for the family to eat. On New Year's Day care is taken to be very well-behaved so as to ensure a good year. Children are given red packets of 'lucky money'. On the eighth day the stars are worshipped from 8 to 12 p.m., with the table put outside with a picture of the god of the stars on it. T'ang yuan (rice and sugar balls), red candles, incense, yellow paper spirit money and a spirit ladder of yellow paper are put out. The paper is burnt and the family eat the food. Every day the ancestor tablets are worshipped as incense is burnt and food presented. On the 16th day the tablets are returned to their box.

Ching Ming. This April festival which means 'clear and bright' after the weather, is the time for visiting family graves. Weeds are cleared away and inscriptions repainted. Then incense sticks and red candles are lit and rice, wine, tea and other foods are set out. Whole roasted pigs are offered and paper clothing and other paper items as well as spirit money (see p. 233) are burnt. A family picnic on the grave hillside follows.

Dragon Boat Festival (or Fifth Month Festival). One of the legends behind this is that a royal official in 459 BCE committed suicide by drowning after failing to quell a rebellion. But river folk decided his task had been impossible and he ought to be honoured, so they gave him food for the next life by wrapping rice, sugar and fruit in reeds and throwing them in the river.

Dragons symbolize Yang and a dragon fight in heaven will cause heavy rain. Four heavenly Dragon Kings are under the control of the Jade Emperor. Boats measuring 24–36 m (78–118 ft) by 1.6 m (4.8 ft) with crews of fifty and a drummer to keep time, have a dragon on their bows and the rowers throw sticky rice cakes on the water to tempt the fish so as to leave the official's body intact. Then mock battles are held to bring on the rain.

The Festival of Lanterns (Yuen Sui) takes place on the 15th day of the first month. It involves paper or cloth dragons 52 m (170 ft) high with 18 kg heads being carried by 23 men through the streets. The dragons were derived from the Yellow River alligators. Taoists visualized them with a camel's head, deer's horns, rabbit's eyes, cow's ears, serpent's neck, frog's belly, carp's scales, hawk's talons and tiger's pad palms. The festival is a call for spring rain.

Taoist priests.

The Hungry Souls Festival (or Ghosts Festival, P'u Tu) falls on the full moon of the seventh month and lasts three days to care for the souls with no descendants to look after them. At the temple a huge effigy of Yen Lo, King of the Underworld, is set up, and facing him Ch'ing Hsu the 'lenient magistrate' flanked by four ghosts who serve him. There are images of the Three Pure Ones behind the altar: the Jade Emperor; Tao Chun, who controls the relations of Yang and Yin; and Lao-Tse. Incense burns. The 'dark altar' dedicated to the nine gods who protect mortals from devils and calamities is furnished with miniature fiends from Hell. A percussion band starts the evening ceremony. Red-robed priests with black hats and coloured battery-illuminated pompoms invoke the neglected spirits to come to the feast.

The second day is a quiet one. For the third day an evening service is held by the shore for unattended spirits to gather there. An altar is set up and an image of the

Hungry Ghosts Festival. Miniature paper palace, Ching Chung Koon temple, Hong Kong.

King of Hell is positioned with a pig's head with candles and incense sticks in its skull at its feet. Children make nine sandcastles for burning paper money on. Bands play, priests call the spirits to come. Tea and wine are put out and the paper offerings burnt. The long list of names of those who have paid for the entertainment for the spirits is read out. The priest slips many genuine coins, which have been donated, into his wide sleeves.

A final service involves the Lion dancers before the Queen of Heaven's shrine and then all the effigies are carried to the shore and a paper junk laden with tea, wine and oil is pushed out to sea.

4. *How do these festivals compare with the Shinto ones?*

5. *Briefly describe the Chiao Rites of Union and the Hungry Souls Festival. What is similar in them?*

BUDDHISM

Tea-ladling over statue of the Buddha.

Theravāda Buddhism has festivals recalling the life of the Buddha. **Magha-pūjā** in February records the occasion when he preached to 1250 Arhats on the rules for monks and announced that he would pass away in three months. It is marked by lighting 1250 candles; Magha is the name of the lunar month.

Wesak (or Vesak), the Buddha day, is named after the Sri Lankan month in which it occurs – at the full moon in April or May. It commemorates three events in the Buddha's life, his birth, enlightenment and entry into Nibbana, and so lasts three days. Houses and streets are decorated with flowers and paper lanterns, and presents given to monks and the needy. Colourful processions take place. It marks the beginning of the Buddhist year. Greeting cards are exchanged with a lotus on them. In India Buddhists show kindness to animals, buying caged birds and setting them free or paying butchers to save animals from slaughter. In Mahāyāna Japan the three events are commemorated on separate days. The first is Hana Matsuri (Flower Festival) in April when model flower gardens are made to recall his birth place, Lumbini Garden, and model white elephants are made, as his mother dreamt of such a rare animal when he was conceived. Children ladle sweet-smelling tea from long-handled ladles over small Buddha statues to recall his first bath in perfumed water or the nectar which rained from heaven at his birth. His enlightenment is marked on 8 December with Jodo-e and his entry into Nibbana on 15 February called Nehan-e.

Asalha (Asala)-pūjā in July marks the Buddha's first sermon on the Middle Way in the deer park, Sarnath, near Benares. The day afterwards sees the beginning of Vassa, the Rains Retreat, when monks stay at their base for three months.

The Water Festival in Burma and Thailand is held at the new year in April when water is splashed on everyone as decorated floats pass by and Buddha images are ceremonially bathed. In Laos and Kampuchea the monks are splashed by the bystanders as they pass. The legend is that a king once had a bet with Brahma, and when Brahma lost his head was cut off in spite of the Buddhist no-taking-of-life rule. The head was said to be hot and had to be cooled with water.

At the end of the rainy season there is another full moon festival marked by the illumination of pagodas and houses – signifying the return of the Buddha to earth when the gods lit his route for him. It marks the end of a period of retreat during which no festivals or weddings have occurred while the Buddha is said to be in heaven preaching to the gods. Robes are given to monks and alms to the poor.

Esala Perahera is the processional fortnight at Kandy, Sri Lanka, in July or August. Four processions honour the four Hindu gods who protect the vicinity while the fifth honours the sacred Tooth of the Buddha, said to be kept there. Thousands of dancers and drummers precede some 50 elephants with one elephant carrying a replica casket in the form of a stūpa. A carpet way of white linen is laid in front of the elephant so that it does not step in any dirt.

Mahāyāna Buddhists hold a similar festival to Wesak and holy days are observed at the full moon each month. Some hold festivals for the dead called Festivals of Lanterns. These are like the Chinese Festival of the Hungry Souls. Offerings are made to the dead and lighted candles placed in paper boats to guide their spirits. Higan ('other shore') is a Japanese festival in March and September when prayers and gifts are offered to the dead. Water is poured over tombstones to transfer merit to the deceased to help them over to the 'other shore'. Mahāyāna Buddhists also recognize the Shinto Bon festival.

6. *What are the main purposes of Buddhist festivals? In what ways are they different from Taoist festivals?*

JUDAISM

Festivals have been the life-blood of Judaism for centuries and have done much to keep the Chosen People united in the absence of a homeland until Israel was established in 1948. The festivals recall God's care for the Jews. Feasts always begin at dusk on the preceding day.

Pesach (or Passover, or Feast of Unleavened Bread) begins on 15 Nisan (March/April) and lasts eight days to mark God's 'passing over' the Jews in Egypt sparing their first-born during the plagues (Exod. 11:1–12.39), and their freedom from enslavement about 1300 BCE.

The house is thoroughly cleaned and no trace of leaven is left. Leaven is the raising agent used in bread-making. This is because the Jews ate unleavened bread the night before they left Egypt, having no time to leaven it. During the week Jews use no leaven, yeast or baking powder. The Orthodox use special dishes and cooking utensils – one set for meat and another for milk dishes – which have never come into contact with leaven, for this one week of the year. Thus a family has four sets of utensils in all, the other two being for the rest of the year.

The first night of Pesach fathers search their homes with a candle to see if the leaven has been removed. A ceremonial meal called Seder (Order of Service for Passover Night) takes place and is repeated on the second night, too, among Orthodox Jews outside Israel. A number of items of food and drink are put out:

- Three matzoth (singular matzah), 'bread of affliction', which look like water biscuits and are flat cakes of unleavened bread
- One roasted shank bone of lamb (symbol of the lambs eaten in the last meal in Egypt)
- One roasted egg (for the new life and the Passover Temple sacrifice)
- Horseradish (for their bitter slavery in Egypt)
- Parsley (for the herbs used to mark the Jews' doors in Egypt)
- A bowl of salt water (slaves' tears)
- Haroseth (paste of apples, nuts and cinnamon, for the joy and sweetness after slavery and the mortar used when brick-making)
- A wine glass for everyone
- An extra wine glass called the Cup of Elijah (who will come before the Messiah arrives).

Candles are put on the table, which is covered with a white cloth. When all are ready father says the Kiddush prayer and then passes parsley dipped in salt water representing tears to everyone. Then he breaks a matzah and hides one half. They begin the reading of the Haggadah (or Hagadah, book of the Passover story). Children may have 'pop up' picture versions. The youngest present has to ask four questions about the origin of the festival:

(1) On this night why is there only unleavened bread?

(2) Why are there only bitter herbs?

(3) Why do we dip our herbs?

(4) Why do we eat in a leaning position?

Father reads the Haggadah which gives the answers. A recurring phrase is Ha-kodosh baruh-hu (The Holy One, Blessed be He). While it avoids mentioning God's sacred name, it praises Him. The egg is then dipped in salt water to mark the Temple's destruction, as eggs are eaten by mourners. Wine is drunk in thanksgiving and the Hallel (praise) psalms (Pss. 113–114) are recited. A blessing is said and wine drunk again before hands are washed and the matzoth are eaten as well as the horseradish. The main meal follows. Finally, a search is made for the hidden matzah, called the afikomen, which is regarded like 'hunt the thimble'. More drinking and singing follows to end with.

Shavuot (or Pentecost or Weeks Festival) is held seven weeks after the Passover to mark the gift of the Ten Commandments. Pentecost means it is 50 days since the beginning of the Passover. Before the festival synagogues are decorated with flowers to recall the harvest offering taken to the temple. The Book of Ruth is read as she accepted Judaism so devoutly and it gives an account of harvesting (Lev. 23:9–14). Originally it was a harvest or pilgrimage festival recalling the 'first fruits' offered when the Hebrews travelled in the wilderness (Deut. 26:1–11).

Tish b'Av (or Fast of the Ninth of Av, or Ab) in July or August, commemorates the destruction of the First and Second Temples. The Babylonians destroyed the First on the ninth of Av in 586 BCE, and Titus the Second in 70 CE. In 135

The menorah (Hebrew, *lamp*), the seven-branched candlestick which stands in Jewish synagogues. Beaten out of one piece of metal to stress unity, it represents the Tree of Life, rooted in the earth with the central stem for Grace and Knowledge, the right-hand branches for Right and Mercy, the left for Death and Judgement. It also symbolizes the seven planets.

CE Bar Kokhba's anti-Rome rebellion ended on the ninth of Av, and in 1492 the Jews were expelled from Spain on that day. So it is the saddest day in the Jewish year. Orthodox Jews fast for 24 hours. All ornaments are removed from synagogues, and talliths and tefillins are not worn for the morning service, when readings from Deuteronomy and Jeremiah take place. During the day the Books of Job and Lamentations are read, and the Kinot, or dirges, about the tragedies of Jewish history recited. Reform Jews do not observe this fast.

Rosh Hashanah (or New Year Festival of the Trumpets) in the month of Tishri (September or October) is marked by the sounding of the shofar (ram's horn) a hundred times, each sounding represents a call to penitence. It is both the anniversary of the world's or Adam's creation, and the Day of Judgement, as everyone's fate for the coming year is settled then. You recite the Tashlikh (Hebrew for 'and you will cast'), from Micah 7:19, while standing beside a river, or pool of water, to wash your sins away. Readings in the synagogues are Gen. 21-22; 1 Sam. 1-2:10; Jer. 31:2-20. The festival marks the birthdays of Abraham, Isaac and Jacob. Bread (challah) and apples are dipped in honey in the hope that the coming year will be sweet. The following ten days are called the Ten Days of Return, or Ten Penitential Days when Jews consider their failings during the past year and ask for forgiveness (Lev. 23:23-24).

Yom Kippur (or Atonement Day) comes ten days after Rosh Hashanah. It is the holiest day of the year and all fast except the sick and children under 13, as it is a time of repentance (Lev. 16). 'Atonement' means 'at-one-ment with God'. As a sign of purity white coverings are put on the ark and bimah, and the rabbis and others wear white robes called kittles, which are the shrouds that one day they will be buried in. It is the only day in the year Jews kneel to pray. Members of a family ask forgiveness of one another. In the afternoon the Book of Jonah is read

The sounding of the shofar three times before the Sabbath originally warned those in the fields it was time to return home. The man who sounds the shofar must recite the blessing: 'Blessed are you, Lord our God, king of the universe, who has sanctified us with your commandments and commanded us to hear the sound of the shofar.'

as it tells of God's forgiveness to those who repent. The Kol Nidre, 'all vows', chant is recited just before the sun sets and the festival begins as a prayer of absolution assuring the Jews that they have God's forgiveness for the vows they have broken. The shofar is sounded again at the end of the day (Lev. 23:26–32) in the final service, Neilah, which recalls the closing of the Temple gates as a symbol of heaven's gates closing.

Sukkot (or Feast of Tabernacles) for the harvest comes five days after Yom Kippur and lasts eight days. It is a pilgrim feast remembering when Jews took offerings to the Temple (Lev. 23:33–43). It also marks the time when Jews lived in tabernacles (sukkot) or rough shelters or huts in the wilderness, so sukkot are built in the garden with branches for roofs so that the stars can shine through. It is decorated with flowers and fruit and all meals are eaten there. The congregation forms a joyous procession round the synagogue carrying citron fruit (ethrog) and palms (lulav), myrtle (hadasim) and willow (aravot) branches; citron is for affection and gentleness, the palm for uprightness, the willow for humility and the myrtle for faithfulness. These are the arba minim, the four parts of the body: citron for the heart, palm for the spine, myrtle for eyes, willow for the lips. Their joining together teaches one that God must be worshipped with all one's being.

The photograph opposite shows the Feast of Tabernacles. The girl in the front right is holding the four items. When held together in two hands, the worshipper repeatedly raises them to heaven then brings them down to her heart to channel affection, gentleness, uprightness, humility and faithfulness from heaven to herself.

Simchath Torah (or Rejoicing of the Law) at the end of Sukkot marks the completion of the weekly readings of the Torah for the year and the beginning of the re-reading. The Torah scrolls are carried seven times round the synagogue, amidst a lot of clapping, singing and dancing. The reader of the last verses is called the Bridegroom of the Torah and the reader of the first verses is the Bridegroom of the Beginning as 'beginning' is the name of the Pentateuch's first book. Thus the reading never ceases; it is eternal.

Hanukkah, Hanukiah or Chanukka (Feast of Lights, or Dedication) lasts eight days in November or December. It marks the time when in 165 BCE Judas Maccabeus, the 'Hammerer', led his men to cleanse the Temple after Antiochus Epiphanes had defiled it by setting up idols and forbidding Jews to practise their religion (Apocrypha, 1 Macc. 4:36–59). The menorah eight-branch candlestick is lit in remembrance that Judas lit a lamp with a day's oil in it and it lasted eight days. One candle is lit the first day, two the second, and so on. Today, Hanukka presents are given in the same way as Christians give Christmas presents. It is customary to play with a spinning top (dreidel, or sevivon), with its four sides marked with the Hebrew letters N, G, H and Sh, standing for 'Nes Gadol Hayah Sham' ('A great miracle happened there'). Bets may be placed on which initial comes uppermost.

Purim (or Feast of Esther) in March marks the Persian Queen Esther's foiling of prime minister Haman's plot to destroy the Jews in Persia. The Book of Esther is read in the synagogue. Rattles are whirled whenever Haman's name is mentioned in the story. 'Purim' means 'lots' and refers to Haman casting lots as to which date was best for killing the Jews. Fancy dress parties follow afterwards and liberal drinking is permitted. Giving to the poor is expected.

7. *Read aloud the following verses from Esther and stamp your feet whenever Haman's name is mentioned: Esther 3:1–7, 10–14; 4:1–7, 15–17; 5:1–14; 6:1–14; 7:1–10; 8:1–8, 16–17; 9:5–10; 16–28.*

8. *Make a list of the names, dates and reasons for all the Jewish festivals.*

9. *In what ways do these festivals help to remind Jews of their role in history?*

10. *Why are these festivals centred so much on the home and food?*

11. *What things are done to make the events referred to as real as can be? What different ways of expressing (a) sorrow for sins, (b) joy for God's care are used?*

CHRISTIANITY

Christian festivals are essentially centred round the life of Christ and their celebration methods vary a lot among the different churches.

Advent (coming), four Sundays before Christmas, marks the beginning of the Christian year. It celebrates the approach of Jesus' birth and looks forward to his second coming in glory. Thoughts are concentrated on death, judgement, Heaven and Hell. Near Christmas, carol services take place, often with nine lessons from the Bible, showing how God created Man and cares for him by sending His Son. Nativity plays (on the theme of Jesus' birth) are performed in schools.

A school Nativity play, King's School, Gloucester.

Christmas (Christ's mass), is Jesus' birthday, celebrated by most Christians on 25 December, but by Eastern Orthodox Christians on 7 January. The name refers to the Mass or Communion held on that day. Many Christians go to midnight Communion in candle-lit churches. Manger scenes are set up in church recording how Jesus was born in a stable. Christmas is traditonally a time when families gather and give each other presents. Children also get presents from Santa Claus, an old man with a white beard who is named after St Nicholas. Special food (turkey and pudding) and decorations (holly, mistletoe and a Christmas tree) all add to a merry occasion.

Epiphany ('showing forth') on 6 January records the showing of the baby Jesus to the Wise Men who were guided by the Star to his birth place. Jesus is thought of as the Light of the World.

Lent begins 40 days before Easter on Ash Wednesday. It marks Jesus' 40 days in the wilderness (Matt. 4). It is a time when Christians consider their failings of the past year and, by denying themselves some luxuries, try to make a fresh start. In earlier days priests and people covered their heads with ashes in sorrow and repentance. Nowadays crosses in churches are covered with purple veils. The day before Ash Wednesday is Shrove Tuesday, when a feast of pancakes may be eaten before the period of denial begins.

Palm Sunday marks the last week of Lent and the beginning of Holy Week when Jesus entered Jerusalem and faced his trial and death. When he entered the city on a donkey people threw palm leaves before him. In many churches palm crosses are given to everyone, and often processions take place round the church.

A Palm Sunday procession in Spain.

Maundy Thursday ('command day') recalls the Thursday of Holy Week, when the Last Supper was instituted. The old tradition is that priests wash the people's feet as Christ told his disciples to do (John 13:2–17). This emphasizes that all must be humble. The Pope washes the feet of his cardinals, and in the Orthodox Church bishops wash priests' feet. In England the sovereign gives Maundy Money (specially minted coins) to the poor.

Good Friday is the Friday of Holy Week when Jesus was crucified, and so it is the most solemn day of the year. Often three-hour services of talks, prayers and hymns of his suffering take place during the period in the middle of the day when Jesus was on the cross. No Communion takes place. In Catholic churches people follow the 14 Stations of the Cross, which means they pray at the scenes round the wall of the church depicting the events. Passion plays on Jesus' trial and death may be enacted. In Orthodox churches the priest carries an icon depicting the dead Christ and lowers it into a stand in the middle of the church and the people stand with candles as at a funeral. Later the icon is carried round outside the church in a 'funeral' procession as the bells toll. In England many Christians of different churches join together in processions behind a full-size wooden cross to hold an open-air service to proclaim their faith to others. Hot cross buns are eaten to mark the event.

Easter Sunday, two days later, is the happiest day of the year as it marks the finding of Jesus' empty tomb. In the Orthodox Church at midnight the people come in processions as the women did who found the tomb of Jesus empty. They circle the church and pause before the closed doors, which represent the stone in front of the tomb. Inside the icon has already been moved to the altar. Outside the people hear the thrice-repeated triumphal shout, 'Christ is risen from the dead. By death He has trampled down death. And to those who are in the grave He has given life.' The people repeat the cry and bells are rung as the doors swing open. People greet each other with 'Christ is risen' and reply, 'Risen indeed!' Easter's date varies from 21 March to 25 April, the first full moon after the spring equinox.

Ascension Day, the Thursday 40 days after Easter, records Jesus' bodily ascension into heaven after his resurrection. Special Communion services are held in some churches.

Good Friday procession of witness in Gloucester.

Whit Sunday (white Sunday – referring to white baptism robes, or Pentecost) is 50 days after Easter. It marks the gift of the Holy Spirit to the early believers in Jerusalem during the Jewish Pentecostal feast (Acts 2). This used to be a favourite time for baptizing new Christians. The effect of the Holy Spirit's coming was such that people present began to speak in 'tongues', that is languages they did not know (Acts 2:4–11). The Pentecostal churches regard it as a mark of evidence that the Spirit has entered a member when he or she speaks 'in tongues' today (see pp. 59–60).

Other festival days in some Christian churches are: Corpus Christi (marking Christ's presence in the Bread); the Assumption ('taking up') of the Virgin Mary into heaven, All Saints' Day and All Souls' Day, as well as saints' days marking particularly outstanding Christians. Some Christian churches dislike the emphasis on numerous festivals and keep solely to the major ones which celebrate Christ's life.

12. List the main festivals and briefly state what they commemorate.

13. Christian festivals are mainly concerned with Jesus' life on earth, while Jewish ones are concerned with the Jews' own past.
    (a) Is this true? Give examples when answering.
    (b) Why do you think this emphasis is made?

ISLAM

The Ramadan Fast is described on pp. 138–9. Eid, Idul or Id is the Islamic word for festival, the days of thanksgiving after Ramadan and Hajj.

Ashura ('tenth') is a fast held on the tenth day of the first month, Muharram, to mark for the Shi'ites the climax of the memorial to Husain, Muhammad's grandson who died in battle (see pp. 62–3). For the Sunnis it marks the birth of Adam, the safe landing of Noah and the Exodus of the Jews.

Id al Fitr (or Eid-Ul-Fitr or Little Bairam or Festival of the Breaking of the Fast) is on the first day of the tenth month of the Islamic year. It marks the end of Ramadan. It is celebrated joyfully and people wear new clothes, visit each other and give presents. Graves are visited by relatives. Charity, Sadequah a-Fitr, amounting to the cost of a meal for the whole family, is given to the poor. Potato pasties (samosas), carrot pudding with salad mixed with yoghourt, and syrupy orange jalebi sweets are eaten. Greetings given are 'Assalama Alaykum' ('peace of God be with you') and 'Id-Mubarak' ('Happy Id').

Id-al-'Adha (or Id-al-Kabir, Eid-ul-Adha, Bairam or the Great Festival of Sacrifice) is the feast of the sacrifice at Makkah during the hajj pilgrimage in the 12th month (see pp. 143–5). It recalls Ibrāhīm's willingness to sacrifice Ishmael (Surah 37:100–111; Gen. 22, which names Isaac as the intended victim). A voluntary fast precedes the day of the feast. The Eid prayers are said and a sermon preached, before the sheep, cows or camels are sacrificed. The head of each family slays his own offering or gets a butcher to do it. The animal is placed with its head towards Makkah and killed with one blow by a knife thrust to the throat while the name of God is recited. The flesh is cooked and eaten by the donors with neighbours and the poor have a share too.

Meelad ul-Nabi (or Maulid an-Nabi, or Maulid ul Nabī or Birthday of the Prophet) is on the 12th day of the fourth month. (The original birthday was 20 August 510 CE). Processions, entertainments and poetry readings all recall Muhammad's life, words and sufferings.

Mirāj ('ladder'), Night of Ascent or Lailat-al-Isra, Night of the Journey, is referred to in Sura 17 called Isrā, or Isrā'wal Miraj, Night Journey and Ascension from Makkah via al-Quds (Jerusalem). First Muhammad went with Gabriel on the winged donkey-mule called Burāq from Makkah to Jerusalem. He met Ibrāhīm, Moses and Jesus. Later Gabriel took him up a ladder to see inside heaven and hell. On this journey he learned that Muslims should pray five times a day. The event is marked as a festival on Rajab 27.

Hijrah Day (New Year) marks the beginning of the success and spread of Islam. It recalls the time when Muhammad led his followers away from persecution in Makkah to the welcoming Medina (see p. 27). At Medina they were able to develop their religious community. The festival was first celebrated on 15 July 622. Today greetings are exchanged and stories about Muhammad are related.

14. *Compare the Great Festival with the Jewish festivals ordered in Lev. 6–7.*

SIKHISM

Sikhs have two kinds of festival (a) melas, meetings or fairs, which reinterpret Hindu festivals; (b) gurpurbs, the birth and death anniversaries of the ten gurus.

Hola Mohalla (the Sikh equivalent of 'Holi') includes a three-day fair with horse riding and athletics, begun by Guru Gobind Singh as a form of military manoeuvres as well as to distinguish it from the Hindu Holi.

Baisakhi on 13 April is the New Year Festival begun by Guru Amar Das. It served three purposes, namely initiation of novices, an opportunity to meet the Guru and to allow people of different backgrounds to meet in brotherhood. Guru Gobind Singh took the opportunity of the 1699 Baisakhi to form the Khalsa (see pp. 67–8). People wear new clothes and a service of thanksgiving is held at the gurdwara. During the previous 48 hours the Akhand Path (continuous reading) of the Guru Granth Sahib will have taken place. A cattle market is held outside Amritsar, while elsewhere sporting, music and poetry competitions may be arranged.

Diwali is when Sikhs celebrate the release of Guru Har Gobind (1595–1644) from captivity in 1612. He had been arrested by the Mugal emperor as the Sikh army was a threat to the emperor. Sikhs came to pray outside the prison where the guru was held until he was released. Thus the festival is seen as one of good triumphing over evil. Lamps are lit, fireworks set off and presents given.

Gurpurbs are the anniversaries of the Gurus. The most important are the birthdays of Guru Nanak and Guru Gobind Singh and the martyrdoms of Guru Arjan and Guru Tegh Bahadur. Guru Nanak's birthday celebrations last three days and include a procession in which the Guru Granth Sahib is carried, preceded by five Khalsa leaders with drawn swords, followed by singers and acrobats. On the final day the service begins at 4 or 5 a.m. with singing, lectures and poetry reading, and continues until 1 p.m. Karah parshad and the langar are served to all (see p. 179). When the Guru Granth Sahib is carried in a flower-decked palanquin, five men with drawn swords representing the first five baptized Sikhs, escort it. All gurpurbs involve the Arkhand Path (continuous reading of the Guru Granth Sahib).

15. Why do you think Sikhs have adapted the Hindu festivals?

16. Why does the reading of the Guru Granth Sahib play such a large part in Sikh festivals?

17. Which religions hold festivals primarily in honour of their gods and which in honour of their human leaders? Give reasons for this difference of emphasis.

18. (a) Why hold religious festivals?
    (b) Are they a waste of time and money?
    (c) Do they aid a religion? If so, in what ways?

19. Is there a place for solemn religious festivals as well as joyful ones?

20. What is the place of (a) music, (b) dancing, (c) plays in religious festivals? Which is likely to make the greatest impression?

21. Describe two festivals which have light as a theme.

22. How important do you think festivals and fasts are in keeping a religion alive today?

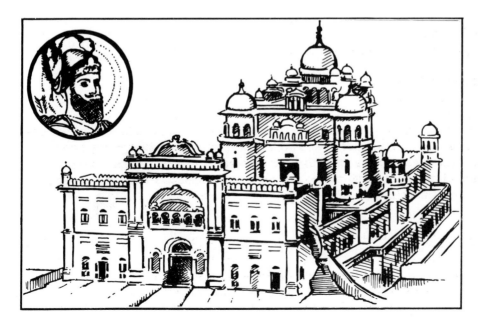

Birthday festival Card of Guru Gobind Singh.

8
ATTENDING
SPECIAL OCCASIONS

In this chapter we shall examine the signing on, coming of age and marriage ceremonies connected with the different religions. Certain rituals may take place to mark the new member with the signs of membership, some form of cleansing may take place to make the person fit for that membership, and finally vows may be taken too. Marriages may be arranged for the couple or they may make their own match, but in each case rituals will be performed to emphasize their new close relationship and bless their future children.

Religious acts or ceremonies are called sacraments. They are outward and visible signs of an inward and spiritual grace which a religion bestows on those involved. They have a mysterious sacred significance. For example, in the Roman Catholic Church, baptism, communion, penance, marriage, extreme unction and the taking of holy orders are such ceremonies.

HINDUISM

Samskāras (ceremonies). A new-born Indian baby is washed and the sacred syllable OM or AUM is written on its tongue with a golden pen dipped in honey. This ceremony is the fourth samskāra of 16 which are performed in connection with a person's life. The first three are to do with conception (so making abortion a great sin) and the last is performed at death. Each samskāra is held in front of a sacrificial fire to the sound of chanting.

Namakarana, the fifth samskāra, is the name-giving ceremony, performed on the 11th or 12th day after birth. A priest works out the baby's horoscope from the exact time and date of birth. The name must begin with one of two or three letters assigned to its zodiac sign, but not a relative's name. Often babies are named after deities.

The Chūdhākarana samskāra is the tonsure, when the barber shaves or cuts a boy's hair and the hair is offered to God. In England this is done at a barber's shop but in India at home or in a temple. It happens in the 15th month of life.

The Sacred Thread Ceremony. This, the tenth samskāra, is the most important. It is called Upanayana ('drawing near') or Yagyopavit or Janeu and occurs for Brahmins between the ages of five and eight, for Kshatriyas at 11 and for Vaisyas

Boys' names
Vjaya (Victory), Shiva, Nataraja (Lord of the Dance i.e. Shiva).

Girls' names
Lalita (Charming), Kumari (Princess), Sita.

Surnames
Gandhi (spice dealer), Desai (chief).

Yagyopavit Sacred Thread Ceremony. What is the thread made of? What is the point of the ceremony? Today the thread is often worn round the waist. The boy is dressed in a yellow cloth with a Munja grass girdle to represent a new body. The girdle goes round him three times as he has to study the Samhitas, Brahmana and Upanishads.

at 12. They are called dvija (twice-born) as they now begin a new kind of life, that of the brahma charya (see pp. 97–8).

This ceremony consecrates the body and entitles it to receive merit. What happens is like a second, or spiritual birth and it marks the start of one's education. Hindus consider spiritual birth to be more important than physical birth. They argue that a mother only carries a baby for nine months, whereas the teacher cares for his pupil for many years. The Sacred Thread has three strings made of cotton, hemp or wool and coloured white, red or yellow, referring to the debts one owes to God, parents and ancestors and one's wise teachers, or representing Brahma, Vishnu and Shiva. The knot in the middle is for the formless Brahman. Only after paying these debts is one entitled to salvation. The knot which ties the strings, each of nine twisted strands, is called the Brahma granthi (spiritual knot), and it means that whoever knows the Supreme Spirit has paid the debts. The thread is put over the left shoulder and under the right arm and worn for the rest of one's life. Wearing the thread, the child stands in front of a fire to hear the prayers said by its father:

> Oh my child this yagyopavit, or sacred thread, is most purified and will lead you to the knowledge of the Absolute. The natural source of the sacred thread is the Lord himself and it is bestowed again and again for eternity. It gives long life and favours thoughts of God. This thread I put round you. By the grace of God, may it give you power and brilliance. AUM, let us meditate on the glorious light of the Creator; may he enlighten your minds.

The boy prays that he may live a good life and follow the truth. Then the teacher says, 'Oh, my pupil, I accept you as one of my children. From now on your happiness and sorrow will be my happiness, and my sorrow.' A boy's head is shaved to mark the start of his new life as the shaving removes any bad karma (evil from a previous life). He now starts the first of four stages of life, the life of a student (brahma charya) (see pp. 97–8).

Five daily obligations of wearers of the sacred thread:
(1) Worship — by offering food and flowers (pūjā)
(2) Reverences for holy men – reciting the Veda
(3) Honouring relatives, elders – offerings of rice and water to ancestors
(4) Helping the poor or holy men with food and shelter
(5) Feeding animals.

1.   Describe what is said and done during the yagyopavit ceremony. Explain its religious meaning.

Marriage. Hindus are expected to marry, to continue the family and care for the welfare of the dead. Girls may marry at 15 and boys at 18 so far as the religious ceremony is concerned. A country's laws may require 16 for a girl. All girls are called kanya devi, girl-goddess of the home. Marriage is the 13th samskāra. Not only must a Hindu marry a Hindu but the couple must come from the same jati (see p. 96). Marriages are arranged by parents, sometimes through advertisements in the Sunday press. The couple may have met socially before the wedding day. Hindus believe their karma destines them to marry a certain person and so parents search for that person.

Hindu wedding costume.

The bride will prepare herself carefully for the ceremony and her friends will rub ointment over her skin. Her kājal eye make-up of ghi (or ghee), herbs, camphor and lampblack was originally intended to keep flies away. She will wear a new sari with gold and red bangles and jewellery. In the centre of her forehead she will put a bindi or kumkum (red spot) of washable powder to show that she is blessed. All married Hindu women put this spot on. She waits for the groom to arrive. Marriages in some parts of India take place at night, starting with a feast at 9 p.m. and the actual ceremony lasting from 1 a.m. to 4 a.m. The groom, dressed in golden clothes and head-dress with threads of beads or silk veiling his face, will arrive on horseback in the midst of a procession lit by neon torches carried by girls and powered by a portable generator. When he arrives the two families exchange presents. Wearing garlands of flowers, the couple will stand under a decorated canopy in front of the priest and the holy fire will be lit as a sign of the pure presence of God. The bride's parents give her to her husband by placing her hand in his, and then her brothers pour fried rice on her hands to show they agree. The couple take seven steps (saptapadi) round the fire, making promises to each other at each step. The last time their garments are tied together. The husband says, 'With utmost love to each other may we walk together . . . May we make our minds united, of the same vows and the same thoughts. I am the wind and you are the melody. I am the melody and you are the words.' On the last step they say together:

> Into my will I take thy heart
> Thy mind shall follow mine,
> Let the heart of yours be mine
> And the heart of mine be yours.

Flower petals are thrown over them before the guests bring forward their wedding presents. Care is taken to worship Ganesha as he holds the key to success in any venture. The groom will not lift his bride's veil until they are finally alone. Married women are titled Shrimati, 'gracious lady' or Mrs.

ENGINEER, Medico, Executive match for tall, slim, pretty Punjabi Arora girl, M.Sc. (maths), post-M.Sc. computer science, father senior executive. Box 154005 Hindustan Times.

VERY WELL SETTLED BUSINESS/HIGH STATUS FAMILY BOY FOR RAMGARHIA, BEAUTIFUL CONVENT-EDUCATED GIRL. DOING MSc (HOME SCIENCE FINAL). 23 YEARS, 162 CMS, ONLY DAUGHTER, PARENTS SETTLED ABROAD IN OWN BUSINESS. CASTE NO BAR. FULL DETAILS BOX 144050 HINDUSTAN TIMES.

MATCH for Brahmin girl, M.A., B.Sc., Primary Teachress, well versed in Household. Write M. Dati, 1513 Laxmi Bal Nagar, New Delhi-110023

New Delhi Sunday newspaper. Compare these advertisements with Sri Lankan ones and an English paper's 'personal' advertisements. See p. 209 for Sri Lankan advertisements.

One major problem of arranged marriages in India is the groom's family's demand for a high dowry from the bride's parents, with items such as refrigerators being listed. In Delhi alone, between January and March 1984, 228 brides died of burns or suicide forced on them by their in-laws. Cases are reported daily in the papers. Few cases come to court, as the reason given for death is usually an accident in the kitchen with the cooking stove, often of the bottled gas type. The Indian government is trying to tighten the law against demanding dowries but it still has to go a long way to ensure that wife-deaths are properly investigated when they occur.

The husband does no housework and the Laws of Manu say that the wife must respect and obey her husband even if he is unfaithful. Orthodox Hindus will not consider divorce, although the Hindu Code of the Indian government does permit it. Hinduism allows polygamy, but Indian law has recently forbidden it. Outside the family organization women are seen as inferior to men. Widows are now allowed to remarry, which was once impossible for them. Women play an active role in government and no political party candidate expects to win against a female candidate.

2. *Why do Hindus have to marry into the same jati?*

3. *Draw up a list of priorities which you might consider as a parent seeking a partner for your son or daughter. What factors do you think parents would consider important, which young people might not?*

Sakaki twig. The
flowers are
yellowish white and
the berries
yellowish brown.

The bride's
headdress is called
the horn hider as it
is said to cover a
woman's horns of
jealousy. It is white
to show she has
'died' as far as her
own family is
concerned.

SHINTOISM

Shrine visiting. The Hatsu-miyā-maiiri (first shrine visit) or Muja-Maiiri (temple visit) takes place on a boy's 32nd day of life and a girl's 33rd day. They are put under the care of the local ancestor god, Ujigami. The priest chants and claps his hands to arouse the god's attention, and gives the baby a small wooden charm, which is worn round the waist in a little bag. He gives the father a sakaki twig intertwined with white paper to symbolize purification. Later on, Shinto followers visit their shrine whenever a new stage is reached in their lives, such as adolescence, marriage, getting a job or retirement. It is felt right that respect should be paid to the local god's befriending of oneself. The ages of 7 and 13 for men and women, also 19 and 33 for women and 25 and 42 for men, are considered yaku (unlucky) years, so they will visit the shrine to drive the evil away by prayer and a money gift.

Marriage. The kami accept sexuality and there is no shame attached to it. Notice the contrast of this attitude to sex to that of most other religions which tend to take a high moral approach to the subject because of their teachings on sin. It is part of human nature, which should be appreciated and fulfilled. Anyone wanting to marry will visit the Ujigami's shrine. The older village style of marriage (mukoiri-kon) involves the couple living at the bride's house for a few years before moving to the husband's. The only rite is the offering of the saké cup (rice wine) by both families to each other. In cities the yomeiri-kon style involves the couple living at the husband's house from the beginning. An arranged marriage may be fixed simply by a miai (an interview to fix the yuino, contract terms) arranged by nakōdo (match-makers, a husband-and-wife team). Sometimes famous people are asked to be nakōdo for the sake of a big announcement party. The nakōdo help the couple in their preparations.

Ceremonies vary a lot, but usually the bridegroom in grey and black visits the bride's house with the nakōdo on the wedding day and a saké party is held. Then the bride in a red, gold and white kimono goes to the husband's house for saké with her mother-in-law. The couple will visit the shrine of their Ujigami where they were taken as babies. The priest will wave his purifying wand over them as part of the Harai purification rite (see p. 104). This wand is called a haraigushi and it is made from a sacred tree with white linen or paper attached to it. Love matches are usual but some marriages are arranged. The new couple may take over the running of the household of the husband's parents if they 'retire' from the task. Some temples have special halls for Shinzenkekkon (weddings) and rent out luxurious bridal gowns.

To divorce a wife, the husband writes a Divorce Letter of three and a half lines. Wives wanting divorce used to have to escape to an enkiridera (temple of cancellation) for three years. Today divorces are granted on grounds of incompatibility.

TAOISM

Protection ceremonies. Children under 16 are protected by the 'Mother' goddess. Three days after birth a ceremony is performed at which red candles are lit and people are careful to say pleasant words in the presence of the hordes of spirits which are believed to be there. The baby is washed and its wrists are tied with red cotton, on which are hung coins and miniature silver toys. They are removed on the 14th day. The idea is to make the baby obedient. Sacred writings may be tied round its waist or neck for protection. On the 14th day the baby has its first haircut in front of the Mother shrine and a feast takes place. Until the age of 16, the rite of 'passing through the door' is held each year, although this is not done in Hong Kong. Priests set up a ceremonial paper arch 2 m high and 1 m wide, an altar and images of the gods. Gongs and trumpets sound as the gods are asked to protect the child. The priests hold swords and bells. Rice is offered as a sacrifice. Then all the family, holding candles, follow the priest, who brandishes his sword against invisible spirits, while going through the arch to the sound of drums. The arch is moved to the four corners of the room and the rite repeated. Each time a small wooden statue to represent the child is made and it is kept until the child is 16 years old. Thus, children pass from a dangerous world into a better one.

At 16 the 'thanking the Mother' ceremony is much the same, the door being the boundary between childhood and adolescence.

4. *What similar things can you find in the ceremonies connected with early life in Hinduism, Shintoism and Taoism?*

5. *(a) What part of the ceremonies would you call superstitious?*
    (b) What superstitions do people in your home area hold today?
    (c) Are these superstitions connected with religions?

6. *The Taoist baby has a copy of the sacred writings round his waist, the Hindu child wears his sacred thread and Christians often wear crosses, while school children carry lucky charms at exam time. Do you agree with the claims made for the possession of such objects?*

Marriage is part of Yang and Yin and the joining of these male and female forces produces Tao (the Way) which is one man and one woman together. Sexual intercourse is part of nature, and in marriage two people are bringing Yang and Yin together in harmony as they should. To stay unmarried is unnatural. In Hong Kong marriage is a civil ceremony.

Mei-jen (friends, relatives or professionals) are go-betweens who make the preliminary arrangements. All-important are the 'Eight Character' certificates which give the hour, day and year of the couple's births. An astrologer is asked to pronounce on them. Certain years are out of harmony with others, and the couple's elements may not match. The Five Elements are identified with the planets. Water (Mercury) produces Wood (Jupiter), but extinguishes Fire (Mars). Fire produces Earth (Saturn), but melts Metal (Venus). Earth is the source of Metal, but soaks up Water. Thus, for example, a 'Fire' girl would consume a 'Wood' man and their marriage would be unhappy.

Likewise their animal signs may be incompatible. Each year, in a 60-year cycle, has a combination of one in five elements and one in 12 zodiac animals. 'A white horse will not share a stall with a black cow.' 'The boar and monkey are soon parted.'

The bridegroom's marriage contract is on red dragon-decorated paper and the bride's on green with a phoenix. An auspicious day is chosen. The bride has a

Bottles of whisky
and other presents
for a Chinese
wedding.

ceremonial bath and pays respect to the ancestral tablets before a long farewell with her parents. They do not attend the ceremony. She says she is dying or wants to die and her relatives reassure her in the ritual farewell. Finally, she is carried off in a decorated red sedan chair which contains a mirror to shield her from evil spirits. Cars are often used now. The journey is accompanied with fire-crackers to scare off spirits. On her arrival at the house of her parents-in-law, the groom will fire three unheaded arrows under the chair as a further precaution. The chair will be carried over a red charcoal fire. Red is the predominant colour of the day as it symbolizes life and joy. Presents are wrapped in red and the bride wears red.

They bow in front of the tablets of the gods and ancestors before meeting their guests. The presents include a pair of red chopsticks as red is lucky and the word for chopsticks sounds like the phrase for 'quickly a son'. They get pomegranates to symbolize a future birth of sons and apples for peace, as the same word is used for both. The couple sit on the wedding bed and the groom raises her veil before they eat and drink together.

The husband can obtain a divorce by writing down all his wife's faults.

7. *Why do you think a couple's home is at the groom's parental home and not the bride's?*

8. *Give some examples of incompatible (a) elements,
    (b) zodiac animals.*

BUDDHISM

Act of Homage. You cannot become a Buddhist until you are old enough to think for yourself. The Buddhist life begins with an Act of Homage, in which you say, 'Praise to Him [the Buddha], the Blessed One, the Worthy One, the Fully Enlightened One [one who has seen the Light of Truth].' You must face a statue of the Buddha and think of his teaching about giving up evil, seeking the spirit of truth within you and helping others. Incense is then offered and you say this:

> All the evil things which I have committed in past lives were done out of ignorance and I ask to be cleansed of these impurities. They are all due to greed, anger, and ignorance which I have cherished for aeons, and they have been practised through my body, speech and mind. Now, without exception I make full confession of them and repent of them, resolving not to commit them after this until the end of time.

You accept the Three Refuges, which refers to the Three Jewels of Buddhism, by saying, 'I take refuge in the Buddha; I take refuge in the Dhamma (Buddhist teaching, see p. 157); I take refuge in the Sangha (brotherhood of Buddhist monks).' Finally, you undertake to live by the Five Precepts (guidelines, see p. 110). All Buddhists chant the Three Refuges and Five Precepts daily.

Marriage. Traditionally parents help their children to find suitable partners. No ceremony takes place at a temple, as a wedding is seen as a secular, not religious affair. The Buddha made no attempt to bring the married state or ceremonies under religious control. The groom says, 'Towards my wife I undertake to love and respect her, be kind and considerate, be faithful, delegate domestic management, provide gifts to please her.' She replies, 'Towards my husband I undertake to perform my household duties efficiently, be hospitable to my in-laws and friends of my husband, be faithful, protect and invest my earnings, discharge my responsibilities lovingly and conscientiously.'

The couple can go to a temple after the ceremony to be blessed and hear a sermon on the Buddha's teaching on married life, but usually invite the monks to their house for this. They bow three times to the Buddha and recite the Homage, 'Honour to the Blessed One; the Exalted One; the Fully Enlightened One', then they recite the Three Refuges and the Five Precepts. After the monks have recited the Buddha's advice, the couple put food in their feeding bowls. The ceremony is called Dāna ('giving').

Divorce and remarriage does occur among Chinese Buddhists but it is very rare, although not rare in Sri Lanka. Theravāda Buddhists believe women automatically have worse kamma than men and so cannot get to Nibbana. Their best hope is to send their sons to be monks, as they then obtain credit for them in the next life. However, some Buddhist sects point out that Buddhism holds that women are born free and with equal rights, intelligence and endowments to those of men. The new Japanese Buddhist sects, such as Rissho Kosekai, stress equality of opportunity to attain Nibbana and have many women religious leaders.

9. Why might parental intervention in finding a partner be (a) a help, (b) a hindrance to a happy marriage?

10. (a) Would you be satisfied with the promises made by the couple to each other or would you disagree with anything promised?
   (b) What other points could be included in such promises?

Karawe Catholic parents seek suitable partner below 33 years for their daughter, typist clerk in a Commercial Bank, salary Rs. 1700/- per month, slim, fair, 5' 7", age 27 years. Dowry cash Rs. 50,000/-. Full details with first letter, P.O. Box 5531 Colombo.

Govi Buddhist parents of Ratnapura seek suitable partner for their fair and pleasant looking daughter age 29. University-qualified pre-school teacher in a leading school in Colombo. An Accountant, Engineer, Bank Manager, Lecturer, Corporation Executive preferred. Apply with details of family and copy of horoscope. Substantial cash. Dowry with a tea property. P.O. Box 5317 Colombo.

A Buddhist qualified partner is sought for Hons. Graduate working as a Lady Scientific Officer (Salary 2,000/-), 28 years, 5' 6". P.O. Box 9327 Colombo.

Advertisements in a Sri Lankan Sunday paper. Notice the Christian's advertisement alongside the Buddhist ones, and the concern for horoscope details which is quite common. See p. 205 for Hindu marriage advertisements.

JUDAISM

Jewish ceremonies connected with birth and joining the faith are designed to stress that you are becoming members of God's Chosen People. Jews believe that God selected them as the people through whom He would disclose Himself and His plans for all mankind. After giving birth, a mother has a ritual bath, mikveh, just as some Hasidim Jews do before the Sabbath.

Brith Millah, or Brit Milah (circumcision, a medical operation performed by the mohel) is performed on boys on the eighth day after birth. The operation's effect is to make a permanent sign on the boy's skin as a mark of membership. The event is a great family one. When old enough a child will learn as his first prayer the Shema ('Hear'), from Deut. 6:4–9, 'Hear, O Israel, the Lord our God, the Lord is One . . .' Note its stress on there being only one God. Jews recite it every morning and evening. Mezuzahs containing the Shema are put on the right-hand door posts of all doors in the house, to be touched as a reminder.

Bar Mitzvah, or Bat Mitzvah ('son of the Commandment') is the coming-of-age ceremony held on the Sabbath (Saturday) following the day after a boy's 13th birthday. A course of instruction in the faith is necessary. The boy may use this prayer:

> *Heavenly Father, at this sacred hour of my life, I stand before Thee in the midst of this holy congregation to declare my duty ever to turn to Thee in daily prayers, and to observe the Commandments of Thy Law by which a man may live worthily. I pray humbly and hopefully before Thee to grant me Thy gracious help . . . Implant in me a spirit of sincere devotion to Thy service, that I may hold fast to what is holy and just and good and resist all evil and sinful temptations. As I grow into full manhood . . . may bodily strength, mental power and moral courage be developed in me, that I may fulfil my duties to Thee . . . as well as . . . to my neighbour . . . Aid my resolve never to separate myself from the [Jewish] community . . . May the noble example of our ancestors inspire me.*

Mezuzah 8 cm long. What do the two tablets pictured on it stand for? What is the name of the seven-branched candlestick above them?

Then he reads the Torah. He is presented with his tallith ('cloak', prayer shawl; see Num.15:37–41). It is made of silk or wool and it was once the sign of distinction and learning to wear one. The strands and knots at each corner represent the Torah's 613 regulations. He will wear it on many occasions and when he dies he will be buried in it. He may also receive his siddur (prayer book). The day finishes with a party, at which he will make a speech thanking his parents and the rabbi for guiding him in the faith, as well as for the presents he has received.

Bath Mitzvah is the corresponding girl's ceremony. In the Reform synagogue she will be allowed to read the Torah. Large family feasts follow the ceremony. Before the Bar and Bath Mitzvah one must have at least two years' instruction in Hebrew and the tradition on several evenings a week from the rabbi (teacher) and possibly have to pass a qualifying exam. Liberal communities also have confirmation services for 15–16 year olds since they feel that 13 years is really too young to make promises.

11. *The Buddhist Act of Homage and the Jewish Bar and Bath Mitzvah ceremonies stress the need for good behaviour. Do you think this should be an important point to be stressed when joining a religion? Give reasons for your answer.*

12. *(a) Do you consider it reasonable or sensible that someone becoming an adult member of a faith should pass an exam to provide his or her knowledge of that faith?*
     (b) Would this help to strengthen the religious group concerned?

13. *Why do you think boys and girls are sometimes treated differently by some religions?*

Marriage. As the divinely-appointed vitality of people's nature, sex is seen as a good thing which must be honoured in marriage. As it enables the Chosen People to continue, Jews are expected to marry. The Old Testament times made it plain that God expected them to 'be fruitful and multiply' and in those days if a young husband died, his brother was expected to marry his widowed sister-in-law so that she could have children (Deut. 25:5). Men were to marry from the age of 18 and girls from the age of 12. A groom was advised not to join the army or to be away from his bride on business for the first year of marriage (Deut. 24:5). Polygamy was finally forbidden in the eleventh century CE. Adultery is considered a serious crime.

Marriage is regarded as a holy covenant and is called Kiddushin, or Kedushin, meaning 'sanctification'. It is rare for a Jew to marry a non-Jew, as religious life is centred on the home – for example, the kitchen where diet is so important. Yet 30 per cent of British Jews marry outside their faith. The wedding need not take place in the synagogue, so houses or gardens are often used.

Inside this Bar Mitzvah card is written: 'We want you to be happy, That's our wish for you, Not only on your Bar Mitzvah Day, But on each future day too. We want you to be happy, In your Manhood, that's just begun, And enjoy life's finest always, For we love you dearly, Son'.

Kiddushin, a Jewish wedding. What is the name of the canopy they stand under and what does it represent?

The rabbi will officiate and the bride will wear white while the groom will have his cappel on. They stand underneath a chuppah (canopy supported by four pillars) to emphasize the 'royalty' of the occasion as the couple are considered king and queen of the day. It also represents their future home. The two witnesses sign the ketubah (marriage document). The groom says, 'I faithfully promise that I will be a true husband to thee. I will honour and cherish thee, I will work for thee; I will protect and support thee'. He and his father will stand under the chuppah and await the bride's arrival as the cantor (prayer leader) sings in Hebrew, 'Blessed be the one that cometh in the name of the Lord . . . May He bless the bridegroom and the bride.'

The rabbi then addresses them before they drink wine from a goblet, the cup of joy. The groom puts a gold ring on the first finger of the bride's right hand, saying, 'Behold thou art consecrated unto me by this ring according to the Law of Moses and Israel.' The Ketubah is read over and seven blessings are pronounced and they again drink from the goblet before the groom crushes a glass under his foot to symbolize the destruction of the Jerusalem Temple and hence the sufferings of the Jewish people. Everyone shouts 'Mazel Tov' ('Good luck').

All Jewish couples are expected to have at least two children to help keep the community going, and a rabbi must set his followers a good example by having his own family. Contraception is permitted in certain circumstances. Divorce is allowed and encouraged if life together has become intolerable. However, divorces are rare. The beth din (see p. 162) issues the document (Get). It is said that a love-filled home is a sanctuary, but a loveless one is a sacrilege. The Talmud says a husband can divorce his wife for a burnt supper – but if a burnt supper takes on such great importance, something must be wrong with the marriage! The importance of sons and the sign of divine favour in the form of a large family often encourages couples to stay together. The person wanting a divorce must get the consent of the other. One safeguard against divorce is that it requires the repayment of the dowry, although a wife's bad conduct (e.g. loud cries, cursing the children in her husband's presence, talking with men, going out with the head uncovered) can stop this compulsory requirement.

14. *Buddhists see a wedding as a secular affair, Jews as a religious one. What arguments can be put forward for both views? Which view do you prefer and why?*

15. *Should a religion indicate the minimum number of children parents should have?*

16. *Should a religious leader marry and have children as rabbis are required to do, or stay unmarried as Roman Catholic priests must? Give arguments for both viewpoints before giving your verdict.*

17. *How do you think Jews square their practical attitude to divorce with their solemn attitude to the contract of marriage?*

Baptism (or Christening) is the name given by most Christians to their joining ceremony. In the Church of England babies are brought by their parents to the church for the ceremony. The parents choose relatives or friends to be godparents whose function is to see that the baby is taught the faith. A boy usually has two godfathers and one godmother, and a girl the reverse. Parents, godparents, the baby and a priest gather at a font. This is a large water container, usually made of stone and situated just inside the church door. The position of the font indicates that the baby is entering the fellowship of the Church. The priest uses water to make the sign of the Cross (mark of Christ's death) on the forehead of the baby. He says, 'I baptize you . . . [name] in the name of the Father, Son and Holy Spirit.' Christians believe that this ceremony marks the spiritual birth of the child as it renounces evil and washes away any sin. It also stresses the spiritual equality of all Christians.

Parents and godparents are asked to ensure that they carry out their duties properly. In the Roman Catholic ceremony, the priest says to the parents, 'You have asked to have your child baptized. In doing so you are accepting the responsibility of training him/her in the practice of the faith . . . Do you clearly understand what you are undertaking?' To godparents he says 'Are you ready to help the parents of this child in their duty as Christian parents?' Both groups are challenged point by point on their belief in Christianity.

One Christian church, the Baptist Church, believes that one should not baptize anyone until they are old enough to say they accept Christianity for themselves. They have baby-blessing ceremonies (Dedication of Children).

When a Baptist has reached at least teenage, he or she undergoes 'New Testament Believers' Baptism' after instruction in the faith. Men wear white shirts and trousers; and women, long white robes. The minister says:

> In Baptism we are united with Christ through faith, dying with Him unto sin and rising with Him unto newness of life. The washing of our bodies with water is the outward and visible sign of the cleansing of our souls from sin through the sacrifice of our Saviour.

Wearing fisherman's waders, he then descends into the waist-deep pool set in the floor of the chapel. The person to be baptized enters too, down one of the two sets of steps. 'Do you make profession of repentance toward God and of faith in our Lord Jesus Christ? Do you promise . . . to follow Christ to serve Him forever in the followers of His Church?' The minister then puts his right hand over the person's nose and mouth and, supporting him with his left hand, bends him backwards until submerged. The person leaves the pool, by the second set of steps, so showing that he is not turning back to the old life.

Conscious of the differences between infant baptism and believers' baptism, a world meeting of churches at Lima in 1982 stressed that baptism should be seen as symbolic of a life-long process which starts with the washing away of sin and being received into the church. The conference called on those who used believers' baptism to find a way of more obviously stressing that children are placed under the protection of God's grace, while those who use infant baptism

Salvation Army crest. Why do you think it has (a) 'S' round the cross, (b) two swords, (c) a crown?

should take greater care to see children are brought up in the faith. All baptized members of the church are expected to help proclaim the Gospel.

18.   *Draw a picture of Believers' Baptism taking place. Describe what happens.*

The Salvation Army does dedicate babies to God's service, but the real signing on comes at a minimum age of seven, usually not less than 16. After instruction the person signs the Articles of War while standing beneath the corps' flag. The flag's red background stands for Christ's blood, its blue for God's purity and its yellow in the middle for the fiery power of the Holy Spirit. The 33 spikes represent Jesus' 33 years on earth; the crown is the crown of life given to those who are saved; the crossed swords are for the fight for God.

Some of the Articles may be summarized as follows:
(1)   The Bible is God-given
(5)   Our first parents were created in a state of innocence, but, by their disobedience, they lost their purity and happiness and [that] in consequence of their fall all men have become sinners, totally depraved and as such are justly exposed to the wrath of God
(6)   Christ suffered to bring forgiveness to mankind; belief in him brings salvation
(9)   We believe that continuance in a state of salvation depends upon the continued obedient faith in Christ
(11)   The soul is immortal and there will be a final judgement resulting in eternal happiness for the righteous and endless punishment for the wicked.

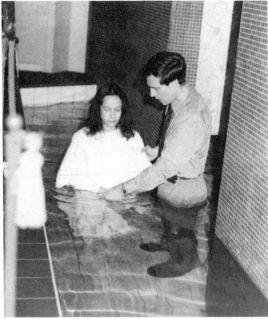

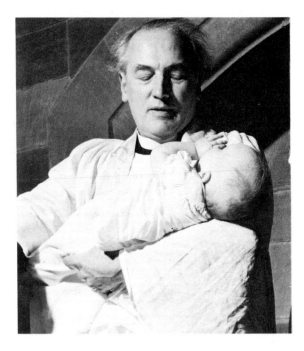

Two styles of baptism. Explain the differences.

Pentecostal churches have Believers' Baptism similar to that of the Baptists, but they also expect their members to undergo the experience of Baptism by the Spirit. This experience can come at any time or place when God so decides, and a person knows it has occurred if his heart is warmed in the faith. Usually this leads to 'speaking in tongues' (Acts 2:1–21), which can mean speaking in a foreign language or in no recognizable one. Speaking in tongues occurs in Pentecostal services and then someone else interprets the message they believe they have heard the speaker convey from God.

Confirmation is a second ceremony held by churches which allow infant baptism. At this ceremony the grown-up child can confirm the promises made on his behalf by declaring his faith in Christ. Confirmation is based on the belief that the first Christians received the Holy Spirit after Christ had left them (Acts 1:7–8; 2:1–21).

During the special Church of England service the bishop (senior priest) asks those who are being confirmed these questions:
'Do you turn to Christ? Do you repent of your sins? Do you renounce evil?' Each must be given a positive answer. The bishop then lays his hands on each believer. By this means, the believer receives the Holy Spirit (Acts 8:17; 9:16) and becomes a full member of the church. The Church of England usually confirms children during the teenage years, but the Roman Catholic Church may confirm children as young as seven. Sometimes girls being confirmed dress in white, like brides.

Methodists receive a Ticket of Membership annually and renew their covenant with God at the annual covenant service.

Church of England confirmation. What is the name of (a) the church official performing the ceremony, and (b) his hat?

ticket of memBership
1990-91
The Methodist Church

a shoRt guioe to chuRch memBeRship

All those who confess Jesus Christ as Lord and Saviour and accept the obligation to serve Him in the life of the Church and the world are welcome as full members of the Methodist Church.

In the Church
Members are committed to worship, holy communion, fellowship and service, prayer and bible study, and responsible giving.

In the World
Members are committed to the working out of their faith in daily life, the offering of personal service in the community, the Christian use of their resources, and the support of the Church in its total world mission.

In Christ we who are many form one body, and each member belongs to all the others.

Romans 12:5

Member ....

Minister ....

Methodist Ticket of Membership (both sides). The scallop shell is from the Wesley coat of arms as well as being an ancient symbol of Christian pilgrims. The fish sign is made up of I-CH-TH-US, the Greek word for 'fish', taken as the initial letters of the Greek words for 'Jesus Christ, Son of God, Saviour'.

Chrismation. In this ceremony the Orthodox Church confirms babies at the same time as they are baptized. Their baptism involves being immersed in water three times. In Chrismation the priest anoints the forehead, nostrils, mouth, ears and chest, and makes the sign of the cross with holy oil. Children take Communion with their parents and when old enough are expected to teach, preach and help run the church.

19. *How do the Salvation Army and the Methodists ensure their members stay active Christians? Should all churches have some form of discipline system?*

20. *List the churches which allow full membership (a) before teenage, (b) at teenage.*

Marriage. Christianity began as a religion aimed at reforming Judaism. Unlike any other religion, it was firmly against polygamy from the start. Husbands and wives were expected to live as if they were one person (Eph. 5:25–6:4). Basically, divorce was forbidden (Mark 10:2–12), although Matthew's Gospel allowed divorce for fornication (Matt. 19:3–9). Over the centuries the Church began to think staying single was more holy than being married. So people wanting to be as holy as possible became monks or nuns. Even today the Roman Catholic Church will not allow its clergy to marry and Orthodox bishops must be single. Among other causes this attitude to marriage arose because Augustine of Hippo argued that mankind's original sin was indulgence in sex. So every sexual act was sinful. In fact, mankind's fall from grace was not because Adam and Eve had sexual relations, as this did not occur until after they were expelled from the Garden of Eden. Their original sin was disobedience to God's command not to eat the tree of knowledge's fruit (Gen. 2:7–4:2). For a very long period many Christians felt every conception was a 'sin' by the parents. The 1549 Church of England Prayer Book said marriage was instituted 'to satisfy men's carnal lusts and appetites, like brute beasts that have no understanding.' The baptism service even stated, 'all men are conceived and born in sin' and prayed that 'all carnal affections may die in him.' Gradually it was appreciated that the sexual act was part of God's creation and so something to be encouraged and enjoyed within marriage. The 1980 Alternative Service Book says marriage is for 'comfort and help' that 'in delight and tenderness they may know each other in love, and, through the joy of their bodily union, may strengthen the union of their hearts and lives.' The baptism service no longer refers to the sin of birth. The Eastern Orthodox church was not affected by Augustine's teaching and so did not relate sex with original sin. Like the Jews and early Western Catholic church, the Orthodox teaching about sex was that it was part of God's good work in all creation. Augustine's argument, that sex was a sinful necessity if the human race was to continue, linked it with the doctrine that God redeems sinners by allowing sex solely within marriage and for the procreation of children. Other religions do not seem to have found sex such a worrying problem as Christianity has done.

21. *(a) What is your opinion of the three reasons in the Book of Common Prayer for the institution of marriage, namely (i) procreation, (ii) remedy against sin, (iii) mutual help and comfort?*
    (b) Would you put them in the same order or not? What are the main changes made by the Alternative Service Book in 1980?

Christians are free to marry whom they wish these days although one church may encourage its members to marry someone from the same church. For example, Roman Catholics argue that children of a marriage in which one partner is Catholic must be brought up as Catholics.

CHRISTIANITY

There were no church marriage services before the ninth century (not until 1563 did a priest have to be present) as marriage was primarily a contract between the couple themselves sealed by the 'sacrament' of consummation. Today the church and priest play an active role. Church of England weddings are preceded by three weekly callings of the Banns of Marriage. This involves the priest reading a notice of the forthcoming marriage and calling on anyone who objects to do so. Objections might arise if one of the couple was already married or if they were too closely related already. On the wedding day the groom and the congregation await the entry of the bride usually dressed in white as a sign of purity. The service begins by the priest explaining the purpose, comforts and joys of marriage before the couple are asked if they will love, comfort, honour and protect each other in sickness and in health 'as long as you both shall live' (Alternative Service Book). At one time the bride had to promise to obey her husband but this vow is now optional. After they have promised themselves to each other, the groom puts a ring on the third finger of the bride's left hand and says:

> I give you this ring as a sign of our marriage. With my body I honour you, all that I am I give to you, and all that I have I share with you, within the love of God.

The priest then says, 'That which God has joined together, let not man divide.' During Orthodox services in Russia crowns are held over the couple, while in Greece garlands are used. They drink wine together to show that they will share the basic necessities of life. Then they make a circular procession symbolizing the fact that their union is intended to last, as a circle has no end.

Quaker weddings begin and end in silent prayer, punctuated by vocal prayers and messages appropriate to the occasion. The couple say to each other, 'Friend, I take my friend [name] to be my husband/wife, promising, through divine assistance, to be unto him/her a loving and faithful wife/husband so long as we both on earth shall live.'

Divorce. The Roman Catholic Church will not allow divorce, but will annul (wipe out) a marriage which has not fulfilled the essential conditions – for example, if it was not properly witnessed or the bride consented out of fear. Separation can also be granted, but this does not relieve the partners of their promises of faithfulness, so neither can marry again while the other lives. The Orthodox Church does allow a bishop to grant divorces in extreme cases of distress. Second marriages are performed in church with a slightly different wording to that used for first marriages, as the Orthodox Church sees its role as one of helping rather than condemning people. The Church of England is divided on the whole subject. Some priests will accept divorce as unavoidable at times and charitably remarry divorcees, while others feel that to remarry them would be a mockery of the vows they took in their original marriage.

22. *'That which God has joined together, let not man divide.'*
    (a) Explain, with reasons, why the Church of England is so divided about remarriage in church for divorcees.

217

(b) Compare the different standpoints of the Roman Catholic and Orthodox Churches.

(c) Is there any solution to the dilemma of a solemn 'until death us do part' marriage and the fact that marriages do break down?

23. *The state permits divorce and remarriage while the Christian churches either tend to reject these events or deplore them. If someone is a genuine Christian faced with an unworkable marriage, should he or she primarily follow the law of the land or his or her church's teaching?*

24. *In view of the problems Christians face over divorce and remarriage would the secularization of marriage (i.e. the ending of its religious aspect) solve the problems for (a) active Christians, (b) clergy, or is marriage too basically a religious deed for this even to be considered?*

ISLAM

Initiation. Islam maintains that one is born free of sin, so no baptism is needed. As soon as a baby is born the Adhan ceremony takes place. The baby is washed and the father whispers the Call to Prayer into his/her right ear and then the command to rise and worship into the left ear. Thus the first words the baby hears are the call to worship Allah. A name-giving ceremony (Aqiqa) occurs on the

An Islamic initiation ceremony. What is happening? The mother might want the imam to be present. Why?

seventh day of the baby's life, when the father names the child after reading passages from the Qur'ān. The baby receives one of Muhammad's names or one of his family's or one of Allah's 99 names with 'Abd' ('servant') added, e.g. Abdullah, servant of God. The baby's head is shaved or washed to take away the uncleanliness at birth, then olive oil is put on the head, and money, equal to the weight of hair cut, is given to the poor. Goats or sheep, two for a boy and one for a girl, are sacrificed and the relatives consume two-thirds of the meat and one-third goes to the poor. Circumcision takes place in the hospital shortly after birth in some Islamic countries and in others, such as Morocco, it is deferred until the baby is three to four years old. Then the small boy receives a special haircut and the operation is done at home.

Bismillah ceremony takes place when a child is four years, four months and four days old. It marks the first time that Muhammad saw the Angel Gabriel and the beginning of the child's religious training. The training is done in the mosque school (madrasah, madressa) and includes learning Arabic and much of the Qur'ān.

Marriage (Aqd Nikah) is arranged by fathers for their children, but the girl has the right to refuse the man chosen for her. The contract is business-like, containing whatever the couple want in it about their relationship and their property, so no Muslim official has to be present at its signing. Many Muslims like the imam to officiate, read from the Qur'ān, talk on the responsibilities of marriage, and lead the prayers. The ceremony can be at home or in the mosque. In Morocco the ceremonies last a week. On the first two days the in-laws are introduced to each other in each other's houses; on the third and fourth days similar introductory meetings are made between the couple's friends. The bride and groom promise to do their 'utmost to render their marriage an act of obedience to God, to make it a relationship of mutual love, mercy, peace, faithfulness and co-operation . . .' Big feasts follow the signing. The bride, wearing an elaborate heavy costume, is carried in a special chair by four women and a ceremonial bedding of the couple takes place.

A Muslim woman wearing the purdah veil. The long black robe worn from head to toe is a shador, or abba. A husband may insist his wife wears a purdah out of doors. Islamic dress has a three-fold purpose: (1) To rid self of pride and vanity; (2) Raise the status of women from being mere objects of male attraction and manipulation; (3) Preserve the sanctity of marriage and the family unit.

The groom, resplendent in a pink turban, has to give the bride a marriage gift (mahr) in money, and he cannot claim it back later. Payment may be made over a period of time and the nature of the gift, money, property, etc., will be settled in the marriage contract. The husband has to pay for the housekeeping. His wife does not have to contribute but can use her wealth for whatever she likes. The married woman keeps her own surname while her children take her husband's name.

Muslim men may marry Christian or Jewish women as they believe in the same God. Muslim women do not have this freedom. The Qur'ān permits men up to four wives provided they are treated equally well. Originally this was to ensure care for women who outnumbered men, especially after a war. The modern interpretation of this is that you should have only one wife as you cannot really treat others exactly alike. 'If you cannot deal equitably and justly with more than one wife, you shall marry only one' (Surah 4:3, 129). Today husbands promise not to marry a second wife when they first marry.

25. *The Muslim marriage contract contains a variety of points on the insistence of the couple. How does this indicate their equal position? List what things (a) a husband, (b) a wife might regard as (i) reasonable, (ii) unreasonable.*

26. *What are your feelings about parents choosing your partner? Who is likely to know better – you or your parents?*

27. *What conclusions can you draw from the freedom of a Muslim man to marry a Christian or a Jew which is denied to a Muslim woman?*

28. *Why do you think Muslim men are now less likely to have more than one wife?*

Islam recognizes the strength of the sex drive and stresses that no guilt is attached to sexual indulgence, provided it is a private matter between husband and wife. Any casual 'sexy' behaviour between men and women is therefore entirely ruled out. Adultery is seen as a sin against Allah and not just a personal matter. Thus Muslims view Westerners' sexual behaviour as animal-like and degrading.

'The lawful thing which God hates most is divorce.' Muhammad, *Hadith*

Divorce. Muhammad, in fact, raised the status of women, for previously daughters had inherited nothing. He made the marriage service into a firm contract giving them security. Divorce, which requires reasons to be given, is only to occur in the last resort and then the wife must be properly provided for. A divorced mother retains guardianship of the children up to the age of seven. After that, sons tend to live with their father as he is able to provide for them until they are able to earn for themselves.

The divorce procedure of Talāq (repudiation) follows a set pattern, allowing time ('iddah) for reconciliation. A husband can revoke his first two repudiations of his wife, but the third makes the divorce final. The wife can then remarry after four months. Should the husband and wife want to remarry each other they can only do so if the wife has remarried and been divorced from a second husband. All the three repudiations can be given at one time so making a divorce final immediately. The wife can only force a divorce she wants by persuading the court (Shar'ia) that her husband is incurably ill or has failed to act as a husband. However, she has a right to separation to be followed by a divorce. It is possible for a wife to insist on the same divorce-fixing terms as her husband when their marriage contract is agreed, as it is up to both of them to decide what goes in that contract. Not many Muslim women insert such a divorce equalization clause. Care of orphans and foundlings is important to Islam and families are encouraged to look after them. But adoption – in the sense of their taking the family name and sharing in the family inheritance – is forbidden.

SIKHISM

Initiation. The mother takes her baby and the ingredients for karah parshad (a kind of blancmange) to the gurdwara. The cook takes a bath before preparing it and recites prayers as it is cooking. The ingredients are equal quantities of flour, sugar (called patashas), water and melted butter. The flour is cooked with the butter for five minutes and then dissolved sugar is added. During the thanksgiving ceremony a little amrit (mixture of sugar and water) is placed on the baby's lips and the Guru Granth Sahib is opened at any page and the first letter of the first hymn found will be used as the initial letter of the baby's name, which will be proposed by the Guru Granth Sahib reader. Sikh names have meanings, such as Dhanna Singh, 'wealthy', and Ajit Singh, 'invincible'.

Initiation, Khanda-di-Pahul (Baptism by the Sword). Sikhs are divided into the Sahaj Dharis ('slow adopters', those who have not joined the Khalsa) and the Kesh Dhari Singhs ('long-haired, lion-hearted Khalsa members'). The Sahaj are believers but are not prepared to serve as soldiers. Anyone who accepts the teaching of the Guru Granth Sahib, forsakes idol worship, takes amrit and believes in the one God can be a Sahaj Dhari, but Kesh Dhari of either sex must undergo initiation (Amrit Sanskar, the drinking of the elixir, or water, of immortality; see p. 68). The amrit will make one immortal in the sense that death will be nothing but the casting away of one's physical body so as to enable one to enter a higher realm. Water represents purity and humility; the sugar, sweetness and saintliness. Men receive the additional name of Singh ('lion') and girls Kaur ('princess'), although children of Kesh Sikhs will be given these names at birth in the expectation that they will join one day. Incidentally, having a common name eliminates caste as the easiest way to tell a person's caste was by his or her name. In fact only five per cent of all male Sikhs are initiated.

This initiation can be done at any age from maturity onwards and you must be instructed beforehand. You stand with folded hands before five Sikhs and beg for admittance. They can refuse it if they think you are not yet fit for the ceremony. Those administering and receiving initiation must bathe and wash their hair first. The five are called Piares ('loved ones') and they wear yellow tunics with blue or yellow sashes. They represent the first five Sikhs who answered Guru Gobind Singh's call (see pp. 67-8). They read out the rules and duties required, as well as passages from the scriptures, before asking those seeking initiation whether they will keep them. This involves the following:

> Accepting the teachings of the Guru Granth Sahib and the teachings of the ten gurus (founding wise men)
> Wearing the five K's (Kakars — symbols). See p. 222.
> Abstaining from alcohol and tobacco
> Not committing adultery
> Working honestly
> Putting no trust in magic or charms
> Accepting other Sikhs as brothers
> Giving a tenth of personal savings to charity
> Being ready to sacrifice all for the faith

Amrit is prepared in a steel bowl, representing the human mind and stirred by a khanda (double-edged dagger) while the five squat in the Vir Asan position (warrior's position, with right knee on the floor and left knee raised ready to spring into action) round it, taking it in turn to stir. Those to be initiated cup their hands together to receive the amrit; they consume it five times before more is sprinkled five times on their eyes and hair. They are told, 'From now on your existence as an ordinary individual has ceased and you are members of the

Khalsa (brotherhood). You are to pray to God and God alone, through the scriptures and teachings of the ten Gurus.' They are told to keep the five K's (Panj Kakka, or Panj Kakke) which are Kesh, Kangha, Kara, Kachha and Kirpan.

Kesh means that their hair must be grown long, and in the case of men, beards too, as symbols of devotion to God. A man's beard signifies his strength. Sikhs point out that long hair was customary among Hindu gods, Jesus, the Buddha and Muhammad, and refer to Samson's strength lying in his hair (Judg. 16), as well as giving medical evidence that hair is 'a great factory of vital energy. Hair is living tissue and a functioning entity . . . human hair absorbs solar energy and no life can exist without solar rays.' 'Nature does not err, and if the hair were unnecessary it would not have been provided.' They refer to vitamin D in particular. Sikhs must wash their hair *every* week. They divide their beards and tie the ends together on the top of their heads.

1 Kesh.

2 Kanga.

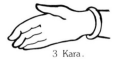
3 Kara.

4 Kachha.

5 Kirpan.

The Five Ks. What are the English words for each of these?

Kangha is a comb, to keep long hair in place under the turban. It is a symbol of cleanliness. The 3–6 m muslin turban is worn to enclose the bound-up hair, and it is seen as a frontier between faith and unbelief, a symbol of generosity, truthfulness and fearlessness. No Sikh will wear anything else on his head and after a long argument with the law courts in England, a special law (Motor Cycle Crash Helmets – Religious Exemptions – Act 1976) was made letting Sikhs ride motorbikes without crash helmets. Boys wear a rumal (small handkerchief) to tie up their hair instead of a turban.

Kara is a steel bracelet worn on the right wrist, symbolizing Sikh unity. It also symbolizes strength in its shape which gives it structural strength. Mathematically it indicates infinity, as any number *(x)* divided by 0 equals infinity. So, regardless of a person's size, *x*, they have strength from their kara. When a Sikh combs his hair in the morning with his right hand and so his Kara goes above his head and he says, 'O Almighty God, Wonderful Lord, you are omnipotent, I am nothing, I am puny, I am zero . . . who has no rival? None but God.' Kara is nearly the same as kari (handcuff) and so it shows one is bound as a disciple to the faith.

Kachha are shorts worn by men and women to give them greater freedom of movement, originally for fighting in battle for their faith. They replaced the Hindu dhoti, a long loose garment.

Kirpan is a short sword, to remind a Sikh of his duty to defend the weak and uphold his faith. Miniature versions are carried today.

The ceremony ends with the distribution of karah parshad. If you break your vows, you would have to apologize publicly to the congregation and do whatever penance (tankha) you were given, such as saying prayers, cleaning utensils or shoes of the sangat (congregation) or preparing the langar (communal meal). Re-initiation is then required as well.

29. *Draw pictures of the five Ks and add a sentence or two under each to explain them.*

30. *Describe the Khalsa initiation ceremony. What Rehat Maryada (code of conduct) rules are required of a Sikh? How do they help a Sikh to cope with life?*

Marriage. Sikhs are expected to marry Sikhs. Parents have a considerable say as to who is to marry whom. Until recently the couple would not have met until their marriage day. Sikhs point to the number of love marriages which fail in England in contrast to the stability of parentally-arranged marriages in their faith.

Sikh wedding. What will the couple walk round while they are holding the scarf?

31. *Is an arranged marriage more likely to succeed than a love match? Give reasons.*

The engagement can be marked by the girl's parents visiting the man's home and presenting him with a kirpan. Sometimes the girl is given a dress, but she may not be present at the engagement parental meeting. The ceremony is called Anand Karaj (Ceremony of Bliss) and sometimes it takes place before sunrise. On this day the mother and other females of the groom's family send him off with his father and male relations to the gurdwara or the bride's home. The men then meet the bride's male relatives at the milani (meeting) and give them turbans. The bride wears a red dupatta (scarf), red or pink shalwar (long trousers) and gold-embroidered kameeze (tunic) and a lot of jewellery. The ceremony can be at the gurdwara, bride's home or in the open air.

They all sit on the floor in front of the Guru Granth Sahib. The granthi (male or female officiant) explains the responsibilities and duties of marriage, stressing its holy status and then asks them to bow before the Guru Granth Sahib to show they accept. The bride's father puts garlands of flowers round the couple's necks and on the Guru Granth Sahib as music and prayers begin. The Guru Granth Sahib is then opened at the Lavan (four marriage vows) and he puts one end of a saffron cotton scarf in the groom's hand, passes it over the shoulder and places the other end in the bride's hand. The granthi reads the first verse and this is repeated by the musicians while the couple rise and walk clockwise round the Guru Granth Sahib holding the scarf. The same procedure is used for three more verses, each of which tells the couple where true happiness lies, namely in devotion to God. Part of the reading is this:

> In the first round, the Lord ordains for you a secular life.
> Accept the Guru's word as your scripture
> And it will free you from sin . . .
> Let your law of life be to meditate on the Name of God . . .
> Fortunate are those who hold God in their hearts; they are even serene and happy.

The congregation shower them with flower petals as they go round the last time. Finally all stand for the Ardas (common prayer) and parshad (see p. 220) is then distributed before the marriage feast takes place elsewhere. No contract has to be signed, and the ceremony takes place before the Guru Granth Sahib.

Wives do not call their husbands by their names but use a term of respect such as 'ji' (roughly 'sir'). Husbands call their wives Ardhangi ('better half') as Nanak made it clear that men and women are equal. The Guru Granth Sahib states:

> It is by women that we are conceived, and from them that we are born,
> It is with them that we are betrothed and married.
> It is the women we befriend and it is the women who keep the race going.
> When one woman dies we seek another.
> It is with women that we become established in society.
> Why should women be called inferior when they give birth to great men?

Guru Nanak made it clear that women could play a leading role in religious services. Widowers and widows may remarry. Divorce and remarriage are allowed, but they are rare.

32. Compare the position of women in Muslim and Sikh marriages.

33. Explain Guru Nanak's comments on Eve in the Garden of Eden.

34. Has Guru Nanak given women a status in Sikhism which women do not hold in other religions? What arguments would Guru Nanak produce to defend his pronouncements on women?

35. Cleansing, washing, or the use of water, is to be found as a main feature of many 'signing on' ceremonies.
     (a) Why? What does it imply?
     (b) Do you think these implications or intentions are sensible ones to make?

36. (a) What should be the minimum age for someone to become a full member of a faith and why?
    (b) Why do you think some religious groups allow signing on at a very young age?

37. (a) What should be done about someone who breaks his or her membership vows?
    (b) Should there be some form of punishment or should this be left to God?

38. (a) Should a person's appearance, e.g. a Sikh's long hair, a Jew's circumcision, mark his membership of a faith?
    (b) Why do non-religious groups mark their membership with special hair styles?
    (c) Why do you think both religious and non-religious groups do such things?

39. Why do special foods or meals play an important role in the worship of religious life? Give examples.

40. (a) What aspects of the joining ceremonies described should be classified as (i) miracles, (ii) superstitions, (iii) supernatural?
    (b) What special elements are essential in such ceremonies?

41. Why are membership ceremonies usually performed by priests or similar people?

42. (a) List religions which allow (i) divorce, (ii) remarriage. List those which do not allow (i) and (ii).
    (b) Is a religion which allows (i) and (ii) setting too low a standard or facing up to what can go wrong in married life?
    (c) Should a religion be content with demanding only minimum requirements or should it set far higher standards for couples than the law of the land might require?

43. (a) Is a religiously performed marriage more likely to last than a registry-office one?
    (b) Do religious beliefs help to keep a marriage going?

44. Give an account of a Jewish wedding bringing out its religious points.

45. Explain the importance of the marriage vows for Christians. What problems can they pose for some couples and clergy today?

46. What is adultery and why do most religions condemn it so firmly?

9
DYING
AND BEYOND

Man is the only animal who knows he is going to die. Naturally, he wonders why and what can be the purpose of living if death is inevitable. Religions claim there is some form of life after death called eternal life. They disagree as to just what form that life will take, but they are convinced it exists. It provides the opportunity to put right the unfairnesses of earthly life. It is argued that earthly life is not in the end tragic for disabled people, the lonely or the poor, as it leads to fulfilment beyond death.

Some religions claim that everything will come to one final climax at the end of time; others do not. If there is life after death a lot of questions arise. Shall we remember our life (lives) on earth? Shall we be able to recognize relatives and friends? Shall we have bodies of some sort? Shall we be able to communicate with others? Can bodiless souls recognize and communicate with each other? Shall we really exist in any form by which we can be identified? Shall we be so absorbed into the Godhead that we cannot be distinguished from any other person? If our identities vanish, what will we have gained by living a good, religious life? Should we think of gaining anything, or just be satisfied with eliminating our selfishness in the worship of God? What can be the purpose of life on earth?

To begin with you must know what you consist of in this life; otherwise you cannot hope to know what might survive on into the next life. Your 'self' is made up of a combination of genes from your parents. Your 'character' is largely built up from these genes but also from the environment and the way you are brought up. If you ask about your 'soul' difficult questions arise. Did God specially create a soul and insert it into you as a baby? Is an embryo a potential soul? Is a soul reborn in countless bodies by reincarnation? Either way that soul must add something unique to your 'self'. But what?

It is claimed that your moral character is built up by your learning to respond or react to your environment – the situation and people around you. Thus you can become a polite, kind person or a ruthless thug. But the word 'soul' implies you are valuable to God as an individual. Think of the popular phrases, 'You have no soul!', 'It's soul-destroying.' To save someone's soul is to save their unique quality as an individual. So the soul is a person's spiritual and moral personality.

Religions feel it is essential to stress that a person is more than just 'self'. A person must have a spiritual side too, and that side is called a 'soul'. They argue that everyone has a 'soul' whether they like it or not. Hence, in you there is a struggle between your self-centred 'self' and your spiritually-centred 'soul'. If you are to find and reach God your 'soul' must conquer your 'self'.

Western religions (Judaism, Christianity, Islam) argue that you have one earthly lifetime only to achieve this. Eastern ones offer several lives by reincarnation as you cannot possibly fulfil yourself and find God in a single, perhaps very short, life. 'One-life' religions may argue there is an extra stage between death and life in heaven — a purgatory state where a soul stays until its failings left over from earthly life can be got rid of. When the soul is made perfect it can go on to heaven.

The Western idea of a new soul being created for each baby born can seem very unjust as some are born malformed or in slum areas while others are far more 'lucky'. The Eastern reincarnation idea removes his criticism of God's unfairness as it claims that your previous way of life determines the circumstances of your next birth – a wicked man may be born deformed, for example.

In the main the Eastern religions tend to say that body and soul are distinct, though they are temporarily joined while on earth. This is a drag on the soul, and so it follows that human life is not God's greatest gift to Man — it is a curse of nature. Man must free his soul from his body's selfishness. Western religions say Man is body and soul together, and death is only their temporary separation. The soul lives on at death and on the Day of Judgement it will be reunited with its body, perhaps in some new spiritual form. Eastern and Western religions disagree as to what a person's construction really is, and hence how he or she will eventually exist in eternity. Eastern religions see the main aim of life as releasing the soul from the 'selfish' body so that they will never be reunited again. Western religions see earthly life as a preparation for the next life — a soul-making time. Easterners see earthly life as a curse which the soul has to suffer and believe you will keep on returning to earth until you have managed to free your soul from your body, i.e. from 'selfishness'.

Other vexing questions are these. Will all people be 'saved' and reach 'Heaven' in the end, or only those who really follow their faith? If we are 'saved', is one really free to reject being 'saved' if one does not want to be? Only those who have died and are in the next life really know the answers. Let us see what the religions teach on the whole subject.

HINDUISM

Funerals. In India the climate makes a prompt funeral (16th samskāra) necessary. The rituals for the dead are called shradda. If possible a dying person will be placed on a floating hurdle in the Ganges and the face washed, as this will save numerous rebirths in the future. Then the dead body will be washed and wrapped in a yellow cloth before being tied to a hurdle. There will be no weeping or wailing, only chanting or silence, as death is welcomed as a release from this life of illusion (maya) to a new and better life. A dead body is called shava which is phonetically close to Shiva.

Cremation at the River Ganges, Manikarnikā Ghat, Benares (Varanasi). The bodies are carried on hurdles. The nearby buildings are blackened by the smoke of centuries. Notice the doms at work, and the body on the hurdle in the river.

The body, wrapped in a red or white cloth, is carried to the riverside steps called the Manikarnikā Ghat. The body is sprinkled with sandalwood oil and garlanded, so honouring it like a god. It is dipped once in the river and put on a pyre (pile) of wood for cremation. Doms (untouchables) supervise the 85 cremations a day and tend the ever-burning sacred fire from which the pyres are lit. They make their living by selling the wood needed and collecting a tax. The eldest son, dressed in white and his head tonsured, will walk round the pyre counter-clockwise – for everything in death is reversed – before lighting the fire by using dried sugar-cane lit from the sacred fire. Ghee (melted butter from which the solid fat has been skimmed off, which keeps well in hot climates) is thrown on the pyre to help the fire burn. When the corpse is almost completely burnt, the son performs kapālakriyā, which involves cracking the skull with a long bamboo pole, thus releasing the soul. Then he puts out the fire by throwing a potful of Ganges water over his left shoulder before walking away. The bones and ashes are collected the next day and lowered into the Ganges in a cloth in the belief that this will prevent further reincarnation and enable the deceased to go straight to Brahman. Hindus in England are cremated at the local crematorium.

Daily ceremonies are performed for eleven days to provide the naked soul of the deceased with a new spiritual body with which it may pass on to the next life. Rice balls called pindā, representing the deceased's body, and milk are offered, for otherwise the soul will remain a ghost to haunt scenes of its past life, irritating relatives. During the transitional time the soul is called preta ('gone forth' from the body); when it arrives at its destination, it is called pitri (ancestor). If the rites are not performed it will stay as preta. Hindus are anxious to have sons as only they are allowed to perform these rites. On the fourth day relatives and friends revisit the deceased's house and comfort the family, giving them presents while prayers are said for the departed soul. A final sympathy meeting, called kriya, is held on the 12th day. Then the deceased's soul is free to pass on to a new life, when a small pindā is joined to a larger one.

Part of the Gītā is recited at cremations:

> Worn out garments are shed by the body,
> Worn out bodies are shed by the dweller.
> Within the body new bodies are donned by the dweller, like garments.

Suttee (literally 'virtuous woman') is the sacrifice a widow was supposed to make voluntarily by which she was burnt on her husband's funeral pyre. This was to wipe out their sins and ensure them millions of years of bliss together in heaven. A widow who did not do this was meant to shave her head, wear no jewels and remain unmarried. Suttee was officially stopped in the nineteenth century, although by some accounts it does continue in villages still today.

Reincarnation. For the Hindu death means the separation of the soul from the body. The soul cannot die or be killed. A person cannot work out his destiny in one lifetime. It would be quite unfair to give him an eternal punishment because he had made some errors during a few years on earth. They believe a person's jīva (soul) (which is sexless; sex belongs to the body) was never born and will never die, for it migrates or moves from one body to another. This is called samsāra (literally 'that which flows together', hence transmigration). So life is complex, mysterious and everchanging.

Starting as a stone a jīva will move to such things as plants and animals quite automatically until it reaches a human being. From then on reincarnation occurs, that is to say it is reborn in people. The new human body that a jīva gets into depends on the life it led in its previous human body. The law of karma (works) applies, and this maintains that you get a position in life according to how good or bad you were in the previous life. So karma is a moral or behaviour law and it works because human beings are self-conscious and can know if they are doing right things or not. Your present condition, your happiness and status are directly the product of your previous life. Consequently you are wholly responsible for your present condition and your future. Notice that God does not judge you for your behaviour as the karma law is an automatic one. No god fixes your future; you do so yourself. Your decide your own fate. Luck plays no part in life at all. You cannot say you have had good or bad luck in a lottery as whether you win or not has been determined in the past by your karma. You can have dukkha (bad experiences) and sukha (good experiences) in your life. You must not feel that you are a condemned person as it is up to you to decide how you will behave and so what your future will be.

1. (a) *State why Hindus almost welcome death and how this affects their funeral customs.*
    (b) *Do you think a person should welcome death when it comes?*

2. (a) *What is your opinion of the Hindu view that one life is too short to find one's atta?*
    (b) *Is it helpful to argue that one has numerous lives on earth?*
    (c) *Is having only one life less fair?*
    (d) *If one's life is affected by a belief in life after death, what differences would it make if one believed one had (i) one life, (ii) numerous lives?*

3. (a) *Is the law of karma just?*
    (b) *Why is it easier to say you will get what you deserve in your next life rather than in your present life? When answering this remember that there are good poor people and wicked rich people in the world.*
    (c) *Will the karma law encourage people to live good lives?*
    (d) *Would you be content to have your life governed by the karma law?*

4. *Is the Hindu right in saying luck does not exist? Give examples.*

The Laws of Manu list punishments for wrong-doing. The man who kills a priest will be reborn as a dog, ass or bull; a man who steals from a priest will be born a thousand times as a spider or snake. Sometimes it is possible for a jīva to find temporary rest in the heaven of one of the gods before returning to earth. Each god has his own heaven, and, to qualify for such a rest, a jīva must have made a pilgrimage, built a temple or some such good deed. The Upanishads claims that a jīva can spend time in one of the numerous heavens or hells between its incarnations. Yama, god of the dead, dressed in blood-red clothes, and holding a noose, judges jīvas by passing them through two fires, in which the righteous will be unharmed but the wicked will suffer.

Although your jīva will go up and down in a zigzag way with transmigration, in the end it will find its atta (real self). Then it will become part of the Godhead and so obtain moksha (release) from the round of transmigration. Until then it can revert to a lower status in life or progress according to its karma. The world is a jīva's gymnasium, its training ground, midway between Heaven and Hell; a mixture of pleasure and pain, good and evil. No social progress, no cleaning up of the world or the bringing of the kingdom of heaven to earth is possible according to Hindus. Notice this contrast with Christianity, which is a religion which seeks to improve life on earth. Hindus believe that Man cannot convert the world into a paradise. Instead the world will develop his character for him.

5. *The Hindu says life on earth is only a temporary business before the real life beyond and the world is only the jīva's gymnasium.*
   (a) What is your opinion of this argument?
   (b) Is life on earth designed to mould your character for the afterlife?

The law of karma leads on to the classification of humans into strict classes and castes, as we have seen (p. 96). Brahmins are nearest to finding their attas as they are the top class but that does not mean that outcastes cannot find their atman. A Hindu welcomes death as a step towards final union with Brahman. Some say that when the jīva passes into the Godhead it loses every trace of its separateness and so it cannot be identified in any way. Others say that some slight differences remain so that a jīva can be identified.

SHINTOISM

Funerals. Everything connected with death is considered pollution but not necessarily an evil. So, when death occurs, a Shinto shrine is covered with white paper to prevent polluted air affecting it. The Japanese see Shintoism as their religion of the living and Buddhism as the religion of the dead. People do not 'die'; they 'withdraw' and 'rise' to heaven. This means that they will have a Shinto marriage but a Buddhist funeral. A recent survey in Japan showed that 93.8 per cent have Buddhist funerals, 3.9 per cent Shinto ones, 1.3 per cent Christian ones and other kinds, 1 per cent.

However, there is a Shinto funeral rite, So-sai, for the 10 per cent of Shintoists who do prefer it to the Buddhist rite. It is usually held at home and not at a shrine so as not to pollute it. An apron (tafusagi) is put round the body's waist, then a knee-length shirt (hadagi) and a tunic, belt and shoes are added. There are two kinds of coffin (kan): nekan, in which the body is lying down; zakan, when it is in a praying position. To the chanting of the chief mourner the coffin or box of cremated ashes is carried out, while the priest purifies the house by sprinkling salt and using his haraigushi (see p. 104). Women wear white veils over their heads and hold a long piece of white cloth which is attached to the coffin or box of ashes, so emphasizing their attachment to the deceased. It is called the rope of life. The service is held inside a curtained enclosure and includes a recital of the person's life. The mourners are purified after the coffin has been buried. Forty-nine days later the Shijūkunichi ceremony installs the Ihai (tablet to the dead) so making the deceased's spirit into an ancestral kami. The Japanese follow the Buddhist custom of grave visiting (Ohakamairi) and carry rice cakes or fruit to show that they treat the dead as living, as kami (see Bon Festival, p. 186).

The soul. Shintoists believe life in this world is more important than any afterlife. As their religion shows little interest in what happens after death, Buddhism has filled the gap (see pp. 236–9). For the first 33 years after death the deceased is remembered at the Buddhist butsudan shrine (which can cost anything up to £2000) in the home's formal entertaining room, but then it is venerated at the Shinto kamidana with the ancestral kami in the ordinary living room (see p. 105). For Shintoists, there is no judgement day to come, souls (tama) are not 'lost' and so do not need 'saving'. Man is called hito, 'human-being-becoming-heavenly'. In other words he is both divine and earthly all his life and so a kami-in-the-making. At death he achieves this new dimension and is called a kami. Moreover a kami which can be near at hand in the kamidana means that death is not so final a break with the living. Relatives have their loved ones near at hand. His soul has two parts: the kunitama, which joins his body at conception, and wake-mitama, which arrives at birth. When these two fall out death occurs and the kunitama returns to the earth from which it came. The old traditional views claim that the innocent wake-mitama go to Takama-no-hara, the High Plain of Heaven, where the kami live. A year of purification can bring the soul to Tok-yo-no-kuni, the Land of Toko-yo, a place of wealth, pleasure and peace. There is also reference to Yomi, the land where the evil spirit Magatsuhi pollutes the dead using aggressive wasps, centipedes and serpents, but where friendly and helpful mice are also to be found. However, modern Shrine Shintoism does not support these traditional views.

6. (a) Why do you think ancient religions like Shintoism raised the status of the dead to that of gods?
    (b) How might this affect the family of a strong-willed granny who had recently died?
7. Shintoism claims life on earth is more important than the afterlife.
    (a) What is your opinion of this view?
    (b) Is it comforting or disturbing?
    (c) Is it likely to affect the way you live now?
    (d) Do other religions hold the same view or do they put eternal life before earthly life?

TAOISM

The Soul. Typical Chinese funeral rites (Sang Li) are connected with ancestor worship. The wealth and status of the deceased will decide how long and elaborate they are. To understand the rite we must find out what the Chinese belief in the soul's structure is. They say a soul is in two parts: the Hun soul is the higher spiritual soul with Yang qualities, while the P'o is the earthly soul with Yin qualities. At death the Hun soul takes on a spirit form (Shen) and has to face a dangerous journey into the underworld. It also enters the green and gold tablet as the Shen Chu Pai with the name, age, birth and death date upon it. This is placed in the house and gold is put there and paper money burnt from 10 a.m. to 4 p.m. for 21 days after death. The P'o soul remains at the grave where it must be ritually pacified and sustained with food to make sure it does not emerge as a wicked ghost (kuei). The purpose of the funeral rite is to aid the Hun soul's Shen spirit in its underworld journey and to ensure its safe transference into the tablet.

Funerals. A dying person's grave clothes are prepared to reassure him that he will be properly buried. Just after death he may be carried outside his home so that his soul will not haunt the house by clinging to the bed. Diviners (Yin Yang Sien Seng) work out when the soul will leave the body as a vapour, saying what form it will take, how high it will be, whether it will be black, yellow or white and in what direction it will go. At the appointed hour everyone leaves the dead person's room.

Taoist coffins.

The diviner will advise on the day, time and place for the funeral. Feng Shui (wind-water) determines where it is natural for the burial site to be – usually a south-facing site with a hill to the east so that spring prevails over autumn, yang over yin. The body is washed and clothed and the feet tied together as it is said it jumps about if chastised by evil spirits. A heavy coffin (113 kilos) of white pine lined with silk and bedding is used. In Hong Kong 50 per cent of funerals are cremations.

On the eve of the funeral a paper stork is burnt as a messenger to deliver the offerings which are to follow. A life-sized paper car with chauffeur, trunks and slave boys and girls is burnt for the soul's journey. A man will precede the procession scattering cardboard 'money' for evil spirits. Professional teams of priests and mourners put on the Huang-lu Chai, Yellow Register ritual for the dead. This involves percussion and wind instruments and acrobatics. A high-ranking Master and his band of 15 can charge huge sums for the ceremony, which will open the way to heaven for the soul. They hang pictures of gods near the coffin. Paper gold and silver money is burnt as well as complete sets of miniature paper clothes for the soul. The female clothes set includes tunic, trousers, and shoes, together with a handbag, mirror, fan, lipstick, earrings, comb, bracelet, and a watch (all these small items are just pictures on a sheet of paper; the main clothes are properly made of paper). Joss sticks are burnt too. On the 21st day a two-storey paper and bamboo house with all its furniture, including paper TV, is burnt for the soul's use.

8. *The Chinese burn paper cars, money, clothing and a house to send to a deceased relative. What does this tell us about their view of life after death?*

In Hong Kong, a memorial mass may be said in which both Taoist priests and Buddhist nuns may play a role. Outside the deceased's house a Spirit Road to purgatory will be prepared by means of a double set of paper and bamboo steps called the Golden and Silver Bridge. Bank notes are pinned at intervals as the soul's travelling expenses along with food and a model of a large house. The shrine with the spirit tablet to the deceased is placed on the Silver Bridge. Relatives then escort the soul along over the Bridge. Afterwards the tablet is returned to its shrine in the deceased person's home or temple memorial hall.

An all night mass will be taken by the shaven-headed nuns who wear special five-pointed birettas. They invite the departed one to attend, listing the person's favourite foods as a temptation. When dawn comes the paper house, ingots and paper clothing are burnt. Baked meats are eaten by all present. The death room is then thoroughly cleaned.

At the final service of remembrance paper clothing is put in envelopes addressed by the priest to the soul and the dot of a cockscomb's blood is put on the ancestral tablet to change the Chinese character from one for Wang (Prince) to the one for Chu (Lord) so changing the deceased from mortal into immortal.

The family wear sackcloth and let their hair grow unkempt during mourning. The deceased's ancestral tablet is put up in the shrine room after the priest has marked it with blood. The length of the mourning depends on the relationship between the mourners and the deceased. The dead are believed to become kuei (ghosts) after three years, and good kuei can be helpful, but bad ones are frightening. So kuei must be honoured. Every day for the first year the family puts food before the tablet as well as before those of the household gods. On the 15th day of the seventh month there is the Ghosts' Feast when food, incense and paper money are burnt as well as a paper boat to take the soul across the river because in that month the door of the unseen regions is opened to the spirits of the dead to walk in.

Taoist paper clothes, money and joss sticks for the next world.

As tablets with their photographs of dead members of a family are put in the shrine room, so the older ones are put in collective ancestral halls in a country setting. The family founder's tablet is on the highest shelf with his descendants below him. All relatives with the same surname use the same hall. In Hong Kong after seven years the body is exhumed. The jade and jewellery in it revert to the relatives. The bones are put in an urn for placing on the hillside. The urns are called chin t'a, golden pagodas.

The journey of the Shen soul is divided into seven periods of seven days each:

Taoist memorial tablets.

First week. It reaches the Demon Barrier Gate and is beset by robbers who demand money, which it pays in spirit money. If the soul has none, it is stripped and beaten. Hence the need to burn paper money bought from the Paper Shop which sells things made of paper for spirits. Hell Bank paper money put in large imposing gold-embossed envelopes, paper gold ingots and cardboard dollars are all available to burn.

Second week. It is put on the scales of the Weighbridge. Good men's souls are as light as air, while sinners' are weighed down by evil deeds. The payment for sinning is being sawn asunder or ground to powder. This is only a temporary ordeal as the soul is restored again.

Third week. The soul arrives at Bad Dogs Village. If it is good the dogs will welcome it, but if not it will be torn apart until the blood flows.

Fourth week. The Mirror of Retribution gives the soul a glimpse of its future; a sinner sees his reincarnation as a pig or serpent.

Fifth week. This week allows the soul a last look back at the past life.

Sixth week. The soul is faced with the Inevitable River Bridge made of a single rope 31 mm (1.25 in) wide and 350 m (1140 ft) high above the rapids and snakes below. The soul is allowed to straddle the rope to get over. Good souls are allowed to bypass the rope bridge and cross by the Fairy Bridge.

Seventh week. The soul reaches the Prince of the Wheel's realm to petition for a speeding up of the transmigration process. Free tea is supplied to wipe out memories of good and bad in the past life. Then the Wheel of the Law is whirled round with the soul trapped between its spokes. If it is allowed to leave by the top right corner it will be a noble person; if by the top left, an orphan, lame or blind person; if by the left or right sides, an animal; if by the bottom right, a scaly creature or shell; if by the bottom left, an insect.

9. *Summarize the stages of the journey a soul takes from the body to purgatory and on to heaven.*

10. *Draw the stages of the journey in a series of pictures.*

Heaven is seen as the place where the ancestors (Pai Tsu) live and from which they control the earth's welfare, so that those on earth should make sacrifices to them. The augury or omen is the connecting language between heaven and earth. Omens can be things affecting the body, such as itchings, tumblings, sneezings, or external signs, like thunder or lightning.

11. *(a) List and explain any omens which have indicated events which did happen, to your knowledge, either to yourself or to someone you know.*
    (b) What is your opinion of omens being the connecting language between the dead and the living? Give reasons for your answer.

The Taoists criticize these Say Pit rites. For example Chuang Tzu (369–286 BCE) when asked about his funeral said, 'Heaven and earth are my inner and outer coffins. The sun, moon and stars are my drapery, and the whole of creation is my funeral procession. What more do I want?' When his wife died, a friend found him singing a song and was shocked. Said Chuang:

> You misjudge me. When she died I was in despair . . . But soon . . . I told myself that in death no strange new fate befalls me . . . If someone is tired and has gone to lie down, we do not pursue them with hooting and bawling. She whom I have lost has lain down to sleep for a while in the Great Inner Room. To break in upon her rest with the noise of lamentation would but show that I know nothing of nature's Sovereign Law. That is why I ceased to mourn.

Finally, Chuang summed up his confidence in facing death when he wrote:

> There is the globe, the foundation of my bodily existence; it wears me out with work and duties, it gives me rest in old age, it gives me peace in death. For the one who supplies me with what I needed in life will also give me what I need in death.

12.   What do you think of Chuang's views on death and mourning?

BUDDHISM

Funerals. 'To realize that life ends in death is to escape from the control of death,' said the Buddha. Buddhist funerals vary a great deal from one country to another. In Sri Lanka a funeral is a modest affair, often by the seashore. For the service the grave area is marked off by a white cloth 'wall' with an entrance arch on one side. White cloth 'arches' are strung between the trees leading up to the area. The mourners, dressed in white, and monks will face each other, sitting on rows of chairs near the entrance arch. The Three Refuges and the Five Precepts are recited. The relatives offer a white cloth to the monks and ask that the merit they receive from this act may be shared with the deceased. A sermon on the Buddha's teaching on death is given and the monks return to give another sermon six days later.

In Hong Kong in 1977 an important grandmother's death, and that of several other relatives who had died sometime earlier, were marked by the employment of a special team of funeral priests costing £20 000. The Taoist-style team included acrobats and in the midst of a varied and colourful programme numerous firecrackers were set off. Bodies can be cremated or buried; in Japan 91.1 per cent are cremated.

In Japan the body is washed, the eyes closed, hands clasped and the body dressed in white as for a pilgrimage. Rice is put out to sustain the soul in the spirit world and a razor or sword for its protection. The priest chants a pillow-sūtra, making the deceased a disciple of the Buddha. The funeral is usually at the temple. Incense and flowers are offered before the coffin which is incorporated into an altar and has a photograph of the deceased on it. Everyone has a photograph taken ready for this purpose. The priest chants sūtras and recalls the deceased's career. Mourners will make their contributions as this extract shows:

Butsudan. The golden metalwork gleams against the black wood.

> Mr Tachi. I was shocked to hear of your tragic, untimely death in a train accident last week. All of us in the office were overcome with grief. You were always so kind to us . . . We hope you are at peace . . . We pray for the happy repose of your soul . . .

The relatives lift the lid for a last look before it is nailed down. The deceased's successor carries a white mortuary tablet before the coffin. At the crematorium the mourners have a meal while waiting for the ashes to be ready. The ashes are put in the urn by the relatives. Hard bones (Adam's apple, knuckles) still remain and these are put in the urn using chopsticks to do so. The urn is then placed in front of the home's butsudan or in the temple for seven weeks. The aim of the rite is to separate the spirit of the deceased from its body so that it can go to the ideal world, and to dispose of the body to ensure no pollution.

A week later the priest will give the deceased a posthumous name as a kind of ordination into buddhahood. Notice that in Japan immediate buddhahood rather than rebirth is the accepted thing. Buddhahood can be obtained even after death. This fits in with the ancestor becoming a kami (see below).

Memorial rites are held on the 49th day after death, as it is believed the soul wanders around the home for seven weeks. Then the mourning ends and gifts are sent to people in return for 'incense money received' (condolence gifts) at the funeral. The urn is then interred and a black mortuary tablet is installed in the butsudan. Thus relatives feel the presence of the deceased in the room and this psychologically supports them. Further rites take place until the 33rd or 50th anniversary, when the spirit changes from being an unstable, dangerous polluting one to a stable, protective and purified ancestral kami. From then on it is honoured in the home's Shinto kamidana (see p. 232).

Before World War II the village carpenter made the coffin, the villagers dug the grave and the priest made all the arrangements, but nowadays a funeral firm sees to everything so separating the functions of priest and funeral director and the role of the community. Many people subscribe to the All-Japan Funeral Directors' Co-operative so as to pay for such costly events by instalments. Funeral directors then tend to charge according to the expected 'incense money' for this is often laid down. For example, when a civil servant dies anyone attending the funeral is expected to give two months' salary to their heirs. Consequently 72 per cent of Japanese think funeral costs are too high and 43.2 per cent want no 'incense money' paid.

13. *Why do Japanese people put food as well as flowers on graves, while Westerners only put flowers? What different ideas about death are implied?*

Japanese tombstones are often decorated with the personal belongings of the deceased such as their umbrellas. Christians believe death is defied by the idea of the dead being resurrected, while the Japanese believe in the continuing presence of the dead. Thus they deny the finality of death and draw comfort from the invisible relative still with them as they daily light incense and offer rice and water at the butsudan.

What happens in the next life is not easy to explain. Buddhists have talked of there being 128 hot hells under the earth, eight cold hells and 84 000 odd ones scattered about the universe for punishment or reward between lives on earth. But such picturesque language can be misleading. The Buddha said that Man is not made up of a perishable 'body' and an eternal 'soul' (jīva), but of five components, the Five Aggregates, skandhas or skeins:

Japanese tombstones.

- Physical features, matter (rupa)
- Feelings (vedana)
- Awareness of senses, sensations which have entered the mind and become perceptions (sannā)
- Intentions, things we do and feel (sankhara)
- Thinking powers, which we have deliberately and consciously made (vinnāna).

All these are constantly changing. For example, a person's skandhas are very different to the skandhas he or she had as a baby. As an adult he looks at things differently. The skandhas dissolve when a person dies. They are not carried on to the next life. What is carried on into rebirth is the kamma, the driving force of desire (tanhā).

Rebirth. The Buddha rejected the Hindu version of transmigration of souls as he said eternal souls did not exist. He offered permanent liberation (Nibbana) instead of a permanent soul. He said that one could break the effects of one's kamma by giving up one's cravings and so cease the Samsara reincarnation cycle by seeking Nibbana. He rejected the Hindu class structure too. It is the things we do and the way we feel that have to be born again and again, until we stop doing wrong, wanting things and having selfish feelings. Only then will there be nothing left to be born again. Rebirth is the endless transmission of an impulse or energy like a billiard ball propelling another it hits while stopping itself!

> All that we are is the result of what we have thought; it is founded on our thoughts, it is made up of our thoughts. If a man speaks or acts with an evil thought, pain follows him as the wheel follows the foot of the ox that draws the wagon . . . If a man speaks or acts with a pure thought happiness follows him, like a shadow that never leaves him! (Path of Teaching)

14. (a) In what way do Buddhist and Hindu teachings on reincarnation differ?
    (b) Which view point do your prefer and any?

Nibbana, or Nirvana. No gods, worship or rituals will enable you to stop your rebirths. You have to achieve it on your own. Buddhism depends on self-help, not on god-help. One can become an Arhat (enlightened person) and achieve Nibbana (literally 'to blow out'; 'to extinguish'). What is 'blown out' is desire. Nibbana is absolute truth, spiritual freedom, freedom from space and time, from illusion, from passion and from all passing things of this world.

'Nibbana is uncompounded – it is made of nothing at all,' said the Buddha, as any compounded thing can be dissolved. It is also unborn – otherwise it would die; it is unmade – otherwise it could be destroyed. Only if Nibbana is uncompounded, unborn, unmade, outside time and space, unperceived by any of Man's senses, can it be really permanent and eternal. If not it would be limited and could be ended. Anything that is born, made, touchable, etc., is merely transient or impermanent (anicca). This does not mean that the human spirit has been wiped out but that it has reached its highest destiny, that of being absorbed into Nibbana. Like wind it is impossible to see. So the Buddha said Man had no soul, a condition called anatta ('atta' means 'soul'). By this he meant that Man had not got a part of him which lasted separately from the universe for eternity. When the Buddha analysed the five skandhas he found nothing behind them which

could be called 'I', 'self', 'soul', and so he declared that Man has no eternal soul.
He claimed the doctrine of anatta does away with the darkness of false beliefs
and produces the light of wisdom. Final and complete Nibbana is called
parinibbana.

15. *(a) Write a full statement of what Nibbana is said to be.*
    (b) Do you think the Nibbana explanation of life after death makes sense
    or not? Give your reasons.

Pure Land. Some Buddhists have developed an alternative idea to replace the
long struggle to reach Nibbana. They argued that there was a nearer goal to hand,
Sukhāvati (The Pure Land of the Western Paradise), a colourful heaven of trees,
streams, bells and birds, which you can reach by having faith in Amitābha
Buddha (Amida in Japanese; O-mi-to in Chinese), King of the Western Paradise.
He has vowed to save all who call on his name in faith. He guides weary
travellers over the sea of sorrow. This is a Mahāyāna (big vehicle) viewpoint (see
pp. 45–6). Faith, rather than the efforts of following the Eightfold Path, will get you
there. Tibetan Buddhists identify particular children as rebirths (tulkus) of
previous spiritual leaders. Their disciples then regard them as rinpoche (precious
jewels). As Tibetan teachings are passed on by such leaders, this is central to their
faith.

16. *Why should it be easier to reach the Pure Land than to work one's way to*
    Nibbana by the Eightfold Path?

17. *'All that we are is the result of what we have thought.' Do you agree or not?*
    Give examples for and against before deciding.

JUDAISM

Funerals. People hearing of a death say, 'Blessed be the true judge.' The
deceased's close relatives make a small tear in their clothing as a sign of
mourning. Funerals are arranged promptly, within 24 hours if possible.
Arrangements are simple as all are regarded as equal in death. No professional
undertakers are involved. The body is dressed in a white shroud (kittel) and tallith
with its tassels cut off. It is placed in a plain wooden coffin with no metal extras.
There are no flowers or music at the ceremony, which consists of a prayer at the
synagogue prior to the burial at the cemetery, Beth Hayyim (the House of
Eternal Life). The coffin is buried and everyone shovels in some earth. The
mourners recite the Kaddish. This praises God and expresses trust in the future
coming of the Messiah to set up his kingdom upon earth. Orthodox Jews will not
allow cremation, as Man is created in God's image and so it would be wrong to
destroy a body deliberately. 'Dust shall return to dust.' When the mourners
return home they are given a hard-boiled egg as a symbol of life – Jews see
death as the doorway to the next life. The family go into mourning (shiva) for up
to seven days. The closest relatives must not leave home and they sit on low
stools. Neighbours visit to offer consolation and help. One of the best deeds a
neighbour can do is to bring the first meal to them. Then for 30 days the
mourners go without amusements until, on the anniversary of the death (called
yahrzeit), they light a candle, recite the Kaddish and set up a tombstone. The
anniversary is marked each year in the home and synagogue by lighting a
candle. It is a religious duty to remember the dead.

Life after death. Jews believe the soul is immortal, but do not try to say what life after death will be like. At one time they did speak of Sheol, a shadowy underground place where the ghosts of the dead went while waiting for bodily resurrection. It was said to be divided up into sections for the good and the bad, and controlled by God (Num. 16:30–33; Isa. 14:9–10, 15; Job 3:11–19; 7:9–10; 10:21–22; 30:23). Jews used to speak of heaven and hell but not very clearly. 'May he dwell in the bright garden of Eden' was a way one could speak of the dead. Nothing was said about what Hell might be like and they did not guess at any tortures which might go on there. They had enough problems to face on earth.

Day of Judgement. Strict Orthodox Jews still look forward to the coming of the Messiah (*not* Jesus) to set up the messianic kingdom after a period of natural disasters and terrors. He will overcome Israel's enemies and set up his kingdom which will end on the Day of Judgement. Then the dead will come alive again in bodily form to await God's judgement. The Messiah is seen to be a strong, wise leader who will carry out a social revolution based on justice. But nowadays Liberal and Reform Jews do not expect an individual Messiah to come, but look forward to the time when the community of Jews will bring in a messianic age of kindliness and justice for all, which will in turn be the Day of Judgement. Some believe the Messiah's kingdom will be blissful and eternal after the Judgement, while others see it as a worldly, temporary affair pending the coming of the judgement. Notice the idea that the soul and body stay together in the end (Isa. 34:1–17; 35:1–10). The blind will see, the deaf hear, the cripples will be whole. Essentially you will get what you deserve on that day. Jews point out that the rewards of a good life are open to all, Jew and non-Jew. They have no exclusive right to heaven, and so there is no need for them to press non-Jews to believe in Judaism.

18.   *Summarize what Sheol was thought to be from the references given above.*

19.   *Summarize the Day of Judgement and its aftermath from the references given above.*

20.   *What reasons do you think the majority of Jews would give for abandoning the earlier views about the coming of the Messiah?*

21.   *Do you think bodily resurrection is essential for an afterlife? Why?*

CHRISTIANITY

Lowering the coffin.

Unction. Roman Catholics help a sick person by giving him the sacrament of Unction or Anointing, which is designed to forgive sins and give spiritual strength to the receiver. The ears, eyes, nose, lips and hands of the sick person are anointed. The consecrated oil (Chrism) made from green wood gives strength, soothes and relaxes but it is not claimed that it restores health. It is not a kind of faith healing. Orthodox Christians use olive oil. Communion given to the dying is called viaticum by Catholics.

Funerals. Burial in coffins is now giving way to cremation as not only do the ashes need less space for interment, but the mourners are less upset by seeing the curtains quietly obscure the coffin in the crematorium than they are by seeing the coffin lowered into the grave and covered with earth. Flowers are often displayed. After a Quaker cremation the mourners gather in their meeting house for prayer and members may rise and praise or recall the life of the deceased.

22. *What are (a) the merits, (b) the drawbacks of (i) graveyard burial and (ii) cremation?*

The Church of England Alternative Service Book quotes Bible passages of hope for the future such as:

> I [Jesus] am the resurrection and the life, said the Lord; he that believes in Me, though he was dead, yet shall he live; and whosoever liveth and believeth in me shall never die. (John 11:25–26)

The service concludes with the words 'We now commit his/her body to the ground . . . in sure and certain hope of the resurrection to eternal life, through

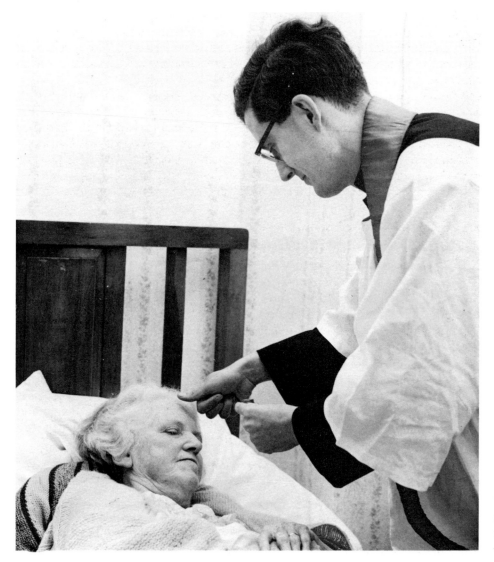

The Christian sacrament of anointing the sick.

our Lord Jesus Christ.' There is a victorious, not sad, nature about the Christian funeral service.

Life after death. The Christian should not fear death but see it as the gateway to eternal life. Having accepted Christ's death as a supreme sacrifice for people, he trusts that sacrifice will pardon his own sins and secure him a place in Heaven. Roman Catholics teach that only those who have led a pure life will enter God's presence immediately. The majority have to undergo a period of purification called Purgatory, where their chief suffering will be the loss of their vision of God. But they will no longer be distracted by the pleasures of the world so their yearning for God will become more intense. Aided by prayers of the living, the saying of masses and the help of the saints, their souls will at last be purged of all sins and see God. The Roman Catholics say that those who died loving evil and hating God banish themselves from Him for ever. They will suffer eternally in Hell. One day Christ will come in final judgement and the dead will rise and the universe be cleansed and changed.

Cremation service showing the coffin disappearing as the curtains close.

Not all Christians would agree with the Catholics. Creeds often include the words, 'I look for the resurrection of the dead,' but do not define what that means. Bible references on the subject are: 1 Cor. 15:20–26, 35–38, 42–44, 53–end; I Thess. 4:13–18. Protestants tend to argue that bodies are mortal and that it is a person's soul which is everlasting. Orthodox churches say that bodies will be restored to life again on the last day. In one way Christianity is unique as it proclaims that the end is already here in that God has entered the world in the substance of Jesus, so that the final outcome of history has already occurred (John 1:1–14). The new age in which God's Holy Spirit is available to believers is with us already, as Christ has saved us from our sins by his death and resurrection. Those who believe in him have eternal life already. The human race now has a new relationship with God available to it.

23. *State the arguments a Christian would give which convince him he should not fear death.*

   They shall recline on jewelled couches face to face, and there shall wait on them immortal youths with bowls and ewers and a cup of purest wine . . . As for those on the left hand . . . they shall dwell amidst scorching winds and boiling water. (Surah 56:4–42)

In another sense the end has not yet come and there have been people who proclaim a second coming of Christ in all his glory which will include the collapse of the universe (Rom. 8; Mark 13:24–27; Rev. 21:1–4). As the Nicene Creed puts it, 'He [Christ] will come again in glory to judge the living and the dead . . . We look for the resurrection of the dead and the life of the world to come.' What form that resurrection will actually take is not clear. However, one thing all are agreed upon, that a person has only one life on earth and that there are no second chances available in future lives here. This gives a sense of urgency to many who preach that one must decide to become a Christian before it is too late. After all one might be knocked down and killed at any time. Christianity, it is claimed, will release you from a fear of death and from a feeling of guilt about your past and give you birth into a new life. Christians believe in the doctrine of Atonement (at-one-ment) by which you can be reconciled to God through Christ's death and resurrection.

24.   *Why does it not particularly matter to Christians that they do not know exactly what will happen at the 'resurrection of the dead'?*

ISLAM

Funerals. A dead body is washed three times (a man's by men, a woman's by women) in the mosque in the wudu way, wrapped in three white sheets (if possible the ones the deceased wore on the Hajj) and carried on a stretcher or plain coffin into the mosque or burial place. After prayers it is buried in a grave with its right-hand side facing Makkah and the head of the body turned toward Makkah. Muslims believe burial should take place if possible on the day of death. Women rarely attend burials. The procession moves quickly so that the deceased can reach heaven sooner. Bystanders each throw three handfuls of earth on the grave, and the first chapter of the Qur'ān is recited. Its third verse stresses the coming of the Day of Judgement, which the deceased will await in a kind of dreamless sleep, so that for the dead it seems instantaneous. They also believe that the body should have contact with the earth and not be contained in a coffin. In Gloucester in 1976 the local council decided Muslims could be buried without a coffin provided that the body was brought to the cemetery in one and then the coffin, minus the lid, was inverted over the buried body so as to cover it. Mourning lasts for seven days and the grave is visited on the seventh day. After burial it is believed two angels visit the grave and question the deceased about his fitness for the next life and prepare him for the Day of Judgement, and for that reason the Shahāda is said over the grave to remind the deceased what to say to the angels.

Day of Judgement. Death is only the end of the present life as Muslims believe in eternal life (Ākhirah, or Akherah). Allah is seen as the God of the Day of Judgement. It is proclaimed in frightening terms:

> When the earth shakes and quivers and the mountains crumble away and scatter abroad into fine dust, you shall be divided into three multitudes: those on the right (blessed shall be those on the right); those on the left (damned shall be those on the left); and those to the fore (foremost shall be those). Such are they that shall be brought near to their Lord in the gardens of delight . . .

When the sun shall be folded up, and the stars shall fall, and when the mountains shall be set in motion . . . and the seas shall boil . . . then shall every soul know what it hath done. (Surah 81)

The turmoil will begin suddenly when angels sound the trumpet once; at the second blast all living creatures will die and at the third all will rise from death and await God's judgement when He has heard the angels' reports. Everyone will be made to read through the report on himself. Then all will pass over the abyss of Hell by the As-Sirat Bridge which is 'finer than a hair and sharper than a sword's edge'. The righteous will cross into Paradise while the wicked will fall into Hell – where purification as much as punishment will take place.

25. *Compare the end of the universe description in the Qur'ān with other religions' theories on the end of the universe.*

26. *Compare the As-Sirat Bridge to the Taoist Inevitable River and Fairy Bridges.*

The arrival in Paradise is described thus:

A state banquet shall they have of fruits; and honoured shall they be in the gardens of delight, upon couches face to face. A cup shall be born round among them from a fountain. (Surah 37:38)

They will live in mansions waited upon by servants while those in Hell will suffer from molten metal, boiling liquids and fire. Only those in Heaven will see Allah. Islam is clear cut and positive about the fruits of life on earth. You will get what you deserve. This also means that what you enjoy in Heaven will be what you are capable of handling; thus some will get more than others.

27. *Why would the Qur'ān's description of paradise delight desert tribesmen?*

SIKHISM

Funerals. When a Sikh dies the body is washed and clothed and placed in the coffin (kwan), complete with all the five symbols of the faith. Cremation follows during which the Sohila (bed-time prayer) is read: 'Strive to seek that for which thou hast come into the world, and through the grace of the Guru, God will dwell in thy heart.' The ashes are thrown into a river. A continuous reading (Akhand Path) of the whole Guru Granth Sahib in which all relatives and friends may take part then goes on for about 48 hours. Alternatively, a Saptah (seven-day) or Dussehra (ten-day) recitation of the Guru Granth Sahib is started at the home of the deceased. A deliberate show of grief is forbidden. Memorials are never erected. Mourning lasts about ten days during which furniture is removed and everyone sits on the floor. No memorial will be erected, as Sikhs do not remember the dead for that person is alive through reincarnation.

Reincarnation. A person is made up of a body and a soul. The body belongs to the Physical Universe where it is born and dies, but the soul belongs to the Spiritual Universe, which is God. This Spiritual Universe is as vast and infinite as the Physical one. Sikhs believe that a person will be reincarnated again and again until his soul is united with God. Man is not basically evil. He was originally good but evil has overshadowed him. A person's soul, being a minute part of the Eternal

Soul, God, has existed from the time of Creation, and until the time it is reabsorbed into Him, it remains separate. The Hindu ideas on reincarnation have been altered by the Sikhs, who stress that all are equal in God's eyes and reject the Hindu class system. A person's soul passes through all stages of existence as with the Hindu transmigration of souls. This is called the evolution of the soul. The highest form of life is the human one. 'You have been granted the human form,' said Guru Arjan, 'now is the time to meet God!' So, the purpose of human life is to enable the soul to appreciate its relationship with God, and by living the life of a good Sikh achieve reunification with God. Your deeds follow your soul like a shadow. Your good deeds, as well as God's grace, will enable you to achieve salvation. Your future is not settled; it is up to you. By repentance, prayer and love, you earn God's grace which neutralizes your previous karma. The fate of the wicked is to be condemned to endless reincarnation until they finally repent and deserve God's grace.

> Mind is the paper, actions are the ink; the good and the bad – virtue and vice – are both recorded therewith.

Guru Nanak thought only reincarnation could explain why some get undeserved miseries and others riches in a particular life. The only explanation could be how such people had lived in their previous lives. Although Guru Nanak said nothing about whether a person lives one life or many on earth, Sikhs came to accept the idea of rebirth. But whether one is reborn or not depends as much on God's will as it does on one's past deeds.

28. How many ways can you think of for the disposal of dead bodies? What are the different religious reasons for these different ways?

29. Some religions state clearly that you get what you deserve in the next or reincarnate life. (a) Is this fair? (b) Can anyone ever live a sufficiently good life to enter into God's presence? (c) Is God's mercy essential if a reconciliation is to be made possible?

30. Is life simply a preparation for eternity, or is it an end in itself?

31. By religions, list in two columns (a) the hopes, (b) the warnings, that religions proclaim on the subject of death and the afterlife.

32. What would you say by way of comfort to a mourner as a (a) Buddhist, (b) Christian, (c) Muslim?

33. (a) Must religions have some theory about life after death if they are to attract and keep followers? (b) Does it help or hinder a religion to be (i) vague, (ii) very positive, in its theories?

34. Everlasting life is the continuance of life in time; eternal life is beyond time and space. (a) Do you agree with this distinction and can you see any other such distinctions between the two lives? (b) Which religions believe in which?

35. Do you agree with the Sikh belief that memorials or monuments to the dead are wrong? How should the dead be remembered?

36. Do you think it is important to have a ceremony such as a funeral service when a person dies? What should such a ceremony consist of?

CONCLUSION

What conclusions can we draw? First, it is clear that people's urge to worship has created, and still creates, endless forms of religious activity. A mosaic of beliefs, attitudes and practices has appeared over the centuries. In all ages and in all countries people have sought to solve the mystery of life.

Secondly, a person's religion is usually determined by where and when he or she is born. Anyone born before Jesus' time on earth cannot possibly have been a Christian – just as anyone born in England is very unlikely to be a Shintoist. If there is one truth to be found, it seems there must be several routes to find it.

Thirdly, history with its scientific and technical changes must lead people to finding different answers to their questions. Earthquakes and volcanoes, rain and drought can now be explained scientifically whereas they once obsessed primitive Man with his fear of spirits. Supernatural causes do not have to be sought for, once natural ones are known. Superstitious healing rites can give way to modern medical knowledge and skill too. Contraception offers a new dimension to sexual relations. Psychology has brought a new light to bear on how our minds work.

Thus the changes and development of history have affected Man's search for truth. Old problems (e.g. earthquakes) have been solved, but new ones (e.g. artificial insemination, mercy-killing) arise. Polygamy of old has been replaced by 'serial polygamy' as a result of divorces and remarriages becoming easier. How should religions believing in life-long marriage react to this? Such questions are open to endless arguments.

Geographical differences have had deep effects on mankind's religious questions. The richly endowed nature of Japan produced a religion – Shintoism – which sought to awaken people's senses of the divine around them. A love of life itself was natural. Judaism, however, was born in the silence and severity of the desert and Protestant Christianity in the cold dark waters of the north with endless cycles of disease and war. It followed that the world was seen as a symbol of Man's sinful nature and life was a battleground of good and bad. The dust of the Middle East and India probably led to Muslim wudu and the Hindu, Buddhist and Sikh custom of removing shoes on entering temples.

Sometimes the beginning of a new religion depended largely on the personality of its founder or revealer getting it 'off the ground'. The Buddha's every hand movement was noted by his disciples; Jesus' magnetic personality drew people to him; Muhammad's inspired leadership commanded absolute obedience, for example. The emphasis of a religion may reflect what its prophet is most influenced by. The Buddha went out and saw the old man, the sick man and the corpse – the natural conditions of individual human life. Moses went out and saw frustrated and enslaved man – the natural conditions of human relationships when one person exploits another for his own ends. Muhammad went out and saw tribes of people worshipping numerous gods — the natural result of groups of people in competition with each other. Jesus went out and saw lonely people, fallen, suffering and unfulfilled — often the natural conditions of individuals in society.

The Buddha thought life was a wheel of futility – everything was transient, just passing by. He left out the fact of progress. Perhaps he saw progress could be as bad as it could be good – is progress from bow to bomb worthwhile? He saw that Man was caught in the trap of attachment; Man has an instinctive drive to acquire worldly possessions. The way out of the trap was to grasp the fact that possessions were a valueless passing illusion and not really worth anything in the end. His Eightfold Path could lead Man out of the trap without the need to believe in a god.

Moses saw the need for action to release his people and so he led them out of captivity. As they were dazed by their new-found freedom, he pressed on them the need for keeping God's law. Muhammad saw the solution of tribal rivalry in the form of an incomparable God who insisted on submission and dutiful obedience. 'Let God be God,' a transcendent, remote divine form who inspires awe in Man. Allah guides man and sends His prophet, but He does not come Himself. In Christianity God comes in human form as Jesus, the Saviour. For Jesus, God was 'My God, My God . . .' No Muslim would add 'my' as a person cannot 'possess' God. For Jesus God was a 'Father' figure with whom one can have fellowship.

Notice the different relationships between God and Man in different religions. Consider whether the difference between religions lies in how far Man thinks God's relationship with him goes, or what type of relationship is involved. Compare your relationship with different people. Who do you love, have friendship with, look up to in awe, obey out of respect, and so on? Then ask yourself whether your mother has the same relationship with your father, your aunt, your brother/sister, your teacher *as you do*. Relationships vary according to who is involved. So Man looks towards God in different ways.

Broadly speaking we have found that religions fall into two groups, the Western and the Eastern. If we take the Western ones – Judaism, Christianity and Islam – on their own, we find that they all believe there is only one God and that He has made special revelations or disclosures of the truth to them. The disclosures they have received are similar in some respects and different in others. Because they believe it is God who has made these disclosures to them they tend to criticize the points on which they disagree more than emphasizing what they have in common. So they dismiss each other's religions as untrue, or only partially true. The Christian argues that the Jews ignore Jesus, while the Muslims say that Christians have ignored Muhammad and the Qur'ān.

Let us look for points they agree on before we examine the disagreements any further. They agree that God sometimes intervenes in the events of history – for example God helped the Jews to escape from Egyptian slavery; He sent Jesus

Christ; He revealed the Qur'ān to Muhammad. Eastern religions would not accept that God acts in such ways.

They also agree that God is the Creator and Commander of all and that He created people to manage the earth for Him. It follows that people should serve Him in return. Thus people have an important role to play in God's plan and must obey God's commandments – Jewish, Christian or Muslim. If such commands are kept, then God will judge fairly, show his compassion and be willing to forgive. Jews, Christians and Muslims agree that God acts in this way.

But it is obvious that people have failed to give a good account of their care of the world throughout history (wars, massacres, neglect of the needy, etc.). They are reluctant to face the implications of creating nuclear bombs or allowing abortions to end life, for example. So people are lawless in the sense that they have failed in their responsibilities. Did God miscalculate when He chose to let people run the earth? Muslims and Christians say 'no' but they offer different explanations.

The Muslim answer to mankind's lawlessness is that people have no excuse as the Qur'ān has revealed what they should be doing. Surah 20 says people are weak and forget, but they can be reminded and helped by the routines of regular prayer and fasting. People can do things by habit and so be 'habituated' into the life God requires of them. Furthermore the government can give a religious lead to the community. In this Muslims are similar to Zionists who talk of a Jewish state, a homeland. Christians may argue that one can defy training by habit, regardless of the fear of severe punishments. Habit training will not cope with a lost sinner, they claim – only the grace of God, the love which suffers alongside the sinner (Christ on the cross) can do that. They argue that, to solve the impasse, the spirit God made Himself into flesh in the form of Jesus so as to be able to demonstrate how He wanted people to live. Then He could also demonstrate His love for the sinner by the crucifixion. For the Christian the relationship between God and people is not only one of commanding and obeying: it is also one of loving and being loved.

Thus Islam claims God sent His messenger, Muhammad, with the message of the Qur'ān, while Christianity claims He sent His Son to lay down his life for mankind. In both these religions therefore, it is God who is searching for us rather than we who are searching for Him. Muslims see qualities of love and compassion in Allah, but do not accept the redeeming love theory of Christ on the cross. Who God is, what mankind's role is and the need for commandments are agreed upon. The disagreement is on what is to be done about people who do not live up to the role required of them. It is not surprising that people's efforts to find the truth should result in disagreements as to how mankind can be brought to fulfil its role.

If we now turn to considering all religions, we find that one basic problem facing them is evil. Where does it come from? Is there an evil god, a devil, behind it? Do we all have evil within us? Christians say that although creation was originally good, evil is now built into the human race. Buddhists claim that life is inevitably bound up in suffering and only the elimination of selfish desire can save one. Buddhists, Hindus and Sikhs claim that suffering is the result of karma, or kamma. Jews and Muslims see it as a test that one must face in life. Christians argue that evil can be overcome and that sin can be forgiven by the believer turning to Christ on the cross. Shintoists argue that evil is not in-built. A purification ceremony is sufficient to restore a person's goodness. No list of do's and don't's is needed for them.

If we ask the question, 'What is the goal of history?', we shall get a different viewpoint to consider. Is history's climax to be a religious or a non-religious one? Karl Marx and his followers expect a marvellous, secular, classless society to emerge. Jews, Christians and Muslims see the goal as the Day of Judgement leading to the life after death. It seems that a person really lives two lives: one here on earth, another in the 'life after death'. For Hindus, life on earth is not real as this world is an illusion (it is not permanent) and the real life will only come after countless attempts to break from this illusion. For any religious person, history acquires a meaning and a purpose when it is related to the truth – when you look beyond the changes and chances of this life to what is to follow. Life on earth by itself is an inadequate answer to the mystery of life as a whole.

Easterners are concerned with the soul's search for immortality, release from this world. Westerners are more concerned to obey God's commands. Easterners do not have a clear idea of God as Creator, Law-giver and Judge, whereas Westerners do. In the West, God commands and Man obeys, and a close relationship is built up between God and His obedient servant. In the East it does not really matter if you believe in one god, several or none, as you can still find Nibbana or Brahman.

In the search for truth, it is noticeable that Easterners are more willing to learn from the experiences of each other. Buddhas can be found in Taoist temples; the Japanese go to Shinto priests for marriages and the Buddhist priests for funerals. Eastern religions are more likely to appreciate that each religion presents the same truth from a different angle. Buddhism sees life on earth as a burden one must escape from and offers salvation by losing oneself in Nibbana, in sharp contrast to the humanists' Marxist offer of salvation on the collective farm – a spiritual solution versus a material or earthly one.

So how can we get all these religions into some kind of focus? It will help if we picture a high mountain with God, the truth of all things, sitting on the top. Down below, on all sides, humans are hunting for ways to climb to the top and find out the truth. They are bunched together in religious groups to help each other, for the climb is going to be a difficult one. Some routes will be dangerous, deceptive and misleading, so it will be sensible to follow a guide who speaks our own language. In the wooded foothills each group starts off along a different way, convinced that it is on the right track. Each religion seems to have arguments among its own members, so the Southern Buddhists set off on a different way from the Northern Buddhists, while the Orthodox Jews reject the way the Reform Jews have chosen, to say nothing of the squabbles among different Christian groups such as Roman Catholics, Quakers, Baptists and the Church of England. But as they climb higher they get clear of the woods and find their routes begin to merge. Orthodox Jews find that their strict keeping to the Jewish laws is not really so important as the fact that they and the Reformed Jews, who are not so strict, both believe that God chose the Jews as a special people. The Christian groups realize their arguments about the types of service they hold are less important than the fact that they all believe Jesus is unique as He is the Son of God in their eyes. Without the wood in the way our religious climbers can see so much more clearly what is important to believe in.

As they approach the summit those who have come up one face of the mountain will be able to see those who have come up the other side. They may find they can help each other to climb the last few metres. One thing is certain, and that is that those who arrive at the top will all meet each other. In the end there can only be one truth to find. In this book we have set off up that mountain from many different routes to see what happens. We have found a lot of arguments over the different starting points, the rules the groups must obey to keep them together, and how the actual climbing is to be tackled. In fact there have even been arguments about what is to be found on the top of the mountain. If there were no arguments this climb of a lifetime would be a dull one indeed.

All this is important to us here and now. Worldwide travel and the migration of refugees and those seeking work has thrown us all together in the twentieth century. The multi-racial, multi-religious society is on our doorstep. We are trying out each other's ways, even if only on the level of curry and sweet-and-sour pork. Punjabi Hindus and Sikhs in Bradford are close and it is not unknown for Sikhs to frequent the Hindu temple and sometimes participate in the leadership of devotion there. Some Christians are trying versions of Hindu meditations to help them in their prayers, while Japanese Buddhists are enjoying the singing they find in Christian churches. Clearly a Buddhist is unlikely to replace the Buddha with Muhammad, any more than a Christian will abandon Christ for either, but this is not so important as recognizing the good points in each other's religions. Jews make it plain that all religions have their routes to God and that Judaism is simply the best route for themselves.

> The need of the moment is not one religion, but mutual respect and tolerance of the devotees of the different religions … The soul of religions is one, but it is encased in the mulitiude of forms. The latter will persist to the end of time.
> (Mahatma Gandhi, a distinguished Hindu)

We should not be afraid to compare religions but learn to help each other along the road to truth. We shall find a greater appreciation of our own faith if we have something to measure it by. If it cannot answer all our problems then maybe another faith will help to supply them for us. No individual human being can hope to know all.

APPENDIX 1
TABLE OF RELIGIONS

Religion	Gods	Foundation date	Founders or revealers	Holy books	Numbers today (millions)	Distribution today
Hinduism	Brahman and 330 million others	1500 BCE	None in particular	Vedas Upanishads	406	India
Shintoism	Amaterasu and 8 million others	650 BCE	None in particular	Kojika	35	Japan
Taoism	Numerous	2000 BCE 570 BCE	Xuan Yuan Huang Di Lao-Tse	Tao Te Ching	30	China, Hong Kong
Buddhism	Not defined	530 BCE	Gautama The Buddha	Tripitaka Sūtras	300	India, Sri Lanka, Thailand, China, Tibet, Japan, etc.
Judaism	God [Hashem]	1800 BCE	Abraham	TeNaKh Torah	12	Israel Worldwide
Christianity	God [Trinity]	1 CE	Jesus Christ	Bible	983	Worldwide
Islam	God [Allah]	600 CE	Muhammad	Qur'ān	850	Turkey, Africa, Iran, Iraq, Pakistan, Indonesia, etc.
Sikhism	God [Akal Parkh]	1500 CE	Guru Nanak	Guru Granth Sahib	15	India, Britain, East Africa

APPENDIX 2
HUMANISM

Humanism is the term used to describe the system of beliefs which puts human interests first and which rejects the belief in a god, or gods. Humanists may be described as atheists. Some do, however, accept that there is a spiritual aspect to life, but refuse to accept any doctrines (agnostics). The kind of society Humanists seek has its origins in the secular pre-Christian world of Ancient Greece.

Humanists argue that religions divide people by demanding obedience. They reject the idea that a god lays down rules of behaviour, arguing that each individual is responsible for his or her deeds and character. There is no divine guidance or support to turn to, so the questions of prayer and sin do not arise. Humanists stress freedom of personal choice, the right to reason for oneself and a belief in humans having an inborn sense of how to behave. Scientific knowledge is the instrument for improving life.

Humanist morality is based on respect and consideration for others – the effect a person's actions will have on other people. They aim, therefore, to be responsible, tolerant, sincere and caring. As a result, they have a strong sense of social responsibility and support (and work for) such organisations as the Humanist Housing Association (which provides sheltered housing), the Independent Adoption Society (for people who wish to adopt, but who do not practise a religion), Oxfam, Age Concern, Amnesty International, the British Pregnancy Advisory Service, the Howard League for Penal Reform and CND. Some Humanists work independently in the community as prison and hospital visitors, nurses, teachers and magistrates. The national body in the UK is the British Humanist Association, but there are also local groups.

Marriage. Humanists are primarily concerned with the human relationship side of marriage. They support the idea of marriage as a long-term partnership but, realizing that some marriages are rushed into too quickly, they suggest a couple might try living together first. They stress that such a pre-marital experiment may not be best for all. Physical love is regarded as one of the greatest human joys, provided it is based on mutual love and consideration. A sense of responsibility between couples is vital.

To offer something in addition to a registry office ceremony, for non-religious couples who want to make something more of their wedding day, the British Humanist Association has produced *To Love and To Cherish: A Guide to Non-Religious Wedding Ceremonies*, with four alternative ceremonies. These offer meaningful rituals, yet underline important values and beliefs. In the ceremonies, 'aspirations' rather than 'vows' are expressed. Although they state firm hope and intention of achieving aims and honouring commitments, they realize that such hopes may not last forever, as people and circumstances change. Men and women are equal in Humanist marriages. Parenthood is important as, not believing in immortality, they hope to leave a better world behind them by producing independently-minded children. Should a marriage break down, feelings of failure will be seen as natural, and not due to any failure to honour 'vows' made before a god.

Death. Euthanasia is accepted by most Humanists. Their *Guidelines for Officiants at Non-Religious Funerals* is a very practical guide, covering every aspect. It suggests a crematorium or burial ceremony procedure so that relatives and friends can say farewell to the deceased in a community atmosphere. Introduced by suitable music, a short opening statement is followed by a tribute to the deceased, the actual committal (to cremation or burial) and concluded with some closing words and music. The tribute will cover the person's life-story and friends and relatives may be encouraged to add their tributes too.

APPENDIX 3
A NOTE ON CALENDARS

BCE = Before the Common Era. It replaces the old BC, Before Christ.
CE = Common Era. It replaces the old AD, Anno Domini, The Year of the Lord. The dates themselves remain the same.

The Gregorian calendar is used in the West and Japan. It is a solar one based on the time it takes for the world to go round the sun.

The *Jewish calendar* is a lunar one with normally 12 months alternating 30 and 29 days each as a lunar month is actually 29½ days. The year starts on Rosh Hashanah in the autumn. Jewish tradition calculates the world as created in 3760 BCE, so add 3760 to CE years to get the Jewish year. For example, 1986 CE is 5746.

The Islamic calendar is a lunar one with 12 months alternating 30 and 29 days; a total of 354 days. Each year begins 11–12 days earlier than the previous one, completing a cycle in 32½ years. 1986 CE is AH 1407. The first day of the year is called the Day of Hijrah. The years are numbered from 622 CE when Muhammad left Makkah. AH means Anno Hegirae, The Year of the Hijrah.

The Hindu creation cycle is made up of four yugas (ages), each worse than the previous one. (1) *Krita* or *Satya yuga*, 1 728 000 years, is the ideal age. (2) *Tretā yuga*, 1 296 000 years – people have become selfish and righteousness is declining. (3) *Dwāpara yuga*, 864 000 years – righteousness is halved. (4) *Kali yuga*, 432 000 years. This age began in 3102 BCE and is now current. Only a quarter remain righteous, religion is declining and calamities are occurring. The whole cycle lasts 4 320 000 years and is followed by a cosmic night of 4 320 million years before a new universe is created.

The Saka calendar of Southern India became the official calendar of India in 1957. It is used alongside the Gregorian calendar. But festival dates may be calculated by other calendars in use in India.

The calendar in China: here the Gregorian calendar was accepted in 1912, but festival dates are calculated from the old lunar calendar, which begins on the first full moon after the sun has entered into the constellation of Aquarius.

The Shap Working Party compiles an up-to-date festivals calendar each year. It is published by the Commission for Racial Equality, Elliot House, 10–12 Allington St., London SW1E 5EH.

INDEX AND GLOSSARY

Arjan (S) (1563-1606), a guru, 31, 67, 91, 201, 245

Arjuna Pandava (H), hero of the Bhagavad Gita, 77-8

Ark of the Covenant (J), cupboard for the Torah, 18-19, 160, 162, 193

Arkan (I), see Five Pillars of Wisdom

Aron Hakodesh (J), see Ark

arti (H), the worship of light, 102, 151-2, 183

Articles of War (C), Salvation Army's statement of beliefs, 213-14

Arya Sama (H), Vedic Movement, 36

Aryan (H), Twice-born, 33-4, 74, 96, 202-3

Asath-puja (B), the Buddha's first sermon festival, 190

asanas (H), body postures, 100

Ascension Day (C), the day Jesus returned to heaven, 24, 90, 196

Ash Wednesday (C), the day on which Lent begins, 197

Ashkenazim (J), Central European Jews, 52

ashram (H), retreat centre, 36, 103

Ashramas (H), four stages of life, 98

Ashura (I), Muharram fast day, 199

Ashoka, (273-232 BCE) Emperor, 42

asr (I), afternoon prayer, 138

As Sirat Bridge (I), crossed by the dead above the abyss of hell, 244

Assassins (I), a sect, 65

Assemblies of God (C), a Christian church formed in 1924, 59

Association of Shinto Shrines, 39

Assumption of the Blessed Virgin Mary (C), her going up into heaven, 199

Assyria, 19

Athanasian Creed (C), statement of Christian beliefs, see Creed

Atharva-Veda (H), a samhitas, 74-5

atheist, one who believes there is no god, 2

Atonement Day, day of penitence to secure good relationship with God (J), 193; (C), 243

atta, or atman (H), one's real self, 7, 34, 75, 78, 97, 101, 230-1

Augustine of Hippo (C), medieval Christian leader, 216

AUM or OM (H), sacred syllable which is said or chanted, 7, 99, 152, 202, 204

Aurangzeb (I) (1658-1707), Emperor, 34, 67

Auspicious Alliance Canon Register (T), priest's list of spirits, 41

Authorised Version (C), Bible translation, 87

avatar, avatāra (H), the form in which a god appears, 8, 50

Avot (J), see Patriachs

ayat (I), a verse of the Qur'ān, 87

ayatollah (I), religious leader, 64-5

Ayatollah Khomeini (I), ruler of Iran, 64-5

azzan (I), call to prayer, 138, 218-19

Baal Shem Tov (J), miracle worker, 51

Babylonia, Babylonians, 19, 20, 50, 53

Bad Dogs Village (T), where souls are put to the test, 235

Badr, Battle of (I), 28

Baghdad, 64

Bahā'u'llāh, 66

Bahā'īs, 66

Bairam (I), see Id-al-'adha

Baisakhi (S), Khalsa's festival, 67, 200

Bait-ul-hah (I), House of God, 143-5

Balfour Declaration on Zionism, 1917 (J), 52

Banda Singh (S), military leader, 68

Bandais (S), followers of Banda, 68

Bani, or gurbani (S), hymns, 70, 179

Banns of Marriage (C), public announcement of marriage-to-be, 216

baolī (S), pilgrims' well, 67

Baptism, initiation ceremony (C), 56, 59, 165, 199, 212-14, 216

Baptist Church (C), church founded in 1612, 57, 170-1, 213-14, 249

baptistry (C), building or pool for baptism, 165

Bar Mitzvah (J), boy's coming of age ceremony, 210

Bat Mitzvah, or Bath Mitzvah (J), girl's coming of age ceremony, 210

Beatitudes (C), sayings of Jesus, 81

Beautiful Names of Allah (I), 29, 90, 175, 217

Believer's Baptism (C), adult baptism of a believer, 59, 213-14

Belur, centre for Ramakrishna Mission, 35

Benares (H), pilgrimage centre, India, 15-16, 100-1, 228

Benedictine Order (C), monks' rule, 133-4

benediction (C), blessing at the end of worship, 167

beth din (J), house of law, court, 162, 212

beth ha knesset (J), house of assembly, see synagogue

Beth Hayyim (J), the House of Eternal Life, 239

Bethlehem (C), place of Jesus' birth, 22

Bhagavad-Gita (H), 'Song of the Lord', holy book, 8, 77-8, 99, 152

bhajans (H), hymns, 103, 152

Bhakti Vedānta Swami (H), religious leader, 36

Bhakti Yoga (H), path of love and devotion, 9, 34, 35, 76, 78, 99, 103, 151

Bharatas, Wars of (H), 76-8

bhāvanā (B), meditation, 115-16

bhikkhu (B), monk, lit. 'one who shares', 116, 117-21

Bible (C), Christian holy book, 17, 32, 54, 58, 83, 85-8, 130, 132-3, 152, 164, 165-6, 170, 173-4, 196, 241-2, 251

big raft (B), see Mahāyāna

bimah (J), reading dais in synagogue, 160-1, 193

bindi (H), red spot on woman's forehead, 204

Birmingham, 36, 48, 65, 69, 160, 174, 177

birth ceremonies (H), 202; (Sh), 206; (T), 206-7; (J), 209; (C), 212-14; (I), 217-18; (S), 220, see Baptism, initiation

Birthday of the Prophet (I), festival of Muhammad, 200

bishop (C), leading priest of an area (bishopric), 57, 163, 168, 170, 197, 214-15

bismillah (I), beginning of religious instruction ceremony, 218

Black-headed (T), Taoist Master, 42

Black Muslim movement (I), 65

Black Stone (I), sacred stone in Ka'ba, 143

Blessed Sacrament (C), consecrated bread, 165-6

boar god (H), see Vishnu

Bodh Gaya (B), site of Buddha's enlightenment, 121

Bodhi tree (B), sacred tree, 15, 121, 157

Bodhisatta, or Bodhisattva (B), enlightened person, 37, 44-8, 82, 119, 158-9, 187

Bodhisharma (B), founder of Ch'an, 46

Body and Blood of Jesus (C), sacraments, 163-6, 167

Bon (Sh), festival of the dead, 186, 191, 231

bonze (B), abbot, 47

Book of Chuang Tzu (T), 13, 80, 106

Book of Common Prayer (C), Church of England prayer book, 56, 216

Book of Revelation (C), last book of the New Testament, 85, 87

Booth, William (C) (1829-1912), founder of Salvation Army, 59

Brahma (H), creator god, 8, 76, 91, 190, 203

Brahma granthi (H), spiritual knot, 203-4

Brahma Samāj (H), a society, 34-5

Brahma Vihāra (B), Four Sublime States, 114

brahma charya, or brahmachārin (H), student stage of life, 74-5, 98, 103, 203-4

Brahman (H), the one great spirit god, 7-8, 10-11, 30, 33-6, 75, 77, 96-7, 99, 203, 229, 231, 249, 251

Brahmana (H), 'Belonging to the Brahmins', part of the Vedas, 74-5, 203

brahmin (H), priestly class, 8, 16, 33, 35, 76, 81, 96, 97, 112, 184, 202, 231

Bridegroom of the (a) Beginning, (b) Torah

crucifixion (C), execution of Jesus, 24-5, 56, 86, 89, 130, 132, 165, 170, 181, 197-8, 242-3, 248

crusades (I), Christian v. Muslims, wars, 64

Cultural Revolution in China, 48

Cup of Elijah (J), cup put out for Elijah, 192

curate (C), assistant clergyman, 58

dāgoba (B), relic chamber and temple, 157

Da'if (I), weak rules, 90

dal (S), platoon, 68

Dalai Lama (B), Gelugpa sect, 47, 48

Damascus, 62, 63

Dāna (B), giving ceremony (H), 101; (B), 209

dancing (H), 152, 181-4; (Sh), 153-4, 184; (J), 194

Darazī (I), sect leader, 64

Dark Night of the Soul (C), 131

darshana (H), sight of an image, 152

Dasam Granth (S), poems by Gobind Singh, 92

Da Sera (H), Durga's Festival, 182-3

Dashara (H), see Da Sera

David (J), Jewish leader, 18, 88

Day of Judgement, 227; (J), 193, 240; (C), 214, 242; (I), 27, 90, 142, 143, 243-4

Dayānanda Sarasvatī (H), (1824-83) religious leader, 36

deacon (C), trainee priest or lay helper, 58, 170

dean (C), senior priest at a cathedral, 58

death (H), 35, 101, 227-31; (Sh), 106, 186, 231-2; (T), 156, 188, 232-6; (B), 111, 236-9; (J), 239-40; (C), 166, 240-3; (I), 174, 243-4; (S), 244-5; see also Chapter 9 and Spirits of the Dead, ancestors, burial, coffins, cremation

Decalogue (J), see Ten Commandments

Declaration of the Truth (I), Shahāda or Kalimah, 137-8

Dedication of Children (C), Baptist Church ceremony, 213

Deepvali (H), see Dīvālī

dekwat (B), temple boy, 118

Delhi, 34, 67, 70, 76, 182, 205

Demon Barrier Gate (T), stage post on soul's journey, 235

demons, see devil

Dengyō Daishi (B), (767-835) sect founder, 47

destroyer god (H), see Shiva

Deutero-Isaiah (J), second Isaiah, 20-1, 22-3

Deuteronomy (J, C), books of the Old Testament, 83

devil, demon (H), 9, 34, 76, 182-4; (Sh), 186; (T), 109, 189; (C), 22, 59; (I), 135, 144; see also Chia demons, Satan

dhamma (B), duty, 111, 113, 158, 208

dhamma-chakra (B), wheel of the law, 113

Dhammākarabiksu (B), see Amida Buddha

Dhammapada (B), Way of Virtue, Path of Teaching, 81, 238

dhan (S), material service a Sikh has to do, 147

dharana (H), concentration, 100

dharma, duty (H), 76, 96-7

dhikr, or zikr (I), reciting Allah's names, 175

dhyana (H), meditation, 43, 100

dhyani buddhas (B), meditation buddhas, 44

Diamond Sutra, or Scripture (B), on Buddha's knowledge and teaching, 82

Diamond Vehicle (B), 45

Diaspora (J), dispersion of Jews, 19

diet, see food

diocese (C), area controlled by a bishop, 58

Dipavali (H), see Dīvālī

Direct Action Day, 1946 (S), 70

disciples (C), Jesus' twelve followers, 22-4, 56, 85-6, 162, 197

Displaced Persons Camps (J), 53

Dīvālī, Festival of Lights (H), 183-4; (S), 67, 200

divination, forecasting of the future, see omens

diviners (T), see omens

divining blocks (T), 156

divorce (H), 205; (Sh), 206; (T), 208; (B), 209; (J), 212; (C), 215, 217; (I), 28, 90, 219-20; (S), 224

Diwali (H), see Dīvālī

doms (H), cremation attendants, 221

Dragon Boat Festival (T), 188

Dragon, Dragon King (T), 189

dreidel, or sevivon (J), spinning top, 194

Druze (I), a Muslim sect, 63

Du'a (I), 'Cry of the heart' prayer, 141

Dual Shinto, Ryōbu, 37

Dukkha, unsatisfactoriness of life (H), 97, 230; (B), 111-12

dupatta (S), scarf, 178, 223

Durga (H), Earth Goddess, wife of Shiva, 10, 34, 150, 182

Durga Puja (H), Durga's festival or Navaratri, 182

Dusehra (S), ten-day reading of the Granth, 244

Dussehra, or Vijaya Dashami (H), tenth day of the Durga Puja, 182

Dusts, The Eight (Sh), human weaknesses, 104

dvija (H), twice-born, 96, 203, see Aryan

Dwāpara (H), third era, iv

Dwarf god (H), see Vishnu

Dyer, General, 68

East India Company, 34

Easter Sunday (C), the day Jesus rose from the dead, 24, 197-9

Eastern Orthodox Church (C), 56-7, 60, 132, 162-4, 196-7, 215-17, 242

Ecclesiastes (J), book of the Old Testament, 88

Ecumenical Movement (C), for Christian unity, 60

Edinburgh World Missionary Conference (C), 60

Egypt, 18, 20, 50, 62, 64, 83, 162, 191-2, 247

Eid, see Id, Id-al-'adha, Id-al-Fitr, Id-al-Kabir

Eight Character Certificates (T), astrological birth details, 207

Eight Dusts (Sh), human weaknesses, 104

Eighteen Blessings (J), 162

Eightfold Path (B), way to Nibbana, 16, 17, 81, 113-15, 157, 238, 247

Ek Oankar (S), 'God is one Being', 31, 177

elder (C), Quaker administrator, 59

Elders, Doctrine of, or, Way of, see Theravāda Buddhism

Elements, the Five, see Five Elements

Elijah (J), prophet, 19, 192

Elim Pentecostal Church (C), founded 1915, 59

ema (Sh), prayer tablets, 106, 154-5

Emperor of Japan, 12, 38, 153-4

Enlightened One, see Buddha, Buddhism

enlightenment (B), finding Nibbana, 44-5, 113, 115, 118-19, 120-1

Epiphany (C), the manifestation of Jesus, 197

episcopacy (C), church government by bishops, 58

Epistles (C), N. Testament letters, 54, 85-7, 166

Eretz Israel (J), Land of Israel, 51

Esala Perahera (B), festival, 191

Esther, Queen of Persia, 194

ethrog (J), citrus fruits, 194

eucharist (C), see communion

evangelical, or low church (C), 58, 129

evangelist (C), gospel writer or preacher, 86

Eve, Adam's wife, 73, 216

Evensong (C), evening prayer service, 166

evil spirits (H), 181; (Sh), 104, 153-4, 186, 206, 232-3; (T), 109, 189, 208, 232, 234; (B), 15; (C), 60, 172; see also devil, exorcism

Exile of the Jews, 20-1, 53

Exodus (J), Hebrews' journey from Egypt to Canaan, 18, 83, 191, 199, 247

Exodus (J), an Old Testament book, 83

exorcism, expulsion of evil spirits (T), 109; (C), 22, 60

Ezekiel (J) (593-571 BCE), prophet, 20, 21, 83

258

Great Awakening (B), when Buddha realized the meaning of life, 15-6, 121
Great Festival (I), see Id-al-adha
Great Going Forth (B), when Buddha left his family, 15
Great Schism (C), split between Orthodox and Catholic, 56
Greece, 43, 56, 217
Gregorian Calendar, iv
grihastha (H), householder, 74-5, 98
Guide of the Perplexed (J), 49
gurbani (S), see bani
gurdwara, or gurudwara (S), temple, 91-2, 147, 177-80, 200, 220, 222-3
Gurmat (S), 'instruction to the gurus', correct name for Sikh religion, 6
gurmukh (S), God-centred person, 146
Gurmurkhi (S), 'Guru language', 66
gurpurbs (S), guru anniversaries, 200-1
guru (H) lit. gu (darkness), ru (remover), wise man, 75, 152; (S), 29-31, 66-8, 91, 200-1, 220-1; see also Nanak, Gobind Singh, Har Gobind, Arjan, Tegh Bahadur, Ram Das, Har Rai, etc.
Guru Granth Sahib (S), 'Teacher Book, Sir', holy book, 31, 67, 69, 91-2, 147, 177-80, 200-1, 220-1, 224, 244, 251

hadasim (J), myrtle, 194
Hadith (I), sayings collection, 90, 136
Hadj (I), see Hajj
Hafiz (I), one who knows the whole Qur'ān, 90
Haftarah (J), a selection of the Prophets, 162
Hagadah, or Haggadah (J), Talmud narratives, Passover story book, 84, 192
Hagar, or Hajarah (I), Isma'il's mother, 144
haiden (Sh), hall of worship, 152-4
Hail Mary (C), prayer to Virgin Mary, 132
Hajj (I), pilgrimage to Makkah, 143-5, 174, 199, 243
Hajji (I), person who has done a Hajj, 145
Hakhamin (J), sage, rabbi, 49
Hakim (I), kalif, 61
Halachah, Halakah, Halahah (J), legally binding statements, 84
halakhot (J), oral law, 49
Halal (I), permitted behaviour, 136
Hallel (J), psalms, 192
Haman, Persian prime minister, 194
Hana matsuri (B), flower festival, 190
Hanukiah, Hanukkah, or Chanukiah (J), Feast of Lights or Dedication, 49, 194
Hanuman (H), monkey god, 10-11, 76
Har Gobind (S) (1595-1645), 6th guru, 67, 200
Har Krishan (S), 8th guru, 67
Har Rai (S), 7th guru, 67

Harai (Sh), ritual purification, 104, 154, 206, 231
haraigushi (Sh), priest's purifying wand, 104, 206, 231
Haram (I), forbidden behaviour, 142-3
Harappan (H), Indian race, 33
Hardwar (H), pilgrimage centre, 30, 102
Hari Mandir, Golden Temple (S), 67, 68, 147, 180
Harijans (H), 'God's people', 36, 96
Haroseth (J), paste eaten at Passover, 192
Harvest (Sh), 179; (J), 194-5
Hasan (I), sound rules, 90
Hasan ibn Sabbāh (I), sect founder, 64
Hashem (J), lit. 'Name', God, see God (J)
Hashishis (I), Assassins sect, 64
Hasidism (J), 'pious' sect, 51
Hasmonean family (J), 49
Hatsu-miya-maiiri (Sh), first shrine visit, 206
haumai (S), self reliance, 146
Havan (H), fire offering, 151-2
Havdalah (J), conclusion ceremony, 162
hazan (J), see cantor
Heaven (H), 9, 230; (Sh), 12, 78, 231-2; (T), 41, 187-8, 235-6; (B), 238-9; (J), 240; (C), 128-9, 196, 198, 242; (I), 28, 244; (S), 91
Heaven, Queen of (T), 14-15, 187-8, 190
Hebrew, 87, 160-1, 210, 212
Hebrew Union College, 51
Hegira (I), Muhammad's migration to Medina, 27, 200
Heian period, 47
heiden (Sh), hall of offering, 153-4, 184
Hell (H), 230; (T), 15, 41, 187, 190, 235; (B), 237; (J), 240; (C), 196, 242; (I), 240, 244; (S), 91
Hell Bank paper money (T), 233-5
Henry VIII (C) (1491-1547), 57, 134
Herod the Great (J) (37-4 BCE), 49, 126
Herzl, Theodore (J) (1860-1904), founder of Zionist movement, 52
Higan (B), Japanese festival for the dead, 191
high church (C), Catholic style of worship in Church of England, 129
Hijrah, see Hegira
Hillel (J), The Elder, 49
himorogi (Sh), ritual site, 37
Hinayāna (B), 'small raft or vehicle', 43, 46, 117
Hinduism, 6-11, 16-17, 29-30, 33-7, 49, 67, 69, 70, 73-8, 91, 95-103, 104, 112, 122, 145-6, 150-2, 157, 181-4, 200, 202-5, 221, 227-31, 238, 245, 248-51
Hirsch, Samson (J), (1810-88) a rabbi, 52
Hitler, Adolf (1889-1945), 53, 126
Hoko (Sh), ornamental processional tower vehicle, 186

Hola Mohalla (S), see Holu Mohalla
Holi (H), spring festival, 181-2; (S), 200
Holocaust (J), Hitler's extermination of the Jews, 53, 126
Holu Mohalla (S), spring festival, 200
Holy books, see (H), Vedas, Upanishads; (Sh), Kojika; (T), Tao Te Ching; (B), Tripitakas, Sutras; (J), Torah, Old Testament; (C), Bible, New Testament; (I), Qur'ān; (S), Guru Granth Sahib; see Chapter 4
Holy of Holies (J), part of the Tabernacle, 18
Holy oil (C), 237
Holy Spirit, or Ghost (C), part of the Godhead, 22, 24, 28, 54-6, 127, 129, 132, 135, 199, 213-15, 242
holy table, or throne (C), 163
Holy Week (C), week including Jesus' crucifixion, 197
Homage, Act of (B), ceremony accepting Buddhism, 209-10
homily (C), helpful talk, 166
honden (Sh), god's living room, 153-4
hondō (B), main hall, 121
Hōnen (B) (1133-1212), founder of Jōdo-Shū, 47
Hong Kong, 4, 42, 155-6, 187, 189, 207, 233, 234, 236, 251
Hosea (J), prophet (active 750-735 BCE), 20-1
Host (C), consecrated bread, 166
hot cross buns (C), eaten on Good Friday, 197
house groups (C), prayer and study groups, 133
House of Eternal Life (J), cemetery, 239
Hsiang Kuo (T), Neo-Taoist leader, 41
Hsin Nien (T), New Year Festival, 188
Huang-lu Chai (T), Yellow Register ritual for dead, 233
Huang-Ti (T), 13, 251
Hui-neng (B), founder of Ch'an, 46
Hui-Yuan (B), Pure Land monk, 45
hukam (S), God's will, 70
humanist, one who rejects the idea of god, 2
Hun (T), heavenly soul, 232
Hungry Souls, or Ghosts Festival (T), 189-91
huppah, see chuppah
Husain (I) (626-80), a martyr, 64, 199
hymns, religious songs (H), 74, 103, 152; (T), 80; (C), 129-30; (S), 91, 179

ibādah (I), worship, 175
iblīs (J), the devil, 144
Ibrāhīm, see Abraham
I-ch-th-us (C), 'fish', symbol, 215
icon, ikon (C), religious painting, 162-3, 197

monks (B), see Sangha; (C), 57, 133-4, 216

monotheism, belief in a single god, 6

Mool Mantra (S), sacred chant, lit. 'basic secret', 91

Morocco, 218

Moses (J), leader (c.1300 BCE), 6, 18-20, 51, 66, 83-4, 88, 121, 160, 200, 212, 247

Moses ben Maimon, see Maimonides

Moshe Rabbenu (J), 'Moses our Teacher', see Moses

Moslem, see Muslim

mosque (I), place of worship, 62, 64-6, 90, 137-8, 141-2, 174, 218, 243

Mother goddess (T), 206-7

Motor Cycle Crash Helmets (Religious Exemptions) Act, 1976 (S), 221

Mount Arafat (I), involved in Hajj pilgrimage, 144

Mount Fuji (Sh), 106

Mount of Mercy (I), see Mount Arafat

Mount Sinai (J), place where God gave Moses the Ten Commandments, 18, 83, 121

mourning (H), 227; (Sh), 231; (T), 233-4; (B), 236-7; (J), 239; (C), 240-1; (I), 243; (S), 244

Muawiya (I), a kalif, 64

Mudita (B), sympathetic or joy meditation, 114

mudra (B), symbolic gesture, 45

Mughal Emperor of India (I), 14, 34, 67, 69, 200

muezzin (I), prayer leader, 138

Muhammad (I) (570-632 CE), Allah's prophet, 6, 26-8, 62-4, 65, 66, 87-90, 136, 138, 142, 174, 199-200, 217-19, 221, 246-8, 250-1

Muharram (I), festival, 64, 199

Muja-Mairi (Sh), temple visit, 206

mujtahidun (I), doctor of law, 64

mullah (I), teacher of Qur'ānic law, 91

murti (H), statue of a god, 150

Mūsā (I), Islamic name for Moses, see Moses

musalta (I), prayer mat, 141

Muslim (I), 'a surrendered man', follower of Muhammad, see Islam

Muslim League, 70

Muzdalijah (I), 144

Nabī (I), prophet, 28, 88

Nagasena (B), a monk who explained Buddhism in Milinda-Panha, 81-2

Nagunuma Myōkō (1889-1957), founder Risshō Kōsekai, (B), 40

Nakayama Miki (1798-1887), founder Tenri-kyō, 39

nakōdo (Sh), matchmaker for wedding, 206

Nam (S), 'Name', Sikh word for God, see God (S)

Nam japna (S), remembering God, 147

Nam Simran (S), 'calling God to mind' meditation, 147

Nāmakarana (H), name giving, 202

Nanak, Guru (S), (1469-1538), founder of Sikhism, 6, 29-32, 91, 145-7, 201, 224, 245, 251

Nanakana, village in Pakistan, 29

Naorai (Sh), communion meal, 184

Nara-Sinha (H), Man-Lion God, fourth incarnation of Vishnu, 8

National Taoist Association, 42

Nativity play (C), Christmas play about Jesus' birth, 196

Navaratri (H), Durga's festival, 182

nave (C), congregational part of a church, 162-5, 167

Nazareth, 134

nebim (I), see nabi

Nebuchadnezzar, King, 20

Nei Tan (T), inner elixir, 109

Neilah (J), final service of Yom Kippur, 193

Nembutsu (B), invoking Amida, 47

Neo-Taoists, 41

ner tamid (J), lamp of perpetual light, 160

Nero, Roman emperor, 54, 86-7

Nevi'im (J), The Prophets, section of the TeNaKh, 83

New Religions in Japan, 39-40

New Testament (C), section of the Bible, 54, 85-6, 126-8, 166, 213

Nibbana, Nirbana, or Nirvana (B), 'going out', 'cooling off', the extinction of earthly self, 33, 43-5, 82, 113, 115-17, 119, 157, 190, 209, 238-9, 249

Nicene Creed (C), statement of Christian beliefs, 55-6, 166, 243

Nichiren (B), sect leader, 48

Night of Ascent or Journey (I), 200

Night of Power (I), see Lailat-al-Qadr, 27

Nihongi or Nihon Shoki (Sh), Chronicles of Japan, book compiled 720 CE, 79

nikku (Sh), worship, 154

Nine Hells Litany of Repentance (T), 187

Ninigi-no-Mikoto (Sh), Amaterasu's son, 12

Nirodha (B), Third Noble Truth, 112

Nisham Sahib (S), flag-pole, 177

Nitnem (S), private devotion collection, 92

Niwano Nikkyō (B), sect founder, 40

Niyama (H), rules, 96, 100

Noah (J), survivor of the great flood, 6, 8, 17, 53, 54, 199

Noahide Law (J), law for God-fearers, 54

nonconformist (C), one who does not conform to the Church of England, 59-60

Northern Buddhism, see Mahāyāna Buddhism

Numbers (J, C), a book of the TeNaKh or Old Testament, 83

nuns (B), 113-14, 226; (C), 57, 133, 216

Nusa (Sh), see haraigushi

Nyingmapa (B), 'Old Ones', 44, 46

Obon (Sh), see Bon

offerings, see alms, sacrifice, (H), 74, 100, 151, 181, 183, 204; (Sh), 105-6, 154, 184, 186; (T), 110, 156, 190, 234; (B), 116-18, 121, 157-9, 190-1, 209; (C), 166; (I), see zakat; (S), 177-8

offertory (C), almsgiving, 166

Ohakamairi (Sh), grave visiting, 231

Oharai (Sh), see Harai

Old Testament (J, C), holy book collection, 83-7, 166, 192-3, 211

OM (H), see AUM

omamori (B), amulets, 48

Omar (I), a kalif, 62

omens (H), 202; (Sh), 37, 154; (T), 155-6, 207, 232-3, 235; (B), 158; (J), 194

O-mi-to-Fu (B), Amida, Lord of the Western Paradise, 38, 44-8, 119, 158, 238

Oral Law (J), 18, 49-50, 84

organ (J), 161; (C), 165, 167, 171

Origen (C), Bible critic, 55

original sin (C), 129, 136, 216, see sin

Orthodox Church (C), see Eastern Orthodox Church

Orthodox Jews, 51-3, 85, 123, 161, 191-2, 239-40, 249

Othman (I), a kalif, 62, 64

Our Father (C), see Lord's Prayer

outcasts (H), see pariahs

overseers (C), 57

Padmā, wife of Vāmana (H), 8

pagodas (B), relic chambers, 157-8

pahul (S), initiation, 220-2

Pai Tsu (T), ancestors' heaven, 235

Pakistan, 29, 64, 65, 70, 251

palanquin, god-carriages (Sh), 185; (T), 156, 187-8; (S), 180, 201

Palestine, 17, 52-3, 62

Pali (B), ancient Buddhist scriptures language, 80-1

palki, or chanani (S), canopy over the Granth, 177-8

Palm Sunday (C), festival of marking Jesus' entrance into Jerusalem, 197

Pancha-shila, or Pans'il (B), see Five Precepts

pandā (H), pilgrim priest, 101

Pandavas (H), part of the Bharata royal family, 76

pangat (S), seating row in the gurdwara, 179

panj kakka, or panj kakke (S), the Five K's, 221

264

Panj Piares (S). Five Loved Ones. 67-8. 220-1

Pannā (B). wisdom steps of the Eightfold Path. 113

panth (S). Sikh community. 177

paper boats (Sh). 186; (T). 234; (B). 191

paper cars. clothing. money (T). for dead person's use. etc.. 232-5

parables (C). short stories with a moral purpose. 22

paradete (C). comforter. see Holy Spirit

paradise. see Heaven

Paradise. Western (B). see Western Paradise. Land of

Pāramitā (B). perfection method. 44

parev. parve (J). neutral foods. 124

pariahs (H). outcasts. 96. 228. 231

parinibbana (B). final Nibbana. 239

parish (C). a church's area. 58

Parliament of Religions. 35

Parochet (J). ark's curtain. 160

parousia (C). second coming of Christ. 24

parshad (H). any consecrated food: (S). see karah parshad

Pārvatī (H). goddess. 10

'Passing Through the Door' Rite (T). 207

passion (C). death of Jesus. 24-5

Passions. King of (B). see Māra

Passion play (C). play of Jesus' death on the cross. 197

Passover. or Pesach or Feast of Unleavened Bread (J). festival marking the sparing of the Jews. 191-2

patashas (S). sugar used in amrit. 220

Path of Knowledge (H). see Jnana Veda Yoga

Path of Love and Devotion (H). see Bhakti Yoga

Path of Psychological Exercises (H). see Raja Yoga

Path of Teaching (B). see Dhammapada

Path of Works (H). see Karma Yoga

patriarchs (J). Abraham. Isaac. Jacob. 17: (C). senior bishops of Orthodox church. 56

Paul. St (C). originally named Saul. early Christian leader and writer. 54. 86

Pavana (H). God of the Wind. 10

Peace Testimony (C). held by the Quakers. 127

Peking. 48. 156

penance. penitent (J). 193: (C). 131-2: (S). 222

penitent's form (S). see mercy seat

Pentateuch (J). five books of Moses. see Torah

Pentecost (J). Shavuoth or Weeks Festival marking gift of Ten Commandments. 181. 192. 199

Pentecost (C). Whit Sunday. marking gift of

Holy Spirit. 59. 199

Pentecostal churches (C). 59. 199. 214

Persia. see Iran

Pesach. or Passover (J). festival of unleavened bread. 191-2

Peter. St (C). Jesus' disciple. 86

Pharaoh of Egypt. 18

Pharisees (J). Separatists. 49. 54

Philosophical Taoism. see Tao Chia

phylactery (J). small scripture container. 123-4

Piares (S). 'loved ones'. 67-8. 220

Pilate. Roman governor of Jerusalem in Christ's time. 23-4. 56

pilgrimages (H). 101-3. 182: (Sh). 106: (B). 121. 236: (J). 126. 192: (C). 134-5: (I). 64. 90. 143-5. 199: (S). 67. 92. 147. 180

pinaka (H). trident. 10

pinda (H). rice balls. 229

Pirkei Avot (J). ethical sayings. 85

Pius XII. pope. 60

plagues (J). 161. 191

P'o (T). earthly soul. 232

Pochama (H). God of Smallpox. 10

pogrom (J). massacre of Jews in Russia and Romania. 53

Poitiers. battle of. 64

polygamy. multiple marriage. 246: (H). 205: (J). 211: (C). 215: (I). 219

polytheism. belief in many gods. 6. 33-4

Pope (C). head of the Roman Catholic Church. 56. 57. 60. 134. 197

Popular Shinto. 37-8

pradakshina (H). processional passage of temple. 150-1

prānāyāma (H). controlled breathing. 100

prasad (H). sacred food. 151-2

pratika (H). symbol. 99

pratima (H). image. 99

pratyahara (H). 'being alone'. fifth step of Raja Yoga. 100

prayer (H). 99-100. 151-2. 183. 204: (Sh). 153-4. 184: (T). 187: (B). 158-60. 208: (J). 162. 192-3: (C). 130-1. 133. 165-6. 242: (I). 138-41. 175. 199-200: (S). 146-7. 178-9; see also meditation

Prayer Book (C). Church of England. 56. 216

prayer flags (B). 159

prayer-mat (I). musalta. 141

prayer wheels (B). 159-60

Presbyterian Church (C). 59

preserver god (H). see Vishnu

priest (H). 101-2. 151. 202. 230: (Sh). 104. 153-4. 184-5. 206. 231: (T). 41-2. 80. 109. 187. 189-90. 207. 233: (B). 118-19. 236-7: (J). 19. 83. 160: (C). 58-9. 132. 134. 163-9. 197. 213-15. 217: see also clergyman. brahmin

Prince of the Wheel (T). 235

Prinknash Abbey (C). 133-4

Progressive Jews. see Liberal Jews

Promised Land of the Jews. 17-19. 52

prophet (J). divinely inspired man. 19-22. 28. 50. 83: (I). 64. 88. 137; see also Muhammad

Prophets (J. C). section of the Tenakh or Old Testament. 83-4. 162

prostration (I). a position during prayer emphasizing submission. 140-2. 175

Protestant churches (C). those rejecting papal rule. 54. 57-60. 85. 242. 246

Protocols of the Elders of Zion. 53

Psalms (J. C). book of songs in TeNaKh or Old Testament. 83. 162. 192

P'u Tu (T). Ghosts' Festival. 189

pūjā (H). an act of worship. shrine room or god-shelf. 99-100. 151-2. 182. 204: (B). communal worship. 116. 158-9. 190

pūjāris (H). temple priests. 151

pulpit. place where preacher delivers a sermon (C). 165. 167. 171: (I). 174. 176

Punjab. 36. 66. 69

Punjabi Suba. Punjabi-speaking state. 70

Puranas (H). 'Old Writings' popularizing the Vedas. 78

purdah (I). veil. 219

Pure Land of the Western Paradise (B). a Buddhist sect. 44-8. 116. 119. 158-9. 239

Purgatory. stage between earthly life and heavenly life (T). 233: (C). 227. 242

purification rituals (H). 98. 101. 150-1: (Sh). 104-5. 152-3. 184. 186. 206. 249: (T). 187: (B). 121: (C). 212-14. 242: (I). 138-9. 141-2. 174: (S). 220-1

Purim (J). Feast of Esther who saved the Jews in Persia. 194

Purusa (H). the first man. 96

pyre (H). wood pile for funeral. 228

qiblah. or qibla (I). the 'direction' wall of a mosque on side facing Makkah. 141. 174. 176

Quakers (C). see Society of Friends

Quraish. or Quraysh (I). a tribe. 63

Qur'ān. or Koran (I). holy book. 6. 27-9. 32. 62-3. 66. 87. 90. 92. 135-8. 141-3. 174. 217-19. 243-4. 247-8. 251

Rabbanites (J). Rabbis' side. 50

rabbi (J). learned man. leader. 49. 51-2. 84-5. 160-2. 193. 210-12

ragas (S). tunes. 91

ragis (S). musicians. 177

Rahiras (S). Holy Path prayer. 147

rain control (T). 189

265

stoning the devil (I), part of the Hajj pilgrimage, 144

stoup (C), basin containing holy water, 165

stūpa (B), relic chamber, temple, 157, 191

suba, state, 70

subha (I), rosary for counting Allah's names, 175

Sudras (H), unskilled class, 33, 96

suffering (B), see Dukkha

Suffering Servant (J), term for Israel, 20; (C), term for Jesus, 23

Sufis (I), 'wearers of undyed wool', mystical sect, 30, 64

sukha (H), good experiences, 230

Sukhākara (B), see Pure Land of Western Paradise

Sukāvati (B), see Pure Land of Western Paradise

sukkah (J), rough shelters, tabernacles, 194

Sukkot (J), Feast of Tabernacles, harvest time, 194-5

Sun goddess (Sh), see Amaterasu

Sunday (C), holy day as Jesus rose from dead on a Sunday, 170

Sunnah (I), rules of life, 62, 66, 90, 136

Sunni (I), largest Islamic sect, 62-4, 199

Surahs (I), chapters of the Qur'ān, 87-8

surplice (C), priest's and choir's white robe, 169

Susanoo (Sh), storm god, 12

Sūtras (B), 'threads', teachings of the Buddha, 46, 81-2, 236, 251

Sūtras, Yoga, see Yoga Sūtras

Sutta Pitaka (B), Teaching Basket, one of the Tripitaka books, 81

suttee (H), widow's death on husband's funeral pyre, 35, 229

swami (H), teacher, 103

swastika (H), 'well-being' symbol, 7

synagogue (J), place of worship, 49, 51, 84, 123, 160-2, 192-3, 210-11, 239

Synod, General (C), governing body of the Church of England, 58

Synoptic Gospels (C), Matthew, Mark, Luke and John, 'one view' accounts, 86

sze (B), temple in China, 158

tabernacle (J), shelter built for Sukkot, 194-5

Tabernacle (J), first house of worship, 18

Tabernacle (C), cupboard for the Blessed Sacrament, 165

Tabernacles, Feast of (J), Sukkot, 194

Tablets of the Law (J), see Ten Commandments

Tai Chi (T), the pattern of Yin and Yang, 106

Taiwan, 14, 42, 48, 156, 187

takbīr (I), saying 'Allāhu Akbar', see Allāhu Akbar

takht (S), 'throne', the stand for the Granth, 177-8

Talāq (I), repudiation for divorce, 219

talisman (Sh), 154, 206; (T), 80, 187; (B), 48

tallit, or tallith (J), prayer shawl, 123, 161, 210, 239

Talmud (J), 'traditions', holy book which explains the Torah, 50-1, 84-5, 212

Talwandi, 29

tama (Sh), soul, 232

tan (S), physical service, 147

tanhā (B), craving for things, 111-14, 238

tanka (S), penance, 222

Tantra (H), 'Rule System', books on Shaktism, 78

Tantric (systematic) Buddhism, 45-7

Tao (T), 'The Way', 13-14, 41, 79-80, 106-9, 187, 207

Tao Chia (T), Philosophical Taoism, 14-15, 42, 107-8

Tao Chiao (T), Religious Taoism, 14-15, 40-1, 80, 107-9, 187

Tao-ch'o (B), Pure Land leader, 45

Tao Chun (T), controller of Yin and Yang, 15, 189; see also Three Pure Ones

Tao-Te Ching (T), the Way and Its Power, holy book written 350-300 BCE, 13, 79-80, 108, 251

Tao Tsang (T), collection of books made in 1436, CE, 41, 80

Taoism, 6, 13-15, 41-2, 79-80, 106-10, 119, 155-6, 158, 187-90, 206-8, 232-6, 249, 251

Taoist Master (T), priest, 109, 187, 233

Targum (J), Aramaic translation of Torah, 84

tashlikh (J), washing away sins, 193

Tauhīd, Tauheed (I), oneness of Allah, 28-9

tawaf (I), pilgrim's walk round the Ka'ba, 143

Te (Power) of the Tao (Way) (T), 13-14, 79-80, 109, 187

teamim (J), Torah grammatical signs, 84, 123-4, 161

tephilin, or tefillin (J), small scripture container, 123-4, 161

Tegh Bahadur (S), ninth guru (1621-75), 67, 91, 201

Tel Aviv, 52

Temizu (Sh), a purifying wash, 152

temples, Chapters 5, 6; see also (H), mandir; (Sh), jinjas; (T), kuans, miao; (B), chedis, chorten, dāgoba, pagodas, stūpa, szes, wats; (J), synagogue, Jerusalem temple; (C), cathedral, chapel, church, citadel, meeting house; (I), mosque; (S), gurdwara

Temple at Jerusalem (J), 19-21, 49, 53, 62, 85, 126, 162-3, 192, 212

Temple of Heaven, Peking (T), 156

Temple of the Sacred Tooth of Buddha,

Kandy, Sri Lanka, 158, 191

TeNaKh (J), holy book containing Torah, Prophets and Writings, 83-4, 251

Ten Commandments, Decalogue (J, C), 18-19, 83, 88, 121-3, 126, 136, 160-1, 181, 192, 248

Ten Days of Return (J), Ten Penitential Days, annual penance period, 193

Ten Penitential Days, see Ten Days of Return

Tendai (B), a sect, 47

Tenri City, 40

Tenri-kyo (Sh), Divine Wisdom sect, 39-40, 104

Tent of Meeting (J), Ohel Mo'ed, see Tabernacle

Thailand, 43, 47, 117-18, 157, 190, 251

Theravāda Buddhism, Way of the Elders or Southern Buddhism, 42-3, 45-8, 80, 117, 121, 157-8, 190-1, 209

Thirteen Principles of Belief (J), 50

Three Baskets (B), Tripitaka, scriptures of Theravāda Buddhists, 80-2

Three Jewels (B), Buddha, Dharma and Sangha, 157-8, 208; see also Three Refuges

Three Ms (B), 45

Three Precious Ones (B), 158

Three Pure Ones (T), San Ch'ing, the Lords of Heaven, Earth and Man, 14-15, 187, 189; see also Jade Emperor, Tao Chun, Lao Tse

Three or Triple Refuges (B), referring to the Three Jewels, 157-8, 208-9, 236

Three Treasures (T), 79, 107

Three Universal Truths (B), 111

Thunder Magic (T), 109

thunderblocks (T), vajra, used to summon the thunder power, 109

Tibet, 43, 47-8, 118, 158-9

Ticket of Membership (C), Methodists' commitment card, 215

tilaka (H), red spot on forehead indicating blessedness, 101, 151

Tipitaka, or Tripitaka (B), Three Baskets, scriptures of Theravāda Buddhists, 80-2, 251

Tisarana, Trisharana, or Triratna (B), see Three Refuges

Tish b'Av (J), Fast of Av, 192-3

Tokyo, 149

Tok-yo-no-kuni (Sh), Land of Tokyo, 232

tombstones (B), 237; (J), 239; (C), 166

tongues, speaking in (C), Holy Spirit speaking through a person, 59, 199, 214

topi (I), small cap, 138

Torah (J), The Law, section of the TeNaKh holy book, 18, 20-1, 23, 49-52, 54, 83-5,

Worms, Diet of, 1521, 57

worship, see Chapter 6, chapel, prayer, puja, matsuri, communion, salat, rakat, etc.

wrestling (Sh), 184

Writings (J, C), part of the Tenakh, or Old Testament, 83–4

wu (B), awareness of enlightenment, 46

wudu (I), act of cleansing before prayer, 138–9, 174, 243, 246

Wu-wei (T), the non-effort way, 108

Wycliffe, John (C), Bible translator, 87

Xuan Yuan Huang Di (T), founder of Taoism, 251

yad (J), pointer, 162

Yad Vashem (J), 'A Place and a Name', the Holocaust Memorial, 126

Yagyopavit (H), Sacred Thread samskāra, Janeu, 96, 98, 202–4

Yahweh (J), Christians' name for Jewish God, see God (J)

yahrzeit (J), anniversary of a death, 239

Yajur-Veda (H), 'sacrificial Veda', second book of Vedas, 74–5

yaku (Sh), unlucky years of a person's life, 206

Yama (H), self-control rules, or God of the Dead, 95, 100, 230

yāna (B), vehicle, 117

Yang and Yin (T), nature's two energies which govern all life, 13–15, 80, 106–7, 109, 156, 187, 189, 207, 232–3

Yang-Chu (T) (440–360 BCE), 13

yantra (H), symbolic pattern for worship, 99

yamulkah, or yarmulke (J), skull cap, see cappel

Yathrib, see Medina

Yethuda, see Judah ha Nasi

Yellow Court Canon or Register (T), Tao Chiao spirit list, 233

Yellow Hats (B), sect of monks, 47

Yen Lo (T), King of the Underworld, 189

Yin, see Yang

Yin Yang Sien Seng (T), diviners, 232–3

Yogas (H), paths to Atman, Jnana Veda, Bhakti, Karma and Raja Yogas, 9, 34–5, 74–8, 97–101, 103, 151; (S), Sahaj, 146

Yoga Sūtras (H), yoga exercises (written 100–200 CE), 78, 101

yogi (B), trainee monk, 116

Yom Kippur (J), Atonement Day, repentance day, 193–4

yoni (H), female image, 151

Yuga (H), timespan or age, iv, 8, 76

Yu-Huang, or Yah-husang, Shang-ti (T), see Jade Emperor

zaddic (J), saint, 51

Zaid (I), Muhammad's friend, 28, 88

Zainab (I), Muhammad's wife, 28

Zakah, or Zakat (I), almsgiving, 90, 141–2, 174

Zamzam, Well of (I), where Ishmael found water, 144

Zazen (B), Zen Buddhist seated meditation, 119, 121

Zealots (J), those who expected a military-leader Messiah, 21

Zen Buddhism, 42, 46–7, 119–21

zendō (B), meditation hall, 119, 121

Zionism (J), movement begun by T Herzl in 1897 with the idea of a Jewish state, 52–3, 248

Zohar (J), 'Splendour' book, 51

zuhr (I), noonday prayer, 138

zulm (I), wrongdoing, 137